Tax Implications on Far

Tax Implications on Family Breakdown

Sofia Thomas,
Chartered Tax Advisor, Director of Sofia Thomas Ltd

James Pirrie,
Solicitor, Director of Family Law in Partnership Ltd

LONDON • DUBLIN • EDINBURGH • NEW YORK • NEW DELHI • SYDNEY

BLOOMSBURY PROFESSIONAL
Bloomsbury Publishing Plc
41–43 Boltro Road, Haywards Heath, RH16 1BJ, UK

BLOOMSBURY and the Diana logo are trademarks of Bloomsbury Publishing Plc

Reprinted 2021

British Library Cataloguing-in-Publication Data

A catalogue record for this book is available from the British Library.

ISBN: PB: 978-1-52651-234-5
ePDF: 978-1-52651-236-9
ePub: 978-1-52651-235-2

Typeset by Evolution Design & Digital Ltd (Kent)
Printed and bound by CPI Group (UK) Ltd, Croydon, CRO 4YY

To find out more about our authors and books visit www.bloomsburyprofessional.com. Here you will find extracts, author information, details of forthcoming events and the option to sign up for our newsletters

Forward

Sofia Thomas and James Pirrie have written an interesting, informative and very readable book. It deserves to be on every family lawyer's bookshelf.

Benjamin Franklin famously said that in this world nothing can be said to be certain except death and taxes. This book gives an interesting historical survey of, and explanation for, the ubiquity of taxes. It reminds us of the epigram of Denis Healey that the difference between tax avoidance and evasion is the thickness of the prison wall. It cites the famous dicta of Lord Clyde and Lord Tomlin that there is no moral imperative imposed on a citizen to arrange his affairs to allow the Inland Revenue to put the largest possible shovel into his stores. I would myself add the dictum of Justice Learned Hand in *Helvering v Gregory*, 69 F.2d 809, 810–11 (2d Cir. 1934) that 'anyone may so arrange his affairs that his taxes shall be as low as possible; he is not bound to choose that pattern which will best pay the Treasury; there is not even a patriotic duty to increase one's taxes.'

In bygone days income tax was strongly resisted as a gross intrusion into a citizen's freedom and privacy. Although it had made a temporary appearance during the Napoleonic wars in order to finance the same it did not arrive permanently on the scene until 1842. Generally, taxes were raised by means of imposts on land or other commodities. Window tax, for example, was maintained in England and Wales from 1696 until 1851. Avoiding that tax by bricking up windows was regarded as perfectly moral and reasonable. No one should feel uncomfortable about using this book to achieve a divorce settlement with maximum fiscal efficiency. It is reasonable and fair to the hard-pressed taxpayer when negotiating the divorce to brick up the windows.

However, great care should be taken when constructing a settlement designed to achieve maximum fiscal efficiency. HMRC now adopts an enhanced aggressive stance against taxpayers they regard as delinquent. There is a sobering story in the book about HMRC even pursuing as far as a tribunal a claim for a penalty against a homeless person who had not filed his return on time: *K Pokorowski v HMRC* [2019] UKFTT 86. The book tells us that now HMRC publish online details of the most delinquent taxpayers and their defaults. The book should help to avoid most pitfalls.

The book is arranged in a very logical order. It is well illustrated by tables and flowcharts. The table illustrating which welfare benefits are, and are not, taxable was certainly for me an eye-opener. I could not discern any underpinning logic; the demarcation appeared to be completely arbitrary.

Chapter 16, and the appendices, are devoted to the use of tax experts in a financial remedy case. Paragraph 16.14(4) rightly states that expert evidence can be submitted on any issue, save for evidence on English law. An opinion from an expert as to the taxes that would arise on the sale, for example, of a business is literally an opinion as to the impact of UK revenue law on that asset. Strictly speaking, therefore, such an opinion is not admissible as evidence. Rather, it is a matter that should be elucidated and imparted by the advocates. However, I think we can safely say that the ship has sailed, just as it has sailed in relation to the opinions of pension experts. Expert opinion on tax is commonplace and is usually extremely helpful. The appendices set out with great clarity exactly what needs to be done and which documents need to be prepared. Nobody should make an application for a Part 25 order for a tax expert without having carefully considered these pages of the book.

The authors are to be congratulated for having produced what will surely become the standard *vade mecum* in this field.

Hon Mr Justice Mostyn
London, 6 May 2020

Preface

'Why would they care!'

'Why would they care!' is a post-it stuck on my computer that greets me every morning and underpins all the work that I do. 'Why would they care!' is the reminder to me to convert the things that I know into what those using me need to know … without any of the extraneous stuff. It underpins the lectures I give, the reports I write and this book that I have written.

I have been working with family lawyers for many years listening acutely to all that they have to tell me and in particular all that they complain about. It seems to me that they have incredible amounts to manage in the cases that they run. So what they need is clear information – sometimes of considerable complexity – but they don't need the 'surround stuff' which may be the bits that interest us on my side of the industry. They need dependable, usable answers.

They also may need background, because so often what I find you are dealing with is options: *'ok we get that Sofia, but if it wasn't that but this, then what…'*.

The best way through this jungle seems to be that these things come in stages and people have different needs at different points in a case:

1. At the outset, solicitors need ranging shot answers so that you can draw a broad map of the emerging financial realities in a case.
2. But at a later stage, you are going to need pin-point accurate answers to specific scenarios for example: *'what taxes would this person with in this situation incur doing this? What sums will be due? When? With what consequences if not paid?'*
3. At a later stage, perhaps at FDR or final hearing, you are likely to need to have answers that can flex… the raw number proves not to be 854,000 but 837,358… so what is that going to mean for the net in pocket?

The purpose of this book is to help family lawyers deal with stage 1. I have tried to create standalone chapters for readers to identify scenarios and read into the relevant background. My intention is to slim the information in each section down to what you have to know to provide a reasonably decent number and one that hopefully is enough for your plan in the case to start to coalesce. I have tried to deal with some of the major red-flags but to deal with them all would produce the sort of turgid manual that risks meaning that the ranging shot never gets done at all or is only completed in the most crude 'rule of thumb' way.

My assumption is that in cases involving any level of complexity, a proper report by SJE under FPR Part 25 will be obtained. This is not least because of issues of provenance: you may be comfortable relying on your ranging shot and over time you may come to develop significant expertise in producing certain sorts of calculation. However, the other party in a contested case will usually want to have an approved/neutral set of numbers on which to build the negotiations at FDR for example.

We look at the form of instructions to experts in Part 3. It will be worth seeking opinions in the form that we consider there so that when you end up with a change of digits at FDR or FH (the 837 not 854 scenario described above), you will still be able to generate reasonably decent working models.

I accept that this is not perfect: ideally you would have instantly and with limited effort, the robust answer that stands up in all scenarios. But I can't do that. I would if I could. However, our tax system is complex and is riddled with exceptions and special circumstances which may well have profound impacts on the tax numbers. So this book is the best that I can do.

- It is a manual of the information that I think that you would care to know.
- It is intended to help you generate the numbers in a more accurate way than may currently be possible for the stage one need.
- I have tried to arrange the chapters in a way that makes the relevant information easy to find: I have looked at the common scenarios that I see emerging in the cases in which I am instructed and which family law colleagues tell me about and I have considered the tax rules applicable to those circumstances. There is an element of overlap between some chapters as I have tried to make each pretty standalone (with cross-referencing where required).

I have set the book up in three parts, part one is intended as an overview and to provide the basics of the most common taxes in divorce. Capital gains tax, income tax and land taxes each have their own chapter detailing the rates, payment dates and applicability of the taxes. Part 2 goes into details and scenarios such as selling the main home and valuing complex earning structures. Part 3 is the process; when and how to appoint an expert and what to expect. Throughout the book there are flowcharts and checklist which I hope will distil the complex conditions into easy to follow guidelines for understanding if a particular relief or exemption may be available for your client.

Sofia Thomas, Chartered Tax Advisor,
Director of Sofia Thomas Ltd

James Pirrie, Solicitor,
Director of Family Law in Partnership Ltd

May 2020

Acknowledgements

James and Sofia would like to thank Paul Cobley for his incredible support with the pensions chapter (and for providing much of that help on a Sunday!). We would also like to thank Roger Isaacs and Kate Hart for allowing us to build on their publication for Resolution in Chapter 16. Thank you to Kiran Goss for all her efforts in getting this project off the ground and her ongoing support. Finally thank you to our editor Chris Harrison who has been very understanding of the many last minute changes.

Sofia

Thank you to my partner Ro for their complete unwavering support and to TJ for being my biggest cheerleader. I promise never again to try and combine a house move and book deadline all in the same month!

Thank you to my Mum for the continuous encouragement and food deliveries. Thank you to my Dad for being a sounding board and reviewing many chapters.

I would like to thank Heather Self who has been a pillar of support and encouragement since we met and Ray McCann for his professional support and kindness. I would also like to thank my friends, Charlotte Watson, Charlotte Pollard, Eleanor Curtis, Ogonna Agwa and Abi Ayodele who have always been on hand throughout the process with many words of encouragement. Thank you to Rebecca Trowbridge for keeping me sane with Pilates and undoing all the damage I created by sitting crossed legged hunched over my laptop. Thank you to Denise Green and Richard Price at Bloomsbury who were so welcoming and supportive. Thank you to Jenny Lank also at Bloomsbury for her dedication in marketing the book.

Finally, thank you to James Pirrie for agreeing to embark on this project with me and for making it so enjoyable.

Contents

Table of Cases

Table of Statutes

Table of Statutory Instruments

Table of International Legislation

CHAPTER 1

Overview of the UK Taxation System

Contents at a Glance

1.1 To provide some background for the labyrinth we are about to delve into, a brief summary of the UK tax system may help to provide some context for the differing and at times counter intuitive way tax applies in the case of divorce. The tax system in the UK professes to do many things and, whilst it is hugely successful in some areas, there are a multitude of areas where the system categorically fails. There are so many paradoxes within the current system that it begins to defy logic and reason. We have tax amnesties for paying undeclared tax, twinned with record penalties of up to 200% of the tax due. We have access to the financial data of individuals from over 200 jurisdictions but failings within the UK's own system have left millions of parents with missing pension credits. HMRC have declared that they want to be the most digitally advanced tax system in the world, but this race forward means that the errors in the system are often unseen and unrectified leaving many individuals unheard.

1.2 Taxes are an ingrained part of public life in the UK, regularly debated in the mainstream media and often a prominent feature of election campaigns. Public attitudes towards those who do not pay their taxes have changed. Be wary of being seen to imply that someone has deliberately been underpaying their taxes! The general result is that most individuals want to (or want to be seen to) pay their fair share of tax; the difficulty is that what people think is their fair share is often lower than what they are actually required to pay and this is where some income tax issues on divorce arise.

1.3 The system is immensely complex and whilst HMRC has created facilities for individuals to do it themselves, we do not have a tax system that is easily understood. In a recent case an individual's penalty for failing to declare the right income was upheld by the courts even though he took his income figure directly from his P60. The tribunal comments that whilst the taxpayer made an honest mistake the law 'does not provide shelter for honest mistakes' and the penalties still applied. Creating DIY facilities for tax reporting without ensuring that there are clear rules to follow is effectively leading the taxpayer into the dark and exposing them to penalties and enquiries which sometimes only come to light during a separation.

WHAT ARE TAXES USED FOR?

1.4 Taxes are a function of the government. They are multifunctional and not singularly to raise money for government spending. The Tax Justice Network helpfully simplifies this area into the four Rs of taxation:

> **Revenue** – Taxes provide the government with revenue for public spending. The government also raises money from rentals of public buildings etc. However the gap between total receipts and receipts from tax is closing, meaning the government is more reliant on tax to meet its spending responsibilities. The backdrop of the pressure of taxes being the majority of revenue the government raises provides some insight into the changing face of HMRC.
>
> **Re-distribution** of wealth – the benefits system in the UK is there to provide additional support to those who require it. £222 billion is expected to be spent on welfare in the UK in the coming year – this figure includes pensions so it is hard to extrapolate the value that is directly for income/welfare benefits. Even so, the total figure is still just over half of what is 'given away' each year in tax reliefs.[1]
>
> **Re-pricing** of goods – this is when the government imposes a tax as a way to change behaviour (think tobacco and the sugar levy). Some argue that the government is turning to tax legalisation to try and solve issues which would be better served by well implemented social policy. This rush to use tax when it is not always the most effective tool for the desired outcome has created some bizarre situations which lack cohesion and in some cases common sense.
>
> **Representation** – policy makers have long urged the government not to forget the power of representation when individuals are taxed and that they have the ability to demand accountability from government.

1.5 The tax system is highly complex and is not aided by the many changes implemented each year by an often revolving door of Chancellors aiming to implement policies for short-term goals. In 2010 the government set up the Office of Tax Simplification (OTS) to try and tackle the ever-growing complexity of the tax system. The OTS has since produced reports on how tax affects people throughout their major life events and has highlighted the tax complexities individuals face during divorce.

A NEW HMRC

1.6 'How will they know?' is one of the most common questions I get asked by clients when I explain that some unreported income needs to be reported

1 www.gov.uk/government/publications/benefit-expenditure-and-caseload-tables-information-and-guidance/benefit-expenditure-and-caseload-tables-information-and-guidance and www.ifs.org.uk/publications/11692.

on their tax returns. It is also often a dilemma with couples if previous tax underreporting comes to light. Many clients feel that it would be better to stay hidden rather than draw attention to themselves. However, in reality the ability to hide from HMRC is rapidly diminishing. HMRC has in recent years embraced the digital age. HMRC announced that it wants the UK to have the 'world's most digitally advanced tax system'. From September 2018 it began receiving fiscal data from over 200 different jurisdictions, the data is provided automatically and details an individual's name, date of birth and account balances. Combine this with information already being provided from the DVLA and the land registry and HMRC can quickly start to build up a picture of a person's life. HMRC has also joyfully joined in with social media. It is making better use of publicly available information, including Facebook, Instagram and Twitter to see if the lives people are living match the income they are reporting.

1.7 It is not only the potential tax which is at stake, HMRC also name and shame tax avoiders and at the end of each year they announce their top ten prosecutions for tax evasion.[2] In 2018 the list included:

- a church leader;
- a manager of a stripping troupe; and
- a businessman who owed more than £53 million in taxes.

1.8 HMRC is able to use the full range of both criminal and civil powers and continues to be successful in around 90% of criminal cases it brings to trial. The average time individuals spend in prison for tax fraud has now jumped up by 10% to an average of two years and five months.[3]

1.9 All these reasons and more are why individuals should want to get their tax position on divorce correct and to correct any previous indiscretions quickly.

1.10 There is an emerging consensus for greater transparency and simplicity within the tax system, however, there is a problem reconciling simplicity and fairness; it seems the system can have one or the other but not both. The system must retain its complexities to allow and provide for specific situations and individuals and to provide flexibility for the government.

1.11 There is a prevailing sense in what is seen day to day that individuals still think of HMRC as this old clunky organisation that will never know if they 'overlook' declaring that little bit of income they make off eBay nor come after them for a bit of bank interest in Spain and that is fundamentally not the case anymore. HMRC is wiser, better resourced and increasingly systemised to permit it to close the tax gap by ensuring the right amount of taxes are being paid. The current reality is the balance of power has shifted in favour of HMRC. On the one hand, it has unprecedented amounts of computing power to mine data

2 www.gov.uk/government/news/hmrc-announces-top-10-prosecutions-of-2018.
3 www.taxation.co.uk/Articles/average-prison-sentence-for-tax-evasion-jumps-10.

and on the other, the system is complex and likely to remain complex which places a huge burden on individuals to get it right. And if they do not, they will face consequences of investigations which could result in high penalties and reputational damage.

CHAPTER 2

HMRC Powers: Penalties and Investigations

Contents at a Glance

2.1 This chapter looks at the widening powers of HMRC and its increasing intolerance of what would have been regarded as legitimate tax planning in earlier years. The consequences of the change in HMRC's approach for the family lawyer are obvious: for those clients, who have engaged in creative financial arrangements, there is a risk of a late-arriving investigation and claim. This is hard enough where a carefully calculated structure is being built to address the needs for the risks it carries in undermining those computations. But more worryingly, such claims will often fall on one party rather than on both. Practitioners may need to keep a weather eye on the latest round of HMRC potential targets for fear of overlooking in-coming claims – or perhaps more routinely take advice on where risks may lie for clients. Claims may need to be resolved before settlements can be agreed. Alternatively, pressure-valve arrangements may need to be built in to orders to address tax debts that should fall to the couple rather than to one party only if the intention of the financial arrangements on divorce is not to be undermined.

POWERS

2.2 HMRC's functions include the collection of tax and the payments of certain benefits.[1] Their three primary strategic objectives are:[2]

1. To maximise revenues and bear down on avoidance and evasion.

1 Annex D – DISCLOSURE OF INFORMATION BY HM REVENUE AND CUSTOMS (HMRC): HMRC'S POLICY AND LEGAL FRAMEWORK.
2 Corporate Report, Our strategy, published 20 Jul 2017.

2. To transform tax payments for our customers.

3. To design and deliver a professional, efficient and engaged organisation.

2.3 The majority of the powers that HMRC has been given by government are to aide HMRC in meeting its primary stated objective of maximising revenues. In recent years these powers have grown exponentially and have been designed to help HMRC collect more tax with fewer staff. In 2019 the House of Lords Economic Affairs Committee conducted a report on the powers of HMRC. The Committee raised many concerns but with one overarching theme: that the taxpayers' safeguards are being systematically eroded. Unfortunately, this can make an individual's experience with HMRC challenging at best.

2.4 'Maximising revenues and bearing down on avoidance and evasion' – this objective should be taken seriously. It suggests that evasion and avoidance are to be treated singularly which is a shift from the previous view. Denis Healey, a former Chancellor and Exchequer, once said that the difference between tax evasion and tax avoidance was the 'thickness of a prison wall'. If under the new approach, there is in fact no distinction between avoidance and evasion does this mean both activities result in individuals being on the wrong side of a prison wall? The accountancy profession is discussing whether there has been a practice of re-categorisation of avoidance – that in effect it is to be regarded as illegal. In the past the differences were relatively easy to define:

- evasion is illegal;
- avoidance is (to use an apt analogy for this book) like having an extra marital affair, not advisable but not illegal;
- tax planning is (currently) squarely within the realms of what is allowable.

The blurring of the lines between evasion and avoidance assists HMRC in using their most obtuse powers to try and reclaim taxes under the guise of possible evasion. Clients who entered into legitimate arrangements many years ago would be wise to seek advice on HMRC's current view of such arrangements.

2.5 The legality and morality of these issues are not new. The most famous quotes about acceptable tax planning are from Lord President Clyde in *Ayrshire Pullman Motor Services v Commissioners of Inland Revenue* (1929) 14 TC 754 and Lord Tomlin in *Duke of Westminster v CIR* (1935) 19 TC 490. Lord Clyde said:

> 'No man in this country is under the smallest obligation, moral or other, so to arrange his legal relations to his business or to his property as to enable the Inland Revenue to put the largest possible shovel into his stores. The Inland Revenue is not slow – and quite rightly – to take every advantage which is open to it under the taxing statues for the purpose of depleting the taxpayer's pocket. And the taxpayer is in like manner entitled to be astute to prevent, so far as he honestly can, the depletion of his means by the Revenue'.

Lord Tomlin was more succinct: 'every man is entitled if he can to order his affairs so that the tax attaching under the appropriate Acts is less than it otherwise would be'.[3]

2.6 The prevailing sense had been that provided it was legal (meaning the actions taken fit comfortably within the legislation) and it did not involve any contrived transactions, then it was acceptable planning and it would not be considered evasion. But things are now moving on.

2.7 HMRC now states that 'tax avoidance involves bending the rules of the tax system to gain an advantage that Parliament never intended…it involves operating within the letter, but not the spirit of the law'.[4] As it sets out in its own guidance: 'if it sounds too good to be true it usually is.'[5]

2.8 Why taxpayers find this harsh is that generally individuals enter into tax planning only with the guidance and support of a tax advisor (usually paying a high fee for the advice). They then assume that the planning is totally legitimate and not open to being challenged. HMRC have come under criticism for failing to target the orchestrators of the schemes and instead targeting the individuals who have less resources (both in finances and expertise) to object to HMRC's findings.

2.9 Also consider some recent changes such as the *Pensions Freedom Act 2005*, where individuals can now withdraw 100% of their pension at any time and 25% of the pension can be drawn down tax free. Individuals investing in EIS shares can claim up to 30% back off their income tax bill.

2.10 With a little bit of planning, married couples with a home and children can pass up to £1m when they die without incurring an inheritance tax (IHT) charge.

2.11 Could all the above be argued to be too good to be true? If that sentence is the barometer for individuals to use when deciding whether they are likely to fall foul of HMRC's attentions or not, they will likely fail to commit to any planning and possibly end up failing to take advantage of tax reliefs the government actually allows.

2012 onwards

2.12 Since 2012 a number of powers have been added to HMRC's toolkit. The powers are aimed at tackling tax evasion and avoidance in response to the demand to increase tax revenues. The new powers include:

- the General Anti-Abuse Rule (the GAAR) introduced to tackle 'the most egregious tax avoidance'. If taxpayers pursue an appeal and lose, they risk a heavy penalty (up to 60% of the tax owed);

3 *IRC v Duke of Westminster* [1936] AC1 (HL).
4 www.gov.uk/guidance/tax-avoidance-an-introduction.
5 Gov UK Guidance. Dealing with Avoidance: An introduction.

- a power allowing HMRC to recover unpaid tax directly from taxpayers' bank accounts;
- doubling taxpayer penalties to 200% of the tax owed for offshore evasion with further increases if taxpayers fail to comply.

2.13 Ever keen to amass more data without constraint, HMRC proposed new powers in July 2018. The proposal included the following:

- the ability to submit information requests directly to financial institutions, accountants, lawyers and other third parties (with related obligations on such professionals to respond);
- the ability to obtain bank statements and transaction histories directly from banks.

The information, HMRC argued, would only be used where it was 'reasonably required to check a taxpayer's position'.

2.14 HMRC already has access to the above powers but tribunal consent is required. The proposed removal of this oversight raises the prospect of unregulated and extensive use of powers without recourse where abused.

2.15 In one particularly notable case hitting the headlines in 2019, *Pokorowski v HMRC*,[6] HMRC demonstrated spectacularly poor judgement in pursuing a homeless man for late-filing penalties. The judgement concluded 'for HMRC to expect a homeless person to keep HMRC up-to-date with their address is ridiculous and just needs to be stated to show its absurdity'. That this ended up at a tribunal, with HMRC attempting to defend its position demonstrates the level of the new zeal on the part of HMRC in current times.

2.16 Individuals not trained in tax will rely on their common sense and sense of logic to help them navigate through their personal tax affairs. Many are confident that HMRC will not be interested in them as there will be someone who owes more tax or who is doing something worse than they are. The reality though is that HMRC is increasingly focusing on the individual, the self-employed trader or the accidental landlord. The large amount of data to which HMRC has access and the algorithms we can only assume its staff are building, means that it will be increasingly quick, easy – and profitable – for HMRC to identify those who have not been paying the correct amount of tax. The excuse of misunderstanding or of having acted honestly but just having made simple mistakes will not be accepted.

2.17 At the point of separation, a stock-take may be crucial if we are to avoid one party bearing the main burden of uncrystallised tax liabilities and the associated professional fees, fines and interest that will go with it as we divide up a share of assets burdened with an underlying tax liability.

6 *K Pokorowski v HMRC* [2019] UKFTT 86 (8 February 2019).

'Spouses know where the bodies are buried'

2.18 HMRC has paid whistle-blowers millions of pounds for tip offs that identify tax fraud and it is no surprise that they love to hear from those formerly in a close personal relationship with the taxpayer. The common-sense internal guidance for HMRC's investigative officer is to listen carefully to the disillusioned former spouse as 'they knew where the bodies were buried'.

2.19 Anyone wanting to make a disclosure to HMRC about their spouse, neighbour or colleague can do so by either calling the Fraud Hotline or by completing a quick e-form. Whilst the spouse whose share of the assets depends on amicable consent might want to make such disclosures with some care – the opportunity for the 'schedule 1 former partner' to get even is obvious. Indeed, where CMS awards are likely to depend on HMRC data, the incentives to identify those shallow graves is likely to be very compelling indeed.

2.20 It is difficult to think of the circumstances in which we would not be encouraging clients to rectify any tax discrepancies with HMRC before HMRC come knocking, but where there is a former partner who may be spilling the beans, the urgency may be all the greater.

2.21 This topic will be discussed further in the following chapters. The point though is hopefully clear: some actions HMRC allow and some they do not and HMRC's opinion on what is allowable and what is not appears to be tightening consistently. Clients who recognise that their affairs are likely to be coming under the magnifying glass are usually only wrong to the extent of how quickly it will happen. Volunteering information will reduce the financial pain of HMRC completing the reckoning up and will at least ensure that the burdens are shared within the matrimonial regime. This prevents only one side having to economise on their needs to enable the debt to be discharged. The court may be slow to re-open a case to discharge a later-arriving tax debt (because such debts are likely only to have been overlooked as part of the taxpayer's previous financial conduct and non-disclosure and because the spouse may well have arranged their affairs in reliance on the dependability of the award).

INVESTIGATIONS

2.22 This section covers HMRC enquiries into self-assessment returns of individuals and companies. Partnerships are subject to similar enquiry provisions but these are not covered in detail here.

To enable HMRC to combat misreporting, it has:

- powers to require information;
- powers to impose fines (called penalties);
- power to impose interest on the tax.

2.23 These powers are circumscribed to some extent and the more innocent the default by the taxpayer, the more limited the scale of powers to investigate. The taxpayer and their advisor will be seeking to rely on:

- the innocence of the error;
- the speed with which information has been volunteered; and
- that the information was volunteered unprompted (rather than only coming to light through HMRC initiatives).

INVESTIGATIVE POWERS OF HMRC

2.24 HMRC enquiries are usually opened because they suspect that there may be an error in the return. Some enquiries are random but some estimates suggest that only 1 in 1,000 enquiries are random. Therefore, if your client receives an enquiry from HMRC the chances are that HMRC have reason to believe they have made a mistake on their tax return.

Who is at risk?

2.25 Some typical behaviour which may peak HMRC's interest includes:

- spouses not correctly (if at all) reporting rental income;
- spouses who are directors of companies where the dividends have not been correctly administered;
- individuals who have sold a property and not reported the gain;
- individuals who have taken part in tax avoidance/disguised remuneration schemes; and
- individuals with income or gains overseas which has not been reported in the UK.

2.26 Some of the forms of correspondence individuals might receive from HMRC are below.

Nudge letter

This is not a formal enquiry, it is a process used by HMRC to prompt individuals to check their tax returns and notify HMRC of any misreporting. No formal enquiry is issued. A nudge letter can be sent at any time.

Enquiry notice

Notice from HMRC that they intend to enquire into a taxpayer's tax return. These must be issued within 12 months of the tax return being filed. HMRC have extended deadlines to issue enquiry notices where they discover that tax has been underassessed and this is due to careless or deliberate behaviour or something which HMRC could not have been expected to be aware of at the time the enquiry window closed.

The extended time frames are:

4 years	Normal time limit
6 years	Careless error
20 years	Deliberate error

Formal enquiry notice

This is issued to the individual with a letter asking for information that the HMRC officer believes is 'reasonably required for the purposes of checking the taxpayer's position'. If a taxpayer replies providing information, they are providing the information voluntarily.

Formal information notice

Formal request for information, the individual has to provide this information unless the request can be legitimately challenged.

These are usually issued to the individual but can also be issued to third parties. Third party notice requests have to be approved either by the taxpayer or by the first tier tax tribunal.

DISCOVERY ASSESSMENT

2.27 HMRC can make an assessment on an individual known as a discovery assessment[7] if it identifies that:

- an amount which ought to have been assessed has not been assessed;
- an assessment is or has become insufficient; or
- relief has been given which is or has become excessive.

2.28 There are restrictions on HMRC's ability to raise discovery assessments. A discovery assessment can only be made if:

- a loss of tax was brought about carelessly or deliberately by or on behalf of the taxpayer; or

7 Taxes Management Act 1970, s 29.

- the HMRC officer could not reasonably have been expected, on the basis of the information available to them at the time, to have been aware of the facts giving rise to the loss of tax.

2.29 For example, where the taxpayer has not adequately disclosed information within the tax return, the HMRC officer could not have been expected to realise that the return was incorrect or incomplete and therefore HMRC can issue a discovery assessment to pursue the as yet unrecovered tax.

2.30 On the other hand, if sufficient information was disclosed within the return to enable an officer to be aware of the situation giving rise to a loss of tax, then once the one-year enquiry period discussed above is over, no 'discovery' can be made and the additional tax that would otherwise be due cannot be collected.

2.31 The general time limit for HMRC making a discovery assessment is four years from the end of the tax year to which the assessment relates. However, if the loss of tax is due to careless behaviour by the taxpayer, the deadline is extended to six years and if the loss of tax was due to deliberate behaviour the deadline is extended to 20 years.

SOLICITORS AND REPORTING OBLIGATIONS

2.32 This is covered in the broadest of ways; please seek advice from your professional body if you feel you may have an obligation to disclose relevant information.

There are three main circumstances when solicitors may have to disclose information to HMRC:

1. **Third party notices** – HMRC write to solicitors to request client data.
2. **Money Laundering Regulations** – Solicitors are required to make a notice under the Money Laundering Regulations.
3. **Corporate failure to prevent the facilitation of tax evasion** – The firm is required to report tax evasion committed within the company.

Third Party Notices

2.33 There are two factors to consider when determining what information HMRC can compel an individual to provide (without direction from the First Tier Tribunal). The first is the capacity that someone is acting in and the second is the type of the information requested. HMRC can request relevant data from **relevant data holders** (there are 16 broad categories of data and data holders – listed at the end of the chapter). Most family solicitors will not be data holders in their capacity as family solicitors.

2.34 Where firms are relevant data holders, HMRC can request information about their clients. HMRC has recently tried to gather client data from law firms by defining them as relevant data holders.

2.35 In a case of *Wilsons Solicitors*[8] HMRC were criticised for their attempt to obtain client information about offshore income from lawyers. HMRC had served an information notice on the Wilsons partnership. The notice required Wilsons as a 'relevant data holder' to provide 'relevant data'. The data HMRC was requesting included details of beneficial owners of offshore companies. Wilsons appealed the notice on the ground that they were not relevant data holders. HMRC argued that they were relevant data holders as Wilsons kept records relating to the beneficial ownership and interests (under Money Laundering Regulations). HMRC felt that these records met the test of maintaining a register and therefore made them a data holder. Of course if this argument held, then this would bring into the scope all firms who keep records for Money Laundering purposes.

2.36 The FTT found that HMRC was wholly incorrect and its interpretation in parts 'requires violation to be done to the wording and meaning' of the legislation. The judge also found that the information notice sent to Wilsons amounted to a fishing expedition by HMRC to try and obtain client data.

2.37 This case shines a light on the different methods HMRC are using to gather ever more data. Worryingly HMRC sent the notice to ten law firms and seven of the firms complied with the notices. The clear lesson here is to seek advice before responding to a HMRC request for information.

2.38 HMRC can issue an information request asking a taxpayer to provide information or produce a document if it is 'reasonably required for the purposes of checking the taxpayer's tax position',[9] a taxpayer notice. HMRC can also issue a third party notice which requests information or a document reasonably required to check another person's tax position. Currently, these can only be issued with the approval of the taxpayer or the tribunal.

2.39 An individual must comply with the requirements of a notice within the period specified in the notice. If an individual receives a third party notice in their capacity as a professional, they cannot be required to produce privileged information.

2.40 Further, a tax advisor cannot be required to produce relevant communications the purpose of which is to give or obtain advice about a person's tax affairs. This may help to reassure some clients who are seeking advice relating to previously undisclosed tax positions.

8 *Wilsons Solicitors LLP and HMRC* TC06778, TC/17/5726.
9 Finance Act 2008, Sch 36A.

2.42 If a client has failed to declare untaxed income, solicitors have no obligation to notify HMRC unless they believe the client has engaged in tax evasion and they have enabled them to do so. This is discussed further below.

Anti-Money Laundering Regulations

2.43 The Proceeds of Crime Act 2002 (POCA) created a single set of money laundering offences throughout the UK. It also created a disclosure regime which makes it an offence not to disclose:

- knowledge of money laundering;
- suspicion of money laundering;
- reasonable grounds for suspicion of money laundering (regulated sector only).

2.44 Knowledge of money laundering amounts to actual knowledge. Suspicion of money laundering is not defined in POCA but the courts provide some guidance. At a decision at the Court of Appeal,[10] Longmore LJ said that 'a vague feeling of unease would not suffice.' This approach was confirmed in the 2010 Court of Appeal decision in *Shah v HSBC.*

2.45 Therefore, we could assume that suspicion is more than a feeling of unease, however, feeling of unease also lacks definition. At Illustration A we look at a few circumstances which may fall into suspicious activity.

2.46 Under POCA money laundering is defined as:

- concealing criminal property; or
- entering into an arrangement whilst knowing or suspecting that it facilitates the acquisition, retention, use or control of criminal property and acquiring, using or possessing criminal property.

2.47 Therefore, if a solicitors suspects their client has entered into transactions which conceal criminal property or enter into an arrangement whilst knowing or suspecting it facilitates the acquisition, retention, use or control of criminal property and acquiring, using or possessing criminal property, they are required to make an authorised disclosure.

Exceptions to failure to disclose

2.48 There are three situations in which one has not committed an offence for failing to disclose:

10 *R v Da Silva* [2006] All ER (D) 131 (Jul).

1. You have a reasonable excuse.
2. You are a professional legal advisor or a relevant professional advisor and the information came to you in privileged circumstances.
3. You did not receive appropriate training from your employer.

2.49 Solicitors do not have to make a disclosure under POCA if the information comes to them in privileged circumstances. Note that the receipt of information in privileged circumstances is not the same as legal professional privilege.

2.50 Privileged circumstances as defined in POCA means information communicated:

- by a client, or a representative of a client, in connection with the giving of legal advice to the client; or
- by a client, or by a representative of a client, seeking legal advice from you, or
- by a person in connection with legal proceedings or contemplated legal proceedings.

Corporate failure to prevent the facilitation of tax evasion

2.51 The Criminal Finances Act 2017 made it an offence to fail to prevent tax evasion. The Act introduced two new offences: domestic and overseas. Both offences require criminal conduct on the part of the taxpayer and criminal conduct on the part of an associated person. An associated person is anyone who provides devices for or on behalf of the company or partnership. This legislation applies to the company or the partnership and not the individual. The company or partnership could be held responsible for the actions of the individual if they were unable to demonstrate that they had processes and producers to prevent and detect potential tax evasion.

It is unlikely that a family solicitor's practice would fall foul of these rules.

2.52

Illustration 2A

Mira is a family solicitor, she is instructed by her client John in family proceedings. Whilst discussing John's form E he explains that he does have rental income of about £10,000 per year but has never reported it on his tax return and has no intention of doing so. Mira should of course encourage John to rectify this position urgently with HMRC. However, Mira has no obligation to notify HMRC of this underreporting.

Consider a different scenario, John says he makes about £100,000 per year selling undisclosed items which he imports from overseas. Every few years he uses these funds to buy properties. This may appear suspicious to Mira especially as John will not give any information about what he is selling. As Mira has a suspicion this could bring her into the scope of the Money Laundering Regulations, however, as this information came to light in the connection of giving legal advice (privileged circumstances) to a client, she may be prohibited from making a report.

INTEREST

2.53 Interest is always payable on the late payment of taxes. Interest runs from the day after the payment of tax was due until the date of payment. In cases where an individual has overpaid tax and a repayment is due, HMRC will add on interest to the repayment. Not surprisingly this is much lower than the rate an individual pays on their late payment.

2.54 A table of HMRC interest payments is below. If an individual has a liability from, say, 2016, interest on the outstanding liability would be assessed as follows: from August 2016 to November 2017 interest would be charged at 2.75%; from November 2017 to August 2018 it would be charged at 3.00% and so on.

From	**Late payment %**	**Repayment %**
7 April 2020	2.60	0.50
30 March 2020 to 6 April 2020	2.75	0.50
21 August 2018 to 29 March 2020	3.25	0.50
21 November 2017 to 20 August 2018	3.00	0.50
23 August 2016 to 20 November 2017	2.75	0.50
29 September 2009 to 22 August 2016	3.00	0.50
24 March 2009 to 28 September 2009	2.50	0
27 January 2009 to 23 March 2009	3.50	0
6 January 2009 to 26 January 2009	4.50	0.75
6 December 2008 to 5 January 2009	5.50	1.50
6 November 2008 to 5 December 2008	6.50	2.25
6 January 2008 to 5 November 2008	7.50	3.00

Note: Different rules apply for offshore income and gains failures. These are discussed later in the chapter at **2.76** onwards.

PENALTIES

2.55 The nature and level of the penalty are based on several factors:

- the nature of the action;
- the behaviour of the taxpayer;
- whether the disclosure was prompted or unprompted; and
- how helpful the taxpayer is in helping HMRC understand the error.

2.56 Different penalty regimes apply for different actions. There are penalties for failing to keep accurate records, failure to file a return on time and failure to pay taxes on time. The penalty regime for these actions are not based on behaviour and the penalty is clearly defined in legislation. The penalties for these actions can be found at **4.40** in Chapter 4.

2.57 If a tax return has been incorrectly filed, or no tax return has been filed and taxes are due as a result of either the error or the non filing then the percentage of the penalty will be based on the behaviour of the taxpayer.

2.58 Penalties for incorrect tax returns are based on a percentage of the potential lost revenue (the additional tax that would have been payable had the tax return been submitted correctly).

2.59 The relevant percentage is based on the behaviour of the taxpayer. Behaviour is categorised as:

- inaccurate despite taking reasonable care;
- inaccurate through failure to take reasonable care (carelessness);
- deliberate;
- deliberate and concealed.

2.60 The maximum level of penalty HMRC can charge for the different behaviours is driven by whether the disclosure to HMRC was prompted or unprompted. HMRC guidance states 'a disclosure is unprompted if it is made at a time when the person making it has no reason to believe that HMRC have discovered or are about to discover the inaccuracy…otherwise it is prompted'.

2.61 If an individual submitted a return but later became aware that there were errors on the return and disclosed these to HMRC this would be a voluntary (unprompted) disclosure and lower penalties would usually apply.

Reason for penalty	**Maximum penalty**	**Minimum if unprompted**	**Minimum if prompted**
Took reasonable care	0%	0%	0%
Careless action	30%	0%	15%
Deliberate but not concealed	70%	20%	35%
Deliberate and concealed	100%	30%	50%

2.62 This brief table provides some context to how HMRC determines behaviour and what actions are likely to lead to being publicly named or placed under investigation. It then goes on to summarise what investigations clients may be placed under and what clients can expect should this happen to them.

Behaviour	HMRC examples	Examples on divorce	Penalty rate
Took reasonable care	Small arithmetical error A reasonable judgement is made on a valuation The error was made by the taxpayer after seeking and acting on advice from a 'competent advisor'	Reporting a gain on a property transfer at lower than deemed market value.	0% if the taxpayer notifies HMRC within 30 days of discovering the error.
Careless	Not keeping adequate records and making mistakes Failing to report one off gains	Failing to report a chargeable capital gain on a transfer or sale of a property is likely to be considered a careless error	Maximum penalty is 30%, this can be reduced to 0% in the case of unprompted disclosure and 15% in the case of a prompted disclosure
Deliberate and not concealed	Omitting significant amounts of income Describing transactions in a deliberately misleading way	Failing to report rental income on a jointly owned property	Maximum penalty is 70%, this can be reduced to 35% in the case of unprompted disclosure and 50% in the case of a prompted disclosure
Deliberate and concealed	Systematic diversion of income to an undisclosed bank account Destroying books or records Creation of false documents	Creating false invoices to artificially increase the amount of enhancement expenditure to reduce the taxable gain on the sale or transfer of a property	Maximum penalty is 100%, this can be reduced to 35% in the case of unprompted disclosure and 50% in the case of a prompted disclosure and HMRC may seek to prosecute an offence of tax evasion

PENALTY MITIGATION

2.63 Once the behaviour has been determined the maximum rate of penalty applies as default; however penalties can be reduced. The level of the mitigation depends on the quality of the disclosure to HMRC. Disclosure is defined as:

- informing HMRC about the return inaccuracy or under-assessment of tax;
- providing reasonable help to HMRC in quantifying the potential tax loss; and

- allowing HMRC access to books, records and information for the purpose of ensuring that the inaccuracy or understatement has been completely corrected.

2.64 The number of penalties imposed on taxpayers for deliberate errors on tax returns rose by 46% from 2016–17 to 2017–18,[11] during the same period penalties for careless errors reduced, suggesting that HMRC is pursuing the higher categories of blame and seeing their categorisation 'stick'. Where HMRC imposes a 'deliberate error' categorisation, it is permitted to adopt a wider and harsher range of powers to investigate and penalise the taxpayer. Therefore where a client does have errors on their tax return it will be beneficial to instruct a tax advisor to assist the client in negotiating with HMRC to try and mitigate the penalties.

2.65 The philosophy underpinning the arrangement is to encourage careful compliance so generally:

- where errors are found in the tax return of a deceased person no penalties will be charged;
- if a taxpayer can demonstrate that they took reasonable care, no penalty will be charged, however, tax and interest will be charged.

Illustration 2B Penalties

To run through the options let us take the example of Mr and Mrs Jones who are both additional rate taxpayers and jointly own an investment property.

- HMRC is seeking to charge a penalty on their 2020–21 tax returns as they inaccurately claimed a £6,000 in-year deduction for fitting a new kitchen in the property.
- The additional tax of £2,400 (being 40% of £6,000) is payable.
- Whether an additional amount is payable in the form of penalties depends on the behaviour:

Reasonable care (0%)

HMRC states that each person must take reasonable care with their tax affairs, but accept that this cannot be identified without 'consideration of the particular person's abilities and circumstances'.[12]

An individual can demonstrate that they took reasonable care if they can establish that they undertook actions which a reasonable person would undertake in their situation. It goes on to say that it is reasonable to expect a person who encounters a transaction with which they are not familiar to take care to find out about the correct tax treatment or seek appropriate advice.

11 www.ft.com/content/27609006-8504-11e8-a29d-73e3d454535d.
12 HMRC Internal Manual – Compliance Handbook CH81120.

Mr & Mrs Jones

Example of taking reasonable care: Mr & Mrs Jones understood that the costs for the new kitchen might not be allowable so Mrs Jones called HMRC's helpline and asked for further clarification and can prove that advice was given that if they were replacing items then the cost is defined as a repair and is allowed as an 'in year deduction'. What was not made clear and what HMRC accepts is that Mrs Jones innocently failed to establish was that they were not just replacing like for like items: they completely re-modelled the kitchen and made structural changes to the building to do so. This means the expenses are capital in nature and therefore would not properly be allowable at all.

As Mr & Mrs Jones called HMRC and requested further guidance (and can prove that they did so), HMRC agrees that they took reasonable care and so no penalties are imposed.[13]

Careless (up to 30%)

An error is careless if individuals failed to take reasonable care (ie behaviour which a reasonable person would not in the view of HRMC, have undertaken).

Mr & Mrs Jones

Example of carelessness: they completed the tax return and claimed the full cost of the kitchen as a deduction. They sought no further clarification on whether this is an allowable expense or not.

This would most likely be argued as a careless error.

Deliberate (up to 70%)

A 'deliberate act' is one which is done consciously with the intention or purpose of submitting an incorrect document.

Mr & Mrs Jones

Example of deliberate error: two years ago when they were planning to re-do the kitchen of the investment property they spoke to a tax advisor about whether they would be able to claim the costs of the refurbishment. The advisor told them that based on the level of work they were planning on doing to the kitchen this would be classified as a capital improvement and would not be allowable as an in-year deduction. They went ahead and filed the return with the deduction, knowing this was not allowed.

This is a deliberate error.

Deliberate and concealed (up to 100%)

Deliberate and concealed inaccuracies are the most serious level of tax evasion. It is when a taxpayer takes active steps to conceal the inaccuracy.

13 HMRC Internal Manual – Compliance Handbook CH81130.

Mr & Mrs Jones

Example of deliberate and concealed action: Mr and Mrs Jones knew that the level of constructive work they were proposing to do to the kitchen would qualify as a capital improvement (from their previous conversation with their tax advisor). They understood that like for like replacements would be allowable so they asked their builder to exclude certain items from the invoice to give the illusion that work done was purely replacement.

This is deliberate and concealed action.

2.66 Once it is apparent that there is an inaccuracy the taxpayer may secure reduced penalties if they provide a quality level of disclosure. This is often referred to as 'telling, helping and giving'.[14]

- 'Telling' gives a possible reduction of up to 30%.

  Telling depends on the timing, nature and extent of the telling.

- 'Helping' gives a possible reduction of up to 40%.

  Helping includes actively assisting HMRC in the assessment and engaging in the investigation to actively quantify the inaccuracies and volunteering additional information relevant to the disclosure.

- 'Giving access' gives a possible reduction of up to 30%.

  This is achieved where the taxpayer ensures that HMRC has access to the information and documents it has requested and provides the information in a timely manner.

2.67 One of the immediate problems with this form of mitigation is that during divorce, sometimes the party who is trying to correct a previous error does not have the information to help HMRC and cannot provide access to documents which they do not have.

Illustration 2C Penalties – Jerome and Mathilda

Jerome and Mathilda have been married for many years. Mathilda is a financial advisor and managed the money in the marriage. In 2011 Jerome and Mathilda bought an investment property in Scunthorpe. The rental profits were approximately £9,000 per year. Mathilda managed the property herself and all the expenses and income went through Mathilda's bank account. The

14 HMRC Internal manual, Compliance Handbook Penalties for Inaccuracies: penalty reductions for quality of disclosure CH82400.

profits were always used for family holidays. In 2020 Jerome met with a divorce lawyer to discuss his options with regards to divorce. During the meeting he gave details of the rental income, and said that he had never reported it on his tax return and did not think that he needed to.

On the advice of his lawyer, Jerome books an appointment with a tax advisor.

Jerome needs to disclose this error on his tax returns.

Did he take reasonable care? No, relying on his wife to handle the finances is not taking reasonable care.

Was he just careless? In the author's view his actions amount to being more than careless, the income has been received for many years, Jerome is a competent individual who has access to the news and internet, he should have at the very least checked with HMRC or online whether the income is reportable.

Is it a deliberate error? This does not mean that Jerome had a deliberate intention to defraud HMRC and not pay his taxes (it may be that that was the case!). It means that Jerome falls into the definition of deliberate behaviour in that he clearly omitted to tell HMRC about serious amounts of income.

Where there is a deliberate error HMRC can open up investigations for the prior 20 years, however, Jerome only started receiving the income in 2011 and this should therefore limit the scope to this date.

In order to quantify Jerome's exposure, we would assess the liability to tax. To do this fully we would need to know Jerome's income levels from 2011–2020 and the income and expenditure for the property. At the moment we know Jerome is a higher rate taxpayer and the profits were around £9,000 per year.

The total tax Jerome will have to pay is £14,400. We then need to consider penalties.

The maximum penalty that can apply for a deliberate error is 70% of the tax due, being £10,080. It is possible to reduce this to 35% of the tax due being £5,040 as this is the minimum penalty for an unprompted disclosure of a deliberate error.

However, to secure the lower rate Jerome will need to satisfy HMRC with the quality of his disclosure.

Telling

When he makes the disclosure to HMRC Jerome should tell HMRC when the income started and the total amount of profits made.

Helping

The level of help Jerome gives HMRC will depend on what questions they ask and what information they require. Jerome may not have all the details to hand unless he receives the bank statements from Mathilda.

Giving

If Jerome has no access to the bank statements, invoices from builders, tenancy contracts etc it is unlikely he will be able to secure mitigation for giving access to.

Therefore, on that basis, it would be wise to anticipate penalties in the region of 50% of the tax due being £7,200.

A REASONABLE EXCUSE

2.68 Where penalties have been correctly charged by HMRC (ie in line with the above principles), then the only grounds for appeal are that the taxpayer had a 'reasonable excuse' for their failure. The term 'reasonable excuse' is not defined in the legislation, though it does set out what is not a reasonable excuse.

Is divorce a reasonable excuse?

2.69 Insufficient funds and relying on third party advice (unless the taxpayer can show they took reasonable care) are not allowable excuses.

2.70 The reasonable excuse argument has been tried many times with varying levels of success.

2.71 In the case of *Timothy Raggatt v HMRC*[15] Mr Raggatt QC appealed against a decision by the First Tier Tribunal when it dismissed his dispute of penalties for late payment of income tax. Mr Raggatt, who had been a barrister for 40 years, claimed that he had exceptional circumstances between 2012 and 2014 as a result of a divorce settlement with a large lump sum and annual maintenance which reduced his income, combined with the cuts to Legal Aid meant that he 'could not have foreseen the change in the environment'. The Upper Tribunal commented that an insufficiency of funds is not a reasonable excuse and it was the view of the tribunal that

> 'although there is no legal requirement on the part of a self-employed professional person to reserve for his or her tax liabilities, in our view, a person with such an episodic life would be well advised to take reasonable steps to make some provision for tax liabilities or to ensure that he or she has appropriate bank facilities available to meet his or her expected tax liabilities if he or she subsequently wishes to rely on a reasonable excuse defence'.

15 *Timothy Raggatt v The Commissioners for HM Revenue and Customs* [2018] UKUT 0412 (TCC).

2.72 The tribunal here makes the case that all self-employed individuals have a duty to keep sufficient funds to once side to meet their tax liabilities and therefore, insufficient cash flow is not a reasonable excuse.

WHAT IS AT STAKE?

2.73 Naming and shaming – 200% penalties and being placed on HMRCs 'naughty list' are some of the penalties that taxpayers risk if they make errors on their tax returns. We have not quite reached the levels of the US where from 2015 US citizens risked having their passports revoked or denied if they have 'seriously delinquent tax debt'[16] but HMRC has enjoyed a rapid increase in its powers. Further, the amount of time HMRC has to issue a discovery assessment (the means by which it pursues an investigation into the detail of an individual's financial circumstances in previous tax years) is increasing. A recent case at the Court of Appeal has allowed HMRC to issue discovery assessments for errors committed in returns 20 years previously. The potential reputational risk of naming and shaming has prompted some individuals to try and bargain their way through the system by accepting the penalties provided their names were not published (HMRC continued to publish their names).

2.74 For an example of the impact of public-naming, perhaps think no further than Jimmy Carr – whilst our clients may not be so publicly visible, such information is very likely to be known in their profession and personal spheres with potentially devastating impacts.

Consequences of deliberate inaccuracies

2.75 If HMRC determines that the taxpayer made an inaccurate report deliberately then the following armory is opened:

1. *Significantly higher penalty amounts*

   The maximum penalty for deliberate behaviour is 70% and becomes 100% if it is for a deliberate and concealed action. Penalties can be up to 200% in respect of additional tax arising as a result of issues relating to offshore jurisdictions.

2. *No opportunity for suspension of the penalty*

   Where a taxpayer's behaviour has been careless the legislation allows for the possibility of a suspended penalty. However, if the behaviour is determined to be deliberate no suspension is allowed.

3. *'Named and shamed'*

   Under the 'naming and shaming' process HMRC will publish details of deliberate defaulters. Needless to say, this could cause significant embarrassment to the

16 *Fixing America's Surface Transportation Act* HR22, s 7345.

taxpayer. HMRC will only consider the publication of a taxpayer's name if the cumulative tax lost due to deliberate behaviour is more than £250,000.

There is no formal appeal permitted against the decision to name and shame. In the case of Mr and Mrs Chan, Mr Chan argued that publication could harm his reputation as a solicitor. Mr Chan said he was prepared to admit deliberate mis-declaration as long as his name was not published. The judge found that Mr Chan had an 'unreasonable expectation that the settlement encompassed non publication'.

HMRC has one year to publish the details of deliberate defaulters. Specific conditions must be met before HMRC are permitted to publish. However, new legislation makes it harder to avoid publication for offshore-related defaults.

4. *The managing serious defaulters programme*

   As well as the risk of having their name and details published, a taxpayer who has deliberately underpaid tax of more than £5,000 may be brought into the managing serious defaulters (MSD) programme, which involves a more serious monitoring of the taxpayer's financial affairs. If individuals find themselves in the MSD programme HMRC may undertake activities such as asking for records to be delivered to HMRC offices so they can be scrutinised and requiring additional disclosure of information and documents with a tax return.

OFFSHORE PENALTY REGIME

2.76 HMRC are continuing to tackle offshore tax avoidance. The Requirement to Correct (RTC) was introduced in Finance (No 2) Act 2007. It required tax irregularities in offshore matters to be disclosed by 30 September 2018. Coinciding with this is the Common Reporting Standard (CRS), the global standard for the automatic exchange of financial information between governments. It is aimed at worldwide tax evasion. These standards require financial institutions to report information to the local tax authority. This data is then passed to the tax authority where the customer is resident. The home authority (in this case the UK) use the data to tackle avoidance.

2.77 From 1 October 2018 HMRC started to receive financial data from around 200 jurisdictions, the information exchanged includes individuals' names, account numbers and balances. Therefore, if your client has any overseas income or gains which have not been reported to HMRC they should quickly reconsider their position.

2.78 It is going to be very difficult for clients who have overseas income or gains to keep it hidden from HMRC as it is much easier for HMRC to identify avoidance following the exchange of data.

Offshore matters include income, assets and transfers outside of the UK. Typical errors would be:

- non disclosure by UK residents of overseas income or gains;
- incorrect treatment of remittances;
- settlors failing to pay IHT on transfers of overseas assets.

2.79 Those individuals who did not correct their outstanding position by 30 September 2018 are now within the Failure to Correct (FTC) regime, this is effectively an individual who had offshore income/gains pre 30 September 2018 and did not report it to HMRC. This regime applies to income and gains arising from overseas, from bank interest to property income or gains from selling a property overseas. UK residents must report these income and gains on their tax returns. The penalties regime for Failure to Correct is different from the standard penalty regime.

2.80 This regime has stricter penalties than the standard penalty regime. Where taxpayers have failed to disclose overseas liabilities by 30 September 2018, the penalties they face start at 200% of underpaid tax, this can be reduced to 100% in the case of an unprompted (voluntary) disclosure.

2.81 Further, in cases where the tax at stake is over £25,000 in any tax year HMRC can levy an asset-based penalty of up to 10% on the value of the relevant asset.

2.82 Individuals can disclose their worldwide income via the worldwide disclosure facility which can be accessed online through the Direct Gov website. For the best chance of reducing penalties individuals need to voluntarily disclose.

2.83 Further, this regime comes with extended deadlines to enquire. Careless behaviour can be assessed for up to ten years (rather than the usual six); assessments for deliberate behaviour can be assessed for up to 24 years (rather than the usual 20).

2.84 Clients who have income or gains which have not be reported in the UK should strongly consider rectifying their position urgently. Two of the most significant elements of this regime are that HMRC will likely have access to the information (through the CRS) and they have extended time limits to open an enquiry. HMRC investigations relating to offshore activity is matter of when rather than if.

CHAPTER 3

Residency and Domicile

Contents at a Glance

DOMICILE

3.1 An individual's residence and domicile will determine how they are taxed in the UK.

Residency is where a person is currently living and is often determined through the individual's actual presence in the country. Domicile is an old concept and traces back to Roman times where a person had to pay taxes where they had their *origo* (origin). In tax law there are three primary tests that identify the type of domicile. If a person is not domiciled under any of these tests, they may be treated as deemed domiciled in the UK. For tax purposes there is no difference between being domiciled or deemed domiciled for income tax and capital gains tax.

3.2 Domicile is quite a British concept, most tax systems for example in France and Germany, do not have an equivalent for tax purposes. They tax their individuals based on their residency position with no regard to their nationality or domicile. Domicile is a legal concept and does not have a specific definition for tax purposes. It is often defined as a place where a person has their permanent home. Domicile is tied to a territory subject to a single system of law, so a person can be domiciled in England and Wales, Scotland or in Northern Ireland, but not the UK. However, for the sake of simplicity we will use the term UK domiciled.

There are three types of domicile:

Domicile of origin	An individual acquires a domicile of origin in the UK if their father was born in the UK (or from their mother if the parents were not married).
Domicile of dependence	An individual can change their domicile from the age of 16. Until then their domicile will follow the person on whom they are legally dependent.
Domicile of choice	If an individual with a UK domicile of origin wishes to acquire a new domicile, they must either: – leave the UK and settle permanently in that other country; or – if the person is living abroad already, they must intend to remain in that other country permanently or indefinitely.
Deemed Domicile	An individual is deemed domiciled in the UK if they have been resident in the UK for at least 15 out of the previous 20 tax years.

3.3 For people to change their domicile they will need to provide strong evidence that they intend to live in the other country permanently. HMRC will look at the following factors when reviewing a person's domicile:

- intentions of the individual;
- their permanent residence;
- their business interests;
- their social and family interest.

3.4 Couples can have different domiciles (different rules apply for marriages which took place prior to 1974[1]).

3.5 There are slightly different deemed domicile rules for inheritance tax than there are for income and capital gains tax. We will only cover the deeming rules for income tax and capital gains tax. Where an individual is deemed domiciled in the UK, they are taxable in the UK on their worldwide income and gains in much the same way as a UK domiciled individual.

3.6 An individual is deemed domiciled if they meet either of the following conditions:

1 For marriages that took place prior to 1 January 1974, the Domicile and Matrimonial Proceedings Act 1973 (DMPA 1973), s 4 effectively re-imposed the wife's domicile of dependence at 31 December 1973 as a domicile of choice capable of being lost in the same way as any other domicile of choice.

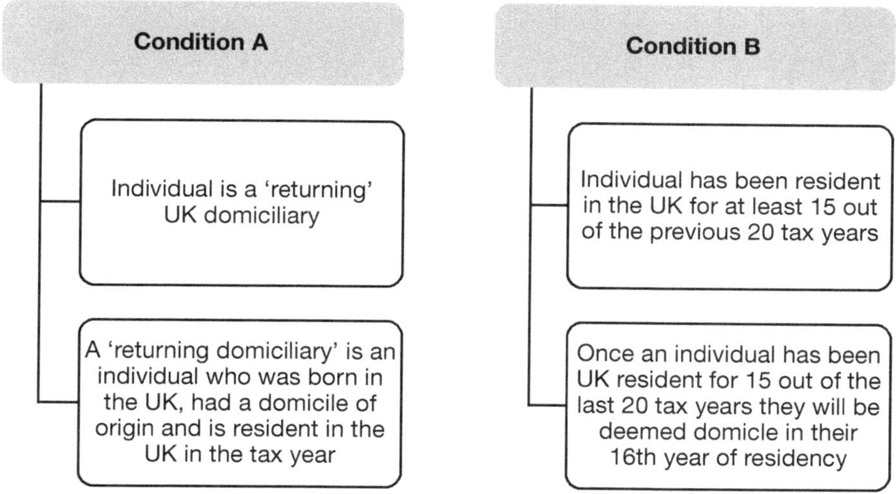

ARISING OR REMITTANCE BASIS

3.7 Individuals who are not domiciled in the UK can choose whether they wish to be assessed on the arising basis of taxation or the remittance basis. This choice is made annually. If an individual does not elect to be taxed on the remittance basis they will be taxed on the arising basis. This means they are taxable on their worldwide income and gains (the same tax position as if they were resident and domiciled in the UK).

3.8 Individuals who are resident and non-UK domiciled (and non-deemed domiciled) can claim the remittance basis of taxation. Individuals who claim the remittance basis are taxable on their UK income and any foreign income and gains earned in the year to the extent that they remit (bring) the money into the UK. Individuals who claim the remittance basis lose their entitlement to the tax-free personal allowance.

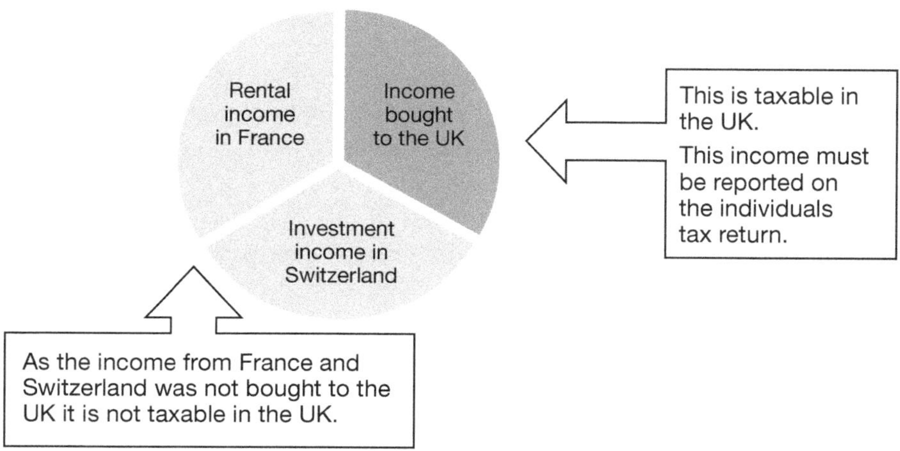

WHAT CONSTITUTES A REMITTANCE?

3.9 The rules on remittances are broad. In brief, there is a remittance if any property consisting of, representing or derived from foreign income or foreign chargeable gains is:[2]

- brought to, received or used in the UK for the benefit of a 'relevant person';
- used to provide a service in the UK to or for the benefit of a 'relevant person';
- used in connection with a loan or debt to provide a UK person with a UK benefit, or
- used to service a debt which relates to property of provision of services in the UK.

3.10 A relevant person includes

- the individual;
- the individual's spouse or civil partner;
- any child or grandchild under the age of 18.

3.11 Remittances only apply to foreign income and gains earned whilst the individual was resident in the UK. Any pre earned capital can be brought to the UK without incurring any tax. This can be helpful if a settlement can be sourced from non-UK funds. We discuss this further at **3.19**.

Illustration 3A

Pre earned capital – Judy

Judy is domiciled in Israel. In Israel she sold her property and had approximately an amount equivalent to £60,000 in her bank account in Israel. In 2020/21 Judy came to live in the UK. The £60,000 in the bank is pre earned capital and can be bought into the UK without triggering an income tax charge.

However, there are special rules about mixed funds. If in 2020/21 whilst Judy was resident in the UK she earned £100 interest on the £60,000 then the interest is foreign income which has been earned by Judy whilst resident. So, £60,000 can be bought into the UK without tax implications but if the £100 is remitted it will be taxed as a remittance if Judy is filing on the remittance basis.

The order of remittances is complex and, in the case where clients have offshore accounts with mixed funds (for example pre earned capital mixed with income or gains earned whilst the individual is UK resident), advice should be sought.

2 Income Tax Act 2007, s 809L.

Illustration 3B

Remittance basis – Taxable income: Tameka

Tameka is 34, she is domiciled in Morocco, she has come to the UK for two years to undertake a part time masters degree. Whilst in the UK, Tameka works part time earning £17,000 per year. In Morocco Tameka has four rental properties generating profit equal to £32,000 per year. She will not bring any of the profits from the rental properties to the UK.

As Tameka is resident in the UK and non-domiciled, she can file her tax return on the arising basis or the remittance basis.

Arising basis – taxation of worldwide income arising in the tax year.

Employment income	£17,000
Overseas rental income	£32,000
Total income	£49,000
Less: Personal allowance	£(12,500)
Taxable income	£36,500
£36,500 at 20%	£7,300

Remittance basis – taxation of UK sourced income and money remitted

Employment income	£17,000
Less: Personal allowance	£–*
Total taxable income	£17,000
£17,000 @ 20%	£3,400

*Tameka does not benefit from a personal allowance as this is removed for individuals filing on the remittance basis.

It is most tax efficient for Tameka to claim the remittance basis of taxation, even with the loss of the tax-free personal allowance. Tameka can amend this choice each tax year according to which will be the most beneficial for her.

Tameka will most likely be given the benefit of her personal allowance through PAYE, therefore she will likely have a tax liability when she completes her tax return as the personal allowance will be withdrawn.

If Tameka does claim the remittance basis she will be taxed on any income from Morocco which she brings to the UK.

SUMMARY OF TAXATION FOR NON-DOMICILES

3.12

Source of funds	**Tax treatment in the UK**
Pre arrival capital	Not taxable in the UK
Cash for Qualifying Business Investments	Not taxable in the UK
Foreign income & gains earned whilst resident in the UK	Taxable to the extent that it is remitted to the UK
UK Income & gains earned whilst resident in the UK	Taxable in the UK

REMITTANCE BASIS CHARGE (RBC)

3.13 As the remittance enables non-domiciles to remove their overseas income and gains from the UK scope of taxation, the government introduced a charge for claiming the remittance basis for long-term residents. Individuals who have been resident in the UK for at least seven out of the last nine tax years have to pay a charge of £30,000 if they wish to claim the remittance basis. Individuals who have been resident in the UK for at least 12 out of the last 14 tax years are subject to a £60,000 charge if they wish to claim the remittance basis. This is known as the Remittance Basis Charge (RBC).

3.14 It will be important to specify how long a client has been living in the UK if they are non-domiciled so that their tax position can be accurately estimated.

3.15 **Note:** if your client is non-UK domiciled this will affect their tax position. If your client has at any time been domiciled in the UK or has been living in the UK for over 15 years, seek advice to ensure that their new non-domiciled position is a strong one. It might be wise to consider the tax implications as both a UK domicile and a non domicile.

Illustration 3C

Mixed Domicile Marriage – Piotr and Magda

Piotr and Magda were both born in Poland. Magda moved to the UK in January 2003 and has lived here from 2003 onwards. She still considers Poland her home and takes regular trips home to visit her friends and family. Magda has said she considers herself to be domiciled in Poland and says she will return there when she retires. Piotr moved to the UK in 2014 and met Magda at a dance class. They married very shortly after meeting in January 2015 and bought two properties together, one in Krakow to rent out and one in Poole to live in as their main home. In March 2020 they separated and decided to divorce. They had no children together and agreed to sell both properties and split the proceeds. At the time of separation both Magda and Piotr were living in the UK.

The property in Krakow is standing with a gain of £320,000 and the property in Poole is standing at a gain of £240,000.

Domicile position

Magda does not have a domicile of origin in the UK as her father was not born in the UK, she does not have a domicile of dependency as she did not move here when she was under 16 and she does not have a domicile of choice as she says she plans to return to Poland in the long term. However, as Magda has been resident in the UK for 17 out of the last 20 tax years (2003/04 to 2019/20) she is considered to be deemed domicile in the UK.

As a deemed domicile and resident, she is subject to tax on her worldwide income and gains in the UK.

Piotr does not meet any of the three types of domicile and he has been resident in the UK for 7 out of the last 20 tax years (2013/14 to 2019/20) so he is not deemed domiciled in the UK.

Tax implications

On the sale of the property in Poole both Magda and Piotr can claim Principal Private Residence relief to exempt the gain. Providing they have been living in the property as their main home since they purchased it, they will have no capital gains tax to pay on sale and they will not need to report the gain on their tax return.

On the sale of the property in Krakow Magda and Piotr will have different tax implications due to their different domicile status.

Magda

50% of the gain (£160,000) will be assessed to tax on Magda. She will have to pay capital gains tax at the property rate of 28% on any gain above her annual exemption of £12,300. Therefore, her tax liability is as follows:

Gain	£160,000
Less: Annual exemption	(£12,300)
Taxable gain	£147,700
Capital gains tax at 28%	£41,356

Magda's capital gains tax liability in the UK on the sale will be £41,356. She will be able to claim a tax credit for taxes paid in Poland on the same gain.

Piotr

3.16 As Piotr is not domiciled in the UK, he can choose to be taxed on either the arising or the remittance basis. However, as Piotr has been living in the UK for seven out of the last nine tax years, he will be required to pay the remittance basis charge if he wants to claim the remittance basis. Piotr's charge will be £30,000.

3.17 If Piotr claims the remittance basis he will not be assessed to tax in the UK on the gain in Krakow. The remittance basis charge of £30,000 is less than the potential capital gains tax liability of £41,356.

If Piotr had been living in the UK for say 4 tax years, he could claim the remittance basis without having to pay a charge and the gain would not be taxable in the UK (on the basis that he would not remint any of the funds to the UK).

Summary of liabilities

3.18

	Capital Gains Tax liabilities	
	Magda	**Piotr**
Poole (FMH)	Nil	Nil
Krakow property	£41,440	£30,000 (RBC)

NON-DOMICILES – SETTLEMENTS AND MAINTENANCE

3.19 The way non-domiciles are subject to tax in the UK means that some tax planning can be undertaken with regards to maintenance and settlements. In the case of *ABX v SBX* [2018] EWFC 81, the husband and wife were both nationals of a mainland Continental European country and not domiciled in the UK. They had three young children who all lived in the UK. As non-domiciles the husband and wife had the option to claim the remittance basis, allowing all non-UK sources of income to only be taxable in the UK if it was remitted to the UK.

3.20 In this case it was agreed that the structure of payments of capital from the husband to the wife should be as follows: the 'funds are paid offshore to her [the wife], she is able to remit them onshore without incurring a tax liability'. As the funds being paid offshore are income earned from the husband and not the wife, the wife can remit them to UK without being charged to tax as she is not remitting income that she earned.

3.21 The judge commented at paragraph 48 that to him this seems 'a remarkable tax loophole, but given that both parties accept that, on advice, it exists and is legitimate' that he would not stand in the way of the wife 'receiving lump sums into an offshore account'. It is later noted that 'every pound received by the wife is worth a pound and every pound received by the husband is worth 55p'. This is the case because if the husband brings money into the UK which he has earned whilst living in the UK, it will be taxed as income at a rate of 45%.

3.22 This type of planning should come with many caveats, as, if the transfer offshore to the wife and then onshore by the wife is considered a remittance then the money is taxable. The definition of a remittance is noted at **3.9** and includes income brought to, received or used in the UK for the benefit of a 'relevant person'. A relevant person includes:

- the individual;
- the individual's spouse or civil partner;
- any child or grandchild under the age of 18

3.23 Therefore, whilst they remain married the wife is a relevant person and any money she brings to the UK will be deemed a remittance from the husband, if it is coming from income earned whilst he was UK resident. He would be charged to tax on the income as if he had bought it into the UK directly.

3.24 Further, the children will remain relevant persons until they reach 18, therefore any funds spent on them even by the wife (who post divorce is a non-relevant person) would constitute a remittance. In this case it may be wise for the wife to undertake not to earmark any funds directly for the benefit of the children.

> **Note:** Where one or more spouses is non-UK domiciled there may be some tax advantages to structuring the maintenance or settlement payments to be paid offshore, or to be directed from pre earned capital.

RESIDENCY

3.25 Generally speaking, individuals who are resident in the UK are taxable on their worldwide income and capital gains arising in that year and individuals who are not resident in the UK are taxable on their UK income and capital gains from property only in that year.

3.26 From April 2013 residency has been determined in the UK through the statutory residency test (SRT). The SRT has three parts, an individual is either:

- automatically non-resident;
- automatically resident;
- resident/non-resident through the sufficient ties test (covered in **3.29**)

3.27 If you think your client may be non-UK resident it will be important to establish this early on for a number of reasons. First as a non-resident they will be treated differently for tax purposes. For example, they will pay no capital gains tax on a disposal of shares (subject to whether they return to the UK – see **3.35**). Secondly, if they are required to spend a significant number of days in the UK due to the proceedings this might impact their residency status which in turn will impact their tax position.

3.28 We will now go through the tests so that you can apply them to your clients. This will only be necessary in cases where a client's residency is in question. The conditions should be read in the order listed below.

3.29 A flowchart for determining residency can be found at **3.30**.

1. Automatically non-resident.

An individual will be non-resident in the UK in the tax year if they meet one of the following conditions:

- they are present in the UK for under 16 days, where the individual has been resident in the UK in one or more of the previous three tax years;
- they are present in the UK for under 46 days, where they have not been resident in the UK in any of the three previous tax years;
- they are working full time overseas.

2. Automatically resident.

An individual will be automatically resident in the UK in the tax year if they meet one of the following conditions:

- they spend over 183 days in the UK in the tax year;
- they have a home in the UK (which they are present in for over 90 days);
- they carry out full-time work in the UK (this is determined by a complex calculation, effectively the individual should be working for 35 hours a week with no prolonged absences from work).

If an individual does not meet the automatic resident or automatic non-resident tests then their residency status will be determined by a combination of how many days they spend in the UK and how many ties they have to the UK. The more ties an individual has in the UK the fewer days they can spend in the UK without triggering residency.

The UK tax system is a self-assessment system, individuals are expected to be honest in their dealings with HMRC. Therefore, whilst some of the below may seem hard to prove the individual is expected to act with honesty when assessing their residency.

3. Sufficient ties.

The ties are:

Family	They will meet this tie if their spouse and or minor children are resident in the UK and the individual sees the child for at least 61 days in the tax year. If a couple are separated the spouse will not create a tie in the UK, however if they have minor children in the UK they will meet the family tie.
Accommodation	This tie will be met if the individual has a place to live in the UK which is available to be used by them for a continuous period of at least 91 days; and they spend at least one night there during the tax year.
Work	This tie will be met if they work in the UK for 40 days or more.
UK Presence	This tie will be met if the individual spent more than 90 days in the UK in either of the previous two tax years.
Country	A country tie is created if the individual spends more days in the UK in the tax year than in any other single country.

3.30 Generally speaking, a day is counted as a residency day if an individual is in the UK at midnight. Where an individual has substantial days in the UK but no midnight stays they may be subject to special deeming provisions.

The number of ties an individual has in the UK directly affects the number of days they can stay in the UK before triggering residency. The day counts are different for individuals leaving or arriving into the UK.

Number of days in the UK	**Not UK resident in any of the three previous tax years (arrivers)**	**Resident in the UK for one or more of the three preceding tax years (leavers)**
<16 days	Always non-resident	Always non-resident
16–45 days	Always non-resident	Resident if four or more ties are met
46–90 days	Resident if four ties are met	Resident if three or more ties are met
91–120 days	Resident if three or more ties are met	Resident if two or more ties are met
121–182 days	Resident if two or more ties are met	Resident if one or more ties are met
≥183 days	Always resident	Always resident

Statutory Residency Test – Automatic Tests – Flow chart – Illustration 3D

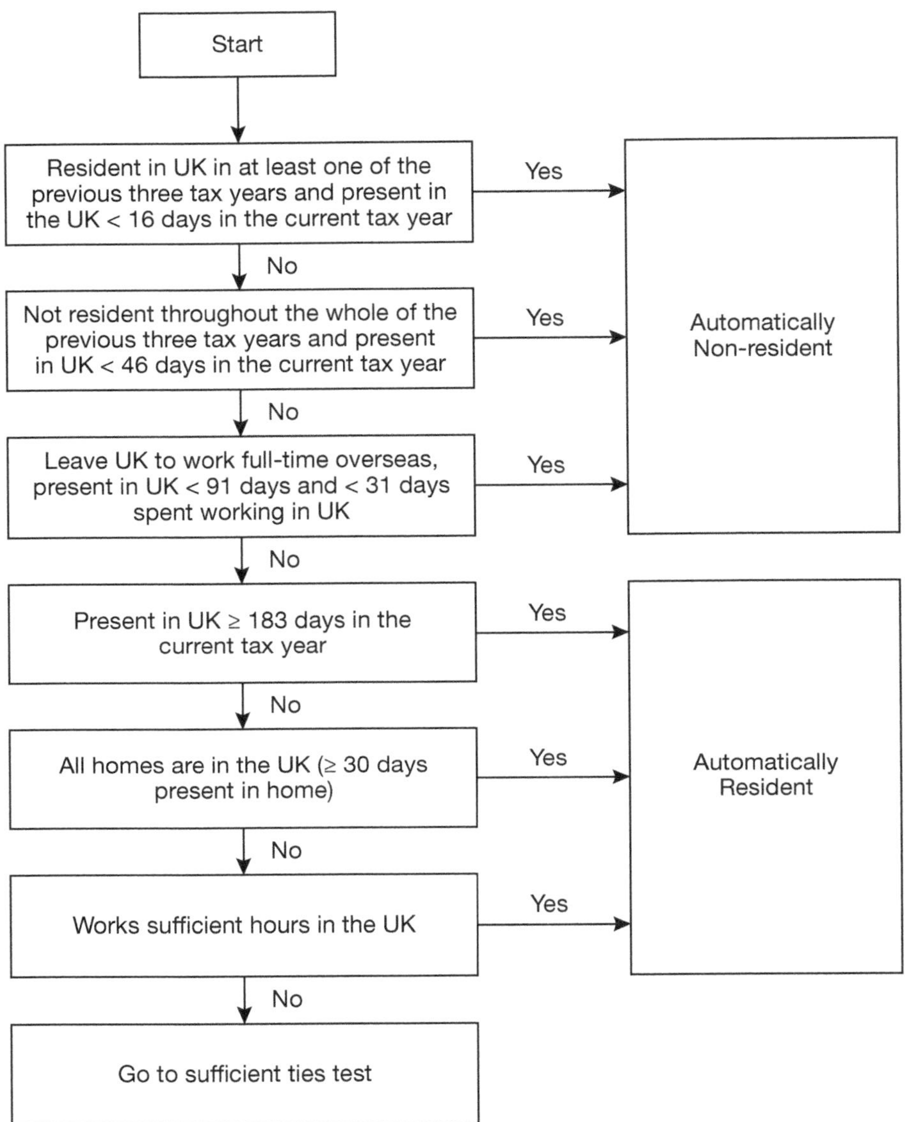
Start
Resident in UK in at least one of the previous three tax years and present in the UK < 16 days in the current tax year
Yes
No
Not resident throughout the whole of the previous three tax years and present in UK < 46 days in the current tax year
Yes
No
Leave UK to work full-time overseas, present in UK < 91 days and < 31 days spent working in UK
Yes
No
Automatically Non-resident
Present in UK ≥ 183 days in the current tax year
Yes
No
All homes are in the UK (≥ 30 days present in home)
Yes
No
Works sufficient hours in the UK
Yes
No
Automatically Resident
Go to sufficient ties test

Statutory Residency Test – Sufficient ties

The number of ties below, together with whether resident at any time in the three previous years and the number of days spent in the UK, determine the individual's residence status for the tax year as shown in the table below.

Has the individual been non resident throughout the three prior tax years?

Yes

UK Resident Family	
Substantive UK Employment ≥ 40 UK days in the tax year	
Accessible UK Accommodation stayed in ≥ 1 night	
Present ≥ 91 days in either of previous two tax years	
Total ties	

Number of days in the UK in a tax year	1 or No UK ties	2 UK ties	3 UK ties	4 UK ties
<16 days	NR	NR	NR	NR
16 to 45 days	NR	NR	NR	NR
46 to 90 days	NR	NR	NR	R
91 to 120 days	NR	NR	R	R
121 to 182 days	NR	R	R	R
>183 days	R	R	R	R

No

UK Resident Family	
Substantive UK Employment ≥ 40 UK days in the tax year	
Accessible UK Accommodation stayed in ≥ 1 night	
Present ≥ 91 days in either of previous two tax years	
Present in UK ≥ any other single country	
Total ties	

Number of days in the UK in a tax year	No ties	1 ties	2 ties	3 ties	≥4 ties
<16 days	NR	NR	NR	NR	NR
16 to 45 days	NR	NR	NR	NR	R
46 to 90 days	NR	NR	NR	R	R
91 to 120 days	NR	NR	R	R	R
121 to 182 days	NR	R	R	R	R
>183 days	R	R	R	R	R

Split year

3.31 Where an individual leaves or arrives in the UK part way through the tax year, split year treatment may apply. Split year treatment is where an individual is treated as resident or non-resident for part of the tax year. This means their income and capital gains may be treated differently in one tax year if part of the year they were resident and part of the year they were non-resident.

Split year treatment applies in the following cases.

Leavers

3.32

- The individual starts full-time work overseas.
- The individual is the partner of an individual who has started full-time work overseas.
- The individual leaves the UK and ceases to have a home in the UK.

Arrivers

3.33

- The individual is starting to have their only home in the UK.
- The individual is working full time in the UK.
- The individual ceases full-time work overseas.

If you think split year treatment may apply to your client seek advice on this and mention it in any request for tax advice.

UK Resident

3.34 If an individual is resident in the UK they are taxable on their worldwide income and gains.

TAXATION OF NON-RESIDENTS

3.35 The taxation of non-residents depends on the nature of the income and gains and the individual's previous residency position in the UK.

Generally speaking, the following applies for non-residents:

Income Source	
UK sourced income	Taxable in the UK
Non-UK sourced income	Not taxable in the UK
UK gains from non-residential property	Not taxable in the UK
UK gains from residential property	Taxable in the UK
Non-UK gains	Not taxable in the UK

We will look at four individuals with different income and different history in the UK.

> *Gerard*
>
> Gerard is UK domiciled, he lived in the UK all of his life until January 2017. In January 2017, Gerard retired and moved to Sweden. After three years in Sweden Gerard missed London and moved back.
>
> *Poppy*
>
> Poppy is a director and shareholder of Pears Pty (an Australian company). Poppy lived in Australia until she was 20, then she moved to the UK, she lived in the UK for ten years and then moved to Germany. Whilst in Germany she drew down income from Pears Pty of £80,000. The following year she returned to the UK.
>
> *Lucas*
>
> Lucas owns two investment properties in France, he has lived in France for the last 15 years. He moved to the UK for one year and then returned to France. Two months after he left the UK, he sold his French properties and then decided to return to the UK.
>
> *Phoebe*
>
> Phoebe is domiciled in Iceland, she lived in the UK from 2007 to 2011 and during that time purchased a property in the UK. She has not returned to the UK since leaving in 2011. In January 2020 she decides to sell her UK property.

3.36 To establish the tax position of non-residents you need to know:

- their residency position in the UK for the 7 years before they left the UK;
- how long they have been non-resident;
- the nature of the income or gain;
- the date of disposal.

Gerard, Poppy and Lucas have income and gains whilst being non-UK resident.

> **Taxation of non-resident gains**
>
> *Gerrard*
>
> Gerrard is UK domiciled, he lived in the UK all of his life until January 2017. In that time, he built up a substantial investment portfolio. The total value of all shares was £2.5 million. His original investment was £1 million. At the end of January 2017 Gerrard retired and moved to Sweden.

In May 2017, whilst resident in Sweden, he sold his entire share portfolio. As he is selling the shares whilst non-resident in the UK there will be no immediate charge to capital gains tax. Therefore Gerrard has no tax liability in the UK at the point of sale.

Poppy

As a non-resident Poppy is not subject to income tax on the income she received from Pears Pty. She does not have to report this income on her UK tax return, nor does she have to pay any income tax in the UK at the point she receives the income.

Lucas

Lucas sold non-UK property, therefore there is no capital gains tax due in the UK whilst he is non-resident.

Phoebe

Even though Phoebe is non-UK resident, as her gains related to a UK residential property she will be liable to capital gains tax in the UK on her gain. The gain will need to be reported and tax paid within 30 days of the disposal.

Temporary non-residence

3.37 The rules regarding non-residents were previously open to abuse. It was common for individuals to leave the UK long enough to become non-resident, sell their assets and return to the UK the following year with no tax to pay. Unhappy with this practice, the government introduced the temporary non-residence rules to try and combat this activity.

3.38 Any income or gains incurred in a period of non-residence will be taxable as earned income or gains when the individual returns to the UK if they return within five years (or five complete tax years if they left the UK before 6 April 2013) of receiving the income or gains.

The rules regarding temporary non-residence can be complex, so a much simplified version is given below.

3.39 If an individual has been resident in the UK for at least four out of the seven tax years prior to becoming non-resident, the temporary non-residence rules are likely to apply.

3.40 Although the non-resident may not be taxable on the income or gain when it arises, if that type of income or gain is caught by the temporary non-resident provisions it will become taxable in the UK if the individual becomes a UK resident within five years.

3.41 The types of income and gains affected by the temporary non-residence rules include:

- flexi-access from a foreign pension;
- pensions under registered pension schemes;
- relevant foreign income taxed under the remittance basis;
- capital gains, including gains from non-resident companies attributed to UK participators;
- a lump sum from a UK pension scheme;
- non-qualifying distributions of UK close companies;
- dividends from an overseas company that would be a close company if it was resident in the UK;
- stock dividends of UK close companies;
- loans from a close company that are written-off during a period of non-residence;
- income distributions from a company that would be a close company if it was resident in the UK if not otherwise taxable in the UK, but which would have been taxable if received (or entitlement arose) in the year of return;
- life insurance chargeable event gains.

Gerrard

Gerard has been resident in the UK for at least four out of the previous seven tax years, therefore the temporary non-residence provisions will apply to him. After three years in Sweden, Gerrard missed his home and returned to the UK. Under the temporary non-residence rules Gerrard is deemed to have incurred the gain on his shares on the date he returns. He returns in December 2019, this is within the 2019/20 tax year. If Gerard had remained outside of the UK for 5 years the gain would not be assessable on his return.

Gerrard's capital gains tax computation will be as follows:

	£
Proceeds	2,500,000
Base cost	(1,000,000)
Gain	1,500,000
Less: Annual exemption	(12,300)
Taxable gain	1,487,700
£37,500 at 10%	3,750
£1,450,200 at 20%	290,040
Total capital gains tax payable	**293,790**

Even though Gerrard has been out of the UK for three years he will only get the benefit of one annual exemption.

Poppy

Poppy has been resident in the UK for at least four out of the previous seven tax years, therefore the temporary non-residence provisions will apply to her. As a non-resident Poppy is not subject to income tax on the income she received from Pears Pty. On return to the UK, Poppy will be taxed as though she received that income whilst she was in the UK.

Poppy's income tax computation is as follows:

	£
Income	80,000
Less: Personal allowance	(12,500)
Taxable gain	67,500
£37,500 at 7.5%	2,812
£30,000 at 32.5%	9,750
Total income tax payable	**12,562**

If Poppy paid any tax in Germany on the £80,000 this will be deductible from the UK tax due.

Lucas

Lucas has not been resident in the UK for at least four out of the previous seven tax years, therefore the temporary non-residence provisions will not apply to him when he returns to the UK. No capital gains tax will be payable when Lucas returns.

Phoebe

Phoebe has already paid tax on the gain of the property. No further taxes will be payable even if she returns to the UK.

Note: If your client is currently non-resident or will be non-resident in the UK and you are seeking tax advice, ensure you ask the advisor to consider the temporary non-residence rules to ensure that if they return to the UK the potential liability is captured.

DOUBLY TAXED INCOME AND GAINS

3.42 Unlike domicile, an individual can be resident in more than one country at a time. If an individual's income or gains are subject to tax in multiple locations, we would first look to the double taxation treaty to determine which country has the right to tax the income and then the other country would take a credit for taxes already paid. As a very general rule, usually the place where the income arises has the initial taxing rights and the other country will take a credit for taxes paid. If any additional tax is due in the other country, the individual will have to pay this tax.

Example of Foreign Tax Credit – Magda and Piotr

When Magda sells the property in Krakow this will likely be subject to tax in Poland of 19%.

19% of the gain of £160,000 is £30,400. As the property is in Poland, they have the primary taxing rights over the property.

The UK will claim a credit for the taxes already paid.

Magda's computation will be as follows:

Gain	£160,000
Less: Annual exemption	(£12,300)
Taxable gain	£147,700
Capital gains tax at 28%	£41,356
Less: Foreign tax credit	(£30,400)
Tax payable	£10,956

If the tax in Poland was £50,000 (ie above the UK liability) Magda would still have to report this on her UK tax return and claim the full credit. No additional taxes would be due but the reporting requirements still apply.

Note: If there is overseas property which is likely to be subject to tax in the overseas location and the UK, ensure both experts are given the potential tax figures in each location. Usually the overseas country will have the primary taxing rights and the UK will take a credit for taxes paid oversees. Tax credits do not apply automatically and must be claimed via the self-assessment tax return.

DUAL RESIDENTS

3.43 It is likely that the position will be complicated in cases of dual residents; therefore seeking advice early on will be necessary.

SUMMARY OF TAX POSITIONS

3.44

	UK Domicile and Deemed Domicile	**Non-UK domicile**
UK Resident	Taxable on worldwide income and gains	Taxable on UK sourced income and offshore income to the extent that it is remitted to the UK
Non-resident	Taxable on UK sourced income and property gains	Taxable on UK sourced income and property gains

Note: If your client is non-resident in the UK ensure they know the number of days that they can spend in the UK before triggering residency. Additionally ensure that you have captured their future plans especially if they are planning on returning to the UK as this will impact their tax position.

RESIDENCY AND DOMICILE CHECKLIST

3.45

		Yes/No/NA	Risk if yes	Mitigation	Ref
Domicile	Is the client non UK Domiciled?	☐ Yes ☐ No ☐ N/A	As a non-domicile individual different tax treatment will apply to them. If they have been in the UK for less than 15 out of the last 20 tax years they can nominate which basis to be taxed on.	Ensure that the client has been filing their self-assessment tax return correctly. In the year of disposals or transfer by divorce it may be more beneficial for the client to claim the remittance basis if non-UK assets are being sold or transferred.	**3.7**
	Has the client been in the UK for the last 15/20 tax years?	☐ Yes ☐ No ☐ N/A	The client will be treated as deemed domiciled in the UK, all of their worldwide income & gains will be taxable in the UK.	Ensure the client understands their tax position and is reporting any overseas income and gains.	**3.6**
	Is maintenance being paid by a non-domiciled individual?	☐ Yes ☐ No ☐ N/A	The settlement may be structured in a certain way so that one party can transfer funds to the other party offshore and then the receiving party remits the income to the UK with no tax charge	If the money remitted is used for the benefit of minor children it will be counted as a remittance and the original party will be charged to income tax on the remittance.	**3.19**

		Yes/No/NA	Risk if yes	Mitigation	Ref
Residence	Is the client currently non-resident?	☐ Yes ☐ No ☐ N/a	As a non-resident they may be taxed differently to residents. Depending on their overseas income and gains, if they return to the UK within 5 years of receipt of the income or gains they may be liable to tax in the UK on returning.	Non residents still have UK filling and payment obligations. Clarify the tax position if the client is thinking about returning to the UK within 5 years of the divorce.	**3.37**
	Selling/ transferring a UK residential property?	☐ Yes ☐ No ☐ N/A	Individuals selling or transferring UK residential property are taxable on the gain even if they are non-resident.	The capital gains tax is payable within 30 days and individuals will have to file a Non-residents Capital Gains Tax Form to report the gain.	
	Is the client resident in more than on country?	☐ Yes ☐ No ☐ N/A	The client is likely to have double filing and payment obligations. Depending on the tax years of different countries they may need to pay tax in both jurisdictions. before the credit can be claimed.	If the same income and gains are subject to tax in two jurisdictions foreign tax credits can be claimed via the UK tax return. The double taxation treaty will determine which country should claim the credits. The gains and income are still required to be reported on the UK tax return.	**3.42**

CHAPTER 4

Income Tax Overview

Contents at a Glance

4.1 For family solicitors, income tax is likely to be the most important tax to consider for calculating net values, therefore understanding the tax base and the allowable tax deductions should help guide you on a client's likely tax position. In this chapter, we cover income tax and national insurance contributions.

Note: sole traders must pay national insurance of 9% on profits over £9,500 therefore it is important to consider the national insurance liability together with the tax liability.

4.2 Later in this chapter is a typical income tax pro-forma. Throughout this and following chapters we will go through the elements of the pro-forma explaining:

- Tax base and payments.
- Rates and allowances.
- Responsibilities and penalties.
- Key points for family lawyers.

The later chapters explore trading vehicles in more detail and for a sole trader, partnership, employee, complex earnings employee and owner managed business we cover:

- What is treated as income.
- Allowable expenses.

- Tax rates.
- Administration.
- Pension contributions.
- Spouses.
- Key points for family lawyers.

THE NON-TAXPAYER

4.3 Around 40 out of 100 adults in the UK do not pay income tax[1] either because they are not working, or their incomes are too low. The tax-free personal allowance in the UK for 2020/21 is £12,500. Any individuals earning under this bracket will not pay any income tax. For taxpayers earning under the personal allowance there is an option to transfer 10% of their personal allowance to their spouse in some circumstances. Other than this there is no ability to transfer or 'bank' unused personal allowances.

Note: Clients who are non taxpayers may have a reduced state pension entitlement as they may not have made enough qualifying years of national insurance payments. Clients can check their state pension entitlement through their Personal Tax Account (see later in this chapter) or by calling HMRC on 0300 200 3310 and requesting the statement to be sent out to them.

UNDERSTANDING THE PRO-FORMA

4.4 For individuals who have employment income only, their tax position will be relatively simple to work out. For individuals who have savings, give to charity, have a side business or are self-employed, the position becomes more complex. For the family lawyer to have a reasonable ranging shot as regards the net position will require an understanding of the source of the income and the rate of income tax which applies to it.

4.5 All income will be taxable unless a specific exemption can be found to exclude it from being taxed. Most forms of income are specifically charged to tax under specific legislation but in the Income Tax (Trading and Other Income) Act 2005 (ITTOIA 2005) there is a catch all provision which imposes a charge to income tax on 'income from any source that is not charged to income tax under or as a result of any other provision of this act or any other act'.[2]

1 Institute of Fiscal Studies – How high are our taxes, and where does the money come from? Briefing Notes 13 November 2019.
2 ITTOIA 2005, s 687.

4.6 The main exempt items for income tax are income from NS&I bonds and gambling winnings. A full table of taxable and exempt income and benefits can be found at the end of this chapter.

4.7 Income tax is charged on income arising in the tax year which runs from 6 April to 5 April. Income is either taxable or exempt from tax. Taxable income tax is then categorised into one of three categories:

1. Non savings income.
2. Savings income.
3. Dividend income.

It is important to correctly categorise this income as the different categories are taxed at different rates and receive different allowances.

4.8 Generally speaking, non savings income is made up of employment income, trading income, rental profits and self-employment income. Savings income is bank interest and dividend income is clearly income from dividends. Foreign income is also subject to tax in the UK, it will sit in whichever category the income is derived from, for example rental profits from Spain would be situated in the Non Savings Income category.

	Non Savings £	**Interest £**	**Dividends £**
Employment Income	x		
Trading Profits **NB – National Insurance is also payable on trading profits*	x		
Property Income profit	x		
Trust Income	x		
Savings Income		x	
Dividends			x
	x	x	x
Less: Deductible payment			
Loan Interest	(x)		
Net Income	x	x	x
Less: Personal Allowance	(x)		
Less: Savings Allowance *		(x)	
Less: Dividend Allowance			(x)
Taxable income	x	x	x
Tax on taxable income			
Tax on non-savings income 20%/40%/45%	x		

	Non Savings £	Interest £	Dividends £
Tax on savings income 0%/20%/40%/45%		x	
Tax on dividends 7.5%/32.5%/38.1%			x

* the savings allowance applies for interest income only where non-savings taxable income is less than £5,000. Interest within an individual's savings allowance is also taxed at 0%

Income tax Liability	x
Less: Tax deducted at source	
– tax on trust income	(x)
– tax paid under PAYE	(x)
Further income tax payable/repayable	X

INCOME TAX PRO-FORMA

Calculating the income tax charge

4.9

1. Establish if the income is taxable or exempt (see table at **4.22** for a summary of taxable and non taxable income).
2. Combine all the sources of taxable income and less deductible payments (see illustration at **4.2.1** for the income tax proforma).
3. Deduct the available personal allowance (see **4.21** for rates and personal allowance).
4. Apply the relevant rates of tax according to the income (see **4.21–4.33** for rates and personal allowance).
5. Any tax deducted at source is deducted from the liability.

EMPLOYMENT INCOME

4.10

Tax base and payments	Employees are subject to income tax and Class 1 national insurance on their cash earnings. Benefits provided by the employer are subject only to national insurance. The tax on employment income is subject to Pay as You Earn (PAYE) which is operated by the employer. The amount individuals receive is called their net pay. The relevant amount of taxes should have already been deducted by the employer. The employer knows the necessary tax to withhold by using

	the individual's tax code which is issued by HMRC. Note that the taxes withheld are not always correct and the individual may have a refund or additional taxes to pay at the end of the tax year. It is likely that an individual who earns between £100,000 to £130,000 will owe additional tax at the end of the year due to the phasing out of the personal allowance.
Rates & allowances	£0 – £12,500 tax free (phased out if income over £100,000) £12,501 – £37,500 taxable at 20% £37,501 – 150,000 taxable at 40% > £150,000 taxable at 45% Employee National Insurance is 12% on earnings between £9,500 and £50,000 and 2% on earnings above £50,000 National insurance on benefits depends on the type of benefit.
Responsibilities & penalties	Keeping accurate records – failure to do so can lead to penalties of £3,000. Employees with total income exceeding £100,000 or earning over £50,000 and claiming child benefit are required to file a tax return. Failure to file a tax return can lead to penalties of £1,600 plus a percentage of the tax due. Inaccuracies on the tax return can lead to penalties of up to 100% of the tax due. Employees with income of over £240,000 may have a reduced annual allowance and may be subject to the annual allowance charge. Termination payments are subject to special rules covered in Chapter 5.
Key points for family solicitors	Gross income and tax withheld is found on the P60. The P60 does not include pension payments made. The March payslip should show pension payments to date. Taxable benefits are found on the P11d
Further Info	We cover the Employee in more detail in Chapter 5.

TRADING PROFITS

4.11

Tax base and payments	Trading income is income which an individual earns with a view to making a profit. This ranges from income from selling clothes on eBay to running a sole trading business. Individuals who have trading income over £1,000 will need to assess their

	income and possibly pay tax on their profits. If an individual is self-employed their profits (assuming they are over £12,500) will be subject to tax and national insurance. All expenses which are incurred **wholly and exclusively** for the purpose of the trade are allowed to be deducted for tax purposes. No taxes are withheld on trading income and tax and NIC due is payable via the self-assessment system.
Rates & allowances	Trading allowance of £1,000 (all or nothing allowance) £0 – £12,500 tax free (phased out if income over £100,000) £12,501 – £37,500 taxable at 20% £37,501 – 150,000 taxable at 40% > £150,000 taxable at 45% Sole traders pay Class 2 & 4 National Insurance. Class 2 NIC is £3.05per week and Class 4 NIC is 9% on profits over £9,500 Must register for VAT if turnover exceeds £85,000 in the period
Responsibilities & penalties	Keeping accurate records – failure to do so can lead to penalties of £3,000. Notifying HMRC of chargeability to tax – failure to do so can lead to penalties of 100% of the tax due. Sole traders have a responsibility to file an accurate tax return. Failure to file a tax return can lead to penalties of £1,600 plus a percentage of the tax due. Inaccuracies on the return can lead to penalties of up to 100% of the tax due as a result of the error.
Key points for family solicitors	Profits (not turnover) are taxable, therefore there can be an incentive to try to maximise expenses and minimise profits. HMRC announced that they will be focusing on the taxes the self-employed pay. Closer attention should be paid for those clients who are self employed.
Further Info	We cover the sole trader in more detail in Chapter 6.

INCOME FROM PROPERTY

4.12

Tax base and payments	Individuals who rent out property or rooms in their own home are assessed to tax on their profits. Taxable profits should be reported on the individual's tax return. For UK resident landlords tax is not withheld on rental income. Tax is declared and paid via the self-assessment system. Losses should also be reported via the tax return to ensure they are available to carry forward and offset against future rental profits.

Rates & allowances	For landlords who share the property with the tenant, rent a room relief of £7,500 is available to deduct from gross rental income. First £12,500 of income is tax free (personal allowance) Next £37,500 is taxable at 20% Next £118,500 is taxable at 40% Income over £150,000 is taxable at 45% National insurance is not payable on rental income.
Responsibilities & penalties	Landlords have responsibilities to keep accurate records – failure to do so can lead to penalties of £3,000. Landlords have a responsibility to file an accurate tax return. Failure to file a tax return can lead to penalties of £1,600 plus a percentage of the tax due. Failure to take reasonable care when filing a tax return can lead to penalties of up to 100% of the tax due as a result of the error.
Key points for family solicitors	Profits are taxable, therefore there can be an incentive to try to maximise expenses and minimise profits. If the expenses are not all allowable this could cause HRMC to investigate. Rent a room relief changed from April 2020 and is only available where the landlord is staying in the property at the same time as the tenant. Therefore, it is no longer available for Airbnb style of lettings where the landlord leaves the property before the tenants arrive. Rental income on properties jointly owned will be assessed on the couple on a 50/50 until the end of the tax year of separation. Even if the underlying ownership structure is different, after the end of the tax year of separation couples will be assessed to tax on their actual ownership.
Further Info	We cover the property income in more detail in Chapter 12.

TRUST INCOME

4.13

Tax base and payments	Trustees are responsible for ensuring the relevant trust taxes are paid on the income arising from the trust. The beneficiaries who receive distributions from a trust will receive a tax credit for the taxes already suffered on the distribution. The beneficiary will be required to pay any additional taxes due or will receive a tax refund for taxes over-withheld by the trustees. The income will be reported on the beneficiaries' tax return.

Rates & allowances	There are two tax regimes for trusts; Rates applicable for trusts (RATs) – these apply for discretionary trusts and rates for Income in Possession Trusts (IIPs). These are the withholding taxes for trust income.

Type of Income	RATs	IIPs
Non savings income	45%	20%
Interest income	45%	20%
Dividend income	38.1%	7.5%

	National insurance is not payable on trust income.
Responsibilities & penalties	Trustees have responsibilities to keep accurate records – failure to do so can lead to penalties of £3,000. Beneficiaries have a responsibility to file an accurate tax return. Failure to file a tax return can lead to penalties of £1,600 plus a percentage of the tax due. Failure to take reasonable care when filing a tax return can lead to penalties of up to 100% of the tax due as a result of the error.
Key points for family solicitors	Trusts are usually complex, and advice should be sought in valuing trust income and potential tax charges when funds leave the trust. Funds leaving the trust can also be subject to exit charges so it is not enough to simply calculate the income tax which may be due.
Further Info	Trust income is not considered further in this chapter.

SAVINGS INCOME

4.14

Tax base and payments	Interest is now predominately paid gross by banks (ie no tax is withheld). Any individual will be subject to tax on their savings income if it exceeds their annual savings allowance.
Rates & allowances	Interest income from ISAs is not taxable Interest income from NS&I bonds is not taxable Savings income is the second column in the proforma so the rate of the tax which is payable will depend on what other income the individual has. For basic rate taxpayers the first £1,000 of taxable savings income is tax free For additional rate taxpayers the first £500 of taxable savings income is tax free Savings income in excess of the savings allowance will be taxed at the individual's top rate of tax, be that 20%, 40% or 45%.

Responsibilities & penalties	If an individual is filing a tax return they will have to report their savings income on the tax return. If their savings income is within their personal savings allowance and there is no other reason to file a tax return the savings income alone will not trigger a filing obligation. If their savings income exceeds the allowance, individuals have a responsibility to file an accurate tax return. Failure to file a tax return can lead to penalties of £1,600 plus a percentage of the tax due. Failure to take reasonable care when filing a tax return can lead to penalties of up to 100% of the tax due as a result of the error.
Key points for family solicitors	As banks no longer withhold interest those with substantial interest income should be aware of their responsibilities. Overseas bank interest is also potentially taxable. The regime for failure to declare overseas income has much harsher penalties, therefore it will be important to establish if any overseas income has correctly been declared in the UK.
Further Info	We cover the offshore income and gains penalty regime in Chapter 2.

DIVIDEND INCOME

4.15

Tax base and payments	Any individual who receives dividends may be subject to tax on their dividend income. Dividends received in the UK are not subject to a withholding tax (or tax credit) therefore tax due will be paid via the self-assessment system.
Rates & allowances	Dividend income is the third column in the proforma so the rate of the tax which is payable will depend on what other income the individual has. Dividends will be treated as the top slice of income. Dividends are taxable when received. Each individual has a dividend allowance of £2,000. Dividends received in excess of £2,000 are taxable income (unless they are by way of a VCT). Dividend income will be taxed at the individual's top rate of tax, be that 7.5%, 32.1% 38.1%.
Responsibilities & penalties	If an individual is filing a tax return they will have to report their dividend income on the tax return. If their dividend income is within the dividend allowance and there is no other reason to file a tax return the dividend income alone will not trigger a filing obligation.

	If their dividend income exceeds the allowance, individuals have a responsibility to file an accurate tax return. Failure to file a tax return can lead to penalties of £1,600 plus a percentage of the tax due. Failure to take reasonable care when filing a tax return can lead to penalties of up to 100% of the tax due as a result of the error.
Key points for family solicitors	As dividends are not subject to a withholding tax, substantial dividends will likely result in a high tax liability. Shares can be transferred between married couples at no gain no loss so there may have been previous movement of shares in the marriage which has no immediate tax consequence, but the recipient spouse should ensure this income has been declared on their tax return.
Further Info	We cover shares in more detail in Complex Earnings, Chapter 8

PAYMENT DATES

4.16 Income tax is payable by 31 January following the end of the tax year. For 2020/21 income tax is payable by 31 January 2022.

PAYMENTS ON ACCOUNT

4.17 If an individual owes over £1,000 at the end of the tax year then they are required to make payments on account for the following tax year. Payments on account are advanced payments to HMRC for taxes due in the following tax year. The payments on account are due by 31 January and 31 July after the end of the tax year and are held on account for the future tax year.

Employees who have underpaid tax in the year can request to have the underpaid tax recovered through their tax code.

4.18 There are no penalties for failure to make payments on account but interest will accrue from the due date of payment. It is possible to reduce an individual's payments on account to nil if they will not have a future liability to tax.

Due to COVID-19 all individuals who had payments on account due by 31 July 2020 can defer these payments to 31 January 2021. The individual does not need to take any action for this to apply. It should be noted that at the time of writing the payments have not been cancelled, just postponed, so in January 2021 an individual could have three payments due:

1. Balancing payment for 2019/20 due 31 January 2021
2. Payment on account for 2019/20 due 31 July 2020
3. Payment on account for 2020/21 due 31 January 2021

Nature of Payment	**Due Date**	**For what tax year**
Balancing payment	31 January 2022	2020/21
1st Payment on Account	31 January 2022	2021/22
2nd Payment on Account	31 July 2022	2021/22

> **Note:** For determining net income ensure that future payments on account are considered to correctly determine available cash flow. Payments on account can be found on a client's tax return.

REPORTING TAX

4.19 Income which has not been subject to tax deduction at source must be reported on a tax return and individuals must notify HMRC of their chargeability to income tax in the year in which they receive the income. Individuals must notify HMRC by 5 October, six months after the end of the tax year in which they became chargeable. Individuals are required to self assess their requirement to tax and report any untaxed income to HMRC.

> **Note:** If a client has received income which has not been subject to withholding taxes and tax is due they must notify HMRC of this chargeability and file a tax return to report the income. This requirement applies for prior years as well. Penalties will apply if an individual fails to notify HMRC.

FILING A TAX RETURN

4.20 In 2015 HMRC declared that 2020 would mark the end of the tax return.[3] That has not happened yet and currently there remain many situations where an individual is required to file a tax return. The following list is not exhaustive and individuals can use HMRC's tool to determine if they need to send a tax return: www.gov.uk/check-if-you-need-tax-return.

3 https://assets.publishing.service.gov.uk/government/uploads/system/uploads/attachment_data/file/413975/making-tax-easier.pdf

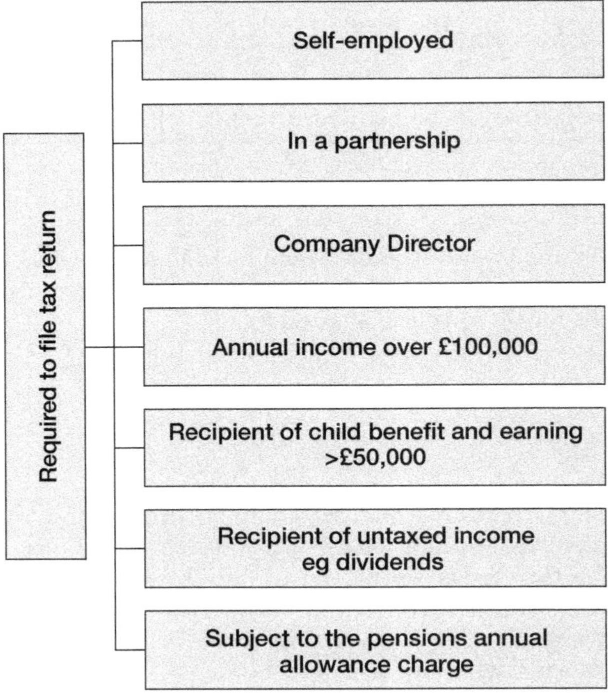

ALLOWANCES

4.21 Broadly speaking, individuals who are resident in the UK will be eligible for the allowances illustrated on the previous pages.

4.22 The personal allowance and savings allowance are impacted by an individual's total earnings levels. The dividend allowance remains available in full regardless of earnings levels. The personal allowance of £12,500 (for 2020/21) is phased out when an individual has total income in the year exceeding £100,000. The personal allowance is reduced by £1 for every £2 earned over £100,000.

4.23 This phasing out of personal allowance is how the top rate of tax at 60% was (unintentionally) created, because it applied only to those with a gross income of between £100,000 – £125,000; for incomes above this rate, the marginal rate of tax drops back down to 45%.

Illustration 4A

60% Trap – Bernard

Bernard earns £100,000. His income is taxed as follows. Bernard buys a rental property and his rental profits are estimated to be £15,000 per year.

This additional income would push his total earnings to over £100,000 meaning his personal allowance would be reduced. The personal allowance would be reduced by £7,500 (being half of £15,000)

	Non Savings Income (£)		Non Savings Income (£)
Salary	100,000	Salary	100,000
		Rental Profits	**15,000**
Total Income	100,000	Total Income	115,000
Less personal allowance	*(12,500)*	*Less: reduced personal allowance*	*(£4,000)*
Taxable Income	87,500	Taxable Income	115,000
£37,500 at 20%	7,500	£37500 at 20%	7,500
£50,000at 40%	20,000	£73,500 at 40%	29,400
Total Tax Liability	**27,500**	**Total Tax Liability**	**36,900**

An increased income of £15,000 has resulted in additional taxes due of £9,400, an effective rate of about 62%.

This tax trap can have major implications for individuals if they are not aware that they will need to keep extra income aside to cover these additional liabilities.

For people who are on the cusp of breaching the £100,000 threshold they can consider paying additional sums into their pensions (provided their annual allowance permits this) to help reduce their income to within the £100,000 threshold.

Note: For individuals taxed under PAYE, if their P60 shows income of between £100,000 to £125,000 they may have additional taxes to pay at the end of the year as they may have been given their full personal allowance through payroll and a bonus or commission payment may have tipped them over the £100,000 level.

Or if an individual earns £90,000 through payroll but has other forms of income which means they will exceed £100,000 they may end up with a disproportionately large tax bill for the year and the family lawyer will want to be vigilant that they are aware of (and have factored in to their calculations) the scale of any up-coming tax hits at the point of reaching their agreement or final hearing.

GIFTS TO CHARITY

4.24 If a charitable donation under Gift Aid is made, the taxpayer's basic rate band is extended by the donation.

4.25 20% relief is given at source and a further relief is given to higher rate and additional rate taxpayers by increasing the amount of income taxed at the basic rate. The relief is only available if the charity is a registered charity in the EEA.

JOINT INCOME

4.26 For 200 years until the end of the 1980s, married couples were taxed as a unit. There was then a rigorous separation process so that each individual was taxed separately. However, recent reforms have seen a muddling of that clear position and some slight return to the earlier regime, for example, in the operation of the higher income child benefit charge and married couples allowance, discussed below.

JOINT RENTAL INCOME

4.27 If a married couple own a property together, the default position is that they will be deemed to receive 50/50 of the rental profits, these profits are likely to be taxable and each party should report them on their tax returns. The tax position is not affected by who actually receives the rental income or the underlying ownership of the property.

4.28 This position is the default position, it will only change if couples have submitted a Form 17 to HMRC which notifies HMRC that they would like to be assessed on their underlying ownership rather than the default 50/50 split.

Therefore where clients jointly own a rental property but only one party has been reporting the income on a tax return, this should be addressed quickly and an amendment sent to HMRC. The same is true if neither party have reported the income on the tax return.

Illustration 4B

Rental Income – Mr and Mrs Keys

Mr and Mrs Keys are married and live in the marital home together. Mrs Keys received a lump sum payment at work and decided to buy an investment property. Mrs Key's income levels meant that she could purchase more of the property than Mr Keys so they bought property 75:25 (Mrs Keys: Mr Keys). The property produces profit of £10,000 per year. As they have not submitted a Form 17, Mrs Keys is taxable on £5,000 of the profits and Mr Keys is taxable on £5,000 of the profits.

If Mr and Mrs Keys wanted to be taxed according to the underlying ownership of the property they could complete a Form 17 and submit this to HMRC, this would result in them being taxed on £7,500 and £2,500 respectively.

> **Note:** couples can only submit a Form 17 when they are married and living together. Once a couple separate they are not eligible to submit a Form 17.

MARRIAGE ALLOWANCES

4.29 There are two reliefs available to married couples: *the married couples allowance* and *the marriage allowance.*

Married couples allowance

4.30 The married couples allowance (MCA) is only available if either spouse was born before 6 April 1935 (so affected individuals are now well into their 80s). The maximum MCA is £9,075 for 2020/21. It is given as a tax reducer at 10%. Therefore, the maximum of tax relief available is £907 (being 10% of £9,075). There are several conditions to be met to qualify for this reduction, including level of earnings. However due to the limited number of people who would likely be claiming this allowance (due to age) we will not consider it further here.

Marriage allowance

4.31 The marriage allowance is 10% of the personal allowance. It is available, subject to conditions, to married couples and civil partners, enabling them to transfer a proportion of the lower earning spouse's personal allowance to the higher earning spouse. (So the recipient spouse then receives a reduction in their income tax liability.)

4.32 To claim the relief both parties must:

- be entitled to a personal allowance;
- not be higher rate or additional rate taxpayers.

4.33 The election can be made online through the Direct Gov website and the relief is given via a tax reduction of 20% of the transferred amount of the personal allowance, resulting in a tax saving of approximately £250 per tax year, with the higher earning spouse benefitting from the savings.

> **Note:** If your client has elected to transfer their personal allowance to their spouse they should contact HMRC to revoke the election, if this is not done the former spouse will continue to benefit from the increased personal allowance.

Illustration 4C

Transfer of the personal allowance – Jen and Ken

Jen and Ken are married and living together. Jen earns £10,000 a year as a teaching assisting. Ken earns £30,000 a year as an administrator.

Jen's total income is under her personal allowance of £12,500. Therefore, she can elect to transfer 10% of her personal allowance to Ken. This would reduce Jen's personal allowance from £12,500 to £11,250. Her income is still below this band so there is no net effect on Jen of making this election.

Ken's personal allowance before the transfer was £12,500, after receiving the 10% top up from Jen's allowance, Ken now has a tax-free allowance of £13,750. This will reduce Ken's tax liability by £250.

4.34 This is quite a common election for couples who are in receipt of pensions where both incomes are relatively low.

Once the election is made the marriage allowance stays in place until one party notifies HMRC.

HIGHER INCOME CHILD BENEFIT CHARGE

4.35 Before 2013, child benefit was a universal non-means tested tax-free benefit. From January 2013 this changed as a rare example of the Chancellor using the tax system as a way of withdrawing a benefit. The charge applies where a member of the household earns over £50,000 and either they or a partner are claiming child benefit. The benefit is then withdrawn at the rate of 1% for each £100 of gross income earned above £50,000.

4.36 It is a complicated scheme:

- it produces aggressive rates of tax for individuals with income between £50,000 to £60,000;
- it applies to households, so the cohabitant-earner could pay the charge for a biologically unrelated child for whom their partner is claiming child benefit;
- it applies if one partner only earns over £50,000 (so two partners earning £50,000 – household income £100,000 – will pay nothing whilst one partner earning £60,000, ie with a much lower overall household income will pay the charge in full).

4.37 These complexities and difficulties have led to many individuals withdrawing claims for child benefit without realising the benefits/arrangements to which otherwise they might have been eligible.

- It is through the registering for child benefit that a non-earning partner is registered to received pension credits.

- By ceasing to register many people have not realised that they have given up these rights to receive pension credits for caring for a child up to the age of 12 (or 17 for children with registered disabilities). Despite pressure from the media and professional bodies the Department of Work and Pensions are currently refusing to backdate any claims for more than one month.

4.38 Individuals should still register for the benefit to protect their state pension entitlement. The form to complete is called CH2 and there is an option to elect not to receive the benefit. Question 68 should be answered no.

There are other implications of course as regards assumptions made by the CMS, treating the child-benefit claimant as the presumptive parent with care.

Note: At the point of separation, the lower earning spouse (earning less than £60,000) will generally want to make the claim. Backdating of only one month is generally permitted. Where their income is above £50,000, then they will need to file a tax return and there will be some benefit clawed back via an assessment.

Illustration 4D

High income child benefit charge – Ken and Len

Jen and Ken have now had a child – Len. Jen still earns £10,000 as a teaching assistant but Ken has been promoted and now earns £45,000. As both of them earn under £50,000 they are eligible to claim full child benefit for their son Len. Child benefit for the year totalled £1,094.

As Jen is the primary carer of Len she completes the application and indicates that the payments should go to her. In January 2021 Ken receives a bonus of £10,000, taking his earnings to £55,000. As Ken's earnings are now in excess of £50,000 and his family is claiming child benefit he must file a tax return and pay the high income child benefit charge.

HMRC make a clear distinction that it is the higher earner who should pay the charge, regardless of who was actually in receipt of the child benefit.

As Ken earned £55,000 the charge will be approximately £547 and will be payable by 31 January 2022.

Note: Clients in Ken's position may not be aware that they have a filing obligation and there may be historical errors which need correcting. If Ken failed to realise he had an obligation to file and filed his return 12 months late his penalty position could be as follows:

Late filing of tax return 6 months: £1,300:

- Plus a behaviour based penalty, careless behaviour is 30% of the tax due: £164.10.

Late payment penalty 5% of the tax due: £27.35

Interest accruing from date payment was due: 3.25% £9.32.

Total Penalties £1,500 + total tax £547 = total payment due to HMRC **£2,047.**

If Ken had a reasonable excuse the 30% penalty of £164.10 would not apply.

PERSONAL TAX ACCOUNT

4.39 HMRC have an online service called a Personal Tax Account. Every person can request access to their personal tax account by going through the steps here (www.gov.uk/personal-tax-account). It is a great tool which allows individuals to check their estimated income tax and has details of their P60. Individuals can also check their state pension entitlements and tax credits through the portal. If your clients have not accessed their personal tax accounts, they should be encouraged to as it can make the completion of the Form E a little simpler.

INCOME TAX PENALTIES – AN OVERVIEW

4.40 The penalty regime is based on the tax due rather than the income. A penalty will apply whether the error is for failure to report trading income or employment income. Therefore the below will apply to individuals who make an error on their income tax returns.

Inaccuracy in return	Penalty based on potential lost revenue Careless inaccuracy – 30% Deliberate but not concealed – 70% Deliberate and concealed – 100% *Reductions for disclosure* Unprompted disclosure minimum penalties nil, 20% and 30% Prompted disclosure minimum penalties 15%, 35% and 50%
Failure to notify HMRC of an error in assessment (within 30 days)	30% of potential lost revenue. *Reductions for disclosure* Unprompted disclosure minimum penalty nil Prompted disclosure minimum penalty 15%
Failure to notify chargeability	Penalty based on potential lost revenue Careless inaccuracy – 30% Deliberate but not concealed – 70% Deliberate and concealed – 100% *Reductions for disclosure* Unprompted disclosure minimum penalties nil, 20% and 30% Prompted disclosure minimum penalties 15%, 35% and 50%

Failure to file return on time	Initial one-day penalty £100 Failure continues for more than three months – £10 per day for up to 90 days Six months late, greater of 5% or the tax due and £300 12 months late – same penalty as for 6 months late unless deliberately withholding the return Deliberate withholding of the return more than 12 months – 70% of the tax due (minimum £300) Deliberate and concealed withholding of the return more than 12 months 100% of tax due (minimum £300) *Restrictions for disclosure* Unprompted disclosure minimum penalty 20% and 30% Prompted disclosure minimum penalties 35% and 50%
Failure to pay tax on time	31 days late – 5% of the tax due 6 months late – 5% of the tax due 12 months late – 5% of the tax due
Failure to keep adequate emails	Maximum penalty of £3,000

LIST OF TAXABLE AND NON TAXABLE INCOME AND BENEFITS

4.41

Type of Income	Taxable	Non Taxable
Bonuses	✔	
Bravery awards – annuities and additional pensions paid to holders of the Victoria Cross, George Cross and most other bravery medals are non-taxable		✔
Commission	✔	
Council tax reduction		✔
Dividend income	✔	
Education maintenance allowance		✔
Foreign earnings	✔	
Gains on life insurance policies	✔	
Gambling winnings		✔
Gifted income		✔
Individual Savings Accounts		✔
Industrial injuries benefits including disablement benefit		✔
Insurance benefits paid to you if you are sick, disabled or unemployed to meet your financial commitments		✔
Interest on child trust funds		✔
Interest up to the time of judgment awarded by a court on compensation or damages for personal injuries		✔

Type of Income	Taxable	Non Taxable
Long service awards		✔
Lump sum bereavement payments		✔
Maternity allowance		✔
National Savings and Investments (NS&I) Certificates		✔
Occupational pensions	✔	
Pension credit		✔
Premium bond prizes		✔
Profits from self employment	✔	
Rental income	✔	
Spousal maintenance		✔
State pension	✔	
Salary	✔	
Termination payments (up to £30,000)		✔
Tips	✔	
TV licence payment for the over 75s		✔
Withdrawals from insurance policies of investment bonds of up to 5% of the amount originally invested		✔
Foreign income	✔	
Bank interest	✔	

Type of benefit	Taxable	Not Taxable
Exempt social security benefits are listed in ITEPA 2003, s 677 and taxable social security benefits are listed in ITEPA 2003, s 660:		
Adoption allowances		✔
Attendance allowance		✔
Bereavement allowance	✔	
Bereavement support payments		✔
Carers' allowance	✔	
Child benefit (repayable if one partner earns over £50,000)		✔
Child maintenance		✔
Child tax credit		✔
Childcare vouchers up to a value of £55 a week		✔
Christmas bonus for pensioners		✔
Cold weather payments		✔
Disability Living Allowance		✔
Employment and support allowance		✔
Guardians allowance		✔
Healthy start vouchers		✔
Higher education student support grant		✔
Housing benefit		✔
Housing grant from local authority		✔

Type of benefit	Taxable	Not Taxable
Income from trusts and settlements	✔	
Income support		✔
Job seekers allowance	✔	
Lump sum pension payments (up to 25%)		✔
Personal independence payment		✔
Return to work credit		✔
Social fund payments		✔
Statutory adoption pay	✔	
Statutory maternity pay	✔	
Statutory paternity pay	✔	
Statutory sick pay	✔	
Universal credit		✔
War disablement pension		✔
War widow's/widower's pension		✔
Widows pension	✔	
Winter fuel payments		✔
Back to work bonus		✔
Council tax benefit		✔

TAX RATES

4.42

Income Tax		
Allowances	**2019/20**	**2020/21**
Personal Allowance (PA)*	£12,500	£12,500
Marriage Allowance†	£1,250	£1,250
Blind Person's Allowance	£2,450	£2,500
Trading Income**	£1,000	£1,000
Property Income**	£1,000	£1,000
*PA is withdrawn at £1 for every £2 by which 'adjusted income' exceeds £100,000. There is no allowance given above £125,000. †The part of the PA that is transferable to a spouse or civil partnership who is not a higher or top rate taxpayer. **If gross income exceeds it, the limit may be deducted instead of actual expenses.		
Rate Bands	**2019/20**	**2020/21**
Basic Rate Band 20%	£37,500	£37,500
Higher Rate Band 40%	£37,500 – £150,000	£37,500 – £150,000

Additional rate 45%	Over £150,000	Over £150,000
Personal Savings Allowance (PSA)		
– Basic rate taxpayer	£1,000	£1,000
– Higher rate taxpayer	£500	£500
Dividend Allowance (DA)	£2,000	£2,000
BRB and additional rate threshold are increased by personal pension contributions (up to permitted limit) and Gift Aid donations.		
High Income Child Benefit Charge (HICBC)		
1% of child benefit for each £100 of adjusted net income between £50,000 and £60,000.		
Remittance basis charge	**2019/20**	**2020/21**
For non-UK domiciled individuals who have been UK resident in at least:		
7 of the preceding 9 tax years	£30,000	£30,000
12 of the preceding 14 tax years	£60,000	£60,000
15 of the preceding 20 tax years	Deemed to be UK domiciled	Deemed to be UK domiciled
Pensions		
Registered Pensions	**2019/20**	**2020/21**
Lifetime allowance (LA)	£1,055,000	£1,073,100
Annual Allowance (AA)*	£40,000	£40,000
Annual relievable pension inputs are the higher of earnings (capped at AA) or £3,600.		
*usually tapered (down to minimum of £4,000) when adjusted income exceeds £240,000.		
State Pension (per week)	**2019/20**	**2020/21**
Old state pension – Single person	£129.20	£134.25
– Married Couple	£206.65	£214.70
New state pension†	£168.60	£175.20
†Applies to those reaching state retirement age after 5 April 2016.		
National Insurance Contributions		
Class 2 (Self employed)		
Flat rate per week	£3	£3.05
Small profit threshold	£6,365	£6,475
Class 3 (Voluntary)		
Class 3: Flat rate per week	£15	£15.30
Class 4 (Self employed)		
On profits £8,632 – £50,000	9.0%	9.0%
On profits over £50,000	2.0%	2.0%
Capital Gains Tax		
Annual exempt amount	**2019/20**	**2020/21**
Individuals, estates	£12,000	£12,300
Most trusts	£6,000	£6,150

Tax rate		
Individual (to basic rate limit)*	10%	10%
Individual (above basic rate limit)*	20%	20%
Trusts, estates*	20%	20%
Business asset disposal relief (BADR)**	10%	10%
Investors' Relief (IR)***	10%	10%
*Individuals are taxed at 18%/20% on gains on residential property and receipts of carried interest. Trusts and estates are taxed at 28% in these circumstances. **BADR is available for lifetime gains of up to £1m. Qualifying disposals include a trading business and shares in a trading company (from a minimum 5% holding) by an officer/employee. Various conditions apply. ***Shares in an unquoted trading company may qualify for IR on lifetime gains up to £10m, if acquired by someone who is not a paid officer or employee of the company and disposal of after 5.4.19. Various conditions apply.		
Corporation Tax		
Year to	**31.3.2020**	**13.3.2021**
Corporate Tax rate	19%	19%
Inheritance Tax		
Rates (for estates)	40%	40%
Reduced rate (for estates leaving 10% or more to charity)	36%	36%
Rate (for chargeable lifetime transfers	20%	20%
Nil rate band limit	£325,000	£325,000
Residence nil rate band limit	£150,000	£175,000
Child Benefit per week		
	2019–20	**2020–21**
Eldest/only child	£20.70	£21.05
Other children	£13.70	£13.95
Guardians allowance per week		
Guardians allowance	£17.60	£17.90

CHAPTER 5

The Employee

Contents at a Glance

INTRODUCTION

5.1 Many years ago, there used to be three main categories of workers for tax purposes: employee; self-employed; and directors. As the way individuals worked changed the use of agency workers and personal service companies became more popular, particularly given the tax advantages that could be harvested along the way: agency workers previously were deemed to have received employment income for tax purposes, however for example, by working through an intermediary, personal service company agency workers sought to be treated as self-employed and thus could be paid gross (outside the PAYE scheme) without the deduction of tax and national insurance and permitting various deductions for tax purposes. These and other changes meant that the historical simplicity of defining an employee became obscured.

WORKER MATRIX

5.2

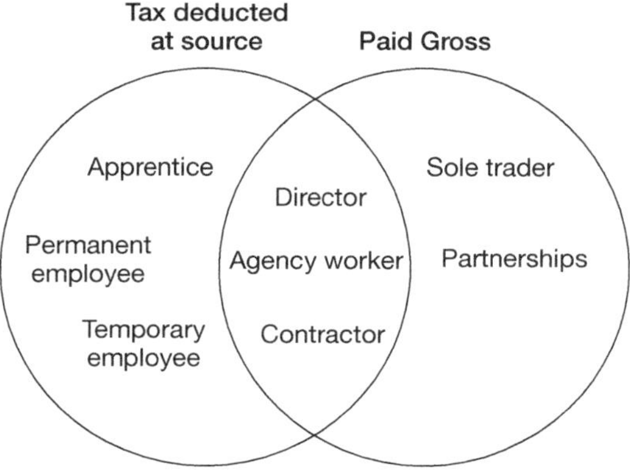

The government's response to this creative, tax-reducing initiative, was to introduce legislation such as IR35 to try to categorise workers as either employed or self-employed. The challenge the government faced was to try to treat people who are effectively working for a company as employees without unnecessarily bringing genuine self-employed people and their clients into the Pay as You Earn (PAYE) regime. Unfortunately, the legislation and guidance from HMRC has not created a clear demarcation and instead has spawned regular reported cases.

Due to the COVID-19 crisis the introduction of IR35 to the private sector which was due to be effective from 6 April 2020 is being deferred and is likely to be effective from 6 April 2021.

5.3 It is an evolving situation and practitioners will want to be aware when encountering some of these situations of the risks of:

- an existing relatively low-tax/high-net-income arrangement coming to an end;
- a claim for historic underpaid tax, accompanied by;
- a need for a significant outlay on professional fees to regularise the situation with HMRC.

5.4 Those who work as contractors, agency workers or work through a personal service company are likely to continue to face a complex blend of taxes for employees and taxes for owner-managed businesses. It is possibly true that these types of structures will start to fall out of favour for individuals for the primary fact that the structures lack certainty and impact companies' ability to plan.

5.5 This chapter will focus on the taxes of people who are (without question) employees. In basic terms, they will have an employment contract, taxes will be deducted from their payslips and they will receive a P60 at the end of the tax year of their employment.

PAY AS YOU EARN (PAYE)

5.6 Pay as You Earn is the system by which employers withhold tax on employment income paid to their employees and pass it on to HMRC. Most cash payments are subject to PAYE but it also applies to readily convertible assets (such as shares on a recognised stock exchange). The record of the employee's pay and taxes withheld is recorded on their P60. If an employee makes pension contributions via salary sacrifice these will not show on the P60. The March payslip should show the total pension contributions. So, in seeking to grasp the full extent of the worker's 'package', you will generally want to always have the March payslip, alongside the other documents that are required to be produced by the form E.

5.7 The form P11D records details of taxable benefits not included in payroll, for example, private medical insurance or a company car.

If an individual changes employer in the tax year a form P45 should be issued by the employer.

	Included on a P60	Included on P11D
Salary	Yes	No
Bonuses	Yes	No
Overtime	Yes	No
Termination Payments taxed under 2.62 ITEPA 2003 (contractual payment for services)	Yes	No
Termination payments taxed under s.401 ITEPA 2003 (ex gratia)		No
– 1st £30,000	No	No
– Excess over £30,000	Yes	No
Payment/reimbursement of genuine business expenses	No	No
Private expenses		
– reimbursed to employee	Yes	No
Readily convertible assets (plc shares)	Yes	No
Private Medical Insurance	No	Yes
Company Car	No	Yes
Cash vouchers	Yes	No
Non-cash vouchers	No	Yes

5.8 On both a P60 and payslips the employee's tax code will be listed. The tax code is calculated by HMRC and tells the employer how much tax to withhold. The tax code sets out the employee's personal allowances. It is reduced by the value of the benefits they receive and can be used to collect tax underpaid in an earlier year, or collect tax on additional income.

THE TAX CODE

5.9 A person's tax code is calculated by HMRC, it tells the employer:

- the amount of tax-free personal allowance to assign to the employee;
- the rate of tax to subject the income to.

5.10 A person's tax code can be found on their payslip and is made up of letters and numbers, the letter is the part of the code to pay the most attention to. The tax code is worked out in the following way:

- HMRC work out a person's tax-free personal allowance;
- calculate income which has not been taxed, for example, part time earnings, or taxable benefits;

- the income which is taxable, but on which tax has not been paid is deducted from the tax-free personal allowance;
- the last digit in the tax-free income amount is removed.

5.11 If an employee has underpaid tax of up to £3,000 in a previous year, they can elect for this tax to be collected via their tax code in the following year. In these cases, the individual's net pay will be skewed by the prior year's underpaid tax. It is not easy to spot when this is happening but most of the time if an individual has a K code it will likely be because they are paying tax they owe from a previous year.

Below is a list of tax codes:

Letters	**What they mean**	
L	Individual is entitled to the standard tax-free Personal Allowance	The code will typically be L1250
M	Marriage Allowance: an individual has received a transfer of 10% of their partner's Personal Allowance	If your client has a tax code starting with M they will need to notify HMRC that they are in the process of separation or divorce and that they no longer wish for the marriage allowance to apply. Note this will increase your client's tax liability by approximately £250
N	Marriage Allowance: an individual has transferred 10% of their Personal Allowance to their partner	If your client has a tax code starting with N they will need to notify HMRC that they are in the process of separation or divorce and that they no longer wish for the marriage allowance to apply
T	Tax code includes other calculations to work out the Personal Allowance	
0T	Individual's Personal Allowance has been used up	This code is likely to be used where an individual's personal allowance has been phased out due to high levels of earnings. Clients who earn under £100,000 with a 0T code may want to request an early P800 calculation to ensure that the tax they owe is correctly reconciled
BR	All income from this job or pension is taxed at the basic rate (usually used where an individual has more than one job or pension)	This code means the client has not been given the benefits of the tax-free personal allowance. Clients with a BR code may want to request an early P800 calculation to ensure that the tax they owe is correctly reconciled. When individuals are on a BR code it means all their income is taxed at 20%, this can result in a large amount of tax being due at the end of the year if they have earned over £50,000.

Letters	What they mean	
D0	All income from this job or pension is taxed at the higher rate of 40% (usually used where an individual has more than one job or pension)	This code means the client has not been given the benefits of the tax-free personal allowance. All of their employment income has been taxed at 40%
D1	All income from this job or pension is taxed at the additional rate of 45% (usually used where an individual has more than one job or pension)	This code means the client has not been given the benefits of the tax-free personal allowance. All of their employment income has been taxed at 45%
NT	Individual is not paying any tax on this income	Usually you would only see this code if an employee is on a tax equalised assignment (eg they are working in a different location to their home and their employer has agreed to settle their taxes).
K	The individual's untaxed income exceeds their tax-free allowance	An individual usually receives a K code when they are paying tax they owe from a previous year or when they are receiving state benefits which they need to pay tax on.

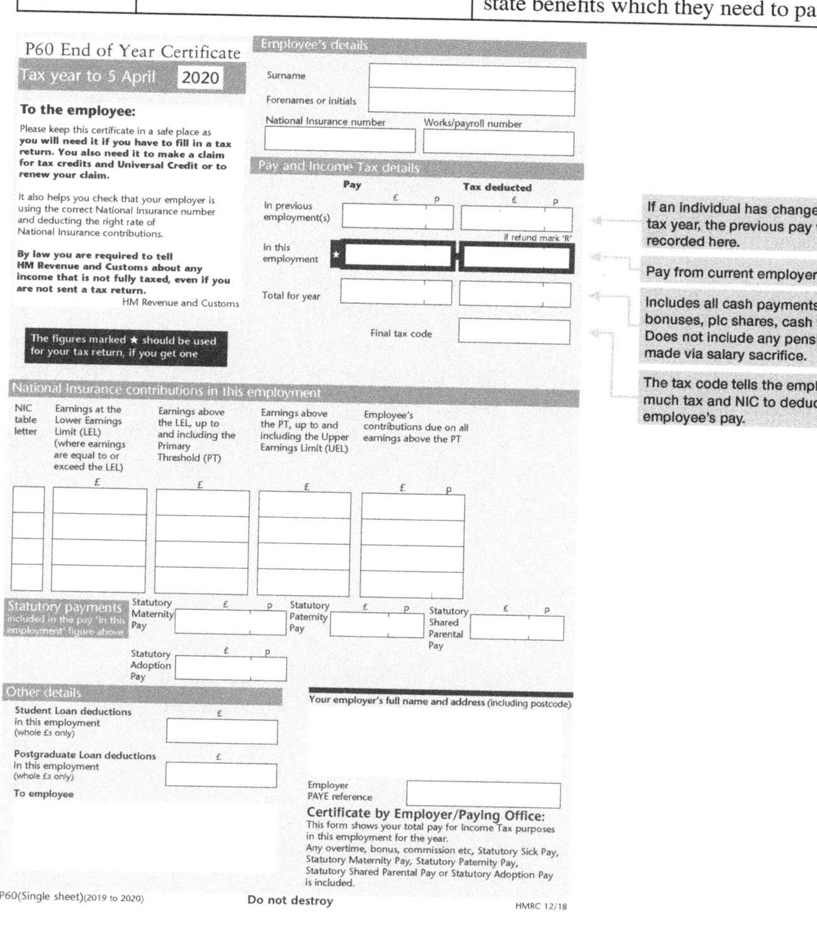

P60 End of Year Certificate

Tax year to 5 April 2020

To the employee:

Please keep this certificate in a safe place as **you will need it if you have to fill in a tax return. You also need it to make a claim for tax credits and Universal Credit or to renew your claim.**

It also helps you check that your employer is using the correct National Insurance number and deducting the right rate of National Insurance contributions.

By law you are required to tell HM Revenue and Customs about any income that is not fully taxed, even if you are not sent a tax return.

HM Revenue and Customs

The figures marked ★ should be used for your tax return, if you get one

Employee's details

Surname

Forenames or initials

National Insurance number

Works/payroll number

Pay and Income Tax details

	Pay £ p	Tax deducted £ p
In previous employment(s)		
In this employment	★	if refund mark 'R'
Total for year		
Final tax code		

National Insurance contributions in this employment

NIC table letter	Earnings at the Lower Earnings Limit (LEL) (where earnings are equal to or exceed the LEL) £	Earnings above the LEL, up to and including the Primary Threshold (PT) £	Earnings above the PT, up to and including the Upper Earnings Limit (UEL) £	Employee's contributions due on all earnings above the PT £ p

Statutory payments included in the pay 'In this employment' figure above

Statutory Maternity Pay £ p

Statutory Paternity Pay £ p

Statutory Shared Parental Pay £ p

Statutory Adoption Pay £ p

Other details

Student Loan deductions in this employment (whole £s only) £

Postgraduate Loan deductions in this employment (whole £s only) £

To employee

Your employer's full name and address (including postcode)

Employer PAYE reference

Certificate by Employer/Paying Office:
This form shows your total pay for Income Tax purposes in this employment for the year.
Any overtime, bonus, commission etc, Statutory Sick Pay, Statutory Maternity Pay, Statutory Paternity Pay, Statutory Shared Parental Pay or Statutory Adoption Pay is included.

P60(Single sheet)(2019 to 2020) **Do not destroy** HMRC 12/18

- If an individual has more than one employment at the same time they will receive two P60s.
- Employers must give employees their P60 by 31 May following the end of the tax year.

THE ANNUAL RECONCILIATION

5.12 PAYE operates best when an individual only has one job which lasts for the duration of the tax year. In other situations, individuals can end up over or underpaying tax. After the end of the tax year HMRC reconcile all the pay and tax data they have received from a person's employer and/or pension provider to check if the right amount of tax has been paid and issue an annual reconciliation form.

This annual reconciliation form is called a P800. Note that individuals who file self-assessment returns may not receive a P800 as the self-assessment return acts as a reconciliation.

5.13 Individuals will get their P800 by September if they are due a tax refund and by October if they need to pay more tax. If an individual does not get a P800 this means that according to HMRC's records the taxes are balanced and no further action is needed.

If a client thinks they may be due a refund they can complete a claim for R38 which may prompt HMRC to reconcile their case earlier.

5.14 It is likely that individuals who have worked less than a complete tax year may have overpaid tax. This is because the PAYE code gives 1/12th of the allowances each month, therefore if an individual has only been working for nine months they will only have received 9/12th of their tax-free personal allowance, rather than 12/12th.

BENEFITS

5.15 Benefits which are taxable will usually be reported on an individual's P11D. The following benefits are not taxable (this list is not exhaustive):

- Employers' pension contributions.
- Mobile phones, provided by a company.
- Childcare, eg a crèche or nursery. The childcare must be open to all employees.
- Workplace parking.

- Trivial benefits including:
  - benefits worth under £50, including:
    - flu jabs;
    - flowers.
- Payments to employees who work from home.
- Eye tests.
- Health screening.
- Workplace gyms.
- Pensions advice (up to £500 per year).

TERMINATION PAYMENTS

5.16 Termination payments receive special tax treatment but only if they are qualifying termination payments. If a client has received or will be receiving a termination payment during proceedings it will be necessary to establish the correct tax treatment. Some employers' payroll departments will be used to these payments and understand the appropriate tax treatment but that is not always the case. The rules around termination payments are complex and a simplified version is provided below. A termination payment is either fully taxable, partially taxable or fully exempt depending on the nature and amount of the payment.

FULLY EXEMPT PAYMENTS

5.17 The following termination payments are fully exempt from tax providing certain conditions are met:

- Termination payment made on the death of an employee (the death does not have to have occurred during working hours).
- Payments made on injury/disability of the employee.
- Payments into a registered pension scheme of an Employer-Financed Retirement Benefits Scheme (EFRB) as part of arrangements for their termination of employments (though the annual allowance charges will still apply).

FULLY TAXABLE PAYMENTS

5.18 Payments in Lieu of notice (PILON) are fully taxable as general earnings. Sometimes the termination payment will include an element of a payment in lieu of notice and in this case the PILON should be calculated to ensure that portion of the award is subject to tax in the correct way.

PARTIALLY TAXABLE PAYMENTS

5.19 After the PILON has been correctly assessed the remainder of the termination payment is taxable only to the extent that it exceeds £30,000. This is known as the £30,000 exemptions. Therefore, payments under £30,000 are fully exempt, otherwise it is only the amount in excess of £30,000 which is taxable.

EARNINGS OVER £100,000

5.20 The rates of income tax depend on which type of income is being taxed. There is further detail on this in Chapter 4.

Every individual who is resident in the UK is entitled to a tax-free personal allowance. The allowance is given each tax year and if it is not used it is lost, it cannot be rolled forward. For 2020/21 the personal allowance is £12,500. The personal allowance is the amount of income that the taxpayer can receive and which will be taxable at 0%. As we have seen in Chapter 4, where an individual's adjusted net income exceeds £100,000 the personal allowance is reduced by one half of the excess.

Example

Ash earns £160,000, their adjusted net income is £160,000 (£60,000 over £100,000) therefore the personal allowance will be reduced by £30,000 (or until it reaches zero). Therefore, Ash will not have a tax-free personal allowance and their income will immediately be taxable from 20%.

For income between £100,000 and £125,000 (the point where the personal allowance will be completely phased out) the effective rate of tax on that income is 60% as shown below:

	A	B
Salary	100,000	125,000
Taxes		
Less Personal Allowance	(12,500)	–
Taxable Income	87,500	125,000
Up to £37,500 at 20%	7,500	7,500
From £37,500–£150,000 at 40%	20,000	35,000
Over £150,000 at 45%		
Total Tax Liability	*27,500*	*42,500*
Net Income	**72,500**	**82,500**

Increase in income	25,000
Increase in tax	15,000
Rate the additional income is taxed at	60%

PENSION CONTRIBUTIONS FOR EMPLOYEES

5.21 There are two main ways of saving funds for retirement:

- personal pension plans (including stakeholder schemes and Retirement Annuities);
- occupational pension scheme (where the employer offers the scheme to its employees).

5.22 Registered pension funds (ie those registered with and approved by HMRC) do not pay income tax or capital gains tax, as such, the income within the pension fund enjoys accelerated rates of growth, untroubled by the taxes that would usually apply to other forms of investment.

On withdrawal, individuals can draw down 25% of the pension fund tax free (subject to any lifetime allowance charges). We will discuss this further in Chapter 9. The rest of the fund is taxed as income when it is drawn down.

TAX RELIEF

5.23 Assuming individuals do not breach the annual allowances, the contributions to a pension are tax free. This means usually tax is not paid on money going into pensions.

Relief is given on amounts contributed to a personal pension scheme at source at the basic rate of tax.

5.24 The taxpayer only pays in 80% of the contribution and 20% is topped up by HMRC. If an individual pays tax at 40% or 45% this higher and additional rate relief is given by extending the basic and higher rate limits which is done via the tax return. For employees, contributions to pensions are usually done by way of a salary sacrifice. This means that no tax is deducted before the payment is made into the pension fund.

ANNUAL ALLOWANCE

5.25 The pensions annual allowance for 2020/21 is £40,000. This is the maximum amount of tax efficient pension contributions that can be made per tax year. The £40,000 is the total of employee and employer contributions. The annual allowance for pensions is tapered down for high income individuals. The annual allowance is reduced by £1 for every £2 of adjusted income in excess of £240,00 but cannot be reduced to below £4,000.

5.26 Prior to 2020/21 the annual allowance was tapered down when individuals had adjusted income over £150,000 therefore, if you are reviewing income from 2018/19 or 2019/20, if the income is over £150,000 the client may have an annual allowance charge.

LIFETIME ALLOWANCE

5.27 The lifetime allowance was introduced from 6 April 2006. It is applied to the total retirement fund of an individual. The lifetime allowance for 2020/21 is £1,073,100. From 6 April 2018, the lifetime allowance has increased annually in line with increases in the Consumer Price Index (CPI).

5.28 The lifetime allowance is the maximum amount of funds an individual can withdraw from a pension without incurring a charge. The tax point is at the point the pension is drawn down and the amount of the tax charge depends on how the pension is drawn down.

- If the total excess of the lifetime allowance is taken out as a lump sum the excess will be taxable at 55%.
- If the excess is retained in the fund and used to pay pension benefits, the excess is taxable when benefits are drawn down at 25%.

ILLUSTRATIONS

5.29 Throughout Chapters 5, 6 and 7 we will talk through several examples to help illustrate the points made in the chapters. There are four primary characters we will use for this. Each person has different levels of earnings:

Jamie	earnings of £40,000
Ryan	earnings of £80,000
Ash	earnings of £160,000
Taylor	earnings of £320,000

Below are illustrations for Jamie, Ryan, Ash and Taylor assuming they are all employed and their employment income is their only source of income in 2020/21.

Employee Income Tax and National Insurance Deductions 2020/21

	Jamie	Ryan	Ash	Taylor
	£	£	£	£
Salary	40,000	80,000	160,000	320,000
Taxes				
Less Personal Allowance	(12,500)	(12,500)	–	–
Taxable Income	27,500	67,500	160,000	320,000
Up to £37,500 at 20%	5,500	7,500	7,500	7,500
From £37,500 – £150,000 at 40%	–	12,000	45,000	45,000
Over £150,000 at 45%	–		4,500	76,500
Total Tax Liability	*5,500*	*19,500*	*57,000*	*129,000*
National Insurance				
Up to £9,500	–	–	–	–
Between £9,500–£50,000 at 12%	3,660	4,860	4,860	4,860
Over £50,000 at 2%	–	600	2,200	5,400
Total National Insurance Contributions	*3,660*	*5,460*	*7,060*	*10,260*
Total Tax and NIC	9,160	24,960	64,060	139,260
Net Income	**30,840**	**55,040**	**95,940**	**180,740**
Effective Tax Rate	22.90%	31.20%	40.03%	43.52%

Jamie and Ryan both earn under £100,000 so they would likely have an L1250 tax code and if this is their only source of income they would not be required to file a tax return. Ash and Taylor both earn over £100,000 so they would be required to file a tax return and their tax code is likely to have an 0T.

THE EMPLOYEE – DOCUMENTS AND KEY CONSIDERATIONS

5.30

	Documents	Details
Documents	P60	The P60 is issued by employers by 31 May following the end of the tax year. It should detail total pay from current employer and total pay from previous employer.
		If a person has two simultaneous jobs in the year they will have two P60s.
	March Payslip	The P60 will not have details of amount contributed to the pension in the tax year. Pension contributions can be found on the March payslip.

Documents	Details
P45	If a client has left work in the year they will be issued with a P45, this will detail their total earnings at that employment in the year.
	The total figure on the P45 should match or be included in the 'total income from other employments' on the P60 so be wary not to double count income.
P11D	A P11D contains details of taxable benefits. Not all benefits will be reported on the P11D as some of the benefits may be exempt from tax or the employer may have a PAYE settlement agreement which allows the employer to settle the tax on the payments in a single annual payment.
P800	If a client has been sent one of these it will show what HMRC has calculated is the correct amount of tax due for the year. Unless the client is disputing the reconciliation, use the total tax on the P800 for calculating net income (rather than from the P60).
Annual Pension statement	If the total contributions to the individual's pension are over £40,000 they may have incurred an annual allowance charge, they should seek tax advice on this to ensure their net pay is correctly documented.
	If their income is over £240,000 they may have a reduced annual allowance. This is discussed in more detail in Chapter 9.
Tax return	If a client is earning over £100,000 or is in receipt of any income which has not been taxed they should be reporting their income on a tax return. If they complete a tax return they will not receive a P800 calculation.
Tax Code	This can be found on the payslip or on a tax code notice.
	If an individual has a N or M code they will need to notify HMRC that they are in the process of separating/divorcing. This will result in the individual with the M code having a larger liability for the year.
	If an individual has a K code, enquire whether this relates to a prior year underpayment of tax, if it does, the net income for the year should be recalculated excluding the tax owed for the prior year.
	If an individual thinks they have been over/under taxed and they are not filing a tax return they can review their P800 which is a reconciliation of the taxes paid in the year. If they do not receive one of these they can call HMRC and request a breakdown for their records.

CHAPTER 6

Self-employed and Partnerships

Contents at a Glance

SOLE TRADERS AND PARTNERSHIPS

6.1 There has been a large rise in the number of self-employed workers in the UK since 2000. The rising number of self-employed people has led to an increase in the number of tax returns filed each year. In HMRC's annual report they reported that the tax gap (the tax due but not paid) from sole traders and partnerships contributed to the majority of the self-assessment tax gap. They went on to report that sole traders and partnerships were more likely to under-declare their tax liabilities.

6.2 Sole traders and individuals in a partnership are broadly treated the same for tax purposes. A sole trader is an individual who undertakes an activity with a view to make a profit. Their business is not separate from them in law and the profits of the business are taxable on the individual following the usual income tax rates. Sole traders and individuals who are members of a partnership do not pay corporation tax. As they have no company which is separate from them in law, sole traders have unlimited liability.

6.3 The term sole trader can apply to any individual who is trading without a formal structure such as a partnership or company. Property developers may be sole traders. Income from property is covered in detail in Chapter 12.

AGENCY RULES

6.4 The agency rules came in in April 2014 and apply to self-employed individuals. An agency is a person or business that makes arrangements for someone to work for a third person, the end client. The agency rules must be followed if all of the following apply:

- the worker personally provides services to the end client;
- there is a contract (verbally or in writing) between the client and any agency;
- as a consequence the worker's services are provided and the end client pays for the services.

6.5 Where all of the above are present, the agency will need to treat the workers as if they were their employees. These rules are different to the IR35 rules as the agency rules apply to self-employed people not companies. There must be a personal provision of services.

Typically workers working through an employment agency will be caught by these rules.

OPENING YEAR RULES

6.6 When a self-employed individual trades, they are required to prepare a set of accounts which show profits or loss made during a particular period. This period is referred to as the period of account or accounting period. Once the trader has chosen their accounting date, they will draw up accounts annually to the date known as the year end. The traders will be taxed on the profits they have made in their basis period. The tax year runs from 6 April to the following 5 April but traders can draw up accounts for any period they want to. Depending on the account date chosen, the trader's first basis period may be under 12 months, for example if they start trading on 1 July 2020 and they chose a year end of 31 December 2020 their first basis period will be six months.

Once a business has been trading for a few years the basis period will be the accounting period which ends in the tax year of assessment. This is known as the current year basis (CYB).

Illustration 36A

Ryan runs a self-employed business which has been trading for many years. Their year end is 31 December each year. Their 2020–21 tax return will show their taxable profits for the period January 2020 to December 2020. The tax return and tax payable will be due under the usual self-assessment timeline, by 31 January following the end of the tax year of assessment.

2020												2021												2022
Jan	Feb	Mar	Apr	May	Jun	Jul	Aug	Sep	Oct	Nov	Dec	Jan	Feb	Mar	Apr	May	Jun	Jul	Aug	Sep	Oct	Nov	Dec	Jan
			2020–21 tax year																					
Ryan's basis period																								
																								tax due

The 'basis period' means the period of trading profits which are assessed to income tax in a particular tax year.

The current year basis will apply unless:

- opening year rules apply (usually when the business is in the first four years of trading);
- the trade ceases; or
- the trader changes the accounting date.

Opening year rules

If your client has started trading in the last three years and is self-employed their taxable profits shown on their tax return may not reflect their actual taxable profits, as opening year rules apply to sole traders.

- The tax for the first year of self-employment is based on the profits for that tax year. If the first accounts end after the end of the first tax year, only part of the profit in those accounts will be taxed in the first tax year.

For example, if the trade started on 1 January 2021 (in the 2020/21 tax year), the first basis period would be 1 January 2021 to 5 April 2021. Profits accruing in this period will be subject to tax in the 2020/21 tax return.

- Tax for the second year of business is based on the profits for the accounting period ending in the year, but if that is not a full year, then it is based on the first 12 months of profits.
- Where the accounting period is longer than a year, assessment is usually based on the profits of the 12 months ending on the accounting date.
- The tax for third and subsequent years is usually based on the profits for the accounting period ending in that year.
- The special rules for the opening year may result in profits of a period being taxed twice. Relief will be given for any period of overlap. This is called overlap relief. Overlap relief will be credited when the business changes their accounting period or the business ceases. The aim is that the total profits taxed will equal the total profits made over the lifetime of the business. If the accounts are always drawn up to the tax year itself there will be no overlap periods.

Overlap Profits

Overlap profits can arise in the opening years of assessment if the trader is subject to tax twice in the same income.

Illustration 6B – basis periods and opening year rules

2020
Jan Feb Mar Apr May Jun Jul Aug Sep Oct Nov Dec
2021
Jan Feb Mar Apr May Jun Jul Aug Sep Oct Nov Dec
2022
Jan Feb Mar Apr May Jun Jul Aug Sep Oct Nov Dec
2023
Jan Feb Mar Apr May Jun Jul Aug Sep Oct Nov Dec
2020–21 tax year
2021–22 tax year
2022–23 tax year
First period of account
six w/e 31 May 2018 £12,000
profits taxed in year 1
period of account, second year rules, 12 months of profit subject to tax
1 Dec 2020 to 30 Nov 2021
profits taxed in year 2
profits taxed twice
period of account undercurrent year basis
w/e 31 May 2021 £18,000
profits taxed in year 3
profits taxed twice
period of account undercurrent year basis
w/e 31 May 2022
profits taxed in year 4

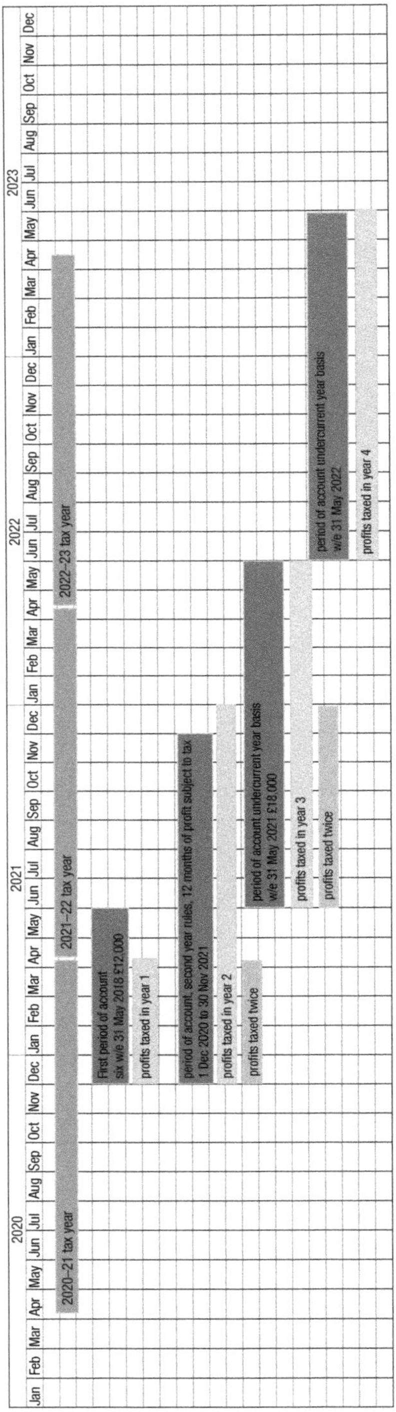

These rules are quite complex and the example is to help illustrate the complexities of trying to determine an individual's actual earnings for the period by using their tax return if they are within the first four years of trading. As a reminder, if an individual's accounting period is the same as the tax year these rules do not apply.

A trader should not be subject to tax on the same income twice so overlap relief will apply when either: the trade ceases or the trader changes their accounting date.

PARTNERSHIPS

6.7 There are three distinct partnership structures, ordinary/general partnership, limited partnership and limited liability partnership.

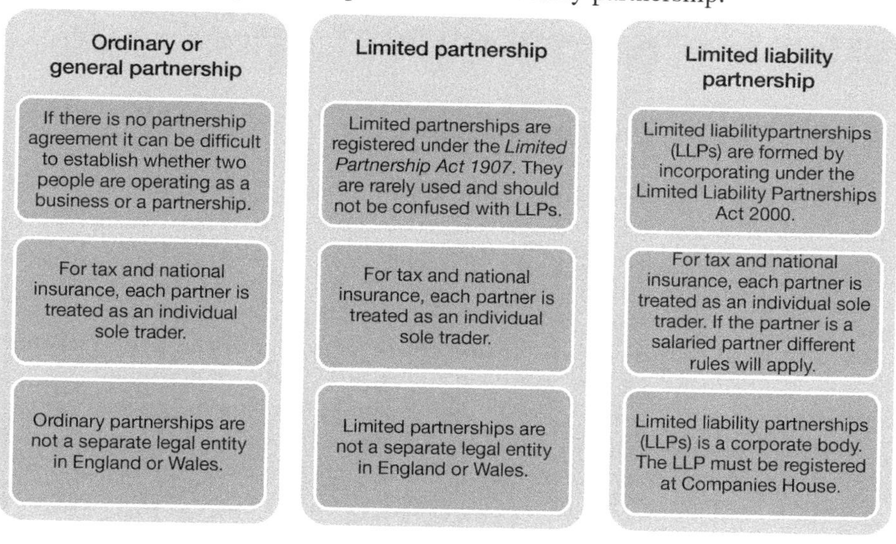

Ordinary or general partnership
If there is no partnership agreement it can be difficult to establish whether two people are operating as a business or a partnership.
For tax and national insurance, each partner is treated as an individual sole trader.
Ordinary partnerships are not a separate legal entity in England or Wales.
Limited partnership
Limited partnerships are registered under the *Limited Partnership Act 1907*. They are rarely used and should not be confused with LLPs.
For tax and national insurance, each partner is treated as an individual sole trader.
Limited partnerships are not a separate legal entity in England or Wales.
Limited liability partnership
Limited liabilitypartnerships (LLPs) are formed by incorporating under the Limited Liability Partnerships Act 2000.
For tax and national insurance, each partner is treated as an individual sole trader. If the partner is a salaried partner different rules will apply.
Limited liability partnerships (LLPs) is a corporate body. The LLP must be registered at Companies House.

The rest of this chapter will look at an ordinary or general partnership only. Individuals who are members of a partnership are taxed under the same principles as those who are self-employed. The basis period will follow the Partnerships accounting period.

TRADING ALLOWANCE

6.8 The trading allowance was introduced from 2017/18. It is a £1,000 tax-free allowance and applies for property and trading income. The first £1,000 of gross trading income is exempt from tax. If the income exceeds £1,000 the taxpayer has a choice of:

– deducting the £1,000 trading allowance from their gross income and being taxable on the excess, or;

– deducting allowable expenses from gross income in the normal way.

The trading allowance can be used against trading and property income and is particularly helpful for tiny businesses, for example individuals selling items on online platforms.

BUSINESS ADMINISTRATION

6.9 Sole traders must file a self-assessment tax return. They will report their turnover and expenses on the self-employment pages of the tax return. An individual can run multiple distinct self-employment businesses in a year. The tax return is due by 31 January following the end of the tax year. For 2020/21 the tax return is due by 31 January 2022.

As partners in general partnerships are subject to the same tax treatment as sole traders this section will apply to them as well. The main relevant distinction for partnerships is that their partnership accounts are also due.

INCOME TAX AND NATIONAL INSURANCE

6.10 National insurance contributions are compulsory contributions to the state system. Several factors affect the level and type of NICs payable including, employment status, age, level of earnings and residence status.

6.11 Sole traders are subject to income tax, Class 4 national insurance and Class 2 national insurance. Income tax will be payable if their profits (or total income) exceed the tax-free personal allowance. The personal allowance is tapered, for every £2 over £100,000 the personal allowance is reduced by £1. Class 2 national insurance is payable if profits are above £6,475 during the 2020/21 tax year. It is assessed weekly and the rate is a fixed amount of £3.05 per week.

Class 4 national insurance is payable where profits are above the lower Class 4 profit limit, this is £9,500 for 2020–21. The rate payable is 9% on profits over this limit.

6.12 Income tax and Class 2 and 4 national insurance contributions are compulsory for self-employed people (assuming they are earning above the thresholds), therefore it is critical to ensure when estimating net income that national insurance has been taken into consideration. Income tax and NICs are payable via the tax return.

SPOUSES IN THE BUSINESS

6.13 Sole traders and partnerships can utilise spouses to reduce their taxable income. They may pay their spouse a wage or treat them as a partner and share profits with them. As there is less formality for sole traders and ordinary partnerships, it is unlikely that there will be any underlying documentation supporting the structure used. Any individual receiving income from a trade or partnership is required to report this to HMRC.

6.14 Individuals are permitted to pay their spouse a wage but the amount of the wage must reflect the work that the spouse is doing in the business. For example, a plumber may pay their spouse £150–200 per week if they are doing bookkeeping, managing appointments, and other business support. It would be unreasonable if they paid their spouse £1,000 per week for these services.

PAYMENTS ON ACCOUNT

6.15 As no tax is withheld from source for self-employed individuals, they will likely be required to make payments on account. These payments are effectively 'pre' payments for the future tax year. These payments are due by 31 January and 31 July. Note that due to COVID-19 any individuals who are unable to meet the 31 July 2020 payment on account payment can make this payment by 31 January 2021

Illustration 6C – Payments on Account

Ryan is self-employed. In 2018–19 he earned £80,000.

Their liability at the end of the tax year was:

Tax	£20,360
Class 2 NIC	£153
Class 4 NIC	£4,086

Total amount owed to HMRC: £24,599.

Their tax liability at the end of the year was £24,599. This balancing payment is due by 31 January 2020.

Ryan will also be required to make payments on account. These will be 50% of £24,599 being £12,299 each.

Therefore Ryan will pay £36,899 by 31 January 2020 being £24,599 as the balancing payment for 2018/19 and £12,299 as a payment on account for 2019/20. Then Ryan will pay another £12,299 by 31 July 2020.

In 2019/20 Ryan earns £100,000. Their tax liability is £32,999. From this we deduct the £12,299 payment on account made in January 2020 and the £12,299 payment on account made in July 2020. Therefore Ryan's balancing payment for 2019/20 is £8,401.

BUSINESS TAXATION

6.16 Sole traders are taxable on their business profits only. The profits will be subject to income tax. Profits are calculated as follows.

Total turnover

6.17

Total turnover	X	This is all the income from sales in the basis period
Less: Allowable expenses	(X)	Sole traders can deduct any expenses that are incurred **wholly and exclusively** for the purposes of their trade
Taxable profits	X	This figure will be inserted into the self-employment pages of the tax return

Allowable expenses

6.18 Expenses must meet the following conditions to be deductible. A painter/ decorator, Suzie, will be used as an example to show some items which would not be allowed:

	Allowable	Not Allowable
Must be actual expenditure incurred by the person in question	Suzie designs some fancy leaflets advertising her services, these cost her £150 to have them printed and delivered to her home	A friend does Suzie a favour and drops some of the advertising leaflets off in their area. Suzie works out that if she had to pay someone to do this it would have cost her about £20
The expenditure must be for the purpose of trade	Suzie buys paints and wallpaper for her next job of re-decorating a home office for a new client	Suzie buys some extra paint to redecorate her own bedroom
The expenditure must be 'wholly and exclusively' so incurred	Suzie travels by train to visit a client – the train costs £120	Suzie travels by train to visit her brother – whilst she is there a new client enquires about her services and she pops in to see them on her way back
The expenditure must be of a revenue rather than a capital nature	Suzie buys some new paint rollers and paint brushes	Suzie buys a new van. Suzie can deduct part of the costs of the van but this is done by taking a capital allowance and not just a straight deduction

6.19 Some of the typical expenses you may see are below:

- office costs, for example stationery or phone bills;
- travel costs, for example fuel, parking, train or bus fares;
- staff costs, for example salaries or subcontractor costs;
- things you buy to sell on, for example stock or raw materials;

- financial costs, for example insurance or bank charges;
- costs of your business premises, for example heating, lighting, business rates;
- advertising or marketing, for example website costs;
- training courses related to your business, for example refresher courses.

Clothing – usually not allowable

6.20 In *Mallalieu v Drummond (HMIT)* [1983] STC 665, Miss Mallalieu, a barrister, claimed a deduction against her income for the dark clothing that she was required to wear in court. The courts found that the expenditure was not incurred wholly and exclusively for the purposes of work as clothes are needed for 'warmth and decency'. Clothes that are allowable as deductions include uniforms, costumes and protective clothing.

Client entertaining – not allowable

6.21 If your client's expenditure seems high and if you notice items in the deductions which seem unusual, they may want to take the time to reconsider their claims. HMRC have announced that they are taking a keener interest in individuals who are self-employed as it is a relatively unregulated area.

Illustration 6D – Expenses

On the self-assessment pages, there is a section to report the expenses of the trade and this is split into several categories.

If a client appears to have excessive deductions this may be an indication that provisions should be made in the case of an investigation and be mindful that this could relate to claims from many years ago.

A recent individual; Alistair Jordan [TC07501] lost his appeal against a closure notice for 2013/14 during which he claimed self-employment expenses of £120,000 against income of just £5,000.

A closure notice means HMRC completed their investigation and issued a notice to Mr Jordan with their findings and requesting additional tax payable. Once a closure notice is issued, if a taxpayer disagrees with the notice they can appeal to the First Tier Tribunal (FTT) which Mr Jordan did.

The claim of £120,000 in expenses arose from an invoice from Mr Jordan's own company for 'value added services'. The invoice was for a total of 1,200 hours at £100 per hour. The FTT found several inconsistencies with this claim, first they found that Mr Jordan was not able to explain what 'value added services' actually were. Further the invoice was for 1,200 hours work between 19 February 2014 and 31 March 2014 – there are only actually 984 hours between these dates.

The FTT refused the appeal and HMRCs assessment to tax of £22,860 was upheld. Strangely HMRC failed to issue a penalty notice for the inaccuracies which would have totalled £11,201, so no penalties were payable by Mr Jordan.

VAT OVERVIEW

6.22 Whilst sole traders and individuals who are part of a partnership do not pay corporation tax they are subject to VAT if their taxable turnover breaches the VAT threshold. Traders must register for VAT if they make taxable supplies above the threshold. The family breakdown process can be long and drawn out and, whilst hopefully the underlying structure of a business will not change throughout the process, if the business becomes liable to VAT the individual will have an obligation to register the business. Once a trader is registered for VAT they must charge customers output VAT. They can reclaim any input VAT incurred on business expenses.

6.23 There are three main rates of VAT in the UK, standard 20%, reduced rate 5% and zero rated. Some products or services are exempt from VAT, this is not the same as being zero rated. A trader providing zero rated products or services can still reclaim input VAT, however a trader providing exempt products or services cannot reclaim VAT. VAT is reported and paid each quarter. The due date for payment and the VAT return to be filed is one month and seven days after the end of the quarter.

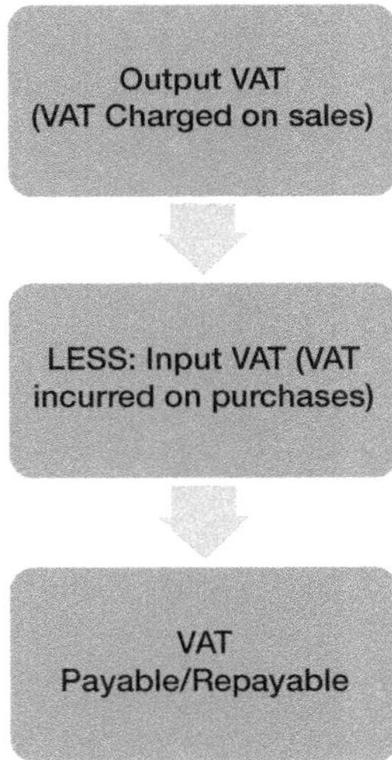

REGISTERING FOR VAT

6.24 A trader needs to be continually assessing whether they need to register for VAT. The VAT registration rules require the trader to look forwards and backwards to assess the level of turnover. Where the value of taxable supplies in the previous 12 months is more than £85,000, the trader has to notify HMRC within 30 days of the end of the month in which the limit was exceeded. They will then be registered from the first day of the second month after exceeding the limit. If the value of taxable supplies to be made in the next 30 days is expected to be more than £85,000, the trader must notify HMRC before the end of the 30-day period. Registration will be effective from the beginning of the 30-day period. Failure to notify HMRC may result in penalties being due. If a trader makes exempt supplies they will not be required to register for VAT. The letting of property is normally an exempt activity from VAT.

Therefore client's whose turnover is close to £85,000 will want to ensure they have considered the possibility of breaching the threshold and needing to register for VAT.

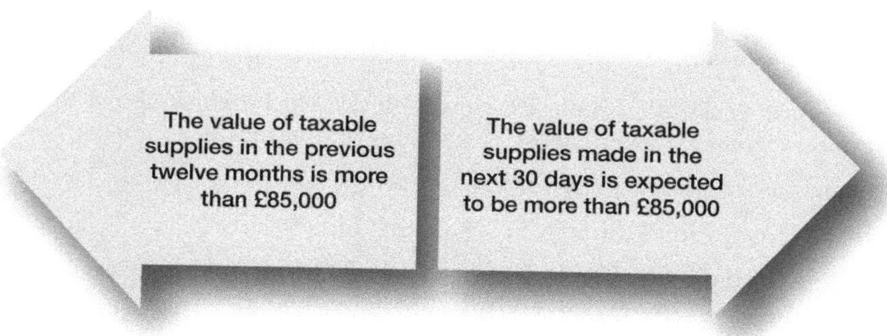
The value of taxable supplies in the previous twelve months is more than £85,000
The value of taxable supplies made in the next 30 days is expected to be more than £85,000

6.25 Individuals can voluntarily register for VAT. Businesses may want to do this for several reasons:

- to appear as a larger business;
- increased levels of credibility;
- reclaim input VAT on purchases.

IMPACT ON SMALL BUSINESSES REGISTERING FOR VAT

6.26 However, if a small business is pushed into registering for VAT because their turnover exceeds £85,000 in one year, they will have to charge VAT on all of their supplies going forward. If they work mainly with individuals this is a 20% hike on their prices.

6.27 Even though that additional 20% is going to HMRC and not to the business this can impact the trader's current client base if they have the choice to work with a similar trader who is not registered for VAT.

MAKING TAX DIGITAL

6.28 Making Tax Digital (MTD) is a government initiative announced in the spring 2015 Budget. It aims to make tax administration more effective and easier for taxpayers to pay their tax online. The current timeline for this is that from April 2019 quarterly reporting was mandatory for VAT for all VAT-registered businesses with a turnover above the VAT registration threshold and it is optional for VAT-registered businesses with a turnover below the VAT registration threshold. This applies for sole traders, companies and partnerships.

6.29 From April 2020 (at the earliest) the plan is that quarterly reporting will be mandatory for income tax and corporate tax for all businesses including landlords with a turnover over the VAT registration threshold. It will be optional for businesses (including landlords) with a turnover below the VAT registration threshold.

Making Tax Digital (MTD) for VAT post April 2019

6.30 Since April 2019, businesses with a taxable turnover above the VAT registration threshold of £85,000 have had to do two things:

- keep their records digitally for VAT purposes; and
- file their VAT return through MTD compatible software.

This is because these businesses are not being asked to keep digital records or to update HMRC quarterly for other taxes until at least 2020.

6.31 For those with a taxable turnover above the VAT registration threshold the digital filing exemption will be extended in cases where:

- the business is run entirely by a practising member of a religious society or order whose beliefs are incompatible with the use of electronic communications; or
- it is not reasonably practicable for a trader to use digital tools to keep their business records by reason of age, disability, remoteness of location; or
- the trader is subject to an insolvency procedure.

6.32 One of the main requirements of MTD for VAT is digital record keeping. The requirement is that the trader files their VAT returns via functional compatible software. Effectively this means that traders cannot input any data directly to HMRC in writing; it needs to be prepared and submitted digitally. This can be done via compatible software or via a bridging software. A bridging software would allow traders to prepare their VAT return on say excel and then submit to HMRC via a bridging software.

Traders will also have to keep a digital VAT account which will keep all of the returns and records.

6.33 For individuals who have businesses but have not yet filed their annual tax returns, requesting copies of the digital VAT records may give some indication of the performance of the business over the last 12 months.

SELF-EMPLOYED AND PARTNERSHIPS – FAMILY SOLICITORS' CHECKLIST

6.34

		Yes/No/ NA	**Risk**	**Mitigation**	**Ref**
Year end	Does the accounting year end coincide with the end of the tax year?	☐ Yes ☐ No ☐ N/A	If it does not, the tax position will follow the trading income earned in the accounting period which ends in the tax year of assessment.	For calculating income use the accounts in conjunction with the tax return and not just the tax return alone.	**6.6**
Starting a trade	Is the business in its first 4 years of trading?	☐ Yes ☐ No ☐ N/A	If the accounting period does not coincide with the end of the tax year different rules will apply for the first 4 years for the basis period of taxation.	Ensure it is clear which income is being subject to tax in the relevant periods. If necessary calculate the availability of any overlap relief. If the business is within the first 2 years of trading, it may have been subject to tax twice on up to 11 months of income. This will depress the amount of income which is available, however this double taxation will be relieved on either the change of accounting date of the cessation of the business	**6.6**
Turnover	Is the business' turnover over £85,000?	☐ Yes ☐ No ☐ N/A	If yes, is the business registered for VAT? If the business or partnership is not registered for VAT they may be subject to penalties and an investigation.	VAT registered traders are required to file quarterly VAT returns electronically. If the business accounts are not available due to timing it may be worth requesting to see a copy of the electronic accounts which would have been used to prepare and file the tax return.	**6.24**

		Yes/No/ NA	Risk	Mitigation	Ref
Expenses	Do the expenses seem dispropor-tionately high?	☐ Yes ☐ No ☐ N/A	The details of the expenses can be found on the tax return. If these seem disproportionately high the client may be more likely to receive an enquiry notice from HMRC. Just because the expenses are high does not mean that they are not legitimate but, if the client, has been filing the returns without the help of an accountant/tax advisor, they may not be aware of what expenses they can and cannot deduct.	Ensure the client is comfortable with the expenses that they have claimed and that they have all the back up documentation to support the claims.	**6.18**

CHAPTER 7

The Owner Managed Business

Contents at a Glance

INTRODUCTION

7.1 The invention of the limited liability business is regarded as a main catalyst for the extraordinary financial growth in England in the early eighteenth century. Now the advantages it offers are more likely to lie in taxation benefits as we will examine below.

7.2 The company of course is a separate entity from the business owner. This permits a variety of different roles within the business:

- as a director (a worker and decision-maker) in the business; and
- as an owner or shareholder of the business.

7.3 However much the business owner may have merged these roles in their mind and started to treat it simply as an extension of themselves:

- the business is a separate entity;
- and is subject to its own tax regimes; thus
- in understanding the receipts of the business owner from the business we need to:
  - differentiate between the two entities of business and business owner;
  - when the business owner receives money as an employee (director), this is a transfer of funds from the business to the employee and there will be a taxation opportunity; and

- when the company pays a dividend, first this is made from its profits which have been subject to corporation tax, then there will generally be a further liability to tax as the dividend is received by the shareholder.

7.4 Within a company the business owner:

- can receive income as an employee (and routinely this will be done to a limited level so as to enjoy the benefits of national insurance contributions);
- more usually, income will be drawn out by way of dividend because this offers distributions without the hit of national insurance payments:
  - either by the employer; or
  - by the employee.
- the business owner also enjoys the flexibility of loans from the company and of having tax breaks for investment in the company.

COMPANY DIRECTORS

7.5 Directors are legally responsible for running the company and ensuring all relevant filing is done on time. In cases where a spouse is director of a company but not actively involved in the day to day running of the company it is vital that they understand their duties as a director still apply.

7.6 Further, even though a company is a separate entity in law, HMRC have powers to issue penalties to directors to pay personally.

A company director or officer can be held personally responsible for a debt owed to HMRC by the company if the debt relates to a penalty issued against the company for a deliberate error on a tax return.[1]

7.7 This was the power used by HMRC in the case of Stephen Bell and Paul Hovers who were issued with a personal liability notice of £89,306 each. In this case HMRC had to prove that the directors knew or should have known that the transaction in question was connected with the fraudulent evasion of tax.

7.8 If during the divorce process it becomes apparent that the company has not complied with their tax obligations it is not only the person who is actually running the company who may be at risk, any directors who may act as sleeping partners are also potentially liable.

7.9 It should be noted that in the case of Bell and Hovers, there was much evidence to show that both directors had enough knowledge to know that their actions may have been suspect and the burden of proof is pretty high on HMRCs end. Nevertheless the point that directors cannot always hide behind a company is one that should be headed by all directors.

1 Finance Act 2007, Sch 24, para 19.

7.10 So in understanding what is making the business tick, the family lawyer is likely to want to grapple with the following and we will look at these topics in turn:

1. How are directors remunerated?
2. How are loans to the director dealt with?
3. How are distributions by dividend made and how are they taxed?

We will look in Chapter 14 at what will happen if a business is sold or wound up.

OFF THE SHELF COMPANIES

7.11 An off the shelf company is a company that has been pre-registered at Companies House but has never traded and is ready to be used immediately. Some individuals choose off the shelf companies when they start trading for a faster and lower cost start. It may also be advantageous as the company will appear longer-lived which may assist with obtaining bank loans or other credit. It is usually quite easy to spot an off the shelf company as on the Companies House list of documents there will be no activity, dormant accounts and then a change of director and that is when either full or abbreviated accounts will start to be filed. There is nothing inherently wrong with someone using an off the shelf company, just be wary that just because the company was incorporated in, say 2003, it does not mean that is how long an individual has been running the company.

RATES

7.12 Corporation tax is charged at 19% on profits of the company. The same rate applies regardless of the size of the company. The tax is a liability of the company. Taxable profit is arrived at by deducting all allowable tax deductible expenses from turnover. The tax liability of the company is influenced by how the profits are calculated. Several tax reliefs for costs or losses are only available to businesses operating as a company; there are also similar provisions only available for sole traders and partnerships.

The company will also pay national insurance at 13.8% on employer salaries.

EXTRACTING MONEY FROM THE COMPANY

7.13 For this section of the chapter it is assumed that the director or company owner will extract almost all available profit out of the business per year. This is relatively commonplace in micro-businesses and helps to illustrate the differing tax treatments at play. The total tax and national insurance burden of the company and the individual tax liability are combined to look at the overall tax position. Clearly in law the company and the individual are separate entities, however for owner managed businesses the reality is that the owners want to see what the whole picture looks like – including the company taxes.

7.14 If an individual is a director of a company there are a few ways they can choose to pay themselves. They can either pay themselves as an employee of the company, or they can pay themselves via dividends. It is most tax efficient to be paid via dividends, however this route is only possible if the company has sufficient after-tax profits.

7.15 Directors can choose to be paid a salary by the company. The salary will be paid by the company via pay as you earn (PAYE) and the company will pay them their net pay. A company can pay wages and salaries even if this will place the company into a loss-making position. Salaries are a deductible expense, therefore paying a salary will reduce the corporation tax liability. However, the company will have an employer's national insurance contribution liability. Consider the following:

J Ltd Company profits before salary £50,000	Jamie's salary	£40,000
R Ltd Company profits before salary £100,000	Ryan's salary	£80,000
A Ltd Company profits before salary £200,000	Ash's salary	£160,000
T Ltd Company profits before salary £400,000	Taylor's salary	£320,000

Illustration 7A shows their tax position if they were taxed as employees.

Illustration 7A

	Jamie	Ryan	Ash	Taylor
Company profit (before salary deduction)	50,000	100,000	200,000	400,000
Less Salary	(40,000)	(80,000)	(160,000)	(320,000)
Taxable Profit	10,000	20,000	40,000	80,000
Corporation tax at 19%	**1,900**	**3,800**	**7,600**	**15,200**
Salary	*40,000*	*80,000*	*160,000*	*320,000*
Taxes				
Less Personal Allowance	(12,500)	(12,500)	0	0
Taxable Income	27,500	67,500	160,000	320,000
Up to £37,500 at 20%	5,500	7,500	7,500	7,500
From £37,500 – £150,000 at 40%	–	12,000	45,000	45,000
Over £150,000 at 45%	–		4,000	76,500
Total Tax Liability	*5,500*	*19,500*	*56,500*	*129,000*
National Insurance				
Up to £9,500	–	–	–	–
Between £9,500 – £50,000 at 12%	3,660	4,860	4,860	4,860
Over £50,000 at 2%	–	600	2,200	5,400
Employer National Insurance at 13.8%	5,520	11,040	22,080	44,160
Total National Insurance Contributions	*9,180*	*16,500*	*29,140*	*54,420*

Total Tax and NIC	14,680	36,000	85,640	183,420
Total Corporation Tax	1,900	3,800	7,600	15,200
Net Income	**23,420**	**40,200**	**66,760**	**121,380**
Effective Tax Rate (personal tax and NIC plus corporation tax)	33.16%	39.80%	46.62%	49.66%

INCOME BY WAY OF DIVIDENDS

7.16 A company can only pay dividends if it has sufficient after-tax profits to do so. The most typical tax efficient director payment structure is where the director will be paid a salary up to the national insurance contributions threshold (this salary will be free of tax and NIC as it will also be under the tax-free personal allowance). Additional income will come by way of dividends.

7.17 The distinction in the share types is usually reflected by the description of the share, eg ordinary, preference, or by the class of the share, eg Class A ordinary shares and class B ordinary shares. The value of the shares will be influenced by the type of shares an individual holds. If all shares are the same type and class the dividends will follow the share percentages.

Revisiting Jamie, Ryan, Ash and Taylor, if they all adopted the above approach.

Illustration 7B

	Jamie	Ryan	Ash	Taylor
Company profit (before salary deduction)	50,000	100,000	200,000	400,000
Less directors Salary	(8,788)	(8,788)	(8,788)	(8,788)
Taxable Profit	41,212	91,212	191,212	391,212
Corporation tax at 19%	**7,830**	**17,330**	**36,330**	**74,330**
Available profits for distribution	*33,382*	*73,882*	*154,882*	*316,882*
Dividends taken	*31,212*	*71,212*	*151,212*	*311,212*
Taxes				
Less Personal Allowance	(12,500)	(12,500)	0	0
Less Dividend Allowance	(2,000)	(2,000)	(2,000)	(2,000)
Taxable Income	16,712	56,712	149,212	309,212
Up to £37,500 at 7.5%	1,253	2,813	2,813	2,813
From £37,500 – £150,000 at 32.5%	–	6,244	36,306	36,563
Over £150,000 at 38.1%	–			60,660
Total Tax Liability	*1,253*	*9,056*	*39,119*	*100,035*

National Insurance				
Up to £8,632	–	–	–	–
Between £8,628 – £50,000 at 12%				
Over £50,000 at 2%				
Total National Insurance Contributions				
Total Tax and NIC	1,253	9,056	39,119	100,035
Total Corporation Tax	7,830	17,330	36,330	74,330
Net Income	**40,916**	**73,613**	**124,551**	**225,635**
Effective Tax Rate (personal tax and NIC plus corporation tax)	18.17%	26.39%	37.72%	43.59%

Illustrations 7A and **7B** show that when the income tax, national insurance contributions and the corporation tax liability are factored in, it is more tax efficient to be paid by way of dividends. Dividend payments offer flexibility.

DIRECTORS LOANS[2]

7.18 Directors are able to take loans from their companies. These loans will be accounted for in the Directors Loan Account. Loans taken out by directors are liable to corporation tax at 32.5%[3] if the following conditions exist:

- the company is a close company. A close company is a company under the control of five or fewer participators (including shareholders) or of any of its directors;
- the loan is to a participator of the company – a participator includes a director or shareholder;
- the loan is outstanding nine months after the end of the filing period.

7.19 The tax charge of the loan is the liability of the company.

If the loan is released or written off and if the director remains the director of the company, the amount of the loan released or written off will be treated as earnings for that year.[4]

2 HMRC Toolkit, Directors Loan Account.
3 Corporation Tax Act 2010, s 455.
4 Tax planning annual, payments made on the termination of employment – Income Tax (Earnings and Pensions) Act 2003 (ITEPA 2003), s 188(1).

> **Illustration 7C: Directors Loan Account**
>
> Ryan is the sole director of R Limited which has a year end of 31 May 2020. The company profits before tax were £100,000. Ryan paid himself a total of £80,000 in dividends from after-tax profits. During the year Ryan needed additional cash so he borrowed £25,000 from the company.
>
> At the financial year end of 31 May 2020 the loan was still outstanding.
>
> As R Ltd is a close company and Ryan is a director/participator of the company the corporation tax charge of the loan will be 32.5% of the loan amount, being £8,125.
>
> If Ryan repays the loan before 28 February 2021 the additional tax charge will not apply.
>
> In this illustration we have ignored the loan related interest rules.

TIMING OF THE PAYMENTS

7.20

Corporation Tax	Corporation tax is payable nine months and one day after the end of the accounting year for small companies. Large companies and corporate groups must pay their corporation tax liabilities by quarterly instalments. Companies with profits of over £1.5 million are large companies.
National Insurance	Employers' and employees' national insurance is payable monthly.
Personal Tax	Personal tax liabilities are usually payable by two equal instalments by 31 January and 31 July. These dates will remain the same regardless of the accounting date of the company.

> **Illustration 7D: Administration and Payment Dates**
>
> Ash is the sole director of A Limited which has a year end of 31 July 2020. The company profits before tax were £200,000. Ash paid himself a total of £160,000 in dividends from after-tax profits.
>
> Annual Accounts are due by 31 July 2021.
>
> Company Tax return is due by 1 May 2021.
>
> Corporation Tax is payable by 1 May 2021.
>
> Ash's personal tax will be due by 31 January 2021.

7.21 A summary of filing dates for corresponding company year ends are below.

Year end	Annual Accounts due	Company tax return due	Corporation tax due
31 May 2020	31 May 2021	1 March 2021	1 March 2021
30 June 2020	30 June 2021	1 April 2021	1 April 2021
31 July 2020	31 July 2021	1 May 2021	1 May 2021
31 August 2020	31 August 2021	1 June 2021	1 June 2021
30 September 2020	30 September 2021	1 July 2021	1 July 2021
31 October 2020	31 October 2021	1 August 2021	1 August 2021
30 November 2020	30 November 2021	1 September 2021	1 September 2021
31 December 2020	31 December 2021	1 October 2021	1 October 2021
31 January 2021	31 January 2022	1 November 2021	1 November 2021
28 February 2021	28 February 2022	1 December 2021	1 December 2021
31 March 2021	31 March 2022	1 January 2022	1 January 2022
30 April 2021	30 April 2022	1 February 2022	1 February 2022

SPOUSES IN THE COMPANY

7.22 It does not take much searching to find a huge amount of resources dedicated to advising individuals on how they can use their family to save tax. The outcome of this is often ill-thought-out structures where the underlying planning intention may not reflect reality.

7.23 If an individual:

- is director of a company;
- extracts most of the profits out of the company each year;
- has a spouse or partner who does not work,

it is true that they can reduce their taxable income by diverting some of their income to their spouse.

7.24 The most common structure is that the individual and their spouse will be 50/50 shareholders of the company. Dividends will be paid and taxed equally on both parties.

Where a couple is married transferring shares to a spouse takes place at no gain no loss so there is no event for tax purposes.

7.25 Sometimes an accountant will value the business ahead of a transfer of shares, so it may be worth asking for any valuations done at the time of transfer to assist with any company valuations.

If Jamie, Ryan, Ash and Taylor all adopted this structure their tax positions would be substantially improved.

7.26 In summary of the tax rates, the position for Jamie, Ryan, Ash and Taylor differs according to the structure they choose to adopt. Due to the tax saving that can be achieved through utilising a non-working spouse it is a common structure and it will be helpful to have an understanding of *why* this planning was introduced.

	Paid via salary	**Paid via dividends**	**Spouse in the business**
	Tax rate	Tax rate	Tax rate
Jamie	33.16%	18.17%	16.40%
Ryan	39.80%	26.39%	20.74%
Ash	46.62%	37.72%	28.69%
Taylor	49.66%	43.59%	39.52%

If the spouse is a shareholder of the company the following should happen:

- the shareholder spouse receives dividends in accordance with their shareholding;
- these dividends are reported on the spouse's tax return and taxes are paid on these.

HMRC'S VIEW OF SPOUSES IN THE BUSINESS

7.27 Where individuals pay their spouse a salary or as a contractor (which is tax deductible), the salary must be within an appropriate range for the services the individual is doing. For example, if the spouse is doing administration or secretarial work they can be paid up to what is the average in the industry for that work. If a spouse is paid say £40,000 as a contractor and they are only working one day a week for the company, this would likely be considered unreasonable and be challenged by HMRC.

7.28 The Financial Conduct Authority (FCA) issued a decision on 30 September 2019 where they imposed a fine on Stuart Forsyth for paying his wife a proportion of his salary and thereby reducing his tax liability by about £18,000. Her salary was the second largest in the company (his being the highest). Prior to 2010 Mrs Forsyth was paid between £5,000 and £10,000 per year which was deemed to be reasonable given the level of work she was undertaking. Whilst this is not a HMRC decision it is interesting to see the burden of integrity being placed on individuals in regulated industries.

7.29 HMRC will struggle to challenge payments made by way of dividends as a director can choose the structure of their company and can choose who has shares and how many shares they have.

One area to take care of is if you see dividend waivers between spouses. Dividend waivers are used when one spouse does not want the other spouse to have a large percentage of share ownership but would like to benefit from sharing dividends for a lower tax bill.

7.30 A typical example involves Mr and Mrs Black. Mr Black has 90% of the shares and Mrs Black has 10% of the shares, but at the end of the year Mr Black signs a dividend waiver waiving his entitlement to 40% of the dividend and gifting this to Mrs Black. In cases where this is done the dividend waiver is taxed on Mr Black as though it were his income anyway. It is caught by settlements legislation which is intended to prevent an individual from gaining a tax advantage by making arrangements to divert their income to another person who is subject to tax at a lower rate.

WHEN PLANNING DOESN'T GO TO PLAN

7.31 The below illustration is what should not happen. It illustrates what the author has seen multiple times. There is no suggestion that any accountant would advise the below. It is an unfortunate outcome of individuals interpreting tax planning to suit their own personal situation. In practice the below illustrations 'works' or remains unchallenged until the point of divorce and at that point often the tax return has been filed but the tax payment has not been made.

Illustration 7E: Ryan and Remy

Ryan is director of R Ltd. Ryan is married to Remy. Remy does not work. On advice of their accountant Ryan gifts 50% of their shareholding to Remy. This is not a disposal for capital gains tax purposes as they are married.

Remy is now a 50% shareholder of the company and should receive 50% of all dividends paid out.

However, in 2017 and 2018 R Ltd paid all the dividends to Ryan's bank account. Ryan manages the marital finances. On the tax returns it has been reported that both Ryan and Remy received the same dividends (following the 50/50 split). Ryan manages the payments to HMRC and ensures that both tax liabilities are settled.

In 2019 the marriage became strained, the company made a profit of £100,000. Dividends of £37,004 were reported on Remy's 2019/20 tax return but in light of the strained marriage Ryan did not make any payment to HMRC to settle Remy's liability. The payment of tax is due by 31 January 2020.

The UK has an independent taxation system meaning that Ryan and Remy are individually responsible for their tax liabilities.

The difficulty with the above situation is that what happened after the tax planning took place was incorrect. The dividends should have been paid into Remy's bank account.

If Remy has no income to settle the liability there are a few options which could be taken to remedy their tax position. These are suggested cautiously as it may be possible to find a solution via the family courts. However, if the proceedings are taking many years Remy may not want to be liable for a tax debt for such a long period of time.

As Remy's return will have reported dividends that Remy did not receive there is an argument to say that the tax return has been incorrectly reported and should be amended to reflect their true income position. Tax returns can be amended within 12 months from the submission deadline. The 2018/19 tax return must be amended by 31 January 2021 and the 2019/20 tax return must be amended by 31 January 2022. These amendments can be filed online and are typically processed within 4–8 weeks.

If there is cause to rectify the historical position there is an option to file either an overpayment relief claim or a special relief claim. An overpayment relief claim can be used to correct historic positions going back up to four years. A special relief claim is for use in exceptional circumstances (such as mental health issues leading to an inability to manage tax affairs.

If you are working on a case similar to the above securing tax advice early on can often help to advise how best to collaboratively manage the payments of historical tax liabilities and how to correct any incorrect positions.

7.32 When the figures are compared at **7.26** it is clear to see why so many small companies adopt the approach of splitting income with their spouse.

7.33 For clarity, there is nothing inherently wrong with assigning 50% of the shares to a spouse but:

- the dividend payments must reflect the underlying share structure;
- the spouse must actually receive the dividend income (either into their bank account, or a joint bank account).

PREVIOUS PLANNING

7.34 If there is a structure in the company it may be important to consider the context around the planning and why it was entered into. What was the understanding and intention of both parties when they entered into structural changes of the business? Is it possible to review the advice of the accountants at the time?

7.35 When undertaking any spousal planning it is critical to ensure that both parties fully understand their obligations and the long-term implications of the planning.

7.36 It may be that one spouse has filing obligations as a result of the planning or previous elections may have been made which are now no longer appropriate.

7.37 In the very complex and lengthy case of Dr Martin John Coward and Ms Elena Ambrosiadou CL-2017-000707, on the issue of company ownership, Dr. Coward's position was that all planning was undertaken to ensure a tax efficient structure only and bore no resemblance to the actual underlying ownership of the business.

PERSONAL SERVICE COMPANIES (IR35)

7.38 The off payroll rules were introduced in 2000. The rules effectively treat a person who is effectively employed but working as a contractor as an employee. These rules are known as IR35. An individual's contract with their client can either be within IR35 or outside IR35.

7.39 An individual's work is deemed to be within IR35 when the individual provides services through their own company to the end client and, if the individual was actually providing the services directly to the end client (rather than through a company), the worker would meet the employment status tests that would make them an employee. Individuals who are impacted are those who work through a personal services company (PSC) and provide services to an end client.

Example

John is an IT contractor and has a company called IT solutions Ltd.

If John worked for five different companies offering IT help it would be unlikely any of the engagements would be within IR35. However if John mainly worked for Pink Corporation, and the nature of his engagement was as follows:

- He had a desk at Pink Corp
- He worked there four days a week
- He had contracted for the company for four years with no significant change in his duties

Then even though he is contracting through IT help Ltd he would likely (under the IR35 rules) be deemed an employee of the Pink Corporation.

Public authorities are responsible for determining if a worker is within IR35. They should do this before the contract is entered into. These rules were set to be expanded to private sector bodies from 6 April 2020. This has now been delayed until 6 April 2021 due to the COVID-19 pandemic.

7.40 HMRC have 12 business entity tests which they have drawn up to help individuals identify whether their contract is high, medium or low risk. In brief the tests are:

Business Premises	Does your business own or rent business premises which are separate both from your home and from the end client's premises?
Private Indemnity Insurance	Do you need Professional Indemnity Insurance?
Efficiency	Has your business had the opportunity in the last 24 months to increase your business income by working more efficiently?
Assistance	Does your business engage any workers who bring in at least 25% of your yearly turnover?
Advertising	Has your business spent over £1,200 on advertising in the last 12 months?
Previous PAYE	Has the current end client engaged you: • on PAYE employment terms • within the 12 months which ended on the last 31 March • with no major changes to your working arrangements?
Business Plan	Does your business have a business plan with a cash flow forecast which you update regularly? Does your business have a business bank account, identified as such by the bank, which is separate from your personal account?
Repair at Own Expense	Would your business have to bear the cost of having to put right any mistakes?
Client Risk	Has your business been unable to recover payment: • for work done in the last 24 months • more than 10% of yearly turnover?
Billing	Do you invoice for work carried out before being paid and negotiate payment terms?
Right of Substitution	Does your business have the right to send a substitute?
Actual Substitution	Have you hired anyone in the last 24 months to do the work you have taken on?

7.41 The tax implications of this are:

- the party that operates PAYE/NIC is treated as the employer for tax;
- the net pay paid to the limited company is treated as taxed employment income.

The rules have different variations depending on the status of the end client.

End Client Type	Who assesses the worker's employment status	Who deducts PAYE/ NICs	When from
Public Sector	End Client	Fee payer	6 April 2017
Large or medium-sized Private Sector	End Client	Fee payer	6 April 2021
Large or medium Private Sector (IR35)	Personal services company	Personal services company	Until 5 April 2021
Small Private Sector (IR35)	Personal services company	Personal services company	Ongoing

If your client is a contractor, specifically in the private sector consider if in the future they will be within IR35. If they will, this means it is very likely that their net income in the future will be reduced as they will be taxed as employees rather than through a company.

OWNER MANAGED BUSINESS FAMILY SOLICITORS TOOLKIT

7.42

		Yes/No/ NA	Risk	Mitigation	More Info
Director's Loan	Is there a balance on sitting under directors loan?	☐ Yes ☐ No ☐ N/A	If the loan is not released or repaid within nine months of the accounting year end the company will be charged to tax on the loan amount at 32.5%. If the loan is written off, the recipient of the loan will be taxed on the loan as though they were additional earnings.	If there is a large balance (in reference to the size of the company) on the Director's Loan account future additional tax charges may become payable and these should be factored into valuations. If the loan is written off and therefore taxed as income will this impact the cash flow of the recipient?	**7.18**
Size of the company	Is the company a micro entity, small company, or a medium company?	☐ Yes ☐ No ☐ N/A	Micro entities, small and medium companies can file abbreviated accounts. These accounts do not include a profit and loss or details of dividends paid.	If the financial health of the company is unclear from the abbreviated accounts, consider requesting a copy of the full accounts submitted along with the company tax return (CT600).	**7.12**

		Yes/No/ NA	Risk	Mitigation	More Info
Spousal Structure	Is there a non working spouse entitled to dividends?	☐ Yes ☐ No ☐ N/A	If these dividends were declared on the financial statements (of the company) and on the tax return of the individual then the individual will have a tax liability.	If the spouse did not receive the dividends one possible remedy is to amend the tax returns for the last two years in the first instance. It will be important to consider the impact of doing this. Eg will it cause changes to be required to be made for the company accounts? Will it frustrate the process?	**7.31**
IR35	Is your client a contractor?	☐ Yes ☐ No ☐ N/A	They may be subject to the IR35 rules. If they are they will be taxed as an employee rather than through their company. This will reduce their net income.	If they are in the public sector, their end client is responsible for assessing whether the contract is in or outside of IR35. If your client works in the private sector their net income may differ in the future if they are deemed to have a contract which is within IR35.	**7.38**

CHAPTER 8

Complex Earnings – Employee share schemes

Contents at a Glance

INTRODUCTION

8.1 In this chapter, we are going to cover employee share schemes and share option schemes and how they are treated for tax purposes.

8.2 Employees generally acquire shares in their employer's company in one of two ways:

- through an award of shares by the employer (from a share scheme);
- on the exercise of a share option.

Share schemes are either approved, meaning they often have tax advantages or they are unapproved and subject to tax and national insurance contributions (NIC) in the normal way. A share is simply part ownership of a company. Once an employee owns shares, they may pay income tax on dividends received and capital gains tax on any gain when the shares are sold. The taxation of dividend income is covered in Chapter 4.

8.3 Shares have:

an award date	the date they are promised to the employee
a vest date	the day the employee owns the share
sale date	when the employee sells the share

8.4 Share options are slightly different in that they have:

a grant date	the date the employee is given the opportunity to purchase options at a certain price

an exercise date	the date the employee chooses to exercise that right, eg the date they buy the option at the agreed price
a sale date	when the employee sells the options

8.5 There are four main types of tax advantaged share scheme which have tax and NIC advantages. They are:

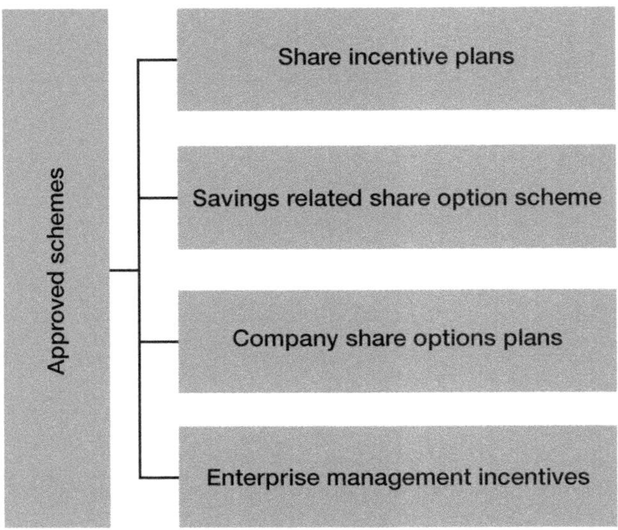

Share options are the right to acquire shares in the employer company in a given period of time.

If shares are gifted (usually as part of renumeration) to an employee this will be treated as taxable earnings. If the shares are readily convertible assets (ie they are listed shares) they will be subject to PAYE and Class 1 NIC.

UNAPPROVED SHARES AWARD LIFE CYCLE

8.6

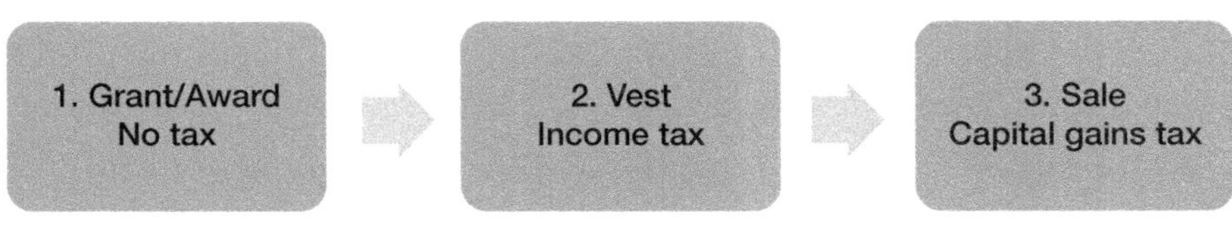

1. Grant/Award

   When a share is awarded/granted to an employee it is similar to a promise of shares. The employer agrees that the employee can receive the shares if certain conditions are met in the future. Usually the conditions include that the individual has to remain an employee of the company. At grant the employee does not own the shares. There is no tax due at award.

2. Vest

   When the shares vest they are delivered into the employee's share account. This is the point the employee owns the shares. Income tax applies at the vest date. Income tax will be charged at the individual's top rate of tax on the market value of the shares at vest. Usually the company will withhold a certain amount of shares to cover the PAYE and NIC liability. The net shares will be delivered into the employee's share account. After the shares have vested the individual can sell or retain the shares. They will still own the shares if the individual leaves the company.

3. Sale

   At the point of sale the shares will be subject to capital gains tax if they have increased in value since the point of vest. The potential capital gains tax liability is calculated as follows, market value at sale and less the market value of the shares at the vest date. If an employee sells the shares on the same day that they vest there will be no capital gains tax to pay (as the share will not have increased in value).

Illustration 8A – Reg – Simple vesting

Reg works for a technology company, he earns £60,000 per year. He has been an employee for two years and in July 2019 he was awarded 1,000 shares as part of his bonus package. At the award date the shares had a value of £2.50. Reg is awarded shares at a value of £2,500, there is no tax to pay at this point. Reg does not own the shares and it is likely that if he leaves the company before the shares vest that he forfeits his right to the shares.

In July 2020 the shares are worth £3.20, per Reg's vesting schedule all 1,000 of the shares vest. At this point Reg is subject to income tax and NIC on the value of the shares.

1,000 shares at £3.20 = £3,200.

Reg's top rate of tax is 40%, therefore tax of £1,280 is due on the vest plus 2% national insurance contributions as the shares are readily convertible assets (ie they are listed on a registered stock market).

The company will withhold 42% of the shares being 420 shares and Reg will receive 580 shares in his share account.

The 580 shares received are net of income tax and national insurance.

In December 2020 Reg decides to sell the shares. At this point they are worth £4.40.

Reg's capital gains tax computation will be as follows:

Sale proceeds	580 × £4.40	£2,552
Less: value at vest	580 × £3.20	(£1,856)
Gain		£696

The gain is well within Reg's capital gains tax annual exemption so there is no capital gains tax to pay and the gain does not need to be reported on Reg's tax return.

8.7 If an employee is a regulated or a senior employee they are likely to have staggered vestings and restriction periods. Staggered vestings are when the share award vests over four years (say) 25% each year, in this case, the individual will only receive their full award after four years.

8.8 Restriction periods occur once the share has vested. The individual is unable to sell the share whilst it is in the restriction period. Some companies will also stipulate that whilst the share is under restriction, it can still be clawed back. A claw back is a contractual agreement where an employee is required to return an amount of variable remuneration (usually shares). If your clients' shares are subject to any claw back provision the claw back is likely to apply to restricted shares in priority to those where the restriction has been lifted.

UNAPPROVED SHARES WITH RESTRICTIONS AWARD LIFE CYCLE

8.9

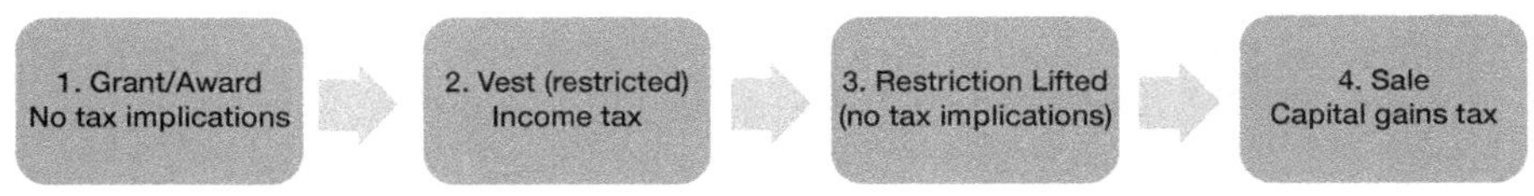

There are no tax implications when a restriction is lifted. The tax points are only at vest and sale.

Illustration 8B – Kathryn

Kathryn works for an investment bank. She is awarded shares in March as part of her bonus. Her shares vest 25% each year but half of the yearly vesting is subject to restriction.

Below is what a typical vesting schedule may look like. All the below numbers are gross. To work out what Kathryn is likely to receive we need to know two things:

(1) The estimated value of the shares

(2) Kathryn's total taxable income

The value of the shares at grant were:

March 2018 – £78

March 2019 – £87

March 2020 – £102

These values are of limited value when working out the potential tax liability. We need to know only the estimated market value at vest.

	March 2018	**March 2019**	**March 2020**
Granted	200	400	600
Vesting in 2019	25		
Vesting in 2019 subject to a 12-month restriction	25		
Vesting in 2020	25	50	
Vesting in 2020 subject to a 12-month restriction	25	50	
Vesting in 2021	25	50	75
Vesting in 2021 subject to a 12-month restriction	25	50	75
Vesting in 2022	25	50	75
Vesting in 2022 subject to a 12-month restriction	25	50	75
Vesting in 2023		50	75
Vesting in 2023 subject to a 12-month restriction		50	75
Vesting in 2024			75
Vesting in 2024 subject to a 12-month restriction			75

As we do not know the future market value of the shares in 2021 the best way to estimate Kathryn's net shares is to work out the percentage of shares that will be withheld.

Percentage of shares

If the client is an additional rate taxpayer you can just take the top rate of tax and apply it to the number of shares.

Kathryn earns over £150,000 so her income is subject to tax at 45% and national insurance of 2%.

In 2021 Kathryn will have:

50 shares vesting from her March 2018 award;

100 shares vesting from her March 2019 award;

150 shares vesting from her March 2020 award.

A total of 300 shares

These are highlighted in grey above.

That is a total of 300 shares. 47% of these shares will be withheld to pay the tax and NIC on the shares. Kathryn will receive 159 shares in her vesting account.

Of course, knowing the number of shares is only helpful if one can then assign a market value to the shares at that future date. It may be worth securing agreed market values early on in negotiations.

Note for tax purposes it makes no difference if the shares are restricted and there are no tax implications on the lifting of the restriction.

APPROVED SCHEMES

8.10 Below we will cover the main features of the four approved share schemes. Where schemes are approved, there are often tax consequences for selling or transferring the shares within a certain time period.

An employee's share plan document will detail whether the shares are from an approved scheme or unapproved, if approved the name will be detailed in the plans.

SHARE INCENTIVE PLANS (SIPS)

8.11 These operate in the following way. A trust is established which acquires shares in the employer company, these are then awarded to employees but continue to be held on trust.

8.12 The following types of shares can be awarded from a SIP:

- **free shares** employees can be awarded up to £3,600 worth of free shares per annum;
- **partnership shares** employees can buy partnership shares up to the lower of £1,800 or 10% of salary plus bonus;
- **matching shares** employers can give up to two further matching shares to the employee for each partnership share acquired;
- **dividend shares** any dividends from plan shares can be reinvested to acquire dividend shares.

8.13 To determine the income tax treatment, you will need to know:

- the type of the share;
- at what point they were withdrawn from the plan.

The income tax and NIC treatment is listed below

Withdrawal	**<3 years**	**3-5 years**	**>5 years**
Free shares	Income tax on market value at withdrawal	Income tax on the lower of market value at allocation or market value at withdrawal	No income tax
Partnership shares	Income tax on market value at withdrawal	Income tax on the lower amount of amount used to purchase shares or MV at withdrawal	No income tax
Matching shares	Income tax on market value at withdrawal	Income tax on the lower of market value at allocation or market value at withdrawal	No income tax
Dividend shares	Dividends used to buy shares are taxable	No income tax	No income tax

8.14 Where there is an income tax charge, PAYE and class 1 NIC will apply if the shares are readily convertible assets (ie they are listed shares).

8.15 The amount charged to capital gains tax is the difference between the value of the shares at the date they are withdrawn from the plan and the value at the date of sale. Therefore, if an employee leaves the shares in the plan for six years and then withdraw them by selling them there will be no income or capital gains tax to pay.

SAVINGS RELATED SHARE OPTION SCHEMES

8.16 A savings related share option scheme is an arrangement whereby employees save a fixed amount each month into a Save As You Earn (SAYE) account and this is topped up by a tax-free bonus from the building society. These funds can then be used to exercise options over employer company shares.

8.17 Exercising an option is taking up the right to buy a share option. The options can be granted at a discount of up to 20% of the shares at the date of grant. The SAYE account must be for three, five or seven years and the length of the contract and monthly savings are fixed at the start.

8.18 Employers can award bonus contributions into the SAYE account, these are tax free. There are no income tax or NIC implications at grant or exercise of the share options. Capital gains tax will be payable on the sale. The capital gain is the difference between the cost of the option at the date it was exercised and the sale proceeds.

COMPANY SHARE OPTION PLANS

8.19 If an employee is participating in a company share option plan there are no income tax or NIC implications on the exercise of the company share option if the exercise is made within three and ten years of the grant. The grant is the point where the individual is given the right to purchase a company option, exercising the option is the point where the individual uses that right to purchase the company option. Therefore, if the employee purchases the option within three and ten years of being granted the right to purchase the option there is no income or NIC at the point of purchase.

8.20 Capital gains tax may be payable on sale. The gain is equal to the difference between the amount of the option at exercise and sales proceeds.

> **Note:** The different rules apply for calculating the gain if the option was exercised out of the three to ten-year window.

ENTERPRISE MANAGEMENT INCENTIVES (EMIS)

8.21 EMIs are share options offered by employers usually to only key members of the company.

In order for the EMI to qualify for favourable tax treatment, the option must be exercised within ten years of grant. There is never any tax charged upon the grant of the option. There is only a tax charge upon exercise of an option within ten years if the option was granted at a discount.

8.22 Income tax would be charged in the following ways:

Lower of	
MV of shares at grant	X
MV of shares at exercise	
Less: Price paid for Option	(X)
Taxable as employment income	X

8.23 There will be a capital gain on the sale of the option. The capital gain is the sale proceeds less any amount paid for the option plus any amount charged to income tax on exercise.

8.24 If there is a disqualifying event between grant and exercise the option can still be exercised but the tax treatment will differ. A disqualifying event includes the employee no longer being eligible because they no longer work for the company or they no longer work for enough hours.

SUMMARY OF TAX TREATMENT OF SHARE SCHEMES

8.25

Share scheme	Conditions	Tax Treatment
Share Incentive Plans (SIPs)	Free and matching shares must be subject to a holding period of between 3 and 5 years (unless employment ceases)	Share is free from income tax if withdrawn after 5 years Income tax charge if withdrawn early Capital gains tax is charged on the sale prices less the value of the share when it left the plan
Savings related share option schemes	Employees must save between £5 to £500 per month for either 3, 5 or 7 years The price of the option must be at least 80% of the open market value	No income tax Only capital gains tax is payable on disposal

Share scheme	Conditions	Tax Treatment
Company Share Options (CSOPs)	No discounts allowed at grant Maximum value at grant is £30,000 Must be held for between 3 and 10 years.	Income tax on exercise if outside the 3 to 10-year period Capital gains tax on disposal
Enterprise Management Incentives	Must be full-time employees Option must be exercised	Income tax on exercise if the options were given at a discount or if exercised >10 years from grant
Non Tax Advantaged Schemes	N/A	Shares are subject to income tax at vest and capital gains tax when sold Share options are subject to income tax at exercise and capital gains tax when sold

CHAPTER 9

Pensions

Contents at a Glance

PENSIONS OVERVIEW

9.1 This chapter is a brief summary of the tax implications of pensions and does not comment on the treatment or law relating to pensions on divorce. For individuals wanting to understand more about the treatment of pensions on divorce we absolutely recommend reading the Report by the Pension Advisory Group 'A Guide to the Treatment of Pensions on Divorce'.[1]

9.2 This chapter aims to provide an overview of the taxation of pensions and some specific pitfalls which can arise in relation to pension sharing and the lifetime allowance. This is a particularly complex area and it is hoped that this chapter may help to highlight when to seek additional advice. Unlike some other areas of the book this is not a chapter which lends itself to a DIY approach.

9.3 Pensions are the main way individuals provide for retirement, generally there are two main categories:

1. Personal Pension Plans (including Stakeholder schemes and Retirement Annuities).
2. Occupational Pension Schemes.

9.4 Largely speaking, there are tax advantages to pensions both when the money is paid in and as the fund grows. The scale and thus value of these advantages has been capped in recent years with changes to the annual allowance and the lifetime allowance, first introduced in 2006.

1 www.nuffieldfoundation.org/sites/default/files/files/Guide_To_The_Treatment_of_Pensions_on_Divorce-Digital(1).pdf

9.5 Individuals who are subject to a pension sharing order should consider whether their ability to pay into their pension is impacted. If the application of a pension debit will impact any protections they have or if the receipt of pension credits will cause them to eventually breach their lifetime allowance.

9.6 This chapter does not comment on investment advice, how to value a pension or how to approach the questions of taking account of their value. An appropriately qualified financial advisor and/or actuary should be engaged for those purposes. A strong orientation is provided by the Pensions Advisory Group's *'A guide to the treatment of pensions on divorce'* published in July 2019 and reference should be made to the guidance provided there which is not duplicated here.

9.7 Personal pensions are flexible schemes as they can remain with the individual throughout their life. If sole traders or individuals in a partnership pay into a pension it is likely to be a personal pension. These schemes operate on a relief at source basis. This means contributions are made net of the basic rate of tax and, if applicable, additional and higher rate relief need to be sought from HMRC through the tax return.

9.8 Occupational pension schemes are schemes administered by (or for) an employer, both in the private and public sectors. Individuals who have had multiple employments are likely to have multiple occupational pension schemes.

9.9 Within occupational pension schemes individuals can be part of a defined benefit scheme (also known as a final salary scheme or career average scheme) or a defined contribution scheme. Defined contribution schemes are the most popular schemes now as the final salary schemes have declined in popularity due to the funding pressure it places on firms.

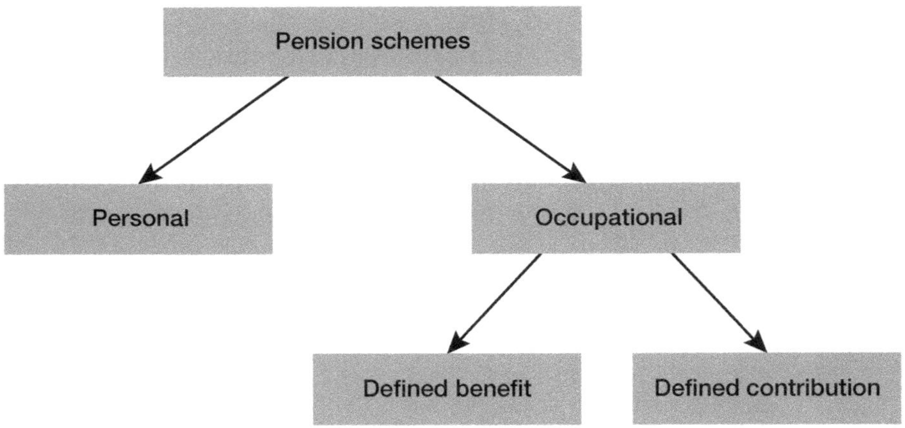

DEFINED BENEFIT (FINAL SALARY/CAREER AVERAGE)

9.10 Under a defined benefit arrangement, regulations or the contract between the member and the employer specifies the final amount of the pension to be paid under the arrangement. This is often expressed as a formula which may be based on the salary in the final year (or last three years of employment).

DEFINED CONTRIBUTION

9.11 Under a defined contribution scheme the member (and perhaps also their employer) will pay into the member's pension, and the pension fund will increase by the value of any contributions and fluctuate in line with the underlying investments. The value of the final pension fund will be the amount paid in plus any growth (or loss) over time.

TAX RELIEF

9.12 Certain conditions must be met for tax relief to be available on pension contributions, and these are summarised in the following flow chart.

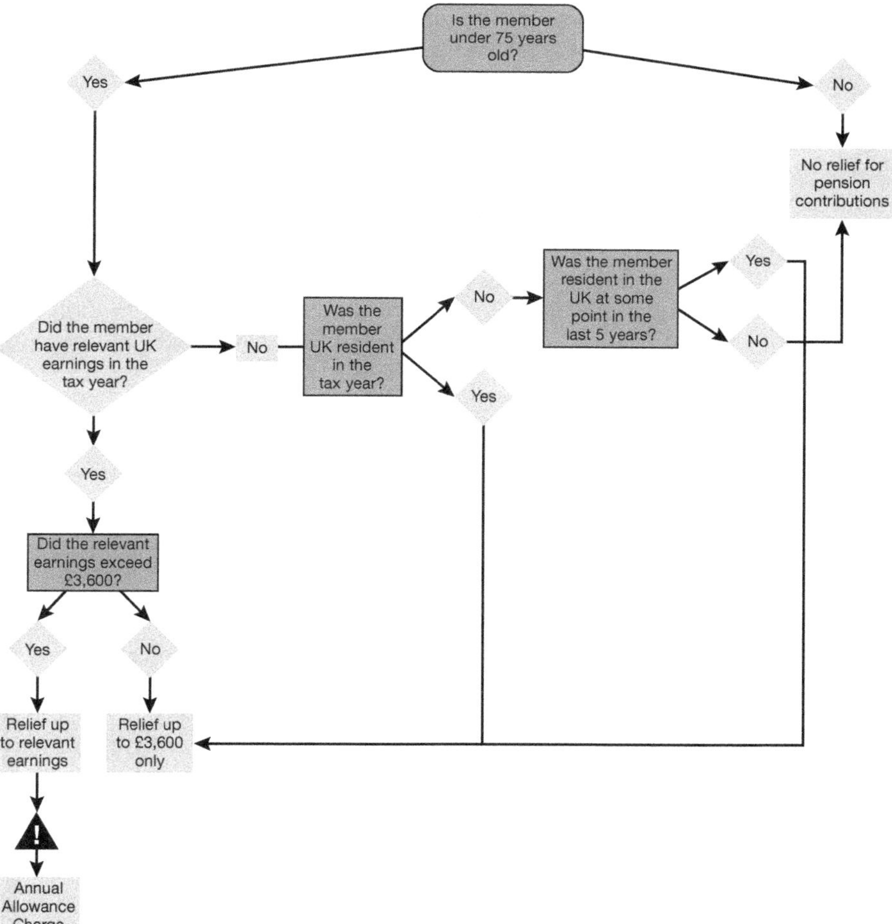

OPERATIONS OF RELIEF

9.13 Providing the individual meets the conditions for relief there are two ways that tax relief is obtained, which depend on how the money is paid into the pension scheme. For the moment we will ignore the annual allowance rules and revisit these shortly. If your client is earning in excess of £240,000 it is important to ensure they have considered the annual allowance charge (both for current and historical positions). Pre 6 April 2020 this amount was £150,000. Therefore, if reviewing 2018–19 or 2019–20 tax returns £150,000 is the income level which may mean the individuals annual allowance has been reduced.

PERSONAL PENSION

9.14 For individuals paying into a personal pension, contributions are treated as being made net of 20% tax. This is known as relief at source, for example a payment into a personal pension of £800 is considered a gross contribution of £1,000 (£800 × 100/80). The contribution is treated as having benefited from £200 tax relief at source. The pension scheme reclaims the £200 from HMRC and this is added to the pension pot.

9.15 For example, Jamie is a basic rate taxpayer and self-employed. She pays £4,000 per year into her personal pension scheme. This payment is deemed to be made net of tax.

HMRC will top up by £1,000 and the total amount in Jamie's pension at the end of the year will be £5,000. As Jamie is a 20% taxpayer, no further adjustments need to be made. Jamie only pays tax at 20% on her income and has already received 20% tax relief at source. This relief is automatic and does not need to be claimed by her.

Illustration 9A

Payments into a personal pension plan (basic rate taxpayer).

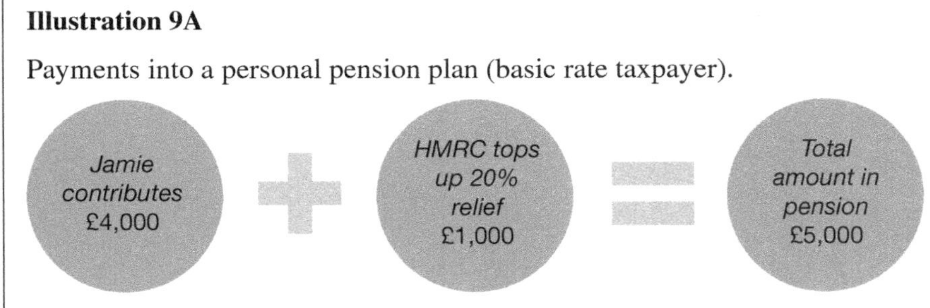

If the taxpayer is a higher or additional rate taxpayer an adjustment needs to be made within the income tax calculation. This additional relief is given by extending the basic rate band. Therefore, if we take Ryan who pays tax at 40%, 20% relief will be given at source and the additional 20% relief will be given via the tax return. This is given by extending the basic rate band by the value of the gross pension contribution.

Illustration 9B

Payments into a personal pension plan (higher rate taxpayer).

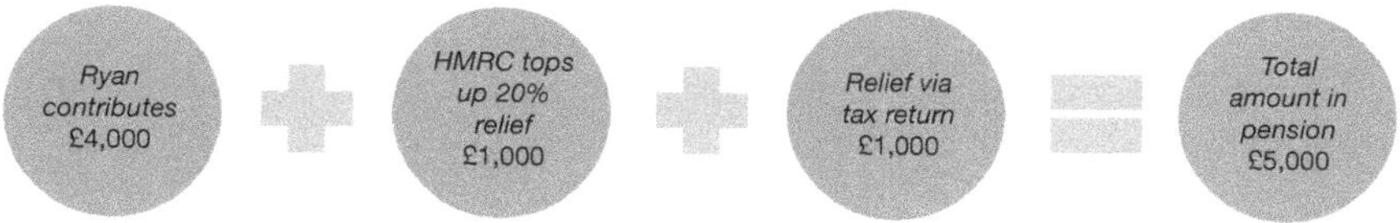

The relief given via the tax return is given by way of either a tax refund or reducing Ryan's tax liability.

OCCUPATIONAL PENSION

9.16 Occupational pension schemes can be processed in a number of ways so it is important to check the underlying documentation. However, contributions made to an occupational scheme are usually made gross (ie before tax has been deducted). This is often done via salary sacrifice. Employers will deduct the member's contributions before calculating their taxable pay. As gross pay is reduced by total pension contributions the gross pay figure on a P60 will not include any payments into a pension. The pension contributions for the year will appear on the March payslip.

9.17 Contributions made to employee pension schemes by the employer are exempt from income tax and NIC (provided the scheme is a registered pension scheme). Note that employer contributions are taken into account for the purposes of the annual allowance charge (discussed later in the chapter).

Note: payments into an occupational pension scheme will not appear on the P60, the total contributions will appear on the March pay slip.

ANNUAL ALLOWANCE

9.18 The annual allowance was introduced in 2006 and limits the total amount that can be paid into a pension scheme and benefit from tax relief per year. It includes all contributions whether made by the individual or another party (for example an employer).

9.19 Contributions in excess of the annual allowance will not benefit from tax relief, the charge effectively removes the income tax benefits on the contributions. Further, much like the personal allowance, the annual allowance is reduced when individuals earn in excess of a certain amount or if they have already drawn down on their defined contribution pension.

9.20 The way pension savings are measured against the annual allowance is different depending on the pension scheme:

- for defined contribution pensions, it is the total contributions from all sources paid in the tax year;
- for defined benefit pensions, it is the capitalised value of the increase in the accrued benefits over the year.

9.21 Even though the annual allowance has been in operation for many years the statistics indicate that many individuals who are liable for the charge remain unaware of their obligations and have not been paying it. One of the reasons for this is that the tapering and the application of the charge must all be calculated manually. Further, most pension statements are issued after the end of the tax year, the pension statements are required to calculate adjusted income and until adjusted income is calculated one cannot work out the reduction in the allowance, making planning quite tricky.

9.22 The amount of the allowance since 2014/15 is £40,000, before any reduction for tapering. This is the total amount of contributions (or value of the benefit accrual for defined benefit) permitted per tax year.

9.23 The annual allowance is tapered for high income individuals and the taper threshold has changed from 6 April 2020. Individuals will have a reduced annual allowance if their adjusted income exceeds the relevant thresholds for the tax year.

9.24 All individuals will start with an annual allowance of £40,000. The amount they can contribute to their pension and receive tax relief on is the lower of their relevant earnings or their annual allowance.

The amount of the annual allowance is reduced by £1 for every £2 of adjusted income over:

- £150,000 for tax years 2016/17 to 2019/20;
- £240,000 for tax years from 2020/21.

The annual allowance is not reduced to zero. For 2016/17 to 2019/20 the minimum annual allowance is £10,000. From 2020/21 the minimum annual allowance is £4,000.

9.25 However, there is another test for income which can help those who may be caught simply because their pension savings exceed £40,000 in the tax year. So even if their **adjusted income** is over £150,000/£240,000, the annual allowance is not cut if their **threshold income** is:

- **£110,000 or less** for the tax years 2016/17 to 2019/20;
- **£200,000 or less** for tax years from 2020/21.

Threshold income is an individual's total income chargeable to tax plus salary sacrifice arrangements, less the individual's pension contributions.

9.26 Therefore for 2020/21 where an individual's adjusted income is over £240,000 and threshold income over £200,000 they will have a reduced annual allowance. The annual allowance will be reduced by £1 for every £2 of adjusted income over £240,000.

> **Note:** adjusted income is not the same as 'adjusted net income'. In simple terms adjusted income is the individual's income plus total employer pension contributions.

9.27 **Money Purchase Annual Allowance** – applies to those individuals who access their defined contribution pension schemes by taking income, but does not apply if only taking the tax free lump sum, or purchasing an annuity. This can be a significant trap for the unwary and the rules are complex so appropriate advice should be sought.

CARRY FORWARD

9.28 Individuals are able to carry forward their unused annual allowance for the last three years on a first in first out (FIFO) basis. If individuals have unused allowances in the past three years, the carry forward may help to reduce any possible charge. Carry forward is only available if the individual has been a member of a registered pension scheme at some point during the carry forward year. They do not need to have made contributions in that year.

9.29 If the pension contributions have exceeded the annual allowance the individual will face an annual allowance charge on the excess amounts contributed into their pension. The amount of the charge is calculated by working out the amounts contributed in excess of the charge and applying tax at the individual's top rate of tax. The annual allowance charge is not a penalty, it is effectively removing the tax relief that would have been available if contributions were within the annual allowance.

PAYING THE CHARGE

9.30 The charge should be reported on a tax return and paid by 31 January following the end of the tax year in which the contribution was made. Individuals also have the option to use the pension scheme to pay the charge. For the scheme to pay the charge individuals must notify the scheme by 31 July in the tax year two years after the tax year to which the charge relates. For charges in 2020–21 the scheme must be notified by 31 July 2022. If all the relevant conditions are met then the scheme is jointly liable with the taxpayer for paying the charge. The funds for the charge will be removed from the individual's pension savings and paid to HMRC.

TAX RELIEF ON DRAWING DOWN A PENSION

9.31 Most pensions allow members to take their benefits from age 55, although with some older pension schemes valuable guarantees could be lost by doing so. Once they reach this age they have total freedom over how they take their pension income. They can withdraw the whole amount in one go, take it over a number of years, purchase an annuity or a combination of these. This flexibility does not apply in quite the same way to occupational pensions, particularly defined benefit or final salary/career average schemes.

The ability to access pension schemes from age 55 may put pension values in a different light during divorce proceedings, particularly for those nearing age 55.

9.32 Assuming the total sum of all pensions does not exceed the lifetime allowance, the member can take 25% of the pension tax free when the benefits are being brought into payment (or crystallised). Generally the tax free cash can be paid up to 12 months after the decision to draw down the tax free amount is made and the pension date has been set.

9.33 For defined contribution schemes up to 25% of benefits crystallised can be paid as tax free cash (providing the amount does not exceed 25% of the individual's lifetime allowance).

For defined benefit schemes, the maximum amount of tax free cash is usually 25% of the value of the benefits brought into payment – again subject to the amount not exceeding 25% of the individuals lifetime allowance.

9.34 The remaining 75% is taxed at the member's marginal income rate of tax. Depending on other levels of income it is common to take the remaining 75% over a lifetime, or at least over a number of years to benefit from the tax-free personal allowance and lower rate income tax bands.

No tax free cash can be paid where a pension credit on divorce is derived from a pension already in payment. Therefore, if an ex-spouse receives a pension credit from a previously crystallised pension, they will not be entitled to the 25% tax free drawdown, as the tax free cash would have already been an option at the point of crystallisation.

9.35 Where someone's life expectancy is less than 12 months, their uncrystallised pension fund can be paid as a lump sum. If this is paid before age 75 it is tax free, as long as it is within their lifetime allowance. After 75 it can only be paid from unused funds and would be subject to a 45% tax charge.

9.36 Further exemptions from the 25% rule include individuals with:

- enhanced or primary protection with registered tax free cash;
- scheme specific tax free cash protection;
- guaranteed minimum pension.

LIFETIME ALLOWANCE

9.37 The lifetime allowance was introduced in 2006 and applies to the amount of a pension benefit that can be taken without triggering an extra tax charge. Benefit crystallisation events including taking tax free cash and pension income.

Individuals are not prohibited from saving into a pension once the value of their pensions reach the lifetime allowance and there is no charge at this point. The charge only applies when benefits are crystallised in excess of the allowance, so it is in effect an exit charge.

9.38 Because the lifetime allowance has changed so much over the years, it is possible for an individual to have a larger lifetime allowance than the standard amount through various protections discussed below.

The amount of the charge also depends on how the funds are withdrawn ie whether as a lump sum or by way of income over time.

VALUES FOR LIFETIME ALLOWANCE

9.39 This is another complex area and advice should be sought. To provide a summary, the lifetime allowance is tested against other crystallised benefits at the time of the benefit crystallisation event. Some benefits can be ignored when testing against the lifetime allowance including

- small lump sum payments (£10,000 or less);[2]
- dependents schemes pensions;
- state pensions.

9.40 The amount of the lifetime allowance has changed frequently. A member's benefits are only tested against the relevant lifetime allowance when a benefit crystallisation event occurs.

Table 9A Lifetime Allowance Rates

Tax Year	Standard Lifetime Allowance	Tax Year	Standard Lifetime Allowance
2020/21	£1.0731m	2010/11 to 2011/12	£1.8m
2019/20	£1.055m	2009/10	£1.75m
2018/19	£1.030m	2008/09	£1.65m
2016/17 to 2017/18	£1m	2007/08	£1.6m
2014/15 to 2015/16	£1.25m	2006/07	£1.5m
2012/13 to 2013/14	£1.5m		

2 PTM063700.

9.41 From 6 April 2018, the lifetime allowance increases annually in line with the consumer price index. Individuals who have pension savings in excess of the lifetime allowance may have protected these through various protection schemes. These are very briefly described below.

9.42 Some of these protections are impacted by pension sharing orders. It will be important to ask clients and their spouses if they applied for any lifetime allowance protections.

A summary of these protections are set out below, with further detail set out later in this chapter.

Tax Year	**Type of protection**	
6 April 2006	Enhanced protection	Members may not make any more pensions savings after 5 April 2006. This protection gives complete immunity from the lifetime allowance charge. If enhanced protection is lost (for example, because the member makes additional contributions) the member could fall back on primary protection if they had it.
6 April 2006	Primary protection	Although primary protection is a fall back for those with enhanced protection members could opt for primary protection, for example if they wanted to continue making pension contributions.
6 April 2012	Fixed protection	The lifetime allowance was reduced from £1.8m to £1.5m from 6 April 2012. To protect individuals who were likely to have pension pots over time in excess of £1.5m there was a facility for individuals to register to protect their lifetime allowance at £1.8m. This was called fixed protection 2012. It was not available if the member had already benefited from enhanced or primary protection and any further benefit accrual after 5 April 2012 would result in this protection being lost
6 April 2014	Fixed protection 2014	From 6 April 2014 the lifetime allowance was reduced from £1.5m to £1.25m. Individuals who had or expected to have pension pots in excess of £1.25m were able to use the 'fixed protection 2014' to protect their lifetime allowance at £1.5m, with similar rules as above.
6 April 2014	Individual protection 2014	As well as fixed protection, individual protection 2014 was available if pension savings exceeded £1.25m on 5 April 2014. This gives the individual a personalised lifetime allowance equal to the value of their pensions on 5 April 2014, known as the relevant amount, (but capped at £1.5m) without the need to cease contributing.
6 April 2016	Fixed protection 2016	On 6 April 2016 the lifetime allowance was again reduced from £1.25m to £1m. Individuals who had or expected to have pension pots in excess of £1m at retirement age were able to use the 'fixed protection 2016' to protect their lifetime allowance at £1.25m, with similar rules applying as per 2012 and 2014 fixed protection.
6 April 2016	Individual protection 2016	As well as fixed protection, individual protection 2016 was available if pension savings exceeded £1m on 5 April 2016. This gives the individuals a personalised lifetime allowance equal to the value of their pension on 5 April 2016, known as the relevant amount (but capped at £1.25m) without the need to cease contributing.

The impact of pension sharing orders on protections is discussed further on in the chapter.

THE LIFETIME ALLOWANCE CHARGE

9.43 The lifetime allowance charge applies at a benefit crystallisation event when there is insufficient lifetime allowance remaining to support the value being crystallised. Even if someone has a pension value over the lifetime allowance before crystallisation, the charge only applies once the lifetime allowance has been used up.

9.44 The chargeable amount is the amount crystallising over the available lifetime allowance.

- If it's paid as a lump sum it's subject to an immediate LTA tax charge of **55%** before it's paid out.
- If it's used to provide a pension income, an immediate LTA tax charge of **25%** applies to the excess. The pension drawn will also be subject to income tax at the individual's appropriate rate. For a higher rate taxpayer, the combined effect of a 25% LTA tax charge and income tax at 40% on the pension income equates to an overall tax charge of 55%. This effective rate would be lower or higher if the individual is taxed on income at a different rate.

9.45 When benefits are crystallised during the member's lifetime, the member and the scheme administrator are equally and separately liable for the whole charge, and payment by one party will reduce the liability of the other. If the scheme administrator does not pay the tax or pays the incorrect amount of tax the liability will fall on the individual. The individual is responsible for completing a tax return and reporting any excess benefits and how they were taken together with the tax paid by the scheme.

The tax charge on the excess over the lifetime allowance depends on how it is used.

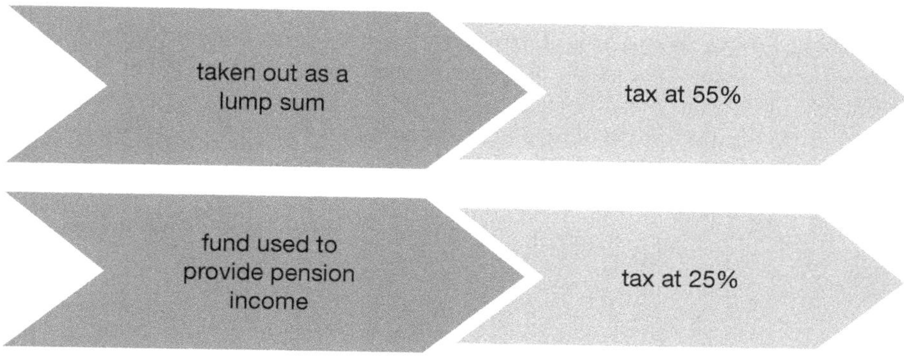

9.46 To decide if a lifetime allowance charge is payable the scheme will test against the lifetime allowance at a benefit crystallisation event (BCE). Generally a BCE will be when benefits from the scheme are taken or when a member reaches age 75.

9.47 As above, the lifetime allowance charge only applies once the lifetime allowance has been fully utilised. As such, individuals with multiple pension schemes will have an option over the order that they crystallise their funds. They could crystallise pension scheme that are not subject to a Pension Attachment Order first, which could cause the ex-spouses pension to be subject to a 55% lifetime allowance charge if the first withdrawal utilises the full life time allowance.

SHARING/ATTACHMENT ORDERS – THE DIFFERING TAX TREATMENTS

9.48 There are three main options when considering pensions on divorce.

1. Pension offsetting.
2. Pension attachment orders.
3. Pension sharing.

9.49 Pension offsetting has no direct tax implications, although when comparing the value of a non-pension capital asset to that of a pension, an adjustment for the taxation difference of these two different assets would usually be made. However, pension attachment (formerly earmarking) orders have different tax implications both for the transferor and the transferee.

For ease, we will not be covering the rules for pre December 2000 divorce petitions.

PENSION ATTACHMENT ORDERS

9.50 Under an attachment order the pension rights remain in the member's pension scheme but part of the member's pension entitlement is earmarked for the former spouse. The attachment pension or tax free lump sum (as appropriate) becomes payable by the pension scheme to the former spouse from the same date as the member benefits become payable. The courts can also require the pension scheme trustees to pay part or all of any lump sum death benefit to the former spouse in the event of the death of the member prior to retirement. The member losing part of the pension suffers a pension 'debit' and the recipient gets a pension 'credit'. This terminology will be used throughout the rest of this section.

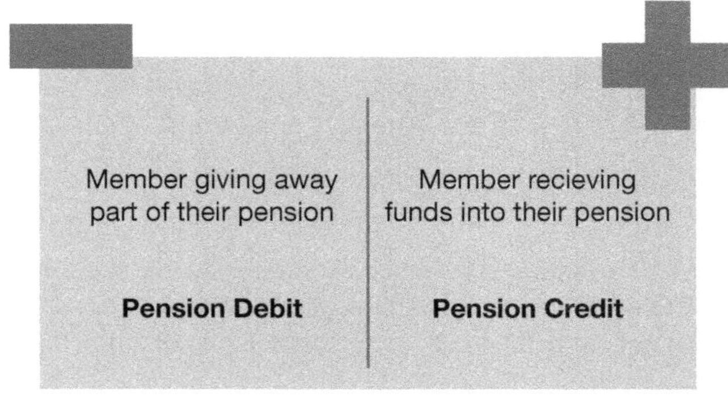

Member giving away part of their pension
Pension Debit
Member recieving funds into their pension
Pension Credit

9.51 When a pension is attached for a former spouse, full beneficial ownership does not transfer to them. The pension scheme member is the one chargeable to income tax on the pension when it is drawn down, with the former spouse receiving their relevant percentage (or often an amount of lump sum) net of the scheme member's highest rate of tax. It therefore follows that the former spouse has no liability to income tax on the amount paid to them; it is effectively considered as a maintenance payment made out of former income and as a form of maintenance payment, it would terminate if the recipient spouse remarries or the scheme member dies.

PENSION SHARING

9.52 A pension sharing order requires the pension scheme to be split by way of a percentage as set out in the order. Pension credit rights awarded to an ex-partner on divorce can be secured within the original pension scheme or by transfer to a new scheme.

We will now consider the tax issues following a pension sharing order.

Contribution rules

9.53 Where the non-member spouse transfers a pension credit into another registered pension scheme it is not treated as a contribution to that scheme. Therefore, there is no tax relief due on the transfer of these funds and it can be ignored for annual allowance purposes.

Impact on lifetime allowance where no protections are in place

9.54 If an individual's uncrystallised benefits are reduced as a result of a pension sharing order, they can continue to contribute to their pension (subject to the usual rules). Having uncrystallised benefits effectively means that the pension has not been drawn down yet and they are under 75.

If the individual suffering the pension debit or receiving a pension credit has protected their lifetime allowance further care is needed and advice should be taken.

9.55 If the sharing order is made on benefits that have been crystallised after 5 April 2006 these will already have been tested against the lifetime allowance. It is not possible for the member to replace the contributions that have been shared, although if they still have unused lifetime allowance they can still make further contributions or crystallise other pension schemes that have not been shared, until the lifetime allowance has been fully utilised.

Pension sharing and Protections

9.56 Most individuals will be subject to the standard lifetime allowance. Individuals' benefits are tested against the lifetime allowance when a benefit crystallisation event occurs. However, there are some circumstances where an individual could be entitled to more or less than the standard amount.

In 2006, two types of protections were initially introduced, primary and enhanced protection.

Primary protection

9.57 Primary protection was for individuals who had over £1.5 million in their pension fund on 6 April 2016. It established a multiplier for the lifetime allowance, meaning the member has an enhanced lifetime allowance when the benefits are drawn.

Receiving a pension credit

9.58 If a pension credit is generated from uncrystallised funds or a pension that was in payment pre 5 April 2006 then there is no change to the amount of primary protection the recipient has. The credits could have the effect of increasing the benefits so that they exceed the protection which would result in an eventual lifetime allowance charge when a benefit crystallisation event occurs.

9.59 However, it is possible to claim a lifetime allowance increase to existing primary protection if the pension credit

- is from a pension already in payment; and
- the original member's entitlement to that pension arose after 5 April 2006.

Being subject to a pension debit

9.60 An individual with primary protection will have their protection recalculated if their pension benefits are reduced as a result of a pension debit.

Individuals who have primary protection must notify HMRC if they become subject to a pension sharing order. They must declare the amount of the pension debit and the effective date of the order. If primary protection remains, HMRC will issue a new certificate showing the revised primary protection amount.

ENHANCED PROTECTION

Receiving a pension credit

9.61 If the individual receiving the pension credit has enhanced protection the way the pension credit is received on divorce will depend on how the rights are secured:

- if the pension credit is paid from the original member's pension into an existing pension arrangement the enhanced protection is not affected;
- if a new arrangement is set up to accept the pension credit directly from the original members pension, the recipient will lose their enhanced protection.

9.62 In certain circumstances it is possible to claim a lifetime allowance enhancement factor when receiving a pension credit. Those with enhanced protection generally would not need to apply for this because as long as the enhanced protection is maintained their benefits are not subject to the lifetime allowance charge.

Being subject to a pension debit

9.63 Enhanced protection is not affected by a pension debit. However, if this resulted in the individual having pension benefits below the current standard lifetime allowance, they may wish to consider losing their enhanced protection in order to make further contributions and rebuild their pension pot.

Fixed protection (2012, 2014, 2016)

9.64 Generally speaking, if an individual has fixed protection the protection will be lost if the individual continues to contribute to the pension on or after the date from which the protection applied eg 6 April 2012 for Fixed Protection 2012. The amount remaining in the fund after the debit will remain protected. However, if the pension debit was so large that it leaves the member's fund well below the standard lifetime allowance, they may consider losing the protection and increasing their fund by making further contributions. This would require careful consideration and input from a regulated financial advisor and pensions on divorce expert.

9.65 A potential trap for people with fixed protection is auto-enrolment, whereby employers are required to auto-enroll their employees into a workplace pension scheme. It is vital that individuals with Fixed Protection inform their employers at the earliest opportunity as there is an exemption that allows employers to exclude such individuals.

Receiving a pension credit

9.66 If the pension credit is paid into an existing pension arrangement of the recipient, then their fixed protection is not affected. However, if a new arrangement is set up to accept the pension credit from the original members pension, the recipient will lose their fixed protection.

9.67 It is possible to claim a lifetime allowance enhancement factor if the pension credit:

- comes from a pension already in payment; and
- the original member's entitlement to that pension arose after 5 April 2006.

This allows the recipient to claim an enhancement factor that will give them an increase on top of their protected lifetime allowance (or the standard lifetime allowance if fixed protection is ever lost) equivalent to the value of the pension credit.

9.68 However, if a pension credit comes from a pension that was in payment before 6 April 2006 then it has never been tested against the lifetime allowance and so there is no change to the amount of fixed protection the recipient had.

This means the additional pension could exceed the available protection, resulting in a lifetime allowance charge when a benefit crystallisation event occurs. If enhanced or fixed protections are lost, HMRC must be notified within 90 days.

Individual protection (2014 or 2016)

9.69 If after 5 April 2014 for Individual Protection 2014 or 5 April 2016 for IP 2016, individuals become subject to a pension debit as a result of a pension sharing order their protection can be reduced or lost altogether as the debit will reduce the value of their relevant amount.

Receiving a pension credit

9.70 The effect on individual protection depends on the source of the pension credit

- if the pension credit is generated from an uncrystallised pension or the original member's pension was already in payment before 6 April 2006 then there is no change to the amount of individual protection the recipient had. This means that the increased benefits could exceed the available protection resulting in a lifetime allowance charge when a benefit crystallisation even occurs.

9.71 It is possible to claim a lifetime allowance enhancement factor increase to existing individual protection if the pension credit:

- comes from a pension already in payment; and
- the original member's entitlement to that pension arose after 5 April 2006.

Being subject to a pension debit

9.72 A member who has individual protection and has their pension benefits reduced as a result of a pension debit will need their lifetime allowance factor to be recalculated. The original valuation or 'relevant amount' used when applying for individual protection (which may be higher than the capped amount) will be reduced by the amount of the pension debit – however, it is possible to reduce the amount of the pension debit.

9.73 This should be done by a pensions on divorce expert but in brief:

Individual Protection 2014 – if the transfer date of the debit is after 5 April 2015, then the value of the pension debit is reduced by 5% for each complete tax year since 2013/14.

Individual Protection 2016 – if the transfer date of the debit is after 5 April 2017, then the value of the pension debit is reduced by 5% for each complete tax year since 2015/16.

9.74 If the result of this is that the remaining pensions are less than £1.25 million (fixed protection 2014) and £1 million (fixed protection 2016), individual protection will be lost. For those losing Fixed Protection 2014, they would still be able to apply for individual protection 2016 if their pension fund exceeds £1 million on 5 April 2016, and they had received no pension contributions into any of their pensions since 5 April 2016, although this would only be worthwhile if the amount being protected was in excess of the current standard lifetime allowance.

HMRC must be informed of the amount of the pension debit and the date of the debit within 60 days.

> **Note:** if a member suffers a pension debit after 5 April 2016 but subsequently makes an application for individual protection 2016, the pension debit must be disclosed in the application so that it can be factored into the amount for the protected lifetime allowance.

PENSIONS CHECKLIST

9.75

		Yes/No/ NA	**Risk**	**Mitigation**	**Ref**
Annual Allowance	Is the individual's adjusted income (total income plus pension contributions) over £240,000?	☐ Yes ☐ No ☐ N/A	They may have failed to report this accurately on their tax return. If there has been historical failure to report this there may be additional tax due The maximum amount an individual can contribute to their pension is £40,000 and this is tapered down if the individual is a high earner	If there has been incorrect historical filing it would be wise to true up the position ahead of the financial proceedings to be sure that the funds involved reflect the true net position of the individual A pension sharing order would not breach the annual allowance charge provided the debit was coming from a registered pension fund	**9.18**

		Yes/No/ NA	Risk	Mitigation	Ref
Lifetime allowance	At the point of the benefit crystallisation event, will the individual have used up their lifetime allowance?	☐ Yes ☐ No ☐ N/A	If an individual's pensions savings are over the standard lifetime allowance, currently £1,073,100, or their protected amount, they will be subject to a tax charge when a benefit crystallisation event occurs. The charge is either 55% or 25% depending on how it is drawn down	Check if the individual has any lifetime allowance protections Ensure the net value of the pension is valued	**9.37**
Pension Attachment	Will the individual's pension be subject to an attachment order?	☐ Yes ☐ No ☐ N/A	The individual will be taxed on the full pension amount when it is withdrawn, not just the percentage which is applicable to them	Ensure that the tax payable by the member is considered within the attachment order, so that the percentage to the ex-spouse applies to the net of tax pension	**9.50**
	Will the individual be the beneficiary of the attachment order?	☐ Yes ☐ No ☐ N/A	The attached benefit will be payable to the former spouse from the same date as the member's benefits become payable The beneficial ownership will not have transferred to them. They will have no liability to income tax on the amount paid to them (so they will not need to report this on their tax return) The member's payment would cease on their former spouse's death or re-marriage	The beneficiary of the order may consider insuring against the death of the former spouse	**9.50**
Pension Sharing	Will the individual's pension be subject to a pension sharing order?	☐ Yes ☐ No ☐ N/A	The individual can continue to contribute to their pension fund subject to the normal contribution rules (annual allowance, lifetime allowance etc)	If the individual has lifetime allowance protection in place they may have to notify HMRC about the pension sharing order. Failure to notify may result in penalties	**9.52**

		Yes/No/ NA	Risk	Mitigation	Ref
	Will the individual's pension be increased by a pension sharing order?	☐ Yes ☐ No ☐ N/A	Will the increase to their pension fully utilise the annual allowance? If so, potential lifetime allowance charge.	Check if the individual will qualify for an enhanced lifetime allowance credit	**9.58**

CHAPTER 10

Capital Gains Tax Overview

Contents at a Glance

CAPITAL GAINS TAX OVERVIEW

10.1 Capital gains tax is a relatively new tax, having been introduced in April 1965. Receipts from capital gains tax make up a small proportion of the overall tax take. However, on divorce, capital gains tax is one of the most important taxes to consider as advantages of transferring assets as a married couple cease after the end of the tax year of separation.

10.2 A capital gain will arise when a chargeable person disposes of a chargeable asset at a profit. A disposal can be a sale or a transfer. In general terms a profit will arise when the proceeds exceed the original cost.

10.3 The total gain is defined as the value of the asset when it is sold (or given away) less its value when originally bought (or inherited). As with income tax there is an annual threshold below which capital gains tax does not have to be paid. This is called the annual exemption and in 2020/21 this is £12,300.

Note: Married couples cannot transfer any part of their capital gains tax annual exemption to each other.

10.4 Further in the chapter is a typical capital gains tax pro-forma. Throughout this and the following chapters we will go through the elements of the pro-forma explaining:

- Tax base and payments.
- Rates and allowances.
- Responsibilities and penalties.
- Key points for family lawyers.

The later chapters explore capital gains tax on the main home, investment properties and chattels and shares.

ALLOWABLE EXPENSES

10.5 Gains are reduced by allowable expenses. From the proceeds of sale individuals can deduct:

- the base cost of the asset (or the value of the asset when inherited);
- all costs of acquisition (this is all costs involved in purchasing the asset);
- incidental costs of disposal (all costs involved in selling or disposal of the asset).

We look at specific examples in later chapters.

THE NON-TAXPAYER

10.6 If all transfers and sales in the tax year give rise to a gain of under £12,300 there is no capital gains tax to pay. In most cases the gain will not need to be reported on a tax return either. If, however, the disposal gives rise to a loss, the loss should be reported on a return to ensure the loss is available to be set against future gains.

THE ORDER OF THE TAXES

10.7 In most cases the rate of capital gains tax depends on the individual's annual income for the tax year. If their income is within the basic rate band (up to £50,000) then some part of the taxable gain will be taxable at the lower rate of capital gains tax. If the individual earns above the basic rate band, the whole gain will be taxable at the higher rate. The rates of capital gains tax are 10% and 20% for non-residential property gains and 18% and 28% for residential property gains. Therefore, you will need to establish the client's annual income ahead of working out their possible capital gains tax liability.

Illustration 10A – Working out the capital gains tax rate to use – Faye

Faye sold a painting in February 2021 giving rise to a gain of £45,500. Faye's total income for the year is £36,000.

What is Faye's capital gains liability for the year?

We first deduct the annual exemption of £12,300 in order to arrive at the amount of taxable gains:

Gain from painting	£45,500
Less: Annual exemption	(£12,300)
Taxable gains	£33,200

In order to calculate her capital gains tax liability for 2020/21 we need to establish the amount of Faye's unused basic rate band:

	£
Income	36,000
Less: Personal allowance	(12,500)
Taxable income	**23,500**
Basic rate band	*37,500*
Less: Taxable income	(23,500)
Unused amount of basic rate band	*14,000*

For a quicker calculation you could deduct Faye's income of £36,000 from the basic rate threshold of £50,000 to arrive at the same figure.

£14,000 of the gain will be taxed at the lower rate of capital gains tax, 10%, amount of the gain in excess of £14,000 will be taxable at 20%.

	£
Taxable gains	33,200
14,000 @ 10% (available basic rate band)	1,400
19,200 @ 20% (excess gain over the basic rate band)	3,840
Capital gains tax Liability	**£5,240**

If Faye's income for the year had been £52,000 she would have utilised all of her basic rate band and her whole gain would be taxable at 20%.

UNDERSTANDING THE PRO-FORMA

10.8 For individuals who have gains from one type of asset, their capital gains tax position will be relatively simple to work out. For individuals with gains or deemed gains from multiple assets, the position will take a little longer to determine. To ascertain the potential capital gains tax liability you will need to know the following:

(a) the date of disposal;

(b) nature of the asset being sold;

(c) individual's income for the year.

10.9 All assets are chargeable for capital gains tax purposes unless they are specifically exempt. All wasting chattels are specifically exempt from capital gains tax. Wasting chattel is defined as tangible moveable property with a useful life of less than 50 years. The main exempt items for capital gains tax are cars, antiques and yachts. A table of the most common exempt assets can be found at the end of this chapter. Chattels are discussed in more detail in Chapter 13.

10.10 If an asset is exempt but it is being bought and sold with an intention to make a profit then this could bring the activity into the scope of income tax as the income may be regarded as trading income.

For example whilst cars are an exempt asset, if an individual was buying and selling cars as a business this would be regarded as trading income and their profits would be subject to income tax.

10.11 Capital gains tax is charged on gains arising in the tax year which runs from 6 April to 5 April. Gains are either taxable or exempt from tax. Taxable gains are then categorised into one of three categories:

1. Gains eligible for business asset disposal relief (formerly known as Entrepreneur's relief).
2. Other gains not eligible for business asset disposal relief.
3. Gains from residential property.

It is important to correctly categorise the gains as the different categories are taxed at different rates and receive different allowances.

10.12 Foreign gains are also subject to tax in the UK if the individual is resident and domiciled in the UK. They will sit in whichever category the gain is derived from, so gains from a property in Spain would sit in the gains from residential property column.

CAPITAL GAINS TAX PRO-FORMA

10.13

	£	£
Gross sales proceeds / market value at transfer	x	
Less: Selling costs		(x)
Net Sales proceeds		(x)

	£	£
Less: Cost /MV 1982		(x)
Less: Acquisition costs		(x)
Less: Enhancement expenditure		(x)
Gain		x
Less: Reliefs (including PPR Relief)		(x)
Chargeable gain		x

	Gains eligible for BADR	Other gains not eligible for BADR	Residential property gain
Current year gains	x	x	x
Less: Current year losses			(x)
Less: Losses brought forward			(x)
Less: Annual exemption			(12,300)
Taxable gains			

Capital gains tax	
Gains eligible for business asset disposal relief @ 10%	x
Gains within the basic rate band @ 10%	x
Gains above the basic rate band @20%	x
Gains on residential property within basic rate band @18%	x
Gains on residential property above the basic rate band @28%	x
Total CGT payable	**x**

GAINS ELIGIBLE FOR BUSINESS ASSET DISPOSAL RELIEF

10.14

Tax base and payments	Business asset disposal relief is a capital gains tax relief available to individuals who make a gain selling or giving away their business. In most instances business asset disposal relief is available to • sole traders/partners selling or gifting whole or part of their business; • company directors and employees holding at least 5% of the ordinary shares and voting rights in a qualifying company who sell or gift all or part of their shareholding.

	The conditions must have been met for two years immediately prior to the disposal. Note this is not an exhaustive list of conditions.
Rates & allowances	£0–£12,300 tax free Over £12,300 taxable at 10% The lifetime limit for business asset disposal relief was reduced from £10 million to £1 million in the March 2020 budget.
Responsibilities & penalties	Keeping accurate records – failure to do so can lead to penalties of £3,000. Notifying HMRC of chargeability to tax – failure to do so can lead to penalties of 100% of the tax due. Required to file an accurate tax return. Failure to file a tax return can lead to penalties of £1,600 plus a percentage of the tax due. Inaccuracies on the return can lead to penalties of up to 100% of the tax due as a result of the error.
Key points for family solicitors	One of the conditions for business asset disposal relief is the qualifying conditions must have been met for two years prior to the disposal. Therefore, if your client thinks business asset disposal relief may be available it is important to seek advice early on ahead of any changes in the business, including if one spouse ceases working for the company as this could remove their entitlement to the relief.
Further Info	We cover business asset disposal relief in more detail in Chapter 14. We cover the owner managed business in more detail in Chapter 7.

OTHER GAINS NOT ELIGIBLE FOR BUSINESS ASSET DISPOSAL RELIEF

10.15

Tax base & payments	Gains which are not eligible for business asset disposal relief and are not gains from property will fall into this category. This includes gains from shares.
Rates & allowances	£0–£12,300 tax free As shown in **Illustration 10A** you will need to determine the level of the client's income to understand if they have any of their basic rate band available. Income under £50,000, gain will be partially or fully taxable at 10%. Income over £50,000, gain will be fully taxable at 20%.

Responsibilities & penalties	Keeping accurate records – failure to do so can lead to penalties of £3,000. Notifying HMRC of chargeability to tax – failure to do so can lead to penalties of 100% of the tax due. Required to file an accurate tax return. Failure to file a tax return can lead to penalties of £1,600 plus a percentage of the tax due. Inaccuracies on the return can lead to penalties of up to 100% of the tax due as a result of the error.
Key points for family solicitors	Employees whose remuneration includes shares should consider the potential capital gains tax implications on the sale of the shares. The shares may also give rise to losses which should be recorded on the tax return to ensure the losses can be carried forward. For clients who are not resident in the UK there is no immediate charge to CGT on shares held in the UK. The gain will likely be exempt, but it is important to seek advice due to rules about temporary non residence.
Further Info	We cover complex earnings in more detail in Complex earnings, Chapter 8. We cover non-resident capital gains tax in in Residency and Domicile Chapter 3.

GAINS FROM PROPERTY

10.16

Tax base & payments	Any individual who sells a UK property will be assessed to capital gains tax in the UK. Non residents are assessed under a different regime but the tax rates are the same. Note there are some restrictions for PPR relief for non residents and periods of non occupation.
Rates & allowances	Individuals selling their main home will be entitled to exempt part or all of the gain under the PPR exemption. Couples transferring properties between them should consider if investment or rollover relief applies. £0–£12,300 tax free. As shown in **Illustration 10A** you will need to determine the level of the client's income to understand if they have any of their basic rate band available.

	Income under £50,000, gain will be partially or fully taxable at 18%. Income over £50,000, gain will be fully taxable at 28%. Certain expenses can be deducted before arriving at the taxable gain.
Responsibilities & penalties	Keeping accurate records – failure to do so can lead to penalties of £3,000. Notifying HMRC of chargeability to tax – failure to do so can lead to penalties of 100% of the tax due. Required to file an accurate tax return. Failure to file a tax return can lead to penalties of £1,600 plus a percentage of the tax due. Inaccuracies on the return can lead to penalties of up to 100% of the tax due as a result of the error.
Key points for family solicitors	Previously there have been exemptions for individuals who were not resident in the UK and for individuals selling commercial properties. From 6 April 2019 these no longer apply, however individuals may not be aware of the changes especially if they have not been living in the UK, therefore it will be important to flag these changes.
Further Info	Selling investment properties in Chapter 12. Selling the main home in Chapter 11. Non residents in Chapter 3.

LOSSES

10.17

Tax base & payments	A loss is a qualifying loss if it has arisen from the sale of an asset which would have given rise to a chargeable gain (had the values been different). For example, a client cannot claim a loss on the sale of their main home if the total (would be) gain would have been exempt from capital gains tax due to principal private residence relief.
Rates & allowances	Allowable losses must be recorded on the tax return in the year they arose to be able to offset them again future losses. Capital losses must first be offset against capital gains in the same tax year. When using current year losses to offset current year gains there is no preservation of the annual exemption. Once current year losses have reduced current year gains to nil the loss is carried forward.

	Carried forward losses are set against the first available gains (the annual exemption is preserved when using carried forward losses). Losses bought forward but not used must be recorded on the tax return.
Responsibilities & penalties	Keeping accurate records – failure to do so can lead to penalties of £3,000. Required to file an accurate tax return. If an individual does not report losses on a tax return there is unlikely to be a penalty, however the losses may not be available in future years if they have not been reported on the tax return.
Key points for family solicitors	As losses can be carried forward it is important to check if the client has any available losses. If clients are selling or transferring multiple properties they may be transferring properties with losses which can be used to offset gains.
Further Info	Selling investment properties is discussed in Chapter 12.

ALLOWANCES

10.18 Broadly speaking, individuals who are resident in the UK will be eligible for the allowances illustrated on the previous pages. The annual exemption of £12,300 is an in-year allowance. If it is not used it is lost. It cannot be carried forward or transferred between couples.

NO GAIN NO LOSS RULE

10.19 Married couples benefit from a capital gains tax exemption which allows them to transfer assets to each other at 'no gain no loss'. This means they can transfer assets between themselves without triggering a capital gains tax charge. The receiving spouse will take over ownership of the property and assume the transferor's original base cost. Married couples cannot share their annual exemption, however the no gain no loss rules enable them to transfer assets and benefit from both exemptions.

The no gain no loss rules apply during marriage and until the end of the tax year of separation.

Illustration 10B – No gain no loss transfer rules for married couples – Kat and Alfie

Kat and Alife are married. Kat works for an investment bank and has a salary of £200,000 and receives 25% of her remuneration in shares. Alfie earns £15,000 a year as a teaching assistant. In February Kat and Alfie decide they would like to purchase an investment property. Most of the funds for the deposit will come from Kat selling her vested shares from her employment. Kat's shares had a value of £50,000 at vest and they are now worth £125,000. Therefore they are standing at a gain of £75,000.

If Kat sells the shares herself her capital gains tax computation will be as follows:

Proceeds	£125,000
Less: Base cost	(£50,000)
Gain	£75,000
Less: Annual exemption	(£12,300)
Taxable gain	£62,700
Capital gains tax payable 20%	£12,540

Alfie is a lower rate taxpayer and has an unused annual allowance, therefore Kat can reduce her potential capital gains tax liability by utilising Alfie's allowances and basic rate band. If Kat transfers Alfie 80% of her shareholding, and then Alfie sells the 80% and Kat sells the remaining 20% the position would be as follows:

Kat	£	**Alfie**	£
Proceeds	25,000	Proceeds	100,000
Less: Base cost	(10,000)	Less: Base cost	(40,000)
Gain	15,000	Gain	60,000
Less: Annual exemption	(12,300)	Less: Annual exemption	(12,300)
Taxable gain	2,700	Taxable gain	47,700
		35,000 at 10% (note 2)	3,500
2,700 at 20% (note 1)	540	12,700 at 20% (note 3)	2,540
Total Tax liability (note 4)	**£6,580**		

Note:

1. Kat's salary is £200,000, she has no available basic rate band so any gains exceeding her annual exemption are immediately taxed at 20%.
2. £35,000 is the amount of Alfie's unused basic rate band. He earns £15,000 per year, £12,300 is tax free, so the portion of his basic rate band he has used is only £3,000 (being his taxable income less his personal allowance). Therefore the first £35,000 of the gain is taxable at the lower capital gains tax rate.
3. Once Alfie's basic rate band has been fully utilised the rest of the gain will be taxed at his higher rate.
4. Kat's liability plus Alfie's liability total £6,580.

This planning results in savings of £5,960.

This types of planning is common and therefore there may be historical transfers in the marriage. The key point to note is that the base cost of the asset transferred will be the original purchase of the asset and not the value of the asset when it was transferred.

TAX YEAR OF SEPARATION

10.20 The no gain no loss principle continues to apply throughout the tax year of separation. This means assets can be transferred between spouses without an immediate capital gains tax consequence.

10.21 For income tax and capital gains tax, married couples and civil partners are treated as living together unless:

- they are separated under an order of a court or;
- they are separated by deed of separation; or
- they are in fact separated in circumstances in which the separation is likely to be permanent.[1]

10.22 The final point on the list provides some scope for interpretation and it may be necessary to seek some advice to ascertain the actual date of separation if couples have been working on their relationship even whilst living apart.

Illustration 10C – Tax year of separation – Tony and Tom

Note this example just considers the authors' opinion on what HMRC might be persuaded to regard as the tax year of separation. It is not commentary around the date of separation for divorce purposes.

Tom and Tony lived together since 2010. In 2014 they married. In 2017 Tom started to become distant and they both became unsure of the future of their marriage. In February 2017 Tom moved out of the family home, Tony and Tom continued to use their joint bank account. In June 2017 after not hearing from Tom for over a month, Tony visited a divorce lawyer to understand his position in a potential divorce. In August 2017 Tom and Tony attended marriage counselling to try to save the relationship. During this time neither Tony or Tom began other relationships and remained committed to each other. In May 2018 Tom started a new relationship and stopped attending marriage counselling.

Options for the tax year of separation

2016/17 when Tom moved out of the home

2017/18 when Tony visited a divorce lawyer

2018/19 when Tom began a new relationship

1 Taxation of Chargeable Gains Act 1992 (TCGA 1992), s 288(3); Income Tax Act 2007 (ITA 2007), s 1011.

We would want to understand substantially more about the prior three years, however, there is a strong argument that the relationship ended in *circumstances in which the separation was likely to be permanent* in 2018/19.

2016/17 Tom moved out of the home

There was still a hope that the marriage would continue. Moving out of the family home does not necessarily signal permanent separation. The fact that the couple continued to share finances suggests some element of continuing a joint fiscal life. Neither of them chose to sever their finances.

2017/18 Tony visited a divorce lawyer

It could be argued that it was reasonable for Tony to visit a divorce lawyer to understand the position should the worst case scenario play out. If Tony held the most assets in the marriage he may want to understand if they are at risk or if Tony was the lower earning spouse he may want to understand what potential rights he has to stay in the family home.

2018/19 Tom began a new relationship

Tom starting a new relationship and ceasing marriage counselling is quite a clear sign that for Tom the marriage is over. Assuming May 2018 is the date of separation, Tony and Tom will benefit from the no gain no loss rules until 5 April 2019. This means they can transfer properties between themselves with no capital gains tax implications

INHERENT GAINS AND RECORDS

10.23 Transferring assets within the tax year of separation can be valuable, however, it will be important to understand the value of the inherent gains which are being moved between spouses.

10.24 Consider two properties worth similar values but one has increased in value by £50,000 and the other has increased in value by £20,000. The party who receives the property which has the higher gain will have a higher exposure for capital gains tax on eventual sale. Further, if these are properties which have had extensive work on them, it will be necessary to establish who has the receipts and proof of works. It is vital that this also be provided to the recipient spouse so that they can claim the necessary deductions on eventual sale. This is discussed further in Chapter 12, Investment properties.

Note: If assets are being transferred inside the tax year of separation there will be no immediate capital gains tax implications, however, it is important to quantify the potential gain so that the net value of the asset can be established.

CONNECTED PERSONS

10.25 From the end of the tax year of separation until the decree absolute, separated spouses are defined as connected persons. This means, any transfers between them will take place at deemed market value.

10.26 Effectively for tax purposes, they are treated as having sold a transferred asset for its current market value and are assessed to tax on the gain, even if no cash has exchanged hands.

Note: Most family members are connected persons, therefore if a client received property from a parent or sibling, or has gifted an asset to their child there will very likely be a capital tax implication of this. It may be important to understand the origin of the asset to ensure all necessary taxes have been paid.

A person is connected to an individual:

- if that person is a relative of the individual;
- the spouse or civil partner of a relative of the individual;
- a relative of the individual's spouse or civil partner;
- the spouse or civil partner of a relative of the individual's spouse or civil partner.

Relative means brother, sister, ancestor of lineal descendant. It does not include nephews, nieces, uncles and aunts.

Illustration 10D – Connected persons – Raj and Sangita

Raj and Sangita separated several years ago. As part of the divorce Raj will transfer 2,000 of his Microsoft shares to Sangita. The tax year of separation has passed, so the connected persons rule will apply to the transfer. Raj bought the shares for £4 per share, they are now worth £85 per share. Raj is deemed to sell his shares to Sangita for £170,000 (being £85 × 2,000). His capital gains tax computation will be as follows:

	£
Market value (2,000 × 85)	170,000
Less: purchase price (2,000 × 4)	(8,000)
Gain	162,000
Less annual exemption	(12,300)
Taxable gain	149,700
Capital gains tax at 20%	**29,940**

Raj will have to report the transaction and pay £29,940 of capital gains tax by 31 January following the end of the tax year in which the gains arose.

Sangita will receive the shares at their market value of £85 per share. If she chose to sell the shares immediately (assuming the shares had not increased in value) there would be no gain, so she would not have any capital gains tax to pay.

DATE OF DISPOSAL

10.27 Possibly the most critical element to establish for capital gains tax is the date of disposal. We talk in more detail about the tax year of separation later in this chapter, however, the timing of the disposal will determine when any capital gains tax has to be paid and the availability of exemptions and reliefs, including the annual exemption and loss relief. Moreover, the value of the asset is likely to change as time goes on and we need to establish the market value at the date of disposal.

10.28 Where an asset is transferred outside the framework of a court order the normal rules apply. The date of disposal will be the date of the actual transfer.

Where a transfer is made in accordance with a court order the situation is more complex. HMRC set out their view at CG22423. A summary is set out below:

Illustration 10E – Date of disposal where a transfer is made in accordance with a court order

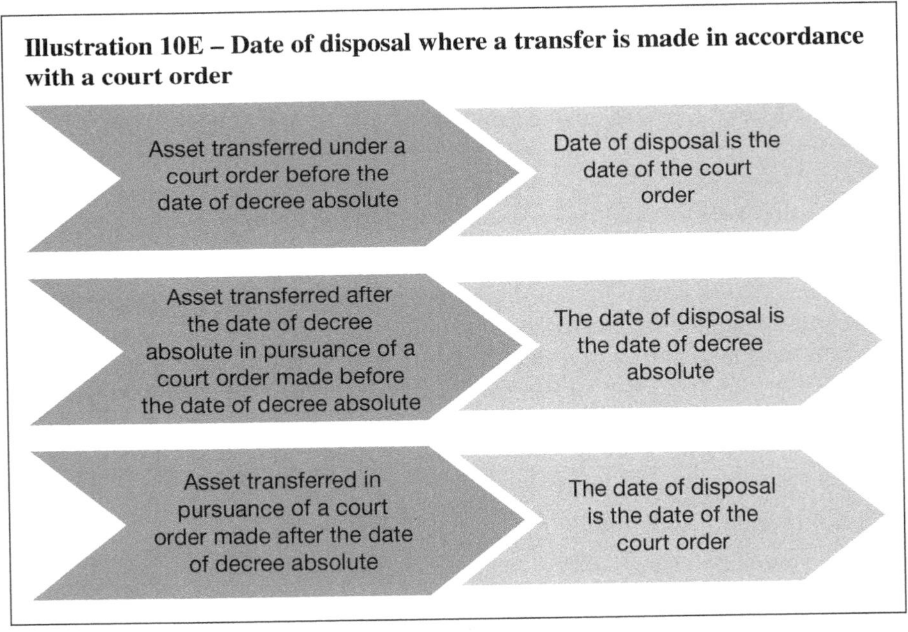

Asset transferred under a court order before the date of decree absolute
Date of disposal is the date of the court order
Asset transferred after the date of decree absolute in pursuance of a court order made before the date of decree absolute
The date of disposal is the date of decree absolute
Asset transferred in pursuance of a court order made after the date of decree absolute
The date of disposal is the date of the court order

10.29 It is important to establish the correct date of disposal as this will determine when the tax is actually payable. Capital gains tax is not payable on the date of disposal but that is the date from when the clock starts. If a disposal of shares takes place in 2019/20 the capital gains tax will be payable by 31 January 2021, if a disposal of shares takes place in 2020/21 the capital gains tax will be payable by 31 January 2022.

In most cases the date of disposal will be the date of the court order even where the assets have been transferred before the decree absolute has been granted.

VALUATIONS

10.30 To arrive at the correct capital gains tax liability the values used will need to be correct. The proceeds will always be the actual amount of consideration unless the transfer is between connected persons (transfers which take place outside of the tax year of separation) or a transfer which is not an arm's length transaction, in which case market value is substituted for actual proceeds.

ASSET	DETERMINING MARKET VALUE
Quoted shares	Valued at the average of the bid and offer prices.
Unit Trusts	Valued at the bid price.
Unquoted Shares	The value of unquoted shares must be negotiated with HMRC.
Property	In practice the average of three estate agents' valuations is often accepted. If there is a disputed market value then clients can request a valuation by the HMRC district valuer.

PAYMENT DATES

10.31 There are different payment dates for capital gains tax for different assets.

Residential property

10.32 For gains on residential property, from 6 April 2020 capital gains tax is payable 30 days from the date of disposal (see **Illustration 10E** for details of the date of disposal). Additionally, clients will have to file a new online property disposal return.

10.33 When completing the online property disposal form the client will take into account their annual exemption and estimate the correct rate to apply.

10.34 The payment of capital gains tax is then made and this is called a payment on account (this is different to the income tax payments on account).

10.35 At the end of the tax year, the client will complete their self assessment tax return, including the property gain. Once their full income, gains and losses for the year are calculated the correct amount of capital gains tax will be determined. Any payment on account over paid will result in a repayment of capital gains tax. If additional tax is payable this will be due by 31 January following the end of the tax year.

10.36 The online property disposal form is not a replacement of the self-assessment tax return, it is in addition to the return. HMRC have introduced this to reduce the amount of time between disposal and eventual payment of tax.

> **Note:** This rapid turnaround time means that clients will need to be aware of their obligations with regards to filing and payment of capital gains tax ahead of the sale or transfer to ensure they are not hit with any penalties for failing to complete the online return.
>
> If assets (including cash) are being transferred it is important to establish a clear timeline to ensure the spouse who is required to pay the capital gains tax has access to funds within 30 days from the disposal.
>
> Currently it takes approximately two weeks to appoint an agent with HMRC, therefore if clients require assistance in filing the returns they should seek to appoint a tax advisor/accountant a few weeks before the proposed transfer.

Reporting and payment requirements for gains on residential property

10.37 Capital gains or losses on land and property must be reported on a property disposal form within 30 days of the disposal. See **Illustration 10E** for establishing the date of disposal.

If the total gain is covered in full by an exemption, for example PPR relief, then no return is due. If the total gain is within an individual's annual exemption for the year then no land transactions return is due.

10.38 In the case that two transactions take place on the same day these can be reported on one land transaction return. If properties are being transferred pursuant to a court order it is likely that the date of disposal will be the date of the court order. In this case all of the property transactions can be reported on the same return.

Brought forward losses can be offset against current year gains on the land transaction return.

10.39 Losses which have occurred in the tax year and before the gain currently being reported can be offset against the gain. Losses which occur in the tax year but after the gain will need to be offset in the individual's end of year self-assessment tax return.

Non residential property

10.40 Capital gains tax due from gains arising from assets which are not residential property are payable and reportable through the usual self assessment system. The tax return is due by 31 January following the end of the tax year.

10.41 Therefore, if a client is transferring shares and selling a rental property they will have two different dates for reporting and paying the capital gains tax.

Illustration 10F – Reporting and Payment of capital gains tax – Dita and Rex

Dita and Rex were married for over 20 years. The assets in the marriage included:

- main home (jointly owned);
- two rental properties (one owned by Dita, one owned by Rex);
- shareholding worth £150,000 (owned by Dita).

They separated three years ago and are now in the final stages of their divorce. The settlement proposal is as follows:

By 31 July 2020 Rex will transfer his portion of the family home to Dita. Dita will keep her rental property and Rex will keep his rental property. Dita will transfer her shareholding to Rex.

The decree absolute is granted on 30 September 2020.

As they are outside of the tax year of separation the reporting and payment dates for capital gains tax are as follows:

Rex will be deemed to sell 50% of the former matrimonial home to Dita. As he has been out of the home for three years, PPR relief will not cover the full gain. Rex is transferring a property under a court order, therefore the date of disposal is the court order. As the gain arises from residential property he will need to file an online property return by 31 October 2020. He will have to pay a capital gains tax payment on account by 31 October 2020. At the end of the tax year Rex will be required to file a self assessment tax return reporting the gain and deducting his payment on account. If there is any additional capital gains tax due he will be required to pay this. The deadline for filing and payment will be 31 January 2022.

Dita will be deemed to sell her shares to Rex for the market value. As her gain is derived from assets which are not residential property, she will report the gain on her 2020-21 tax return which is due by 31 January 2022 and payment is due by 31 January 2022.

Due to the different assets they are disposing of, Dita and Rex have different reporting and filing obligations.

Paying in instalments

10.42 In short, it is not possible to pay capital gains tax in instalments. The only time paying in instalments may be possible is in cases where the consideration is received in instalments. However, if the property transfer is mandated in the court order and this is issued after the transfer this will extend the payment window as the 30-day clock begins from the deemed date of disposal which is likely to be the court order.

Note: It will be important to work out the timing of transfers to ensure parties have sufficient funds to settle any capital gains tax labilities.

Illustration 10G – Summary of capital gains tax consequences at the different stages of the divorce process

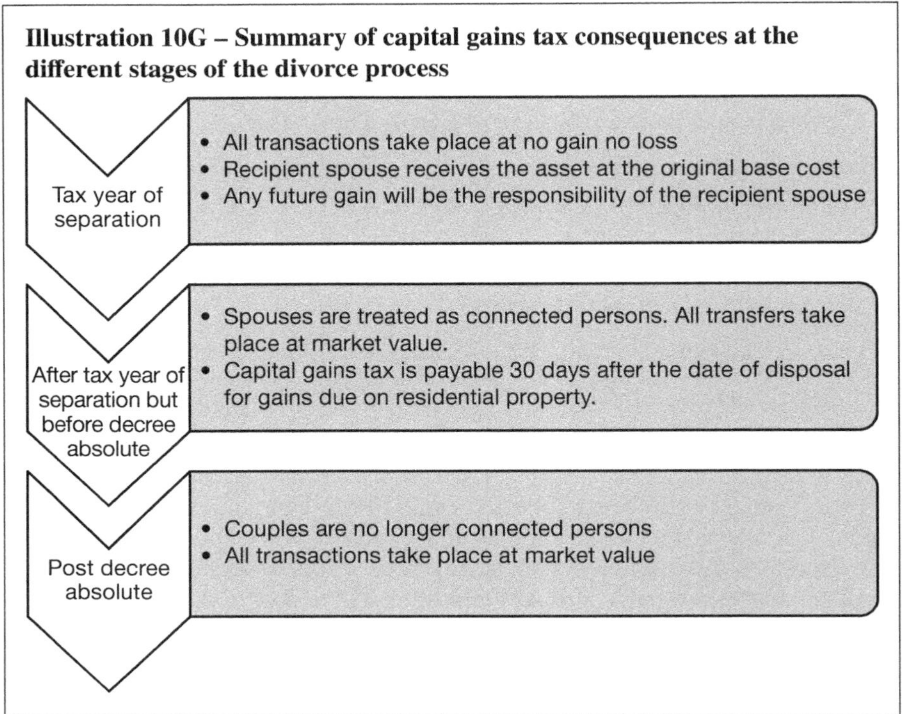

Tax year of separation
• All transactions take place at no gain no loss
• Recipient spouse receives the asset at the original base cost
• Any future gain will be the responsibility of the recipient spouse
After tax year of separation but before decree absolute
• Spouses are treated as connected persons. All transfers take place at market value.
• Capital gains tax is payable 30 days after the date of disposal for gains due on residential property.
Post decree absolute
• Couples are no longer connected persons
• All transactions take place at market value

CAPITAL GAINS TAX PENALTIES – AN OVERVIEW

10.43 The penalty regime is based on the tax due rather than the type of income. A penalty will apply whether the error is for failure to report a gain arising from shares or property. Therefore the below table will apply to individuals who make an error on their self assessment tax returns.

Inaccuracy in return	Penalty based on potential lost revenue Careless inaccuracy 30% Deliberate but not concealed 70% Deliberate and concealed 100%

	Reductions for disclosure Unprompted disclosure: minimum penalties nil, 20% and 30% Prompted disclosure: minimum penalties 15%, 35% and 50%
Failure to notify HMRC of an error in assessment (within 30 days)	30% of potential lost revenue. *Reductions for disclosure* Unprompted disclosure: minimum penalty nil Prompted disclosure: minimum penalty 15%
Failure to notify chargeability	Penalty based on potential lost revenue Careless inaccuracy 30% Deliberate but not concealed 70% Deliberate and concealed 100% *Reductions for disclosure* Unprompted disclosure: minimum penalties nil, 20% and 30% Prompted disclosure: minimum penalties 15%, 35% and 50%
Failure to file return on time	Initial one day penalty £100 Failure continues for more than three months – £10 per day for up to 90 days Six months late, greater of 5% or the tax due and £300 12 months late – same penalty as for 6 months late unless deliberately withholding the return Deliberate withholding of the return more than 12 months – 70% of the tax due (minimum £300) Deliberate and concealed withholding of the return more than 12 months 100% of tax due (minimum £300) *Restrictions for disclosure* Unprompted disclosure: minimum penalty 20% and 30% Prompted disclosure: minimum penalties 35% and 50%
Failure to pay tax on time	31 days late – 5% of the tax due 6 months late – 5% of the tax due 12 months late – 5% of the tax due
Failure to keep adequate records	Maximum penalty of £3,000

CAPITAL GAINS TAX RELIEFS – AN OVERVIEW

10.44 There are several capital gain tax reliefs which may be available for individuals to reduce their gain. For a relief to apply, all of the conditions must be met and usually the relief must be claimed. Some of the reliefs listed below require a claim from both parties for it to be successful.

	PPR relief	**Investment property relief**	**Business asset disposal relief**
Who can claim it	Home owners	Any individual	Sole traders/partners/ shareholders
Type of asset	Main home	Investment properties	Material disposal of business asset
Effect of claim	Exempts up to 100% of gain (for periods of occupation or deemed occupation)	The assets transfer with no immediate CGT, the gain is deferred until the eventual sale of the property	Gains taxed at 10%
Time limit	No claim (it applies automatically)	Joint claim 4 years from the end of the tax year of disposal	Claim 1 year from 31 Jan following the tax year of disposal
Summary of Conditions	Property must have been owner's main home at some point during ownership The property and grounds must be within 0.5 hectares (or the garden and grounds must be within keeping for the size of the property)	Multiple interests in land held jointly by two people One landowner transfers his interest in one or more holdings of land The consideration received by the landowner includes an interest in the jointly held land As a result of the transaction, each of the co owners becomes the sole owner of one or more of the holdings of land formerly jointly held	A business asset includes furnished holiday let, sole trader/partnership, shares in trading co >5% The individual must be a director or employee of the company The conditions must be met for the 24 months prior to disposal
Restrictions	Gains charged where the absence from the home does not qualify as a period of deemed occupation	Both parties must co own at least two properties before the transaction and own (wholly) at least one property each after the transaction	Lifetime limit £1m Non-business use
Considerations on divorce	The maximum period of final deemed occupation is nine months. If couples are transferring or selling the main home within nine months of one of the spouses leaving	This is a valuable relief for couples who jointly own investment properties and will be splitting up their portfolio. There are several conditions which must	The conditions must be met for 24 months ahead of the sale or transfer. One of the conditions is that the shareholder must be working or the director of the

	PPR relief	Investment property relief	Business asset disposal relief
	the home there may be a CGT liability	be met but, providing they are met, the transfers are not time critical	company, therefore it is important that if business asset disposal relief is a possibility, that it is considered before any changes in the company are made
More information	Chapter 11	Chapter 12	Chapter 14

CAPITAL GAINS TAX RELIEFS – AN OVERVIEW CONTINUED

10.45

	Gift relief	EIS reinvestment relief	SEIS reinvestment relief
Who can claim it	Any individual	Any individual	Any individual
Type of asset	Business assets (including furnished holidays lets)	Any asset sold	Any asset sold
Effect of claim	Rollover against base costs of asset for donee	Freezes potential gain until the EIS shares are sold	Gain of 50% of available SEIS expenditure exempt provided shares held for three years
Time limit	Joint claim four years from the end of the tax year of disposal	Invest either 12 months before or 36 months after disposal Claim five years from 31 January following the tax year in which shares are issued	Invest in year of disposal (or following year) Claim five years from 31 January following the tax year in which shares are issued
Summary of conditions	Business assets include, unquoted trading company shares, shares in a personal trading company and an asset used in a business for trade If these are transferred a claim for gift relief can be made	The individual must reinvest the total proceeds in qualifying EIS shares to defer the total gain	The individual must reinvest the total proceeds in qualifying SEIS shares to defer the total gain

	Gift relief	EIS reinvestment relief	SEIS reinvestment relief
Restrictions	Restrictions based on value of current business assets and current assets	Must reinvest in qualifying EIS shares No upper limit	Must reinvest in qualifying SEIS shares Maximum available expenditure £100,000 (therefore maximum exempt gain £50,000)
Considerations on divorce	Gift relief is unlikely to apply in the case of divorce.	Providing the conditions are met there will be no CGT payable on eventual disposal of shares. If the shares are sold within the three-year holding period then CGT may be payable. If premature selling of the share is likely, CGT will need to be considered. A disposal includes a transfer to a spouse	Providing the conditions are met there will be no CGT payable on eventual disposal of shares. If the shares are sold within the three-year holding period then CGT may be payable. If premature selling of the share is likely, CGT will need to be considered. A disposal includes a transfer to a spouse
More information	Chapter 14	Chapter 13	Chapter 13

LIST OF EXEMPT ASSETS FOR CAPITAL GAINS TAX

10.46

Asset type
Cars
Cash (sterling)
Compensation or damages for personal/professional injury
Decorations for valour or gallant conduct
Disposal of a debt
Gambling winnings
Government gilts
Life assurance polices (gain is subject to income tax)
Only or main residence *
Woodlands

Chattels (moveable property with a useful life of 50 years or less) examples include
Computers
Greyhounds
plant and machinery
racehorses
Shares
Approved employee share schemes
Deeply discounted securities (DDS)
EIS Shares *
ISA shares
Junior ISA Shares
Lifetime ISA Shares
Qualifying corporate bonds (QCBs)
SEIS Shares *
Shares in VCTs

* Conditions must be met for the gain to be exempt

CHAPTER 11

The Family Home

Contents at a Glance

THE FAMILY HOME

11.1 There is a lot to cover on this topic so this chapter will make points succinctly and keep the information relevant. The term 'a little knowledge can be a dangerous thing' springs to mind when thinking about tax on the family home. There have been a plethora of changes to the way the main home is treated for capital gains tax purposes so it is wise to ensure you are familiar with the latest changes.

When an individual sells their main home they will be eligible for a relief called Principal Private Residence Relief (PPR). This is a relief which exempts the gain on a taxpayer's main home.

11.2 For the majority of people this means that there is no capital gains tax to pay when they sell the property which they have lived in as their main home. However, there remain many circumstances where individuals will not meet all of the criteria for this relief and the sale of their main home will trigger a capital gains tax liability. Whether PPR relief has been correctly claimed features frequently at the tax tribunals and with the recent changes to the relief I think we can expect this to continue.

11.3 The conditions for the relief are discussed below but it is important to remember that the default position is that the relief is **only available for periods of actual occupation**. If one party has moved out of the home into rented accommodation, it does not matter that they have not bought a second property, they lose the entitlement to the relief for periods when they are absent from the property (save for a few exemptions which we discuss further in the chapter).

11.4 The gain on the main home is calculated in the normal way and then PPR relief is available to exempt the gain, therefore in cases where PPR relief cannot reduce the whole gain to zero it is important to consider if any enhancement expenditure has been spent on the property. This will help to reduce the chargeable gain.

The following are allowable deductions:

- the purchase price of the property;
- costs of acquisition;
- expenditure incurred which enhances the value of the property (providing it is still reflected in the nature of the property at the time of the disposal);
- any expenses incurred in establishing, preserving or defending their title or a right to the asset;
- incidental costs of making the disposal;
- costs of acquisition and disposal include fees, commission or remuneration paid for:
  - Surveyor;
  - Valuer;
  - Auctioneer;
  - Accountant;
  - Agent;
  - Legal advisor;
- advertising to sell the property.

11.5 The deduction of PPR relief is highlighted in the below computation. It is important not to overestimate the allowable deductions as this distorts the capital gains tax position.

Whilst awaiting actual figures these can typically be used, although the selling costs will vary according to estate agent fees:

- 0.5% of the purchase price for acquisition costs;
- 0.5% of the market value for potential transfer costs;
- 1.5% of the market value for potential costs of sale.

PROPERTIES OWNED OR INHERITED PRIOR TO 1982

11.6 Capital gains tax was rebased to 31 March 1982 in the Finance Act 1988 (FA 88). Therefore, if a property was owned or inherited pre-1982 then you will need to use the 1982 value of the property rather than the original purchase price or value when inherited.

Table 11A Capital Gains Tax pro forma

	£	£	£
Gross sales proceeds/market value at transfer	x		
Less: Selling costs		(x)	
Net Sales proceeds		x	
Less: Cost /MV 1982		(x)	
Less: Acquisition costs		(x)	
Less: Enhancement expenditure		(x)	
Gain		x	
Less PPR relief		**(x)**	

	Gains eligible for BADR	Other gains not eligible for BADR	Residential property gain
Current year gains	x	x	x
Less: Current year losses			(x)
Less: Losses brought forward			(x)
Less: Annual exemption			(12,300)
Taxable gains			

Capital Gains Tax Liability:	
Gains eligible for Business Asset Disposal relief at 10%	x
Gains within the basic rate band at 10%	x
Gains above the basic rate band at 20%	x
Gains on residential property within basic rate band at 18%	x
Gains on residential property above basic rate band at 28%	x
Total CGT payable	**x**

CONDITIONS OF PPR RELIEF

11.7 The primary conditions for PPR relief are as follows:

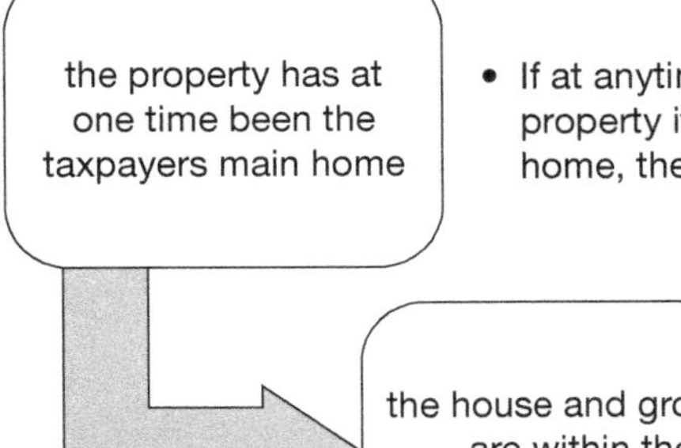
the property has at one time been the taxpayers main home
the house and grounds are within the permitted area

- If at anytime during the ownership of the property it has been the taxpayer's main home, the property will qualify for PPR relief

- The legislation defines the permitted area as half a hectare. A larger area may be allowed if the taxpayer can prove that the larger area is reasonably required for the enjoyment of the house

Therefore, if an individual has never lived in the property as their main home, no PPR relief will be available.

11.8 The legislation uses the term 'dwelling house' when describing property on which PPR relief may be claimed. The legislation does not go on to define dwelling house however, case law has determined that it can be taken to mean not only the house but also outbuildings. Caravans and houseboats are likely to qualify as a 'dwelling house' provided they are static.

> **Note:** If your client has a non-typical home seek advice early on as to whether PPR relief may be prohibited for any reason.

PERMITTED AREA

11.9 For land associated with the property to qualify for PPR relief, on the date of the disposal the land must:

- be occupied and enjoyed with the residence;
- be 'garden or grounds' of the residence; and
- not exceed the permitted area.

The legislation defines the permitted area as 0.5 hectares which includes the site of the property or a larger area which is reasonably required for the enjoyment of the property as a residence. The area must also be in keeping with the size and character of the house.

> **Note:** If your client has a property with large grounds ensure this is made clear to any expert when requesting a capital gains tax report. It may be that the PPR claim will be restricted.

CALCULATION OF THE RELIEF

11.10 The amount of PPR relief available is calculated by way of a fraction. The gain is multiplied by total occupation over total ownership.

Therefore, if a client has lived in the property for the total period of ownership their gain will be fully exempt.

> Gain X period of occupation/period of ownership = Exempt gain

The fraction is always calculated in months. Periods of occupation are a total of actual occupation (ie the period of time the individual was actually physically living in the home) plus periods of deemed occupation, deemed occupation is given in certain circumstances.

Illustration 11B – PPR Relief computation – Tina and Bette

Bette and Tina have been together since 2008 and bought their main home in 2010 for £350,000 and had always lived there. They married in 2014 and stayed living in their main home. In 2018 Bette and Tina decided to start divorce proceedings, however due to their financial situation both of the parties continued to live in the home. In 2020 the divorce was finalised and as part of the settlement both Tina and Bette agreed to sell the home. The home was sold for £390,000.

	£
Sale proceeds	390,000
Less: costs of sale	(5,850)
Less: Purchase price	(350,000)
Less: costs of acquisition	(1,750)
Gain	32,400
Less: PPR relief	(32,400)
Taxable Gain	**Nil**

PPR relief: £32,400 × $\frac{120}{120}$ = £32,400

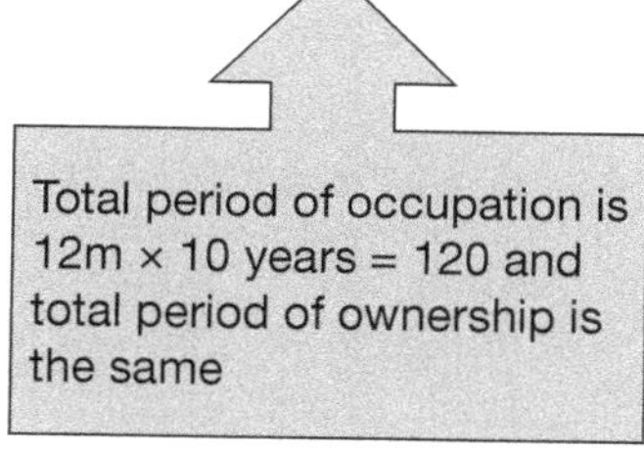

Total period of occupation is
12m × 10 years = 120 and
total period of ownership is
the same

Neither Bette nor Tina have a taxable gain, the whole gain is exempt. They will not need to report this transaction to HMRC and there is no tax to pay.

Once a party has left the home we then need to consider if any of the deemed occupations periods will cover their absence.

FINAL PERIOD OF OWNERSHIP

11.11 From 6 April 2020 the final nine months of ownership always qualifies as deemed occupation. This was previously 36 months and then halved to 18 months, then again to nine months. The halving of the final period of occupation to nine months should be of a concern to family lawyers where one party has left the former matrimonial home. Where there is an absence of over nine months the absent spouse will start incurring a potential capital gains tax liability.

11.12 The change to nine months will not affect people with a disability and those who are long-term care residents in care homes. In these circumstances the 36-month final period of exemption remains.

DEEMED OCCUPATION

11.13 The legislation contains certain provisions for people who have been unable to occupy their home for a qualifying reason. Periods in hospital or on holiday are not qualifying reasons. Further, if a person is prevented from being in the home by their former spouse, that is also not a qualifying reason.

11.14 There are only three periods of absence which will qualify in addition to the nine months. All of the conditions require re-occupation of the main home or prevention from re-occupying due to work.

Reason for absence	**Any reason**	**Employed Overseas**	**Working elsewhere**
Details	Taxpayer can have up to three years' absence from the home qualify as deemed occupation. The time can be made up of separate periods but cannot exceed three years.	If the taxpayer is overseas by way of their employment (not self-employment) or lived abroad with a spouse who was employed overseas, this is a qualifying period.	Taxpayer is prevented from living in the home due to working elsewhere (employment or self-employment) or lives with a spouse working elsewhere, this is a qualifying period.
Qualifying period	3 years	Unlimited	4 years

Reason for absence	Any reason	Employed Overseas	Working elsewhere
Re-occupation of the home after period of absence	The taxpayer must re-occupy the home as their main home after the period of absence for it to qualify as deemed occupation.	If the taxpayer is prevented from re-occupying the home due to their place of work then they will not need to satisfy the re-occupation periods for the relief to apply.	If the taxpayer is prevented from re-occupying the home due to their place of work then they will not need to satisfy the re-occupation periods for the relief to apply.

Illustration 11C – Deemed Occupation in Practice – Pierre and Louis

Pierre and Louis lived in their main home in Hull, they bought the home in 2000 and had lived in the property the whole time of ownership. In 2013 Pierre's job was moved to Frankfurt, Louis joined Pierre in Frankfurt. Pierre worked in Frankfurt until 2019 when he handed in his notice.

From 2000 to 2013 Pierre and Louis lived in their home; therefore, they have 156 months of actual occupation, being 13 years × 12 months.

From 2013 to 2019 Pierre and Louis have been absent from the home for 72 months, being 6 years × 12 months.

The period from 2000 to 2013 will always be covered by PPR relief, plus an additional 9 months of deemed occupation at the end of the period of ownership.

Whether the 72 months will qualify as deemed occupation will depend on what Pierre and Louis do next.

Next steps	Qualifying/Non qualifying period of deemed occupation	Reason
Stay in Frankfurt to spend some time enjoying the country and sell the property in Hull	The 72 months will be non qualifying	The period will not qualify as Pierre and Louis did not move back into the home
They decide that living in Frankfurt had sparked a passion to travel and they decided to move to Florence and sell the home in Hull	The 72 months will be non qualifying	The period will not qualify as Pierre and Louis did not move back into the home
They go travelling for one year and then move back into the home in Hull	The 72 months will qualify for deemed occupation	The 72 months will qualify under the working abroad provisions. The one-year travelling will qualify under the three years for any reason provisions. The period is qualifying as Pierre and Louis re-occupy the property

Next steps	Qualifying/Non qualifying period of deemed occupation	Reason
Move back into their Hull home	The 72 months will qualify for deemed occupation	The period of time they were absent will qualify as deemed occupation and there will be no periods of absence for PPR relief. The period is qualifying as Pierre and Louis re-occupy the property

When considering if clients have any potential capital gains tax exposure on the main home, it is therefore not just the present situation which needs to be considered. It will be beneficial to ask clients for their occupation history of the main home and to understand what they plan to do in the future.

For example, if one party (A) has moved out of the home during the divorce proceedings but will return to the home once B has moved out, then providing A is absent for less than three years, they will not have a capital gains tax liability on the sale as the whole period (up to three years) will be covered by deemed occupation.

MORE THAN ONE HOME

11.15 Where a married couple are living together they are deemed to have one main home between them. Where a couple (or individual) has more than one residence, they can nominate the main residence by notifying HMRC. **The properties must both be a qualifying residence which is defined as 'the dwelling in which that person habitually lives; in other words, his or her home'.**[1]

11.16 If a couple have more than one qualifying residence and no nomination is made, the residence which is the main home based on the facts will be the property on which they can claim PPR relief. Usually the main residence will be the one at which the individual spends the most time. However, there are other factors at play, some of the factors which HMRC will consider are:[2]

- Where does the family spend their time?
- Where do the children go to school?
- Where is the individual's place of work?
- How is each residence furnished?
- Where is the individual registered at the doctors/dentist?

1 CG64427 Capital Gains Manual.
2 CG64545 Two or more residences: No valid election made.

11.17 For example, consider Mr and Mrs Harvey. They live and work in Bristol and also have a weekend/holiday home in St Ives. Both the Bristol home and the St Ives home are residences because they live in both properties. In a standard month they will stay in Bristol from Monday to Thursday and St Ives Friday to Sunday. They keep clothes at both properties and they do not rent out either property. Mr and Mrs Harvey could nominate either property to be treated as their main home. They bought the Bristol home in 2003 for £210,000 and it is currently worth £500,000. They bought the St Ives home in 2007 for £350,000 and it is now worth £600,000.

11.18 This can be a useful election if the holiday home in St Ives is likely to increase in value more than the property in Bristol. It does not matter that the facts might show that the Bristol property is the main residence. Provided that the nomination is valid, it cannot be challenged. Note that, if the St Ives property was an investment property which was rented out and not lived in, no nomination could be made.

11.19 Previously a nomination for the main home (in cases where individuals had more than one qualifying residence) had to be made within two years of purchase, however, the rules have now changed and providing certain conditions are met, the nomination can be made at any time. The nomination must be signed by both parties.

Note: If a couple has more than one residence (ie more than one property that they lived in) it may be beneficial to consider whether it would be worthwhile nominating the property with the higher gain as the main residence for PPR relief purposes.

In the case of a divorce, if a couple have multiple residences, they may consider which property would benefit from the relief.

Illustration 11D – more than one residence

Mr and Mrs Harvey

Mr and Mrs Harvey have two properties which could qualify as their main residence.

A Bristol property owned from 2003 to 2020 and a St Ives property owned from 2007 to 2020. The Bristol property will always qualify for relief up to the date they bought the St Ives property. Therefore, for the period of 2003 to 2007 PPR relief is available, even if they elect for the St Ives property to be their PPR.

To establish which property would benefit from the PPR relief we will work out what the gain would be on each property without the claim for the period from 2007 to 2020. This is the period of time where both properties could potentially benefit from PPR relief.

Bristol

	100%	50%
	£	£
Sale proceeds	500,000	250,000
Less: costs of sale	(7,500)	(3,750)
Less: Purchase price	(210,000)	(105,000)
Less: acquisition costs	(1,050)	(525)
Gain	281,450	140,725
Less: PPR £140,725 × $\frac{57}{204}$		**(39,320)**
Chargeable gain		101,405
Less: Annual exemption		(12,300)
Taxable gain		89,105
Capital gains tax payable at 28%		**24,949**

Mr and Mrs Harvey own 50% of the property each

PPR Computation – As the property was Mr and Mrs Harvey's only home from 2003 to 2007 that period plus 9 months which will benefit from the PPR relief. From 2003 to 2007 is 48 months plus 9 = 57. Total ownership period is 2003 to 2020 which is 204 months.

St Ives

	£	£
Sale proceeds	600,000	300,000
Less: costs of sale	(9,000)	(4,500)
Less: Purchase price	(350,000)	(175,000)
Less: acquisition costs	(1,750)	(875)
Gain	239,250	119,625
Less: Annual exemption		(12,300)
Taxable gain		107,325
Capital gains tax payable at 28%		**30,051**

As the gain on the St Ives property is higher Mr and Mrs Harvey may choose to elect the St Ives property as their main residence, this would exempt the whole gain. They must make this election jointly.

An election to treat the St Ives property as the main home for PPR will mean no relief is available for that period of time on the Bristol property.

INHERITED OCCUPATION

11.20 Another change to the way the main home is treated from 6 April 2020 is the inherited ownership provisions. These provisions state that an individual will inherit their spouses' periods of occupation throughout their periods of ownership.

Prior to 6 April 2020 the following planning could be undertaken:

Illustration 11E – PPR Planning Pre 6 April 2020 – Kaleb and Annalise

Kaleb inherited a house in 2002 when his father died. Kaleb already had an apartment and did not want to move into the house so he rented it out. In 2011 Kaleb and Annalise got married. They decided they wanted to live in a larger property so they moved into the house. In 2019 they decided to sell the property and buy somewhere in the country. When Kaleb inherited the property it was worth £895,000. It was put on the market in 2019 for £1.75 million.

If Kaleb was assessed on the gain his liability would be as follows:

	100%
	£
Sale proceeds	1,750,000
Less: costs of sale	(26,250)
Less: Value when inherited	(895,000)
Less: acquisition costs	–
Gain	828,750
Less: PPR £828,750 × $\frac{\mathbf{84}}{\mathbf{192}}$	**(362,578)**
Chargeable gain	466,172
Less: Annual exemption	(12,300)
Taxable gain	453,872
Capital gains tax payable at 28%	**127,084**

PPR Computation – Kaleb owned the property from 2002 to 2018, 16 years × 12m = 192. He lived in the property from 2011 to 2018, 7 years × 12 months = 84. We do not add on 9 months as the 9 months only applies to the final months of ownership. Kaleb was living in the property in the final 9 months of ownership so we do not need any deemed occupation for that period.

Kaleb would have a capital gains liability of £127,084.

To circumvent this liability, pre April 2020 Kaleb could have transferred his property to Annalise, as they are married the transfer takes place at no gain no loss. Annalise would qualify for full PPR relief on the sale of the property as she has lived in the property as her main home the whole period of time she owned it. However, this planning opportunity is no longer available.

11.21 From 6 April 2020, a spouse will inherit their spouse's periods of absence on transfer. When this is combined with the reduced nine-month exemption, in cases where the property is transferred to the spouse within the tax year of separation but the non-occupying spouse has been absent for over nine months, the receiving spouse will inherit their periods of absence and a possible latent capital gains tax liability.

Illustration 11F – Inherited occupation periods, within the tax year of separation – Tyson and Layla

Tyson and Layla married and bought a property together in March 2012 for £650,000. On 10 April 2020 Layla moved out of the property. In June 2020 Tyson and Layla agree to divorce. It is planned that Layla will transfer her 50% of the family home to Tyson in March 2021 when the property will be worth £1,200,000.

The transfer is happening within the tax year of separation so there is no immediate charge to capital gains tax. However, Tyson will inherit Layla's periods of absence which could result in latent capital gains tax being transferred to him.

The property will have been owned for 109 months, Layla has 97 months of actual occupation and nine months of deemed occupation.

	50%
	£
Deemed market value	600,000
Less: costs of transfer	(3,000)
Less: purchase price	(325,000)
Less: acquisition costs	–
Gain	272,000
Less: PPR $£272,000 \times \frac{106}{109}$	(263,588)
Latent gain	8,412

On the transfer to Tyson, Tyson will inherit a latent capital gain of £8,412. The amount of actual capital gains tax which would be payable on sale would depend on how long Tyson continued to live in the property and whether he had any periods of absence. In this case, Tyson's gain would be fully covered by his capital gains tax annual exemption.

11.22 The implications of this provision will mainly come into play in the following situations:

- spouse has been absent from the property for over nine months;
- the transfer takes place in the tax year of separation;
- If it takes place after the tax year of separation and Taxation of Chargeable Gains Act 1992 (TCGA 1992), s 225B relief is not claimed (see **11.29**).

FAMILY HOME ON DIVORCE

11.23

> If your clients have lived in their main home for the whole period of ownership and are still living together throughout the divorce proceedings then there will be no capital gains tax impact on the sale or transfer of the main home, even if this takes place outside of the tax year of separation because the total gain would qualify for full PPR relief.
>
> The same applies if one party has been absent but the period of absence is under nine months.

11.24 In cases where the above scenario does not apply there is likely to be a capital gains tax exposure on the party who has left the home.

We will now consider: (a) how to calculate the potential CGT charge; and (b) what reliefs are available to potentially mitigate the charge. At **11.39** we discuss how these provisions are applied in the case of Mesher Orders and Deferred Charges.

Illustration 11G – Lin and Andy

Lin and Andy married in 1999, they bought their current home in July 2014 for £650,00. After troubles in the marriage, Lin moved out of the family home and moved in with her sister in May 2015. It is now October 2019 and Lin has come in to talk about a potential divorce. The home is worth approximately £800,000.

The tax year of separation has passed and therefore if Lin transfers the home to Andy the transfer will take place at deemed market value which would likely result in a capital gains tax liability for Lin as Lin has been outside of the home for more than nine months.

A basic calculation:

1. Check with Lin the following:
   a. Has she lived in the property as her main home from July 2014 until the date she left (May 2015)?
   b. Is the property and grounds under 0.5 hectares?
   c. What are her levels of earnings?
   d. Have there been any substantial improvements to the property?
2. Decide on an approximate sale/transfer date.
3. Calculate the periods of:
   a. Ownership;
   b. Actual occupation;
   c. Deemed occupation;
   d. Total occupation (b+c);

4. Work out the potential capital gains tax liability.

Lin provides the following answers:

1. Lin has confirmed:
   a. She has lived in the property as her main home from July 2014 until May 2015.
   b. The property and grounds are under 0.5 hectares.
   c. She earns £52,000 per annum (this means she is a higher rate taxpayer and capital gains tax is payable at 28% on the taxable part of the gain).
   d. There have been no substantial improvements to the property.
2. We chose a date 6 months in the future, May 2020.
3. The periods of ownership in months are:
   a. Ownership = 71 months (July 2014 to May 2020);
   b. Actual occupation = 11 months (July 2014 to May 2015);
   c. Deemed occupation = 9 months (final 9 months of ownership);
   d. Total occupation (b+c) =20 months.
4. Capital gains tax computation for Lin.

	50%
	£
Gross sales proceeds/market value at transfer	400,000
Less: Selling/Transfer costs	(2,000)
Net Sales proceeds	398,000
Less: Cost/MV 1982	(325,000)
Less: Acquisition costs	(3,250)
Less: Enhancement expenditure	–
Gain	69,750
Less PPR	**(19,648)**
$\text{Gain} \times \frac{\text{total occupation}}{\text{total ownership}}$	
$69{,}750 \times \frac{20}{71}$	
Chargeable Gain	**50,102**
Less: Annual exemption	(12,300)
Taxable Gain	37,802
Capital gains tax payable at 28%	**10,584**

Note: When estimating costs including costs of sale and acquisition costs be wary not to overestimate these as they can distort the tax position. If a property is being transferred these costs will be substantially less than if it is being sold.

Lin would have to pay the capital gains tax within 30 days and report the gain to HMRC.

FAMILY HOME TO BE SOLD

11.25 If the family home is to be sold as part of the settlement, the non-occupying spouse will likely have a capital gains tax liability and a requirement to file a tax return. If there is no taxable gain, because this is either covered by PPR relief or the annual exemption, then the client will not need to file a tax return to report the gain.

11.26 In the case of the worked example with Lin and Andy, if the property was to be sold then Lin would have an exposure to capital gains tax. The tax would be payable within 30 days of the sale and Lin would need to report the gain to HMRC within the same 30-day period.

11.27 In the case of a sale on the open market there are not many options to mitigate the tax liability on the gain, therefore quantifying the exposure early on will ensure that the potential liability is considered in discussions. The limited mitigations options are considered below.

11.28 Mitigation options:

- Ensure all of the qualifying expenditure has been deducted from the gain.
- Do any of the deemed occupation periods apply? It is unlikely, but in the event that the separation occurred at a time when the non-occupying spouse was working away from the home they may qualify for the period of time away from the property to be deemed occupation.

FAMILY HOME TO BE TRANSFERRED TO OTHER PARTY

11.29 In the case that it is decided that the family home will be transferred to the other party outside of the tax year of separation, the transferring spouse will be deemed to sell their share of the property to the other spouse for the deemed market value of the property. However, there is a relief at TCGA 1992, s 225B which can exempt the whole period of absence for the non-occupying spouse. Note that this relief only applies when the property is transferred to their spouse. It cannot be used to exempt a gain when there is a sale on the open market.

11.30 Several conditions must be met and understood for the TCGA 1992, s 225B relief to apply.

The full conditions for this exemption are in the TCGA 1992, s 225B. The conditions were previously listed at Extra Statutory Concession D6.

11.31 A summary of the conditions are as follows.

Where an individual:

(a) ceases to live with their spouse in a property which is their main residence, and

(b) subsequently disposes of the property to the spouse, then if conditions A to C are met PPR will apply as if the house continued to be the individual's main home until disposal.

Condition A is that the disposal is pursuant to:

(a) an agreement between the individual and their spouse made in contemplation of divorce or separation, or

(b) an order of the court.

Condition B is that in the period between the individual ceasing to live at the property, the property continued to be the only or main residence of the spouse.

Condition C is that the individual has not elected for another property to be treated as their main home.

11.32 The extended relief shall only apply on the making of a claim by the individual.

Illustration 11H – TCGA 1992, s 225B Relief – Lin and Andy

In the case of Lin and Andy, as a recap, Lin and Andy married in 1999, they bought their current home in July 2014 for £650,00. After troubles in the marriage, in May 2015 Lin moved out of the family home and moved in with her sister. It is now October 2019 and Lin has come in to talk about a potential divorce. The home is worth approximately £800,000. If Lin transfers her share of the home to Andy outside of the tax year of separation, she will be deemed to 'sell' her share of the property to Andy for market value. She will be assessed to capital gains tax on the transfer and her capital gains tax liability would be approximately £10,000 (this calculation is shown at **11G**).

It is possible that Lin may be able to benefit from TCGA 1992, s 225B relief.

We will now run through the conditions to ensure she meets them all:

Is the transfer pursuant to divorce? Yes.

Whilst she has been out of the home, has Andy continued to live in the property as his main home? Yes.

Has Lin elected for another property to be her main home? No.

As Lin meets all of the conditions she should notify HMRC that she would like to elect to use TCGA 1992, s 225B relief.

Once Lin has notified HMRC of this choice, she will have no capital gains tax liability on the transfer of the property and no reporting requirements. This notification should be made as soon as possible and within two years of the transfer of the property.

11.33 This relief can be utilised at the time of proceedings or it may be that the property will be transferred to the occupying spouse in five years time. If so, the relief will still apply (assuming all the conditions are met), however, the client looking to claim the relief should consider the following.

11.34 An individual can only claim PPR on one property per period of time. Therefore, if they chose to buy another home, whilst still owning the former marital home, only one of the properties can qualify for PPR relief. They may want to keep the relief on the former marital property due to its value. This decision means that the second property they purchased will be incurring a latent capital gains tax liability.

This is easier to explain by way of an example:

Illustration 11I – TCGA 1992, s 225B Relief – Cindy and Ken

Cindy and Ken were married for over 20 years. They bought their marital home in Jan 2001 for £390,000. It is now January 2020. They have three children aged 20, 18 and 13. Ken moved out of the home in March 2018 and bought a small flat for £400,000. They began divorce proceedings in 2019. As part of the order, Ken would retain 50% ownership of the property until their youngest child turned 18, at that point he would transfer his 50% share to Cindy (providing she could take over the mortgage), if she could not take over the mortgage the property would be sold.

It is anticipated that the property would be worth £1,500,000 in January 2025. It is also anticipated that Ken's flat would be worth £600,000 in January 2025.

In summary, the family home was bought in January 2001 for £290,000 and will be worth £1,500,000. Ken's flat was bought in March 2018 for £400,000 and will be worth £600,000. Ken will always be entitled to relief on the family home for the period 2001 to March 2018 (plus nine months) as this was his main home. This will not change. The period from March 2018 to January 2025 is the period of time where Ken has two homes and he has an option to claim TCGA 1992, s 225B relief to exempt the gain for his periods of occupation on his main home. However, if he does this, he will not be able to claim PPR relief on his flat for the same period.

What are Ken's liabilities and options regarding his flat and the former matrimonial home?

From March 2018 Ken has two properties. From the facts, Ken's flat would appear to be his main home.

If Ken transfers his share of the former matrimonial home to Cindy in 2025 then he could benefit from TCGA 1992, s 225B relief. However, if he makes this election and in 2025 he cannot transfer the property to Cindy and it is sold, Ken will potentially lose out on the PPR relief on his flat.

Transfer of the main home in 2025

If a TCGA 1992, s 225B relief claim is made Ken's whole period of ownership would qualify as occupation and Ken would not have an exposure to capital gains tax.

Sale of the main home in 2025

If the main home was sold in 2025 Ken's CGT position would be as follows:

1. Ken has confirmed:
   a. He has lived in the property as his main home from January 2001 until March 2018.
   b. The property and grounds are under 0.5 hectares.
   c. He earns £105,000 per annum (this means he is a higher rate taxpayer and tax is payable at 28% on the taxable part of the gain).
   d. There have been no substantial improvements to the property.
2. January 2025 is deemed date of sale.
3. The periods of ownership in months are:
   a. Ownership = 289 months (January 2001 to January 2025).
   b. Actual occupation = 207 months (January 2001 to March 2018).
   c. Deemed occupation = 9 months (final 9 months of ownership).
   d. Total occupation (b+c) = 216.

Capital gains tax Computation for Ken on the family home is as follows:

	50%
	£
Gross sales proceeds	750,000
Less: Selling/Transfer costs	(7,350)
Net Sales proceeds	742,650
Less: Cost/MV 1982	(195,000)
Less: Acquisition costs	(1,950)
Less: Enhancement expenditure	–
Gain	545,700
Less PPR	**(407,859)**

$$\text{Gain} \times \frac{\text{total occupation}}{\text{total ownership}}$$

$$545{,}700 \times \frac{216}{289}$$

Chargeable Gain	**137,841**
Less: Annual exemption	(12,300)
Taxable Gain	125,541
Capital gains tax payable at 28%	**35,151**

Potential capital gains tax on the family home could be £35,151.

However, Ken should also consider the potential gain on his flat for the same period.

	£
Gross sales proceeds	650,000
Less: Selling/Transfer costs	(9,750)
Net Sales proceeds	640,250
Less: Cost /MV 1982	(400,000)
Less: Acquisition costs	(4,000)
Less: Enhancement expenditure	–
Gain	236,250
Less PPR	–
Chargeable Gain	**236,250**
Less: Annual exemption	(12,300)
Taxable Gain	223,950
Capital gains tax payable at 28%	**62,706**

The potential taxable gain on his flat is larger than the gain on the former family home, therefore Ken should consider whether he wants to claim TCGA 1992, s 225B relief and potentially disadvantage himself.

The other consideration is that the tax on the former family home would be payable on transfer. Ken may not have that cash available to pay the tax. The tax on the flat would only be payable when he sells the property, so he would have the funds to pay the capital gains tax.

TRANSFER THEN SALE?

11.35 In the case that the property is going to be sold but one of the parties has a capital gains tax exposure, could that party transfer the property to their former spouse, claim TCGA 1992, s 225B (ensuring the whole period of absence is covered by PPR) and then the former spouse sell the property?

11.36 With any of this type of planning one has to consider whether this would fall foul of the general anti-abuse rules (GAAR). The GAAR was introduced in April 2013 as a catch all anti-abuse regulation. If an action is deemed to be abusive then any tax advantages gained by the action are removed by HMRC.

11.37 HMRC decides whether tax arrangements are abusive or not based on a 'double reasonableness' test. The legislation says that tax arrangements are abusive if they 'cannot reasonably be regarded as a reasonable course of action, having regard to all the circumstances', including:

- whether the substantive results of the arrangements are consistent with any principles on which those decisions are based;
- whether the means of achieving those results involves one or more contrived or abnormal steps, and whether the arrangements are intended to exploit any shortcomings in those provisions.

11.38 Whether these actions would be regarded as abusive would depend on the circumstances. For example if the property was on the market, had a buyer, and ahead of the sale X transferred the property to Y to secure the TCGA 1992, s 225B relief and then the property completed, this may fall foul of the GAAR.

If the property was transferred to the occupying spouse and then they sold it, this is more likely to be within the normal course of action, however advice should be sought on this.

> **Note:** If seeking advice on the potential sale or transfer of the main home include a question similar to the below:
>
> > 'Could you advise on whether either of our clients could benefit from a TCGA 1992, s 225B election? If so:
> >
> > – how should the election be made and within what period of time'.

MESHER ORDERS

11.39 If the family home is subject to a Mesher Order or similar, the non-occupying spouse can still claim TCGA 1992, s 225B relief but only if the property will be transferred to the occupying spouse at the end of the period. If the property will be sold at the end of the period, the non-occupying spouse will (assuming the prices increase) have a capital gains tax liability and filing requirement.

11.40 There is still only one point of disposal for capital gains tax with a Mesher Order and that is the date the property is eventually sold or transferred.

The period the non-occupying spouse lived in the property ahead of moving out will always qualify for PPR relief. The final nine months of ownership will also qualify.

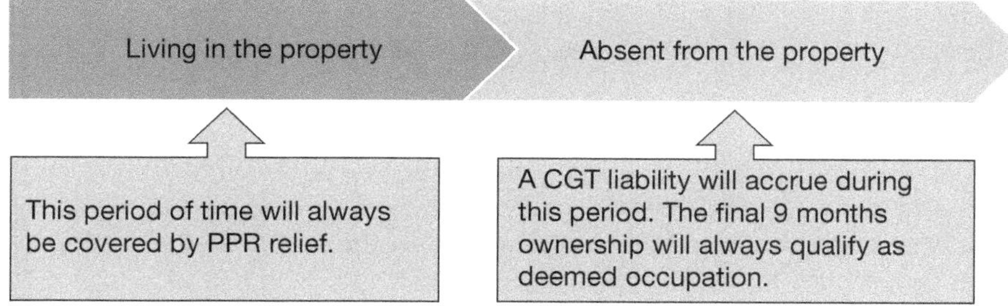

11.41 Valuing the potential capital gains tax liability where Mesher Orders are being used, requires an estimated market value at the trigger event.

11.42 Further, the deemed occupation provisions used to be 36 months before being halved to 18 months. It is possible that parties entered into Mesher Orders when the old rules still applied and believed they would have a limited capital gains tax liability. Therefore, whilst the nine months is somewhat valuable it cannot be relied on that it will remain at nine months in the future.

11.43 If the non-occupying spouse leaves the UK whilst still owning the property different rules will apply for the occupation periods of the main home. Seek advice early on if your client has left the main home and living overseas and this is not by way of employment.

DEFERRED CHARGES

11.44 There are two points of disposal for a deferred charge. The first is the disposal of the main home to the occupying spouse.

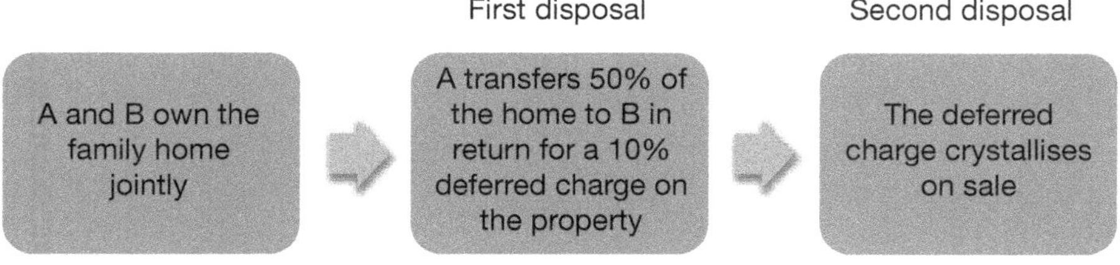

On the first disposal, there is a potential capital gains tax exposure on A if A had been out of the property for over nine months.

11.45 As A is transferring the property to B it may be possible for a TCGA 1992, s 225B claim to exempt the gain on the initial transfer. There is likely to be a second gain on the subsequent disposal. The gain will be a chargeable gain and if it exceeds the annual exemption it will be taxable.

Illustration 11J – Deferred Charges – Nelly and Max

Nelly and Max married in 1996. In July 2002 they bought their family home for £150,000. They have twin boys aged 11. In January 2018 Max moved out of the family home into rented accommodation. In December 2019, the property was worth £620,000, as part of the divorce proceedings they agreed that Max would transfer Nelly his share of the property for a 10% charge over the property when it sells in 10 years' time.

What are the capital gains tax implications on Max?

We need to work out the potential capital gains tax liability on the initial transfer:

	50%
	£
Market value at transfer	310,000
Less: Transfer costs	(1,550)
Net Sales proceeds	308,450
Less: Cost /MV 1982	(75,000)
Less: Acquisition costs	(750)
Less: Enhancement expenditure	–
Gain	232,700
Less PPR	**(217,187)**
$\text{Gain} \times \frac{\text{total occupation}}{\text{total ownership}}$	
$232{,}700 \times \frac{196}{210}$	
Chargeable Gain	**15,513**
Less: Annual exemption	(12,300)
Taxable Gain	3,213
Capital gains tax payable at 28%	**899**

Could Max make a TCGA 1992, s 225B claim? Let us work through the conditions:

- He has ceased to live with Nelly in a property which was their main home (tick).
- He will be disposing of his share of the property to his spouse (tick).
- The disposal is pursuant to an agreement in contemplation of divorce (tick).
- The property has remained the main home of Nelly (tick).
- Max has not elected any other property to be his main home (tick).

Max does meet all the conditions and could make a claim for TCGA 1992, s 225B relief to apply. If he makes the election there will be no capital gains tax liability on the initial transfer.

After the transfer Max has a deferred charge over 10% of the property. The base cost of this charge is 10% of the market value of the property at the date of transfer. Max's deferred charge's base cost is therefore £62,000.

If we assume the property's value in 10 years' time is £950,000 Max will receive £95,000. There is no further PPR available on the gain.

Using the standard proforma:

	£
Proceeds	95,000
Base cost	(62,000)
Gain	33,000
Less: Annual Exemption	(12,300)
Taxable gain	20,700
Capital gains tax payable @ 20%	**4,140**

Max would have a capital gains tax liability of £4,140.

Assuming Nelly continued to live in the property as her main home she would not have a liability when she sold the property as the full gain would be covered by the PPR exemption.

11.46 In practice most deferred charges are based on a percentage of the property price. In the rare case that the charge was for a fixed amount the capital gains tax position would be different.

11.47 If the deferred charge is for a fixed value it is deemed to be a return of a debt (rather than a gain) and therefore it is not assessed to capital gains tax.

11.48 If in the above example, Max had a deferred charge for £100,000 when the property sold, he would not have a capital gains tax liability.

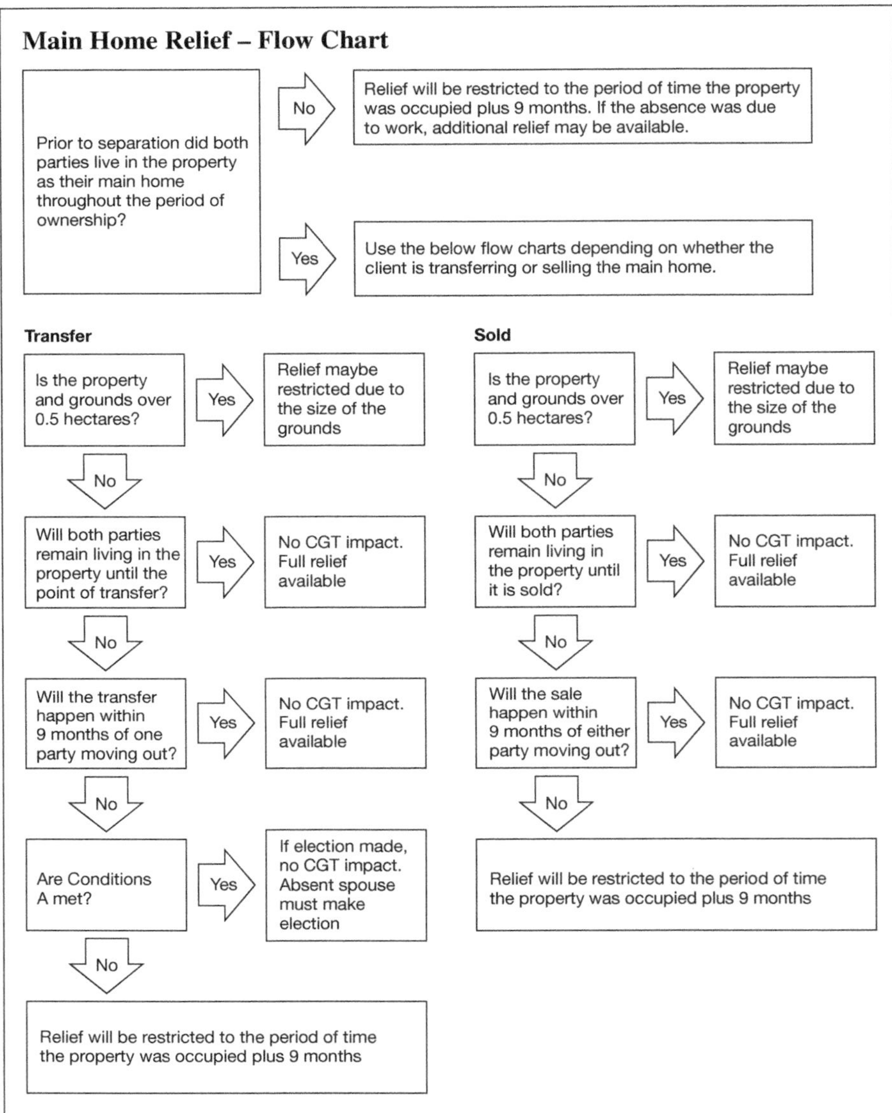

Conditions

The transfer is made under an agreement between spouses/civil partners or under a court order. Throughout the period from the individual moving out to transfer, the house continues to be the only or main residence of the other spouse/civil partner. The individual has not elected another house to be their main residence for any part of that period.

MAIN HOME – CHECKLIST

11.49

		Yes/No/ NA	Risk	Mitigation	Ref
Number of properties	Does the client have two or more properties which they have lived in as their main home?	☐ Yes ☐ No ☐ N/A	If no election is made the PPR will attach the property which is the main home as determined by the facts.	They can elect which property they wish to attach a PPR claim to. It must be a joint claim made to HMRC. Once a claim has been made clients cannot claim PPR for the same period on another property.	**11.15**
Grounds	Are the grounds of the property >0.5 hectares?	☐ Yes ☐ No ☐ N/A	PPR is restricted to the property and the permitted area. The permitted area is 0.5 hectares or grounds reasonably required for the enjoyment of the property.	Seek advice as to whether the PPR will be restricted if the grounds exceed 0.5 hectares.	**11.8**
Pre 1982	Was the property bought pre 1982?	☐ Yes ☐ No ☐ N/A	Capital gains were re-based at 1982 and all values prior to that date should be ignored.	Ignore any periods prior to 1982 and use the 1982 value as the purchase price of the property.	**11.6**
Absence	Has the client been absent from the property for > 9 months?	☐ Yes ☐ No ☐ N/A	They may have a capital gains tax liability for any periods over 9 months. If the property is being transferred in the tax year of separation, any periods of absence will be passed to the receiving spouse.		**11.11**
	Has the client been absent due to work?	☐ Yes ☐ No ☐ N/A	If the client has been unable to re-occupy the property due to work, they may be able to treat the absence as deemed occupation.	See the conditions for these deemed occupation periods at **11.14**	**11.14**

		Yes/No/ NA	Risk	Mitigation	Ref
	Is the client transferring the property to their spouse?	☐ Yes ☐ No ☐ N/A	If no election is made and this transfer is done after the tax year of separation the transferring spouse will be deemed to sell their portion of the property for market value. Where they have been absent from the property for over 9 months they are likely to have a capital gains tax liability on the transfer.	Consider whether TCGA 1992, s 225B relief would apply. This relief applies where an individual: (a) ceases to live with their spouse in a property which is their main residence, and (b) subsequently disposes of the property to the spouse, then if conditions A to C are met PPR will apply as if the house continued to be the individuals' main home until disposal. Conditions A to C can be found at **11.31** **The extended relief shall only apply on the making of a claim by the individual.**	**11.29–11.31**
Transferring to spouse	TCGA 1992, s 225B relief – no other home?	☐ Yes ☐ No ☐ N/A	If this claim is made, the occupying spouse must continue to occupy the property as their main home. If they do not, the conditions will not be met and the relief will not apply.	Ensure this is documented as part of the agreement. This is a sole claim. Only the non-occupying spouse needs to make the election to HMRC.	**11.32**

		Yes/No/ NA	Risk	Mitigation	Ref
	TCGA 1992, s 225B relief – other home?	☐ Yes ☐ No ☐ N/A	If a client claims TCGA 1992, s 225B relief this will impact them if they own another property which they live in, they will not be able to claim PPR on their new property for the period of time the s 225B election covers.	Consider the potential gains on both the former family home and the client's new home. It may be that the s 225B claim is not beneficial to the client. If the claim will be beneficial ensure it is made to HMRC within two years of the transfer.	**11.33**
Non resident	Has the client been non UK resident during ownership of the property?	☐ Yes ☐ No ☐ N/A	Special rules apply to non residents when claiming PPR.	Seek advice early on. You will need to tell the expert: – the dates the client was non resident (or details of their days in and out of the UK); – whether they were working abroad; – whether they spent any days in the property whilst non resident.	**3.35**

CHAPTER 12

Investment Properties

Contents at a Glance

12.1 This chapter considers investment properties owned by individuals rather than properties owned by way of a company. In couples where one or both parties own investment properties it will be important to consider income tax, capital gains tax and land taxes. Ownership of investment properties can have wide ranging tax implications but for the purposes of this chapter we will focus on:

- The income tax treatment of rental income.
- Capital gains tax on sale or transfer.
- The impact a second property can have on stamp duty.

12.2 In this chapter, we will follow Sabrina and Felicity who are going through the process of a divorce. They own three investment properties and a main home. We will look at:

- how they are taxed on their rental income;
- the tax impact if they complete all transactions within the tax year of separation;
- the capital gains tax due if the transfers take place after the tax year of separation;
- the availability of investment property relief;
- how the position changes if they are deemed to be trading in property rather than investing.

Facts for examples

Sabrina and Felicity are married and jointly own four properties. Three investment properties and their main home.

Sabrina is employed and earns £55,000 per year.

Felicity earns £15,000 per year.

We will assume Felicity and Sabrina have both utilised their capital gains tax exemptions for the year.

Property	Ownership	Purchase price	Market value
		£	£
Lavender Close (main home)	Sabrina/Felicity	410,000	750,000
Francis Road (investment)	Sabrina/Felicity	209,000	375,000
Wellington Street (investment)	Sabrina/Felicity	152,000	495,000
Junction Road (investment)	Sabrina/Felicity	85,000	72,000
Total		**856,000**	**1,692,000**

INCOME TAX

12.3 As discussed in Chapter 4, income tax is payable by 31 January following the end of the tax year. Therefore, it will be important to understand at what point in the payment cycle your clients are in with regards to their income tax on their rental properties.

12.4 If an individual is in receipt of rental income from investment properties they need to declare this to HRMC on a tax return and pay tax on the profits.

12.5 For example, if it is July 2020, clients will know what their rental profits were from April 2019 to April 2020 but it is likely that they have not yet paid the taxes due as the final deadline for payment will be 31 January 2021. Rental profits are charged to tax at 20%, 40% or 45% depending on a person's level of income. National insurance is not payable on rental profits.

12.6 If a couple jointly own a property they will be assessed to tax on 50% of the profits regardless of underlying ownership. For example, if A owns 20% and B owns 80%, A and B will be assessed as earning 50% of the profits. This is the case unless the couple submitted a Form 17 which allows them to be taxed on underlying ownership. This treatment continues until the end of the tax year of separation. After the end of the tax year of separation the couple are taxed on their underlying ownership.

12.7 Rental income is reported on the property pages of the tax returns. Losses from UK property can be carried forward and offset against first available profits from UK property. Rental losses cannot be used to reduce other taxable income.

12.8 From 6 April 2017 tax relief for mortgage interest for buy to let landlords was restricted. The restriction was phased in and in 2019/20 full relief for mortgage interest was given on 25% of the interest. From 2020/21 only basic rate relief is given for mortgage interest. Individuals will receive a 20% tax credit at the end of the income tax computation. Individuals who pay tax at 40% or 45% will be liable to tax on phantom income. This change makes it harder to complete a quick estimate for tax on rental income.

12.9 The below table shows the percentage of the mortgage interest payments that can be deducted from rental income and the percentage which will be subject to the new tax credits. As mentioned, from April 2020 all mortgage interest relief will be subject to the tax credit rules but it may be worthwhile to consult the table if calculating the tax liability on rental income for prior years.

	Percentage of mortgage interest payments deductible from rental income	**Percentage of mortgage interest payments qualifying for the new 20% tax credit**
Before April 2017	100%	0%
2017/18	75%	25%
2018/19	50%	50%
2019/20	25%	75%
Post April 2020	0%	100%

12.10 Where the individual is a basic rate taxpayer (ie their total income for the year is under £50,000), they will receive a 20% tax credit – effectively, whilst their computation will look different to pre April 2017, they will still get full relief for their mortgage interest.

Illustration 12A – Income tax on investment properties

Sabrina and Felicity are married and jointly own three properties.

Sabrina is employed and earns £55,000 per year.

Felicity earns £15,000 per year.

2020/21 Income Tax Computation on rental income

To briefly estimate the tax due on rental income you will need to know:

(a) the total income in the year for the individual;

(b) the total rent (before deducting mortgage interest);

(c) the total mortgage interest.

	100%	50%
The total rental profits (without deducting for mortgage interest)	£30,000	£15,000
Total mortgage interest	£12,000	£6,000

Actual profit (total rent less all expenses including mortgage interest)	£18,000	£9,000

Pre April 2017, the taxable profits would have been £18,000 or £9,000 each. Sabrina's income is over £50,000 therefore she is a higher rate taxpayer, therefore she would pay tax at 40% being £3,600 and Felicity earns under £50,000 (even when her rental income is included) therefore she would pay tax at 20% being £1,800.

Under the new rules relief is given for mortgage interest at the end of the income tax computation.

Sabrina – Quick calculation

Sabrina earns over £50,000 and therefore pays tax at 40% on the rental profits and she will receive a 20% tax credit for the mortgage interest:

	£	
Taxable profits	15,000	
Tax at 40%	6,000	
Less 20% tax credit for mortgage interest	(1,200)	
6,000 × 20%		
Tax payable on rental profits	**4,800**	This is £1,200 higher than Sabrina would have paid pre April 2017. As she would have paid 40% on the actual profits of £9,000 which is £3,600

Sabrina is paying £4,800 tax on actual profits of £9,000. Her effective rate of tax on her actual profits is therefore 53%.

Felicity earns £15,000, adding her share of the rental profits means her total income is £30,000, this is below the higher rate threshold of £50,000, therefore all of her income is taxable at 20%.

Felicity – Quick calculation

	£	
Taxable profits	15,000	
Tax at 20%	3,000	
Less 20% tax credit for mortgage interest	(1,200)	This is the same liability Felicity would have had pre April 2017 as she is a basic rate taxpayer
6,000 × 20%		
Tax payable on rental profits	**1,800**	

Felicity is paying £1,800 tax on actual profits of £9,000. Her effective rate of tax is therefore 20%.

It is also important to factor the mortgage interest restriction rules when valuing an assets potential income. For a higher or additional taxpayer, the rate of tax will be higher than their marginal rate of taxation.

Note: as the mortgage interest is deducted at the end of the tax computation an individual's total income for the year will be higher than their actual income. This is because the rental profits will not have had a deduction for mortgage interest. Therefore, this may also have an impact on the ability to claim child benefit even if actual profits mean an individual's income is below £50,0000.

For example, if Felicity earned £40,000 in the year, 50% of her actual profits are £9,000 (as above). This means her total actual income is £49,000.

However, the new mortgage interest rules mean her total income will be deemed to be £40,000 + £15,000 = £55,000. As her earnings are over £50,000, she will have breached the threshold for child benefit. Therefore, if she was in receipt of child benefit, some of this would be subject to a tax charge at the end of the year, even though her income has not actually changed.

Therefore, if one party is planning to claim child benefit post divorce, it will be important to consider whether any income from rental profits will distort this position.

CAPITAL GAINS TAX

12.11 Capital gains tax is charged on capital gains arising on the disposal of an asset. Investment properties may have risen or fallen in value since purchase and the property may have inherent gains or losses. Individuals are able to deduct acquisition and disposal costs before arriving at the chargeable gain or loss.

12.12 The following are allowable deductions:

- The purchase price of the property.
- Costs of acquisition.
- Expenditure incurred which enhances the value of the property (providing it is still reflected in the nature of the property at the time of the disposal).
- Any expenses incurred in establishing, preserving or defending their title or a right to the asset.
- Incidental costs of making the disposal.

- Costs of acquisition and disposal include fees, commission or remuneration paid for:
  - Surveyor;
  - Valuer;
  - Auctioneer;
  - Accountant;
  - Agent;
  - Legal advisor.
- Advertising to sell the property

12.13 Expenditure incurred which enhances the value of the property is commonly referred to as enhancement expenditure. Examples of qualifying expenditure would include adding a conservatory or garage to the property or adding an extension. The enhancement must still be reflected in the property at the point of sale to qualify.

TRANSFERS WITHIN THE TAX YEAR OF SEPARATION

12.14 Transfers of property within the tax year of separation will take place at no gain no loss, meaning there will be no immediate charge to capital gains tax. However, the properties may be being transferred with different levels of gains in the property so a rough capital gains tax computation should be done to ensure the net values of the properties are being used rather than the gross values.

Illustration 12B – Transfer of investment properties within the tax year of separation

Sabrina and Felicity jointly own three investment properties and their main home. They have both continued to live in the main home.

Property	Ownership	Purchase price	Market value
		£	£
Lavender Close (main home)	Sabrina/Felicity	410,000	750,000
Junction Road (investment)	Sabrina/Felicity	85,000	72,000
Francis Road (investment)	Sabrina/Felicity	209,000	375,000
Wellington Street (investment)	Sabrina/Felicity	152,000	495,000
Total		856,000	1,692,000

Total assets are £1,692,000.

It is proposed that as part of the divorce Felicity will own Lavender Close and Junction Road 100% (total market value of both is £822,000) and Sabrina will own Francis Road and Wellington Street (total market value of both is £870,000).

Provided the transfer takes place before the end of the tax year of separation there will be no capital gains tax to pay and Sabrina and Felicity will inherit each other's base cost of the properties.

After the transfer the ownership would be as follows:

Felicity

Property	Purchase price (£)	Current Market value (£)
Lavender Close (main home)	410,000	750,000
Junction Road (investment)	85,000	72,000

Sabrina

Property	Purchase price (£)	Current Market value (£)
Francis Road (investment)	209,000	375,000
Wellington Street (investment)	152,000	495,000

As part of the proposal Felicity will retain the main home. Any gain on the main home will be exempt from capital gains tax (providing all the conditions are met – see Chapter 11). Felicity will also receive a property which has an inherent loss. The availability of the loss to offset against future gains will be impacted when the transfer takes place. As the transfer is taking place whilst the no gain no loss rules apply (ie within the tax year of separation) Felicity's loss can be used to offset future gains.

Summary of taxable and exempt gains

Felicity

Property	Ownership	Purchase price (£)	Current Market value (£)	Enhancement Expenditure	Gain/ Loss (£)	Treatment
Lavender Cls (main home)	Felicity	410,000	750,000		340,000	Exempt
Junction Rd (investment)	Felicity	85,000	72,000		(13,000)	Realisable Loss

Sabrina

Property	Ownership	Purchase price (£)	Current Market value (£)	Enhancement Expenditure	Gain/ Loss (£)	Treatment
Francis Rd (investment)	Sabrina	209,000	375,000		166,000	Taxable Gain
Wellington St (investment)	Sabrina	152,000	495,000	130,000	213,000	Taxable Gain

Considering future gains

After the transfer Sabrina and Felicity's base costs of the properties will be the original purchase price. The values of the property are not re-based to market value. If both Sabrina and Felicity sold the properties immediately, they would have the following capital gains tax position:

Post transfer

Felicity's capital gains tax liability on a future sale would be Nil and a carry forward loss.

Sabrina's capital gains tax liability if she were to sell the properties immediately would be £106,120 this is worked out as follows,

Gain from Francis St	166,000
Gain from Wellington St	213,000
Taxable gain	379,000
CGT at 28%	106,120

Therefore, whilst there would be no capital gains tax impact on the transfer of the properties, Sabrina is disadvantaged due to the nature of the assets she receives.

Felicity

Property	**Ownership**	**Purchase price (£)**	**Market value (£)**	**Gain/Loss (£)**	**Future CGT liability**
Lavender Close (main home)	Felicity	410,000	750,000	340,000	Exempt
Junction Road (investment)	Felicity	85,000	72,000	(13,000)	Nil

Sabrina

Property	**Ownership**	**Purchase price (£)**	**Market value (£)**	**Gain/Loss (£)**	**Future CGT liability**
Francis Rd (investment)	Sabrina	209,000	375,000	166,000	£46,480
Wellington Street (investment)	Sabrina	152,000	495,000	213,000	£59,640

TRANSFERS OUTSIDE THE TAX YEAR OF SEPARATION

12.15 Once a couple are outside the tax year of separation they are treated as connected persons for tax purposes. This means:

- transactions between them take place at deemed market value;

- losses can only be offset against gains incurred from a transfer to the same person.

Sabrina and Felicity – Transfer outside the tax year of separation

All the facts from the previous example are true, but now the transfer is happening outside the tax year of separation.

As such Sabrina will be deemed to purchase Francis Road and Wellington Street from Felicity and Felicity will be deemed to purchase Lavender Close and Junction Road from Sabrina.

Ownership Summary pre-transfer:

Property	Ownership	Purchase price	Market value
		£	£
Lavender Close (main home)	Sabrina/Felicity	410,000	750,000
Junction Road (investment)	Sabrina/Felicity	85,000	72,000
Francis Road (investment)	Sabrina/Felicity	209,000	375,000
Wellington Street (investment)	Sabrina/Felicity	152,000	495,000
Total		856,000	1,692,000

Felicity's capital gains tax computation

Felicity is deemed to sell her 50% share of Francis Road and Wellington Street to Sabrina for market value.

	50%
	£
Market value $\frac{£375{,}000 + £495{,}000}{2}$	435,000
Less: purchase price $\frac{£209{,}000 + £152{,}000}{2}$	(180,500)
Less: enhancement expenditure	(65,000)
Gain	189,500
20,000 @ 18%	3,600
169,500 @ 28%	47,460
Total CGT	**51,060**

Felicity earned £30,000 in the year (including rental income). She has £20,000 of unused basic rate band, so the first £20,000 of her gain is taxable at the lower CGT rate of 18%

Felicity would need to pay capital gains tax of £51,060 to HMRC within 30 days of the transfer.

Sabrina's base cost of the properties will be 50% purchase price and 50% of the market value at transfer.

Sabrina's base cost

Property	Ownership	50% Purchase price (£)	50% Market value at transfer (£)	Total base cost (£)
Francis Road (investment)	Sabrina	104,500	187,500	292,000
Wellington Street (investment)	Sabrina	76,000	247,500	323,500

Sabrina's Capital gains tax computation

Sabrina is deemed to sell her 50% share of the main home and 50% of Junction Road to Felicity.

As Lavender Close is Sabrina's main home the whole gain can be exempted through PPR. Junction road is standing at a loss so there is no gain to charge tax on.

Sabrina will not be able to utilise this loss other than on a gain arising on a transfer to Felicity.

Post transfer

Sabrina's capital gains tax liability is Nil. Sabrina will have a capital gains tax libality of £51,060 when selling in the future.

Felicity's capital gains tax liability is £51,060. Felicity will have no future capital gains tax liability.

SUMMARY

12.16 If the transfer is completed within the tax year of separation Sabrina will inherit latent capital gains tax of approximately £51,000. If the transfer is done after the tax year of separation Felicity will pay capital gains tax of approximately £51,000 and Sabrina's base cost for the properties is enhanced as the 50% of the transfer takes place at market value.

INVESTMENT PROPERTY RELIEF /ROLLOVER RELIEF

12.17 Where couples are transferring investment properties between each other each person may be able to defer the gain by claiming roll over relief. To benefit from the relief **all** of the following conditions must be met[1]:

1 *TCGA 1992, s 248A* Capital Gains Manual.

- One or more interest in land is held jointly by two or more people.
- One landowner transfers his interest in one or more holdings of land to one or more co-owners.
- The consideration received by the landowner for the transfers includes an interest in jointly held land.
- As a result of the transactions both the landowner and each of the co-owners becomes the sole owner of either:
  - part of the land formerly held jointly, or
  - one or more holdings of land formerly held jointly.

12.18 The relief is not available where the property is the main home or which would qualify as a main home within six years. Therefore, if one of the investment properties will be used as the main home after transfer it will not qualify for the relief.

12.19 If the above conditions are met the transfers take place and the gain is held over until the property is sold (or later transferred). It removes the immediate charge to capital gains tax. The base cost of the property going forward will be the original purchase price of the property. It effectively gives the same result as completing the transfer in the tax year of separation.

This relief is not automatic and must be claimed. The time limit for the roll-over relief claim is four years from the end of the tax year in which the exchange took place. **The claim must be a joint claim.**

WILL SABRINA AND FELICITY QUALIFY FOR THE RELIEF?

12.20 Working through the conditions we see:

- they jointly own one or more properties (tick);
- they will each be transferring their interest in at least one property to the other (tick);
- the consideration received by each of them includes an interest in a property (tick);
- as a result of the transaction both Sabrina and Felicity will each become the sole owner of a property (tick).

> **Note:** Sabrina is receiving two rental properties (Francis Road and Wellington Street). If she intends to live in one of these as the main home in the following six years the relief will not apply (or will be withdrawn). In return for these properties, Sabrina is transferring to Felicity Lavender Close which is the main home. If this was the only property she was transferring then the relief would not be available as Felicity intends to live in the property as her main home.
>
> The properties subject to the claim will be Francis Road, Wellington Street and Junction Road.

Illustration 12C – Sabrina and Felicity – Rollover Relief

All the facts from the previous example are true and now we are considering the application of rollover relief.

If Sabrina and Felicity claim rollover relief their position will be as follows.

Ownership summary – pre-transfer

Property	Ownership	Purchase price	Market value
		£	£
Lavender Close (main home)	Sabrina/Felicity	410,000	750,000
Francis Road (investment)	Sabrina/Felicity	209,000	375,000
Wellington Street (investment)	Sabrina/Felicity	152,000	495,000
Junction Road (investment)	Sabrina/Felicity	85,000	72,000
Total		856,000	1,692,000

Ownership summary – post transfer

There would be no immediate charge to capital gains tax. By making the claim both Sabrina and Felicity agree to absorb the other's gain and pay the relevant capital gains tax on the eventual sale of the properties.

Felicity			
Property	**Ownership**	**Purchase price (£)**	**Market value (£)**
Lavender Close (main home)	Felicity	410,000	750,000
Junction Road (investment)	Felicity	85,000	72,000

Sabrina			
Property	**Ownership**	**Purchase price (£)**	**Market value (£)**
Francis Road (investment)	Sabrina	209,000	375,000
Wellington Street (investment)	Sabrina	152,000	495,000

Sabrina and Felicity will each inherits the other's base cost on the property.

The only properties which would be subject to the claim would be Francis Road, Wellington Street and Junction Road.

If Sabrina wanted to live in one of the investment properties it would need to be excluded from the claim. It would not prevent the relief from being claimed as there is still more than one property and both Sabrina and Felicity each own one property 100% after the transaction.

Post transfer

Sabrina's immediate capital gains tax liability is Nil, but she will have future capital gains tax liability of £106,102 being the £51,060 latent gain from Felicity plus Sabrina's gain.

Felicity's capital gains tax liability is Nil, assuming the values of the properties remain the same Felicity will not have any future capital gains tax liabilities on the properties as one of them is her main home and the other one is standing at a loss.

SUMMARY OF SABRINA AND FELICITY

12.21 They jointly own three investment properties and one main home. At the end of the transfers Sabrina will own two investment properties and Felicity will own one investment property and the main home.

The date of the transfers and the claiming of rollover relief will impact the capital gains tax liabilities. A summary of the impact of the transactions is below.

Date of transaction	Claim for rollover relief	Sabrina Immediate CGT Liability	Felicity Immediate CGT Liability	Sabrina Latent CGT liability	Felicity Latent CGT liability
During the tax year of separation	Not necessary	Nil	Nil	£106,120	Nil
After the tax year of separation	No	Nil	£51,060	£51,060	Nil
After the tax year of separation	Yes	Nil	Nil	£106,120	Nil

12.22 As Felicity is deemed to be disposing of her interests in investment properties (which are chargeable to CGT) she will have the immediate charge to tax on a transfer after the end of the tax year. Sabrina's liability will arise when she sells the properties. Her liability is almost double Felicity's as she absorbs Felicity's capital gains tax liability for Felicity's 50% share and she is liable for the gain on her 50% share of the properties. This can be a valuable option if individuals do not have the cash to settle any immediate capital gains tax liabilities as a result of the transfer. By claiming rollover relief the tax becomes payable on a future sale (or transfer) at which point there is more likely to be cash available to settle the liability.

TRADING OR INVESTMENT

12.23 In the above examples we have assumed that the sale would be liable to capital gains tax as this is the applicable tax when selling a capital asset. If it was deemed that Sabrina and Felicity were trading in property, rather than investing in property the applicable tax on sale would be income tax. This might also be referred to as trading tax.

12.24 If a person is in the business of buying and selling properties and that is their trade, they will be subject to income tax and national insurance on their profits. Property letting is not a trade,[2] however the buying and selling of property can be a trade.

Most of the time it is relatively straightforward to determine whether a person is investing in property or is a property trader.

12.25 If Sabrina and Felicity bought three flats and renovated them and then sold them immediately after renovation then this would point to a trade of property developing and they may be liable to income tax and national insurance on the profits of the properties.

If Sabrina and Felicity bought three flats, rented them out and then sold them 10-15 years later this would suggest they were investing in property and the gains would be subject to capital gains tax.

12.26 Looking at their property in Wellington Street, it was purchased for £152,000 and they spent £130,000 on the property and the current market value is £495,000. If the property was bought say six months ago, the amount spent on the property and drastic increase in value might point to this activity being one of trade, especially if they intended to sell the property within a short period of time. If this was the case, the gain of £213,000 would be subject to income tax at 40% and 45% and Class 4 National Insurance at 9%.

12.27 If the Wellington Street property was deemed to be a trade activity it would not necessarily mean that the other properties would be deemed to be in a trade as well. If an individual is trading in property, rollover relief would not be available, however, gift relief, which operates in a similar way may be available.

> **Note:** Where a client may be trading in property it should be established early on whether they are indeed trading in property and then, if they are, whether an income tax calculation would be more appropriate than a capital gains tax calculation.

INCOME TAX ACT 2007

12.28 Trade is defined in ITA 2007, s 989, as including 'any venture in the nature of trade'. The interpretation of the word 'trade' has been left to the courts,

2 In tax law there is a definition for **trading** in the Income Tax Act and the Capital Gains Tax Act. The separation of property (and letting) income from trading income is a long-established principle in UK tax law. In *Salisbury House Estate Ltd v Fry* [1930] 15 TC266, 'A landowner may conduct a trade on his premises, but he cannot be represented as carrying on a trade of owning land because he makes an income by letting it'. This principle has often been applied by the courts, in *Griffiths v Jackson* [1982] 56TC583 'although property income is now computed like trading income, letting is still not trade'.

which have developed a number of tests, commonly referred to as the 'badges of trade', to determine whether somebody is trading.

12.29 These 'badges' will not be present in every case and of those that are, some may point one way and some the other. The presence or absence of a particular badge is unlikely, by itself, to provide a conclusive answer to the question of whether or not there is a trade. The weight to be attached to each badge will depend on the precise circumstances. The approach by the courts in using the badges of trade has been to decide questions of trade on the basis of the overall impression gained from a review of all the badges.

12.30 The following table notes each badge, the corresponding HMRC commentary surrounding the badge and the relevant case law.

Badges of trade	**HMRC Business Manual**	**Cases**
Profit-seeking motive	*BIM20210* An intention to make a profit supports trading, but by itself is not conclusive. Evidence that the sole object of acquiring an asset was to re-sell it at a profit, without any intention of holding it as an investment, is a pointer to the conclusion that a trade is being carried on. **However, the presence of a profit-seeking motive is not necessarily a decisive pointer to the existence of a trade**. It is only one factor to be weighed along with all the other relevant factors. Some assets are more likely to be held as investments than others are.	'mere intention is not enough to invest a transaction with the character or trade'.[3] *Rutlege v CIR* [1929] 14TC490. 'the question is not what business does the taxpayer profess to carry on, but what business does he actually carry on'. *CIR v Hyndland Investment Co Ltd* [1929] 14TC694.
Frequency and number of similar transactions	*BIM20210* Systematic and repeated transactions will support 'trade'. A single isolated transaction can amount to the carrying on of a trade for tax purposes, but it is generally not easy to show that that is the case. The transaction, if it is to be trading for tax purposes, has to be a venture in the nature of trade.	The test to be applied is whether the operations involved in the transaction are of the same kind or character, and carried on in the same way, as those which are characteristic of ordinary admitted trading in the line of business in which the transaction was carried out. *CIR v Livingston and Others* [1926] 11TC538 at page 542.

3 'It has been said, not without justice, that mere intention is not enough to invest a transaction with the character of trade. But, on the question whether the appellant entered into an adventure or speculation, the circumstances of the purchase, and also the purchaser's object or intention in making it, do enter, and that directly, into the solution of the question.'

Badges of trade	HMRC Business Manual	Cases
Nature of the asset	*BIM20250* Is the asset of such a type or amount that it can only be turned to advantage by a sale? Or did it yield an income? The area of difficulty concerns assets that are generally bought: as an investment that usually, but not necessarily, yields income, for example shares.	That presumption can be overturned, but there is, in practice, a greater onus on those who assert that there is a trade, than is the case with assets that are commonly dealt with by way of trade. *CIR v Fraser* [1942] 24TC498. In *Rutledge*, a taxpayer purchased one million rolls of toilet paper in one single transaction. He then sold them in another single transaction. This was held to be trading as there was no other justifiable reason to purchase such a large quantity of toilet paper. *Rutledge v CIR* 14 TC 49.
Connection with an existing trade	*BIM20270* Transactions that are similar to those of an existing trade may themselves be trading.	In *Harvey* a builder claimed that certain properties that he had built and then sold many years later were investments and not part of his trading stock. **On the facts of his case he succeeded** but the court commented: 'We accept the evidence that you intended to hold these as an investment against your old age', they are saying in effect: 'We find that you intended to hold these properties for the income which they are capable of producing and not as stock to be turned over at a profit in the course of trade.' The facts here at p. 165 show that that intention was carried into effect for 20 years, and the properties never became trading stock. In those circumstances when the property is sold it is still sold as an investment, and the proceeds are not assessable to Income Tax under Case I of Schedule D' *Harvey v Caulcott* [1952] 33TC159 at page 165.

Badges of trade	HMRC Business Manual	Cases
Changes to the asset	*BIM20275* Was the asset repaired, modified or improved to make it more easily saleable or saleable at a greater profit? Expenditure on an asset after purchase and before sale is not always strong evidence of a trading motive. You must have regard to the nature and scale of the expenditure.	
The way the sale was carried out	Was the asset sold in a way that was typical of trading organisations? Alternatively, did it have to be sold to raise cash for an emergency?	'I think the test, which must be used to determine whether a venture such as we are now considering is, or is not, "in the nature of trade", is whether the operations involved in it are of the same kind, and carried on in the same way, as those which are characteristic of ordinary trading in the line of business in which the venture was made.' *CIR v Livingston and Others* 11TC538.
Financing arrangements	*BIM20300* Was money borrowed to buy the asset? Could the funds only be repaid by selling the asset? If an asset is purchased using a short term loan that the taxpayer is unable to repay without selling the asset, HMRC may be able to successfully argue that the asset was purchased specifically with a view to selling it and is therefore a trade.	For example, in *Wisdom* the taxpayer was held to be trading in relation to profits made from the purchase and sale of silver bullion. His normal occupation was not in that sort of activity. The purchase of the bullion was financed by loans at a high rate of interest in circumstances that made it clear that it was necessary to sell the asset in the short term, to repay the loan and eliminate the interest obligation. *Wisdom v Chamberlain* [1968] 45TC92.
Method of acquisition	*BIM20315* The way in which an asset was acquired must be considered. If it is by gift or inheritance it will be difficult, although not impossible, to show that a subsequent sale is by way of trade.	

Badges of trade	HMRC Business Manual	Cases
Length of ownership	*BIM20310* Assets that are the subject of trade will normally, but not always, be sold quickly. Therefore, an intention to resell an asset shortly after purchase will support trading. However, an asset, which is to be held indefinitely, is much less likely to be a subject of trade.	'What were the purchasers' intentions as to resale at the time of purchase? If there was an intention to hold the object indefinitely, albeit with an intention to make a capital profit at the end of the day, that is a pointer towards a pure investment as opposed to a trading deal. On the other hand, **if before the contract of purchase is made a contract for resale is already in place, that is a very strong pointer towards a trading deal rather than an investment**. Similarly, an intention to resell in the short term rather than the long term is some indication against concluding that the transaction was by way of investment rather than by way of a deal.' **He went on to say that this factor was in no way decisive by itself.** *Marson v Morton and Others* [1986] 59TC381.

INVESTMENT PROPERTY – CHECKLIST

12.31

		Yes/No/ NA	Risk	Mitigation	Ref
Additional rate taxpayer	Is your client an additional rate taxpayer?	☐ Yes ☐ No ☐ N/A	From 6 April 2020 mortgage interest relief is given as a 20% tax credit. This means an individual's effective rate of tax on their rental profits may be much higher than their effective rate.	If they have not yet filed their tax return ensure the correct net income for rental is used. You will need to work out the tax on profits (before deducting mortgage interest) at their effective rate and then deduct 20% of the mortgage interest from their tax liability.	**12.10**

		Yes/No/ NA	Risk	Mitigation	Ref
Child benefit	Does your client claim child benefit?	☐ Yes ☐ No ☐ N/A	Due to the way the mortgage interest relief is given, total earnings for 2020-21 may be higher even if they have not actually changed. This could mean an individual is paying the higher income child benefit charge because their rental income pushed them over £50,000.	Ensure your client understands how the computation for rental income is done. If your client is receiving rental property as part of the settlement check the total income to ascertain whether this will impact the child benefit claim or not.	**12.10**
Underlying ownership	Do the couple own different percentages of the property?	☐ Yes ☐ No ☐ N/A	Where couples own different portions of a rental property the tax treatment changes after the tax year of separation.	During the tax year of separation rental profits will be assessed on the couple 50/50 regardless of the underlying ownership of the properties. After the end of the tax year of separation tax is assessed on the actual percentage of the property owned.	**12.6**
Multiple investment properties	Transferring properties inside the tax year of separation?	☐ Yes ☐ No ☐ N/A	Any capital gain or loss in the property will pass to the receiving spouse.	Quantify the amount of the gain being transferred. If there have been any works done on the property ensure the receiving spouse receives this documentation so that they can claim the expenses in the future.	**12.14**
	Transferring properties outside the tax year of separation?	☐ Yes ☐ No ☐ N/A	The transfer will be deemed to take place at market value. The transferring spouse will be assessed to capital gains tax on the market value of their share of the property being transferred.	Consider if rollover relief will apply. Both parties will need to make the election. The relief effectively gives the same outcome as if the properties were transferred within the tax year of separation.	**12.15**

		Yes/No/ NA	Risk	Mitigation	Ref
			Any capital gains tax due will be due within 30 days of the transfer.		
	Trading or Investment?	☐ Yes ☐ No ☐ N/A	If the parties are trading in property income tax and national insurance will be payable on any gains/profits.	Look at the badges of trade to determine if it is likely that the activity will be deemed to be trading or not. If unsure, seek advice. If they are deemed to be trading the possible tax implications will be higher as the top rate of income tax is 45% compared to the higher rate of CGT at 28%.	**12.23**

CHAPTER 13

Chattels and Investments

Contents at a Glance

CHATTELS AND INVESTMENTS

13.1 In this chapter we consider the capital gains tax implications of transferring and selling chattels and investments. We will consider listed shares only (analysis of shares in a private company can be found in Chapter 14 – selling a company and Chapter 7 – the owner managed business). Capital gains tax rates for non-property gains are 10% and 20%. Capital gains tax is payable by 31 January following the end of the tax year.

CHATTELS

13.2 Chattels are assets which can be seen, touched and moved – tangible moveable property. It includes assets such as paintings, racehorses and computers. Buildings, shares and land are not chattels as they cannot be seen, touched and moved. The two most common types of chattels are:

- Cheap chattels.
- Wasting chattels.

13.3 There are different rules for chattels when they are used in a business. If business assets are being transferred as part of the divorce seek advice early on about the potential capital gains tax position of the transfer.

Wasting chattels

13.4 Wasting chattels are exempt assets. A wasting chattel is one with a useful life of 50 years or less. Typical examples of these include, racehorses, computers, yachts and cars.

Cheap chattels

13.5 A cheap chattel is a non-wasting chattel, meaning it has a useful life of over 50 years. This includes items such as paintings, jewellery and antiques. Depending on the value of the asset it may be exempt from capital gains tax or special rules will apply.

13.6 If the sale proceeds or deemed market value and purchase price are £6,000 or less, the asset is exempt from capital gains tax.

- Where the proceeds are £6,000 or less and the costs of acquisition are more than £6,000 the capital loss is restricted by deeming the proceeds to be £6,000.
- If the sale proceeds exceed £6,000 and the costs of acquisition are £6,000 or less, the chargeable gain is the lower of:
  - the amount calculated using the normal capital gains tax rules;
  - 5/3 × (gross proceeds – £6,000).

13.7 The following table summarises the capital gains tax position of cheap chattels:

Proceeds	**Cost**	
	≤£6,000	**>£6,000**
≤£6,000	Exempt	Loss restricted (proceeds deemed to be £6,000)
>£6,000	Gain restricted to max of 5/3 of gross proceeds less than £6,000	Normal capital gains tax rules

13.8 See these rules by way of the flow chart below:

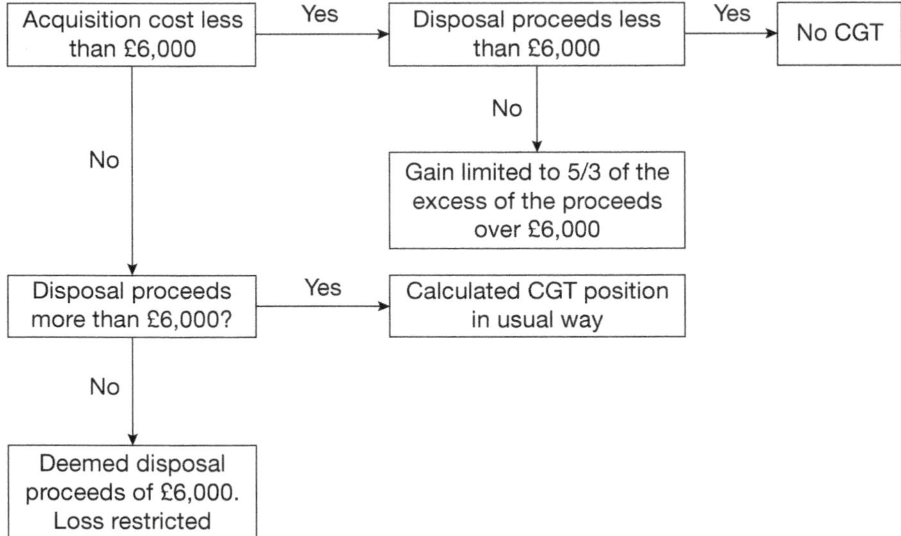

Illustration 13A – Niamh and Sandeep – Cheap Chattels

Niamh and Sandeep are married. In 2010 they inherited some money when Sandeep's mother passed away. They used the money to buy some antiques. It is now 2020 and Niamh and Sandeep are in the process of separating. Rather than dividing up the antiques they have agreed to sell them and split the proceeds.

All of the antiques are cheap chattels as they have a useful life of more than 50 years.

Both Niamh and Sandeep earn £35,000 per year.

Cheap chattel	Purchase price	Sale price
Antique vase	£7,000	£23,000
Antique pot	£2,000	£5,000
Antique watch	£5,000	£19,000
Antique chair	£15,000	£4,000

Vase

As the purchase price and sale price is over £6,000 the normal capital gains tax rules apply. The proceeds less the purchase price produces a gain of £16,000.

Pot

As the purchase price and the sale price is under £6,000 the item is exempt from capital gains tax, therefore the £3,000 gain can be ignored.

Watch

As the watch was bought for under £6,000 we can restrict the amount of the gain, chargeable to capital gains tax. The chargeable gain is the lower of:

- the gain calculated using normal capital gains tax rules which equals £14,000 (£19,000 – £5,000) or;
- the amount by which the disposal exceeds £6,000 is £13,000 multiply this by 5/3 gives a maximum gain of £21,666.

The lower amount is £14,000, therefore that is the gain we will input into the computation.

Chair

The chair made a loss, however the loss will be restricted. The proceeds will be deemed to be £6,000, therefore they will have an allowable loss of £2,000.

Capital gains tax computation

Gain and loss computation	£
Antique vase	16,000
Antique pot	–
Antique watch	14,000
Antique chair	(2,000)
Total gains	28,000

Niamh's capital gains tax computation:

	£
Total gains	14,000
Less annual allowance	(12,300)
Taxable	1,700
At 10%	170

Sandeep's capital gains tax computation:

	£
Total gains	14,000
Less annual allowance	(12,300)
Taxable	1,700
At 10%	170

Niamh and Sandeep both pay tax at the lower rate of 10% as their income is within the basic rate band of tax.

The capital gains tax is due by 31 January following the end of the tax year in which the assets were sold.

SHARES

Listed shares

13.9 Valuing quoted shares for capital gains tax purposes is straightforward. The value of the shares on the date of disposal is the value of the share as listed on the official list published by the Stock Exchange. The value for capital gains tax is the average of the bid and offer prices.

13.10 The gain is the sale price less allowable expenses. Allowable expenses include purchase price of the share and any selling fees.

13.11 If shares have no value, individuals can make a negligible value claim on their tax return to utilise any loss and offset this against future gains. HMRC have a list online of all listed companies where they agree the shares have no current value.[1] Losses are first offset against gains in the current year and are then carried forward to offset against future gains.

Illustration 13B

Craig purchased shares a few years ago and has decided to sell all of his holdings to help finance a property. Craig is a higher rate taxpayer.

Holdings

Company Name	**Number of shares**	**Purchase price £**	**Sale price £**	**Gain/loss £**
Titanwinds	1,200	1.21	4.56	4,020
Funvolution	782	3.45	0.92	(1,978)
Qualivon	2,982	2.9	4.32	4,234
Ozarro	3,110	5.12	9.12	12,440
Avrax	20	147.01	198.02	1,020
Evrum	523	27.98	112.12	44,005

Capital Gains Computation

	Gain/ Loss £
Titanwinds	4,020
Funvolution	(1,978)
Qualivon	4,234
Ozarro	12,440
Avrax	1,020
Evrum	44,005
Gain/Loss	63,741
Less: Annual exemption	(12,300)
Taxable gain	51,441
Capital gains tax at 20%	**10,288**

Capital gains will be due by 31 January following the end of the tax year of disposal.

1 www.gov.uk/guidance/negligible-value-agreements.

Tax efficient investment schemes

13.12 If shares are held in a tax-free wrapper such as an ISA then any gain on the shares are tax free. Gains on shares in EIS and SEIS companies are also exempt providing certain conditions are met.

13.13 There are several options for individuals who want to make tax efficient investments. We will outline the most common below. The aim of the below is to provide enough information to give context to how the schemes operate and the potential for tax to be clawed back if these assets are sold or transferred ahead of the end of the qualifying period.

Enterprise Investment Scheme and Seed Enterprise Investment Scheme

13.14 The EIS and SEIS schemes encourage individuals to invest in certain companies by giving income tax relief on the amount invested. Any disposals of EIS and SEIS shares are also free from capital gains tax provided they have been held for at least three years.

13.15 When an individual subscribes for shares in an EIS or SEIS company they will receive income tax relief on the investment.

13.16 For EIS, the relief is 30% of the amount subscribed. The maximum investment is £1 million, providing relief of £300,000. This relief will be lost (meaning the tax will be clawed back) if the shares are sold within three years. Relief will be withdrawn if these shares are transferred as part of a divorce if this happens within the three-year period.[2]

13.17 For SEIS the relief is 50% of the amount subscribed. The maximum investment is £100,000, providing relief of £50,000. This relief will be lost (meaning the tax will be clawed back) if the shares are sold within three years.

The relief is only available where the companies are qualifying companies and the individual must not be connected with the company.

Illustration 13C – SEIS Share subscription

In 2019–20 Gary was employed and earned £290,000 per annum. His salary was subject to PAYE and his employer paid taxes on his behalf of £118,000.

In the year Gary subscribed for shares in Blue Ltd which was a qualifying SEIS company. He subscribed for shares to the value of £50,000. A subscription for SEIS shares provides income tax relief at 50% of the amount subscribed. Therefore Gary will receive an income tax reduction of £25,000.

2 ITA 2007, s 209(4), or 257FA(4).

Gary's income tax computation will be as follows:

	£
Salary	290,000
Less personal allowance	–
37,500 @ 20%	7,500
112,500 @40%	47,500
118,000 @45%	63,000
Total tax	**118,000**
Less tax reducer	*(25,000)*
Tax liability	93,000
Less: tax paid via PAYE	(118,000)
Tax refund	**(£25,000)**

If Gary sells the shares within three years some of the tax relief will be clawed back. The claw back is the lower of:

- the original income tax reducer (£25,000);
- 50% × sale proceeds received (only if the shares sell at a loss).

13.18 If SEIS or EIS shares are sold within three years, capital gains tax will be payable on any gain and income tax relief will be clawed back.

Note: If a client holds qualifying EIS or SEIS shares the relief they received at the time of subscription will be clawed back if the shares are disposed of within three years of subscription. This could result in a high-income tax charge. If the shares have been held for over three years there will be no capital gains tax on sale or transfer (assuming the other conditions have been met).

Venture Capital Trusts

13.19 When an individual subscribes for shares in a qualifying Venture Capital Trust (VCT) they will receive tax relief on the investment.

13.20 For VCTs the relief is 30% of the amount subscribed. The maximum investment for tax relief is £200,000 providing relief of £60,000. This relief will be lost (meaning the tax will be clawed back) if the shares are sold within three years.

13.21 There is also an exemption for dividends received by an investor on shares in a VCT. Dividends on VCT shares are exempt from tax but this is only available for the first £200,000 invested in a VCT in a tax year. This relief does not extend to EIS or SEIS shares. All dividends on EIS and SEIS shares are taxable.

CHATTELS AND INVESTMENTS – CHECKLIST

13.22

		Yes/No/ NA	Risk	Mitigation	Ref
Chattels	Is the asset used in a business or trade?	☐ Yes ☐ No ☐ N/A	The rules for chattels outlined in the chapter will not apply.	Seek advice if these assets are going to be sold or transferred.	**13.3**
	Does the asset have a useful life of less than 50 years?	☐ Yes ☐ No ☐ N/A	Ensure these assets are not part of a business or trade. If they are not, they are exempt from capital gains tax, they can be sold and transferred with no capital gains tax consequence.	If the asset is exempt, any gains are not chargeable and the gains do not need to be reported on a tax return.	**13.7**
	Does the asset have a useful life of more than 50 years?	☐ Yes ☐ No ☐ N/A	Different capital gains tax rules apply.	See flowchart at **13.7** for capital gains tax rules on cheap chattel.	**13.8**
Shares	Does the client hold any shares with a negligible value?	☐ Yes ☐ No ☐ N/A	Once the shares have no value it will not be possible to sell them so the loss incurred may not be captured.	A negligible value claim should be made with HMRC so that the loss can be offset against either current year or future gains.	**13.11**
EIS/ SEIS/ VCTs	Has your client held EIS/SEIS/ VCT shares for less than three years?	☐ Yes ☐ No ☐ N/A	If these shares are sold, capital gains tax will be payable on the gain and income tax relief will be clawed back.	If possible, EIS/SEIS/ VCT shares held for less than three years should not be sold. If they have to be sold seek advice on the potential tax implications of the sale. Remember it is not just capital gains tax but also the income tax implications which need to be considered.	**13.14**

		Yes/No/ NA	**Risk**	**Mitigation**	**Ref**
	Has your client held EIS/SEIS/ VCT shares for more than three years?	☐ Yes ☐ No ☐ N/A	Providing all the other conditions have been met, no capital gains tax will be payable on the sale of the shares.		**13.14**

CHAPTER 14

Extracting Money from a Company

Contents at a Glance

OVERVIEW

14.1 This chapter covers the options available to individuals and couples who have a small limited company. It covers the tax considerations for individuals who are:

- extracting money from the company;
- planning on selling the company;
- transferring shares to their spouse;
- transferring shares back to the company.

It considers the availability of the following options:

- Business Asset Disposal relief (formerly known as Entrepreneur's relief);
- Holdover Relief/Gift relief;
- Investors' relief;
- Company buy back of own shares.

14.2 This is a very broad-brush approach on complex issues. It provides enough information to highlight the basic tax implications of a variety of actions. However, if it seems one of the above reliefs or a company buy back of shares is an option your clients might consider, **this would be an area where advice should be sought.**

14.3 Throughout this chapter we will follow Marcel as he considers his options on divorce. Marcel runs a successful handmade jewellery company, Gems Ltd. Marcel married Gabby in 2010, in 2012 Marcel transferred 40% of his shares to Gabby. The transfer of shares happened when they were married so there were no capital gains tax implications as transfers between married couples take place at no gain no loss. In 2013 Gabby lost her job and they decided that it would benefit the company if Gabby helped out in Gems Ltd for a few days a week. Gabby developed and ran the small marketing and promotions team. Due to Gabby's hard work Gem Ltd have been approached many times by larger stores who were interested in purchasing the company. Each time Marcel and Gabby have refused. Since 2013 Gabby has only worked for Gem Ltd and had no other income.

14.4 Gem Ltd's turnover, net profit, dividends and retained earnings cash at bank for the last three years are listed below.

Turnover — total sales and receipts for the year.

Net profit — turnover less all allowable company expenses.

Dividends — money taken out of the business as dividends (ie not as a salary).

Retained earnings — net income left after dividends have been paid out.

Year	Turnover	Net profit	Dividends	Retained earnings
2017	£390,000	£142,000	£120,000	£22,000
2018	£690,000	£412,000	£250,000	£162,000
2019	£980,000	£670,000	£250,000	£420,000

At January 2020 the cash at bank is £879,000.

Their accountant has given a company valuation of £1,500,000

14.5 In February 2020 (2019/20 tax year) Marcel moved out of the family home and began a relationship with someone else. By May 2020 Gabby and Marcel agree to divorce. During this time, Gabby reduced her work at Gem Ltd and only worked one day a week for the company. Marcel and Gabby separated in February 2020. By May they are outside of the tax year of separation, therefore any transfer of assets (including shares) will take place between them at deemed market value.

14.6 They agree that Gabby will give up her shares in Gem Ltd and Marcel will pay Gabby a settlement of £500,000.

Two things are happening as part of this proposal:

(a) Gabby is transferring her total shareholding to Marcel;

(b) Marcel is giving Gabby cash of £500,000.

TRANSFER OF SHARES

14.7 Gabby will be deemed to sell her shares to Marcel for the current market value. As this is a transfer of shares in a privately owned trading company there are three reliefs to consider:

1. Business Asset Disposal relief (formerly known as Entrepreneur's relief)
2. Investors' relief
3. Hold over relief

Without considering any of the above, Gabby's capital gains tax computation for 2020/21 would be follows:

	100%	40%
	£	£
Market value	1,500,000	600,000
Less: Base cost	–	–
Less: Annual exemption		(12,300)
Taxable gain		587,700
Capital gains tax at 20%		**117,540**

Gabby would have a capital gains tax liability of £117,540. This would be payable to HMRC by 31 January 2021.

Let's now consider each of the above reliefs

BUSINESS ASSET DISPOSAL RELIEF (FORMERLY KNOWN AS ENTREPRENEUR'S RELIEF)

14.8 Business Asset Disposal relief is a capital gains tax relief available to individuals who make a qualifying business disposal. The relief is available to sole traders, partners and company directors and employees. Qualifying gains are taxed at a reduced rate of 10%. The maximum lifetime limit has been reduced from £10 million to £1 million from 22 March 2020. Therefore only the first £1 million of gains in an entrepreneurs lifetime will be eligible for the 10% rate.

Main qualifying conditions

14.9 The shareholder must:

- hold shares in a trading company or holding company of a trading group;
- be an officer of the company (director or employee);
- hold at least 5% of the shares;
- be entitled to at least 5% of profits on sale/winding up;
- have met the above conditions for 24 months immediately prior to the sale.

The conditions by way of a flow chart are below.

Business Asset Disposal relief conditions

14.10

Flowchart 14A

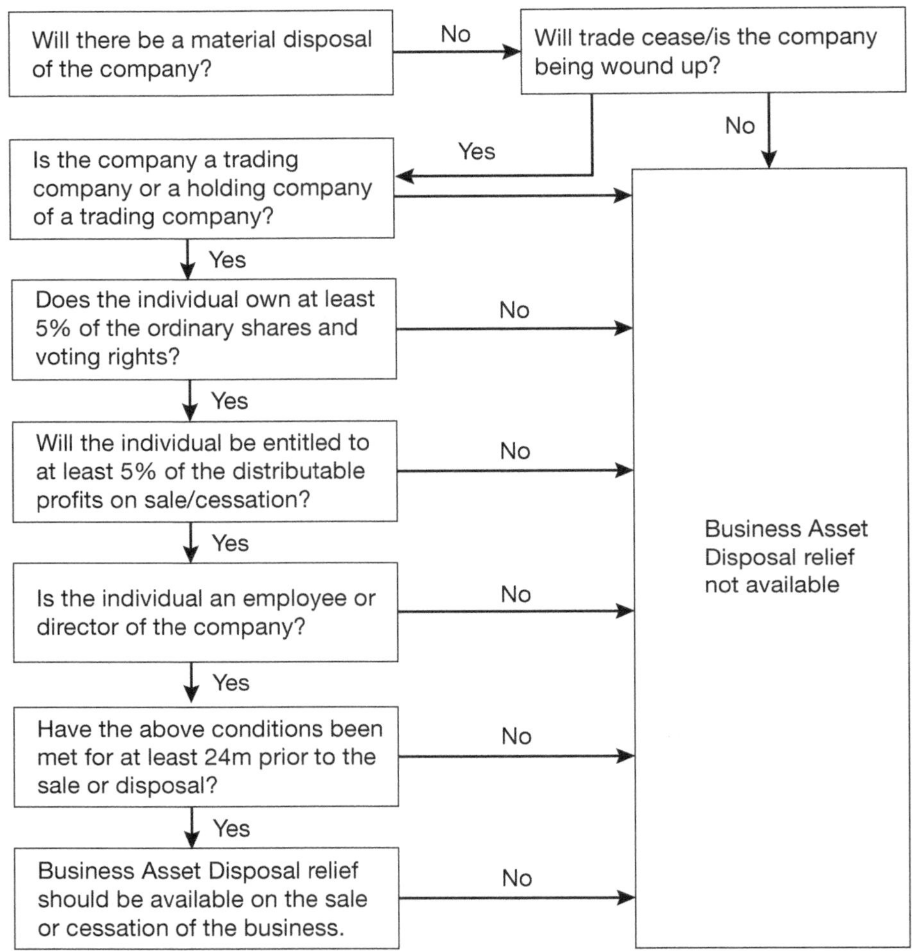

Detail on the conditions

14.11 Each of the conditions must be met for the relief to apply. We will briefly comment on each condition in some more detail below.

Material disposal

14.12 The relief is available where there is either:

- a **material disposal** of **business assets;**

- a disposal which is associated with a material disposal (not considered further in this text);
- a disposal of trust business assets (not considered further in this text).

14.13 **Business asset** means:

- whole or part of a sale trade/partnership business;
- a disposal of an asset used in the business at the time the business ceases to be carried on, or
- a disposal of shares or securities in a company.

Trading company

14.14 Hold shares in a **trading** company or holding company of a **trading** group.

Business Asset Disposal relief is only available for trading companies. A trading company is 'a company carrying on trading activities whose activities do not include to a substantial extent activities other than trading activities'. An activity is carried on for the purpose of trade if it is carried on in the process of conducting or preparing to carry on the trade.

14.15 Note the definition says the activities do not include substantial extent activities which are not trading. HMRC considers substantial to be more than 20% and the 20% test is applied to criteria including:

- Turnover.
- Asset base.
- Expenses.
- Directors time.

14.16 For example, if Gem Ltd had purchased property with some of the retained earnings, the rental income from the shop would count as investment activities. Very broadly speaking if they owned say five rental properties and 50% of their turnover was coming from the rental properties the company would be unlikely to meet the conditions of trading.

Where a company has some investment activities it will be necessary for an expert to determine whether an Business Asset Disposal relief claim is likely to be successful.

Individual conditions

The definition of a material disposal depends on the type of asset sold

14.17 In the case of the sale/gift of shares or securities in a company, the disposal is 'material' if throughout the two years prior to either the disposal of the shares or the date the company ceased to be trading the company is a trading company or the holding company of a trading group and the taxpayers meet the following individual conditions:

- the individual holds at least 5% of the ordinary shares and voting rights of the company;
- is also beneficially entitled to at least 5% of the distributable profits and/or assets at winding up. (This second economic ownership test was effectively bought in to prevent individuals setting up complex ownership structures where they met the 5% ordinary shares and voting rights test but on sale they were actually entitled to less than 5%);
- and the taxpayer is an officer or employee of the company or for another company in the same group (no minimum hours' requirement, so full or part-time employees or directors are eligible).

14.18 Gem Ltd is a trading company, Marcel and Gabby both work for the company and are 60% and 40% shareholders of the company and have been so for over two years. Therefore, when Gabby transfers her shares to Marcel she will be able to claim Business Asset Disposal relief on the gain.

Gabby's tax computation would be as follows:

	100%	40%
	£	£
Market value	1,500,000	600,000
Less: Base cost	–	–
Less: Annual exemption		(12,300)
Taxable gain		587,700
Capital gains tax at 10%		**58,770**

> **Note:** Business Asset Disposal relief must be claimed on or before the first anniversary of the 31 January following the tax year of the qualifying disposal. For a disposal in 2020/21 Gabby would need to make the claim by 31 January 2023.

INVESTORS' RELIEF

14.19 Investors' relief is available where an individual makes a disposal of qualifying shares in a trading company. The definition of a trading company for Business Asset Disposal relief also applies for investors relief.

Where a claim for relief is made the gains will be taxed at 10%. The lifetime limit of £10 million has not been reduced (unlike with Business Asset Disposal relief).

Conditions

14.20 The company must be a trading company (see **14.14** and **14.15**). The shares must have been issued by the company on or after 17 March 2016 and must be held continuously for a period of at least three years. The shares must be new ordinary shares subscribed for by the individual for cash. At the time the shares were issued the company must have been unlisted.

14.21 There is no requirement for the investor to hold at least 5% of the voting rights as there is for Business Asset Disposal relief. The relief is only available to individuals who are officers or employees of the company.

14.22 Investors' relief will not be available to Gabby as her shares were issued before 17 March 2016 and she is an employee of the company. With the reduction of the Business Asset Disposal relief limit family business structures may change so as to give non-working spouses in the business shares which would qualify for investment relief on sale. However, for the relief to apply the shares must have been held for at least three years.

HOLDOVER RELIEF

14.23 Holdover relief (also called gift relief) applies when there is a transfer of business assets. As we have seen, as Gabby is connected to Marcel, when she transfers her shares to him she will be assessed to capital gains tax on the market value of the shares. In situations such as this, hold over relief is available to defer Gabby's gain on the shares. The gain is deferred by holding over the gain against the base cost of the shares in the hands of Marcel.

Gabby CGT computation	100%	40%
	£	£
Market value	1,500,000	600,000
Less: Base cost	–	–
Gain		600,000
Less: Holdover relief		(600,000)

Marcel new base cost	100%	40%
	£	£
Market value	1,500,000	600,000
Less: Held over gain	–	(600,000)
Marcel's base cost		0

Note: per HMRC guidance Holdover relief is now only available in divorce in exceptional circumstances (discussed at **14.26**). However, it is useful to understand how it operates before discussing the exceptional circumstances.

14.24 Therefore when Marcel sells the shares he will have a capital gains tax liability on the held over gain. The relief is only available when the asset gifted is a 'business asset'. Unquoted shares in a trading company are business assets for hold over relief purposes.

Holdover relief restrictions

14.25 Holdover relief is restricted where the donee pays the donor for the business assets. The amount of the restriction is equal to the consideration received.

For example, if Marcel paid Gabby £100,000 for her shares, the maximum hold over relief available for Gabby to claim would be £500,000. The gain of £100,000 would be immediately chargeable to capital gains tax.

Gabby CGT computation	100%	40%
	£	£
Market value	1,500,000	600,000
Less: Base cost	–	–
Gain		600,000
Excess proceeds		(100,000)
Gain eligible for Holdover relief		(500,000)
Chargeable gain		100,000

Gift relief is also restricted when a donor gifts shares in his personal company and that company holds 'non business assets'.

Holdover relief on divorce

14.26 HMRCs view has changed on whether holdover relief can be claimed on business assets in divorce.

Previously the authority for consideration on divorce was based on the case of *G v G* [2002] EWHC 1339 (Fam). Judge Coleridge stated that the idea that the right to a financial provision has a monetary value and stated : 'Neither party has any "rights" as such at all' and he was 'satisfied that...the wife gives no consideration for the transfer of shares that {he} ordered in her favour'. The takeaway from this is that no consideration is received and therefore hold over relief would be available in full providing all other conditions were met.

14.27 This view has now changed based on the judgement of the Court of Appeal in *Haines v Hill* [2007] EWCA Civ 1284. HMRC now argues that where there is a court order this automatically means there is actual consideration for the value equal to the market value of the assets transferred under the court order.[1]

1 See HMRC Capital Gains Tax Manual at CG66886.

14.28 As with the above example, applying the *Haines v Hill* precedent, Gabby would be deemed to have received consideration of £600,000 for her shares and thereby the gain eligible for hold over relief is reduced to nil.

14.29 It should be noted that HMRC manuals are not definitive statements of the law and have been effectively challenged on numerous times. HRMC does allow that 'exceptionally' it may be possible to prove that nothing was given up in exchange for an asset on divorce in which case hold over relief may apply.

14.30 In light of the change of guidance, for planning purposes, assume that hold over relief on divorce would not be available but it would be worth seeking further guidance if the there is significant liability which cannot be met due to lack of liquidity.

14.31 If Marcel and Gabby had separated in 2020/21 (the tax year of separation) then the transfer of shares could be done under the no gain no loss principles, Gabby could transfer her shares to Marcel and not incur a capital gains tax liability.

Extracting Cash from Gem Ltd

14.32 Marcel has very little personal savings, therefore he will need to utilise the retained cash in Gem Ltd to meet the £500,000 settlement. The standard way to extract money from a company would be for Marcel to withdraw the money as a dividend.

Withdraw the money as a dividend

14.33 At January 2020 there was £879,000 in the company bank account, we first need to deduct any taxes payable from that money to arrive at the available cash figure. It is important that all upcoming tax and business liabilities are considered ahead of any withdrawal of cash from the company.

	£	
Cash at bank	879,000	
Less: VAT	(80,000)	
Less: Corporation tax	(127,300)	
Net Cash	**671,700**	**this is the amount of cash available for withdrawal**

14.34 If Marcel withdrew £500,000 from the company this would be taxed as a dividend. It is May 2020 and Marcel has already withdrawn £20,000 as dividends, (£10,000 per month). He thinks he minimally needs £5,000 per month for the rest of the year. We have therefore factored in £70,000 of dividends for Marcel's income in the calculation.

The tax implications of withdrawing £500,000 are as follows:

	£	
Dividend income	570,000	£500,000 for the settlement + £70,000 in dividends
Less: dividend allowance	(2,000)	
Less: personal allowance	–	
Taxable income	568,000	
£37,500 at 7.5%	2,813	first £37,500 of dividend income is taxable at 7.5%
£112,500 at 32.5%	36,563	from £37,500 to £150,000 (which is £112,500) of dividend income is taxable at 32.5%
£418,000 at 38.1%	159,258	dividend income in excess of £150,000 is taxable at 38.1%
Total tax liability	**198,634**	
Total withdrawals	570,000	
Less tax	(198,634)	
Net income	**371,366**	

14.35 Marcel's effective rate of taxation on the withdrawal is 35%, total taxes divided by total income (198,634/570,000 × 100 = 35%). Therefore of the £500,000 withdrawn for the settlement, Marcel would pay tax of £175,000 and would only receive £325,000 net.

14.36 To calculate the gross withdrawal needed we need to gross up £500,000. To do this we multiple the net amount, £500,000 by the grossing up fraction. The grossing up fraction is 100 divided by 100 less the rate of tax. £500,000 × (100/100–35) this equals £769,230. Marcel would need to withdraw £769,230 to have £500,000 after taxes, and this is does not include the £70,000 dividends Marcel needs to live from.

14.37 The tax implications of:

(a) Gabby transferring her total shareholding to Marcel;

(b) Marcel withdrawing cash of £500,000 from Gem Ltd are:

	£
Gabby capital gains tax	58,770
Marcel income tax liability	175,000
Total tax	**233,770**

The company does not have £769,230 cash available so we shall look at other options.

TAKING A DIRECTORS LOAN

14.38 Another option Marcel could consider is taking a loan from Gem Ltd. Marcel could take a directors' loan from the company, the loan would be free from income tax and national insurance. Therefore Marcel could take a loan of £500,000 and have net cash of £500,000 to meet the amount due for the settlement. As Marcel is a director and participator of the company there will be a tax charge levied on any amount of the loan outstanding after nine months after the end of the accounting period.

14.39 Marcel should also be charged interest on the loan to avoid the loan being treated as a benefit in kind which would bring it into the scope of national insurance. After taking the loan, Marcel would then have nine months from the end of the accounting period to repay the loan. If we assume an accounting end date of 31 December, the dates would work out as follows:

> Marcel withdraws a loan from Gem Ltd in June 2020 of £500,000. The company year end is 31 December 2020. If the loan is outstanding at 30 September 2021 Gem Ltd will have a corporation tax liability on the loan of £162,500. The corporation tax paid can be reclaimed when the loan is repaid in full.
>
> If the loan is written off Gem Ltd will be liable to class 1 National insurance on the amount of the loan and Marcel will pay income tax on the loan as though it was a dividend payment. Gem Ltd will not receive corporation tax relief for the amount of the loan written off.
>
> If the loan of £500,000 is written off, the tax implications will be as follows:
>
> Gem ltd – Class 1 NIC liability of £69,000 (13.8% of £500,000)
>
> Marcel will have an income tax of £175,000 (being the effective rate of 35% on £500,000)
>
> Total taxes equal £244,000.

SELLING THE COMPANY – BUSINESS ASSET DISPOSAL RELIEF

14.40 Marcel and Gabby have already been approached by major department stores who are interested in purchasing their company. They think they could achieve a sale value of £1.5 million. The £1 million Business Asset Disposal relief lifetime limit applies to each individual.

If Marcel and Gabby sold Gem Ltd they may be eligible to claim Business Asset Disposal relief on the sale.

Company conditions

14.41 Is there a material disposal of the company? (tick)

Is it a trading company? (tick)

Individual conditions

14.42 Do Gabby and Marcel both own at least 5% of the ordinary share capital and have at least 5% of the voting rights? (tick)

On sale will Gabby and Marcel be entitled to at least 5% of profits on distribution? (tick)

Do Gabby and Marcel both work for the company? (tick) **Note:** there is no minimum hours' requirement so it does not impact Gabby's claim that she works part time.

Have Gabby and Marcel met the conditions for the 24 months prior to sale? (tick)

14.43 Business Asset Disposal relief will be available on sale. The tax computation is as follows:

		Marcel	Gabby
	100%	60%	40%
	£	£	£
Sale proceeds	1,500,000	900,000	600,000
Less: base cost			
Less: annual exemption		(12,300)	(12,300)
Taxable gain		887,700	587,700
Capital gains tax at 10%	**147,400**	**88,700**	**58,700**

The total tax liability would be £147,400.

Marcel and Gabby would have the following net proceeds:

- Gabby £541,300.
- Marcel £811,300.

WINDING THE COMPANY UP

14.44 Business Asset Disposal relief also applies on cessation of trade. If the company is wound up the cash in the company can be withdrawn as capital and if Business Asset Disposal relief applies, tax is paid at 10%. If Marcel and Gabby decided to wind the company up they would be able to claim Business Asset Disposal relief as all the conditions have been met.

The available cash in the company is £671,700:

Wind up		60%	40%
		Marcel	Gabby
	£	£	£
Capital distribution	671,700	403,020	268,680
Less: annual exemption		(12,300)	(12,300)
Taxable gain		390,720	256,380
Capital gains tax at 10%		**39,072**	**25,638**

Marcel and Gabby would have the following net proceeds:

- Gabby £243,042.
- Marcel £363,948.

Clearly there are so many factors to consider before winding a company up, however from a tax perspective one important consideration is what will Gabby and Marcel do next.

14.45 In the past some individuals ran companies, let cash build up in the companies, ceased trading, extracted the cash paying 10% and then started another company with the intention of doing the same thing. This was known as phoenixing. In 2016 the government brought in new rules to target these behaviours. Very broadly the new rules state that individuals will not get the favourable tax treatment on cessation if, within two years the individual is involved with carrying on an activity which is the same as the old company carried on or even one that is similar to it.

14.46 HMRC's aim is to establish whether the company was wound up solely to ensure capital treatment on what would otherwise have been income.

14.47 Therefore, if Marcel wound up the company only to secure lower tax treatment and then set up another jewellery company, Business Asset Disposal relief on his capital distribution would be withdrawn. Not only would Business Asset Disposal relief be withdrawn but the distribution would be treated as income not capital. The withdrawal would be treated as dividend.

Marcel's liability would therefore be:

	£
Income	403,020
Less: dividend allowance	(2,000)
Less: personal allowance	–
Taxable income	401,020
£37,500 at 7.5%	2,813
£112,500 at 32.5%	36,563
£253,020 at 38.1%	96,401
Total tax liability	**135,776**

Marcel's tax liability would increase by approximately £100,000.

SUMMARY OF OPTIONS

14.48 So far we have looked at the tax implications of Gabby transferring shares to Marcel and Marcel withdraws cash available from Gem Ltd. Marcel and Gabby sell Gem Ltd and Marcel and Gabby wind up Gem Ltd.

COMPANY BUY BACK OF OWN SHARES

14.49 One option Gabby and Marcel could consider is a company buy back of shares. This would enable Marcel to use the money from the business without incurring an income tax charge on the withdrawal.

14.50 A purchase of shares by an owner managed company is usually treated as an income distribution meaning that income tax would be payable on the amount paid to the individual (Gabby) by the company. However, if certain conditions are satisfied, capital treatment can apply meaning that capital gains tax will apply.

> **Note:** A company purchase of own shares must meet certain legal requirements otherwise the transaction may not be legal and unforeseen tax implications could arise. Therefore, if clients think this option may be useful to them ensure company legal advice is sought.

14.51 For the purchase of the shares to be treated as capital (and enable Business Asset Disposal relief to apply) the following conditions must be met:

- The purchasing company must be an unquoted trading company.
- The purpose of the payment must benefit the trade and no schemes or arrangement tests are met. The trade benefit test is not determined in the legislation, however HMRC includes the following example as a scenario where the trade benefit test would be met 'Where a disagreement between shareholders over the management of the company is leading to an adverse effect on the trade of the company, then the purchase of own shares removes the dissenting shareholder.'[2]
- The shareholder must be UK resident.
- The shares must have been owned for a minimum of five years.
- The shareholder's interest in the company must be substantially reduced.
- The shareholder must have no continuing connection to the company immediately after the purchase.

2 CG58635 Capital Gains Manual.

- If Gem Ltd purchased Gabby's shares for £500,000 would capital treatment apply?
- Gem Ltd is an unquoted trading company.
- Is the purchase to benefit the trade? As Gabby and Marcel are divorcing this would suggest that there would likely be disagreements between shareholders which could have an adverse effect on the trade of the company.
- Gabby is UK resident.
- Gabby has owned the shares since 2012 so the five-year test has been met.
- Gabby would sell all of her shares, therefore she would meet the test of her shareholding being substantially reduced.
- Gabby does not want to work for Gem Ltd after the disposal of her shares so she would meet this test too. It will be vital that Gabby remains working for Gem Ltd up until the disposal to ensure that she qualifies for Business Asset Disposal relief.
- Gabby's liability on a company buy back of shares would be £48,770. Gem Ltd would have no tax implications.

Company buy back of shares	£
Capital payment	500,000
Less: annual exemption	(12,300)
	487,700
Capital gains tax at 10%	**48,770**

It is possible to obtain HMRC clearance on a company buy back to ensure that capital treatment is given.

SUMMARY

14.52

	Gabby		Marcel		Total Taxes
		£		£	£
Gabby transfers her shareholding to Marcel, Marcel withdraws £500,000 from Gem Ltd	Capital gains tax BADR relief at 10%	58,770	Income tax at dividend rates	175,000	233,700
Sell Gem Ltd, proceeds £1,500,000	Capital gains tax BADR relief at 10%	87,700	Capital gains tax BADR relief at 10%	58,770	147,470

	Gabby		Marcel		Total Taxes
		£		£	£
Wind up Gem Ltd, total capital £671,700	Capital gains tax BADR relief at 10%	39,072	Capital gains tax BADR relief at 10%	25,638	64,710
Company buy back of shares	Capital gains tax BADR relief at 10%	48,770		–	48,770

CHAPTER 15

Land Taxes

Contents at a Glance

LAND TAXES IN ENGLAND AND NORTHERN IRELAND AND WALES

15.1 There is not a huge amount to consider in terms of land taxes and divorce as there is usually no immediate charge to land taxes when land is transferred in connection with a divorce. Land taxes are taxes on land transactions. They are normally applied on the completion of the purchase of land and are charged on the consideration for the property. Therefore, if a property is gifted and no consideration is paid, land taxes will not be applicable. Note that where a property is gifted with a mortgage attached to the property the mortgage is deemed to be consideration.

15.2 There is a catch all provision which states that all transactions which take place in contemplation of divorce are ignored for stamp duty purposes (even when the transaction takes place after the end of the tax year of separation). Therefore, when transferring properties after the end of the tax year of separation, capital gains tax is the most important tax to consider as there will likely be an immediate charge to capital gains tax on transfer. There are some areas where capital gains tax and stamp duty land tax cross over and unfortunately, due to different definitions in the taxes, there can be some complexity when both of these taxes apply.

15.3 Whilst there will be no immediate charge to stamp duty land tax on divorce it will need to be considered in the context of the additional rate of stamp duty and first-time buyers' relief (in limited circumstances).

15.4 Land taxes are devolved taxes, meaning that England and Northern Ireland, Scotland and Wales each have their own land taxes. They each have their own rates for land tax and names.

England and Northern Ireland	Stamp Duty Land Tax (SDLT)
Scotland	Land and Buildings Transaction Tax (LBTT)
Wales	Land Transaction Tax (LTT)

We will only cover the rates applicable to England and Northern Ireland and Wales.

15.5 The rates of the taxes are below:

Figure 15A

Property stamp tax			
Residential Price/ premium payable	**England & NI SDLT**	**England & NI SDLT additional rate**	**Wales LTT**
£1 – £125,000	Nil	Nil	Nil
£125,001 – £145,000	2%	5%	Nil
£145,001 – £180,000	2%	5%	Nil
£180,001 – £250,000	2%	5%	3.5%
£250,001 – £325,000	5%	8%	5%
£325,001 – £400,000	5%	8%	5%
£400,001 – £750,000	5%	8%	7.5%
£750,001 – £925,000	5%	8%	10%
£925,001 – £1.5m	10%	13%	10%
Over £1.5m	12%	15%	12%

PAYMENT AND FILING DATES

15.6 The deadline for submitting a stamp duty land tax return and paying any tax due is 14 days from the effective date of the transaction.

15.7 If the stamp duty land tax return is not filed within 14 days of the effective date there is a £100 penalty and where the return is more than three months late there will be an additional penalty of £200. Interest will be applied to any late payment of taxes.

15.8 If the land transaction return is more than one year late a tax-based penalty may apply depending on the reason for the late return.

TRANSACTIONS IN CONNECTION WITH A DIVORCE

15.9 Transactions made:

- by course order;
- an agreement by spouses in contemplation of divorce;
- as a result of a judicial separation

are exempt from charge to stamp duty land tax. This exemption is not available if the transaction involves someone other than the spouse.

Illustration 15A – Stamp duty in divorce – Richard and Judy

Richard and Judy have been married for seven years. They work together and are higher rate taxpayers. Working and living together proved to be too stressful and they have decided to divorce.

Richard owns six investment properties and the main home. Judy has never owned a property.

As part of the divorce Richard will transfer three of his investment properties to Judy.

There will be no liability to stamp duty land tax on the transfer.

Note: if the transfer takes place after the tax year of separation Richard may have a capital gains tax liability on the deemed market value of the transfer. It may be possible for Richard and Judy to claim rollover relief on the property. See Chapter 12 for more information.

Illustration 15B – Stamp duty in divorce – Piers and Susanna

Piers and Susanna are getting divorced. They are both higher rate taxpayers.

Piers and Susanna own a family home together and an investment property bought for £230,000 is now worth £350,000. Susanna's father, Ian, moved into the investment property a few years ago and has been paying Piers and Susanna rent.

Piers and Susanna are considering selling the investment property as part of the divorce. Ian has said he would like to buy the property and continue living there. As part of the proceedings it is agreed that Ian will pay £300,000 to Susanna and Piers for the investment property.

As Ian is connected to Susanna and Piers they will be assessed on capital gains tax at the deemed market value of the property, being £350,000 rather than the actual amount Ian is paying of £300,000. The stamp duty that Ian will pay on the purchase will be based on the actual consideration of the property.

Piers and Susanna – Capital gains tax computation on the sale of the property:

		Piers	Susanna
	£	£	£
Market value	350,000	175,000	175,000
Less: Costs of transfer	(2,500)	(1,250)	(1,250)
Less: Purchase price	(230,000)	(115,000)	(115,000)
Less: Costs of acquisition	(2,300)	(1,150)	(1,150)
Gain	115,200	57,600	57,600
Less: Annual exemption		(12,300)	(12,300)
Taxable gain		45,300	45,300
Capital gains tax at 28%		12,684	12,684

Ian's Stamp Duty Land Tax Computation:

Total consideration	£	300,000
£0 – £125,000 at 0%		
£125,001 – £250,000 at 2%	£	2,500
£250,001 – £300,000 at 5%	£	2,500
Total	£	5,000

Summary

As result of the transaction:

Piers and Susanna will each have a capital gains tax liability of £12,684, **this is payable within 30 days of the transfer.**

Ian will have a stamp duty land tax liability of £5,000, this is payable within 14 days of the transaction.

FIRST-TIME BUYERS' RELIEF

15.10 Whilst this is unlikely to come into play in many circumstances it is important to consider the potential loss of first-time buyers' relief. It may be necessary to quantify the potential loss of the relief to the receiving spouse.

15.11 First-time buyers purchasing a home to live in as their main residence will pay no stamp duty land tax if the purchase is below £300,000. If the property is below £500,000, they will pay a reduced rate of 5% on the value between £300,000 and £500,000. The relief is only available if an individual has never had a major interest in any other property. This includes by way of gift or inheritance.

Illustration 15C – Loss of first-time buyers' relief – Richard and Judy

Continuing on from the earlier example, prior to the transfer of the properties Judy had never owned a property. After the transfer of the properties Judy will own a major interest in at least one property. Therefore, as a result, she will no longer qualify as a first-time buyer.

After the divorce, if Judy wanted to purchase her own property to live in, she would not qualify for the lower rate of stamp duty as a first-time buyer and she will be subject to the additional rate of stamp duty as she now has a major interest in a residential property.

If Judy was going to spend £400,000 on her new home the SDLT liability differs as follows:

SDLT as a first-time buyer £5,000

0% up to £300,000	£0
5% on £300,001 to£400,000	£5,000
Total	**£5,000**

This will not apply to Judy as she is no longer a first-time buyer.

SDLT single property £10,000

0% up to £125,000	£0
2% on £125,001 to £250,000	£2,500
5% on £250,001 to £400,000	£7,500
Total	**£10,000**

This will not apply to Judy as she owns more than one property and is not replacing her main home.

SDLT additional property £22,000

3% up to £125,000	£3,750
5% on £125,001 to £250,000	£6,250
8% on £250,001 to £400,000	£12,000
Total	**£22,000**

This is the rate that will apply to Judy on her next purchase

HIGHER RATE OF STAMP DUTY LAND TAX

15.12 Since 1 April 2016 there has been a higher rate of stamp duty for individuals purchasing another property. There is a 3% surcharge of stamp duty land tax on purchases of additional residential property.

15.13 If at the end of the day of the transaction the individual will own more than one residential property, the additional rate of stamp duty will apply.

15.14 Individuals are not subject to the additional charge if they are replacing their main home. Therefore, where people own rental properties, in the case that they are purchasing a property to replace their main home, the additional rate will not apply, even though, at the end of the day of the transaction the individual will own more than one residential property.

15.15 The replacement of the main home must be within 36 months for the additional rate not to apply. This 36-month period looks forwards and backwards. If the previous main home is sold then the individual has up to 36 months from that date to purchase a replacement property without incurring the additional charge. Equally, if the periods of ownership overlap, the individual has up to 36 months to sell the original main home and then they can obtain relief of the additional stamp duty paid.

Illustration 15D – Additional Rate – Richard and Judy

In the example of Richard and Judy, Richard owns the family home and investment properties. If Richard was to sell his main home, he is able to purchase another main home without incurring the additional rate of stamp duty land tax. For the additional rate not to apply, Richard must:

- be purchasing a replacement of his main home;
- be completing the transaction within three years of disposing of his first home or buying his second home.

Richard has found a new home he wants to buy, it is £750,000.

He has not yet sold his original main home, therefore the additional rate will apply in the first instance.

SDLT (additional property) £50,000

3% up to £125,000	£3,750
5% on £125,001 to £250,000	£6,250
8% on £250,001 to £750,000	£40,000
Total	**£50,000**

SDLT (single property) £27,500

0% up to £125,000	£0
2% on £125,001 to £250,000	£2,500
5% on £250,001 to £750,000	£25,000
Total	**£27,500**

As Richard still owns his original main home, he will be required to pay the additional rate of stamp duty land tax, meaning he has a liability of £50,000.

If he sells his original main home within three years then he will receive a refund of £22,500. This refund is obtained by amending the original SDLT return and this must be done within 12 months of the purchase of the second main home.

If Judy wanted to purchase a main home she would have to pay the higher rate of stamp duty (see **Figure 15A**), this is because she does not have a main home to replace and she has investment properties. Therefore, at the end of the date of the transaction she has more than one property and she is not replacing her main home so the additional rate applies. If Judy sold all of the investment properties then she would pay the standard rate of stamp duty land tax on her future purchase.

Equally if Judy moved into one of the properties as her main home she would then be able to pay the standard rate of stamp duty land tax if she replaced that property with another main home. Note that if the properties were subject to a rollover relief claim Judy would not be able to move into one of the properties as her main home without jeopardising the relief. Rollover relief is discussed in detail in Investment Properties (Chapter 12).

15.16 In the case of couples who jointly own a main home and investment properties, the date of disposal of the main home will be important to establish as that will be the date the 36-month rule applies from.

15.17 If an individual is purchasing another home during the proceedings, timing is likely to be an issue. Where an individual still owns a main home the additional rate of stamp duty will apply. The individual is then required to submit an amended Stamp Duty Land Tax return once the original property has sold to obtain a refund of the additional rate.

15.18 If a spouse is receiving investment properties and did not co-own the family home they are likely to face the higher rate of stamp duty when they purchase a home for themselves.

Example

Catherine and Alex are getting divorced. They have been separated for three years and it's agreed that Alex will transfer his share of the main home to

Catherine. However, in the interim Alex has found a property that he would like to purchase.

As Alex is going to transfer his share of the FHM to Catherine he is disposing of his main home and by buying another home he satisfies the conditions of replacing his main home. However, if he buys his new home **before** he transfers the FHM to Catherine then he will be subject to the higher stamp duty rates. Once the transfer is complete Alex can then apply for a refund of the additional rate as long as the transfer happens within three years of him buying his second property.

If he buys the new property after he transfers the FMH to Catherine the higher rate of stamp duty will not apply.

REQUIRED TO STAY AS A LEGAL OWNER

15.19 Where a court order is issued which prevents an individual from disposing of their interest in the main home, the property does not count as owned by that person for the purposes of establishing if the additional rate applies.[1] Certain conditions must be met for this to apply.

15.20 The conditions are as follows:

- the person (A) has a major interest in a dwelling;
- the property adjustment order has been made in respect of the interest for the benefit of another person (B) and the dwelling is:
  - B's only or main residence, and
  - is not A's only or main residence.

15.21 If the conditions are met then A is treated as **having no interest in the property**. No election needs to be claimed for this to apply. Clients may want to flag this to their conveyancing solicitor to ensure the higher rate is not incorrectly applied.

15.22 Note that the legislation states 'A is to be treated as having no interest in the dwelling' and NOT that 'A is treated as having disposed of their interest in the property'. Therefore it is unlikely that the replacement property provisions discussed above would apply here.

15.23 As such if a person has other properties this provision will not result in them not being charged the additional rate of stamp duty land tax.

The conditions by way of flow chart are below:

1 FA 2003, Sch 4ZA, para 9B – Finance Act 2018.

Additional rate of Stamp Duty in cases where legal ownership is retained – Flow Chart 15A.

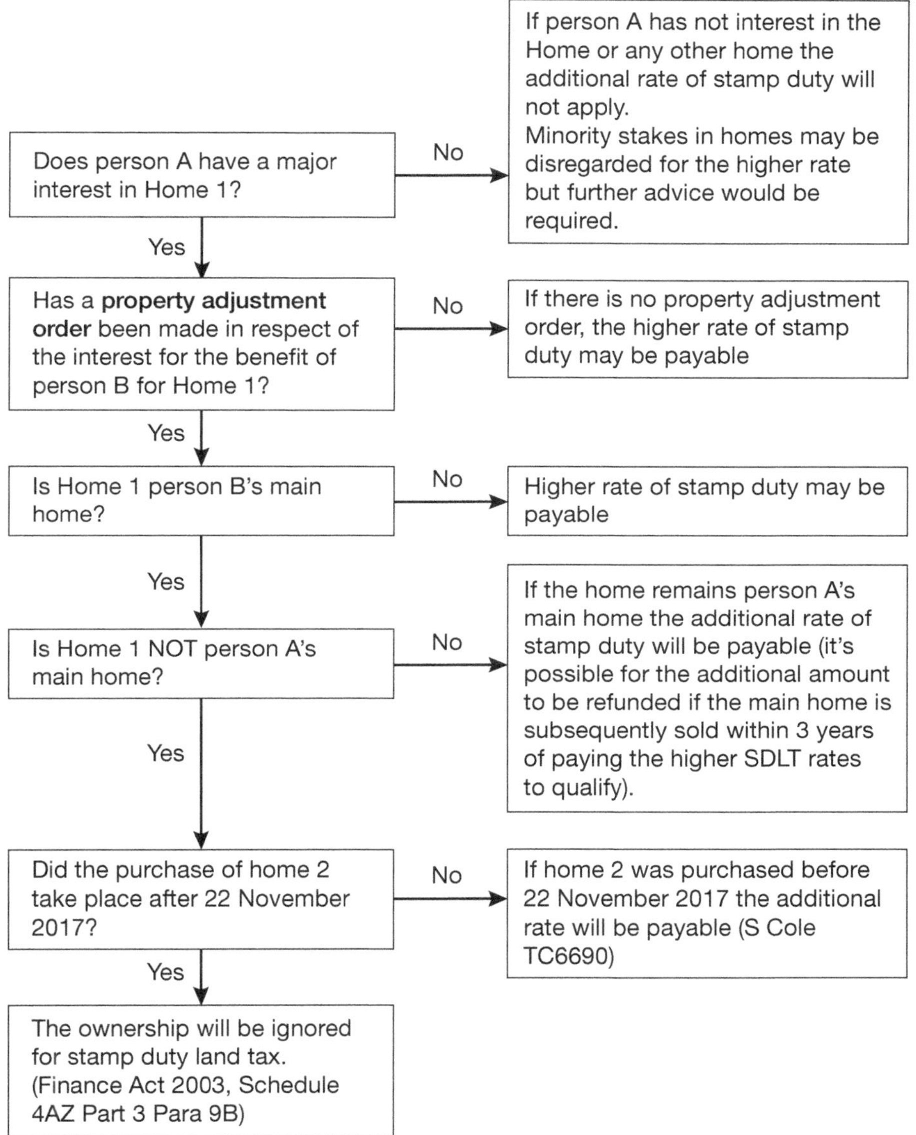

Illustration 15E – Main home subject to a Mesher order – Richard and Judy

If we assume that as part of the divorce Richard was required to stay on as the legal owner of the family home for five years. If during this period Richard wanted to purchase another property to live in, would this purchase be subject to stamp duty land tax at the higher rate? Let us consider the conditions listed above.

Richard has a major interest in the family home (tick)

The property adjustment order has been made in respect of the interest for the benefit of Judy (tick)

The property is:

- Judy's main home (tick)
- It is not Richard's main home (tick)

The conditions have been met, therefore Richard is deemed not to have an interest in the family home.

However, Richard does still have interests in other properties, therefore the additional rate would still apply.

If Richard owned no other properties and this exemption applied, the additional rate of stamp duty would not be payable.

Note: Where clients have a main home and own other properties, consider whether the additional rate of stamp duty may apply in the future.

MAIN HOME

15.24 In Chapter 11 we discussed individuals can elect a main home if they live in more than one property, for example, a property they live in near work and a holiday home. These rules do not apply to stamp duty land tax. The main home for stamp duty land tax is always the property which is the main home on the basis of the facts. Therefore, you could have situations where individuals have a main home for CGT and a different main home for SDLT. As such an individual could sell one home and treat it as their principal private residence but not be eligible to pay the standard rate of stamp duty when they buy another property as they are not replacing their actual main home. An extended example of this is below.

Illustration 15F – Two different main homes – Rhys and Jac

Rhys and Jac met in 2002 and married in March 2014. They are both UK resident. They have two children.

Jac's parents died in February 2004 and left him three properties:

Property address	Location	Current market value	Value when inherited
Ronda Sant Pere	Spain	£3,100,000	£1,400,000
Lockmead Close	London	£450,000	£290,000
Admiral Street	Leeds	£400,000	£280,000

In June 2011 Jac and Rhys purchased their family home in Sussex for £650,000. It is now worth approximately £900,000.

Rhys owns no other properties.

Since 2004 Rhys and Jac have spent four months of each year in the property in Spain. The property has no mortgage and in 2009 Jac transferred 50% of the property to Rhys. The property has never been rented out.

Rhys and Jac separated in March 2020. It is July 2020 and they have agreed to sell the property in Spain and split the proceeds. Jac will keep the properties in London and Leeds and will remain on the title of the Sussex home for three years. After three years Rhys will take over the property if he can secure a mortgage on the property or it will be sold.

Jac has said he will purchase another main home as both the London and Leeds properties are currently let out.

What are the capital gains tax and stamp duty implications of the above?

One can typically start with the capital gains tax position.

1 property is being sold immediately (Spain, Ronda Sant Pere)

50% of 1 property will be transferred (Sussex property)

There are two properties which could potentially qualify as the main home as Rhys and Jac have resided in both properties, the one in Sussex and the one in Spain. Principal Private Residence relief will be available to reduce some of the gain. As PPR is only available for periods of actual occupation (not reduced for holidays) the Sussex home would qualify for the whole gain to be exempt but Ronda Sant Pere would only qualify for partial relief.

Rhys and Jac have spent four months of every year at Ronda Sant Pere since inheriting it.

First let us work out the capital gains tax liability on each property if no relief was claimed:

Ronda Sant Pere – No PPR claim

		Rhys	**Jac**
	£	£	£
Proceeds	3,100,000	1,550,000	1,550,000
Less: Costs of sale	(46,500)	(23,250)	(23,250)
Less: Base cost	(1,400,000)	(700,000)	(700,000)
Chargeable gain	1,653,500	826,750	826,750
Less: Annual exemption		(12,300)	(12,300)
Taxable gain		814,450	814,450
Capital gains tax at 28%		228,046	228,046
Total tax due			**456,092**

Matrimonial Home – Sussex No PPR claim

		Rhys	Jac
	£	£	£
Proceeds	900,000		
Costs of sale	(13,500)		
Purchase price	(650,000)		
Acquisition costs	(3,250)		
Chargeable Gain	233,250	116,625	116,625
Less: annual exemption		(12,300)	(12,300)
Taxable gain		104,325	104,325
Capital gains tax at 28%		29,211	29,211
Total tax due			**58,422**

Ronda Sant Pere – with PPR claim

		Rhys	Jac
	£	£	£
Proceeds	3,100,000	1,550,000	1,550,000
Less: Costs of sale	(46,500)	(23,250)	(23,250)
Less: Base cost	(1,400,000)	(700,000)	(700,000)
Gain	1,653,500	826,750	826,750
Less: PPR	(603,528)	(301,764)	(301,764)
$\mathbf{1{,}653{,}500 \times \frac{73}{200}}$			
Chargeable gain	1,049,973	524,986	524,986
Less AE		(12,300)	(12,300)
Taxable gain		512,686	512,686
Capital gains tax at 28%		143,552	143,552
Total Tax			**287,104**

PPR fraction is total occupation / total ownership. The property will be owned for 16.5 years and Rhys and Jac have occupied the property for 4 months every year for the past 16 years 4 × 15 = 64 months plus 9 months deemed occupation = 73

Matrimonial Home – Sussex with PPR claim

		Rhys	Jac
	£	£	£
Proceeds	900,000		
Costs of sale	(13,500)		

Purchase price	(650,000)			
Acquisition costs	(3,250)			
Gain	233,250			
Less: PPR		(233,250)	(233,250)	PPR fraction is total occupation / total ownership. Rhys and Jac have occupied the property for the whole period of ownership
$\mathbf{233{,}250 \times \frac{112}{112}}$				
Chargeable gain		–	–	
Total tax due			**–**	

Summary of options

Rhys and Jac can only claim PPR on one property at a time. They must both agree which property they wish to nominate as their PPR and they must notify HMRC. If no nomination is made the PPR will attach to the property which is their main home based on the facts (which would be the Sussex home).

If an election is made it would save approximately £100,000 in capital gains tax. However, it would mean no PPR will be available on the Sussex home for the same period.

Option one	£
Sussex (no PPR Claim)	58,590
Ronda Sant Pere (PPR Claim)	287,104
Total Tax	**345,694**

Option two	£
Sussex (PPR Claim)	–
Ronda Sant Pere (no PPR Claim)	456,092
Total Tax	**456,092**

Therefore if Rhys and Jac elect to treat Ronda Sant Pere as their main home they will pay approximately £100,000 less tax on disposal.

They will have to make a joint election to HMRC.

No PPR will be available on the Sussex home for the period 2011 to 2020. Therefore, when Jac transfers the Sussex home to Rhys in the future, there will be a capital gains tax liability on the transfer and when Rhys sells the property in the future he will also have a capital gains tax liability.

Stamp Duty Land Tax

Jac is planning on using the proceeds from his half of the sale of Ronda Sant Pere to purchase a main home for himself in London.

The additional rate of stamp duty will be payable on this purchase. This is because Jac is not replacing his **actual** main home, which on the facts is the Sussex property. Whilst his requirement to legally remain owner of the Sussex home can be ignored for SDLT purposes, Jac still owns two other properties.

Therefore the additional rate at 3% will apply on the purchase on Jac's next property.

LAND TAXES – CHECKLIST

15.24

		Yes/No/ NA	Risk	Mitigation	Ref
Transfers outside the marriage	Is a property being transferred to anyone outside of the marriage?	☐ Yes ☐ No ☐ N/A	The stamp duty land exemption on divorce only applies when the properties are being transferred within the marriage. Properties being sold or transferred to other parties outside of the marriage will be within the scope of stamp duty land tax.	Stamp duty land tax is charged on consideration. The purchaser of the new property will be assessed to stamp duty land tax on the amount they are paying for it. This is slightly different to the capital gains tax rules where sometimes market value is subsisted for actual proceeds.	**15.13**
First-time buyers' relief	Has one party never owned a property before?	☐ Yes ☐ No ☐ N/A	If one party has never owned a property before and they are receiving property by way of transfer then they will lose any future entitlement to first time buyers' relief. The relief is 0% on property purchases up to £300,000 and a reduced rate of 5% on properties up to £500,000.	Quantify the potential loss and ensure your client is aware that the receiving of a property will mean they lose their entitlement to the relief. It is irrelevant that they are not buying a property.	**15.10**

		Yes/No/ NA	Risk	Mitigation	Ref
Additional 3% rate	Is one party buying a replacement main home before former main home is transferred or sold?	☐ Yes ☐ No ☐ N/A	If an individual buys a new home before they sell or transfer their share of FMH they will be subject to the additional rate of stamp duty land tax on the purchase.	The additional amount of stamp duty land tax paid will be refunded if the original home is sold/transferred within 3 years of the second home being purchased. The refund is obtained by amending the original stamp duty land tax return. Therefore this is likely to be more of a cashflow issue, but the values can be substantial.	**15.12**
	Is one party remaining legal owner of the property?	☐ Yes ☐ No ☐ N/A	If an individual has to remain an owner of the property through a court order the interest in this property is ignored when considering if the additional rate is payable.	If the interest in the property can be ignored this means the additional rate will not be payable if that property is the only property that individual owns. If the individual owns other properties the additional rate will still apply.	**15.19**
	At the end of the transactions will one party have investment properties but no main home?	☐ Yes ☐ No ☐ N/A	As they own properties they may be subject to the additional rate of stamp duty when purchasing another property. However if the property they buy is intended to be their main home the additional rate should not apply if it is within 3 years of the original transfer.	If they have transferred or sold their main home they have 3 years to purchase another property and benefit from paying the standard rate of stamp duty land tax.	**15.21**

CHAPTER 16

We let down our clients by making insufficient use of available experts

Contents at a Glance

16.01 Generally, the positive contribution from experts in financial remedy work reaches further along the continuum of our cases than we might assume. Or put it another way, whilst the court might be seeking to contain provision of experts' reports, by and large solicitors may be failing to invite in the help as often as they should:

- experts are generally much cheaper than we, solicitors, think (they cost far less to provide a detailed authoritative report than we would take splashing about in the shallows trying to get even a ranging shot); and
- it is, perhaps a small miracle that we escape without criticism or complaint quite as often as we seem to. (But in an increasingly consumer society, that strategy is probably a flawed one to depend upon for the long-term.)

The pros and cons might line up as follows:

In favour of getting help	*Against*
(1) The risk of getting it wrong … or of not having the numbers wholly right/ accessing all possible benefits or exemptions for the client.	(2) Knowing who to use/when to use them/ how much the help is likely to cost or how best to access it.
	(3) The cost and admin 'hassle' of issuing the instructions and the delay of getting back the answers. The need to process the guidance at the end.
(4) Meets the need of providing an authoritative answer when acting in a partisan process.	
	(5) May ask the wrong question and need further help.

In favour of getting help	*Against*
(6) Builds connection/ skills and experience for the next case.	

16.02 The focus of this section is to recognise that solicitors are generally responsible for developing and implementing case strategy and its purposes include:

- recognising the need for experts;
- building familiarity and expertise in spotting that they are needed;
- clarifying how they should get involved and when the process for doing so should start; and
- helping systemise how experts are involved and how to work with them.

16.03 The table above summarises the arguments for and against involving a tax expert. By helping with the problems on the right-hand side, the benefits on the left-hand side can flourish and then expertise will build through experience.

16.04 The materials in the Appendix are designed to provide a comprehensive and safe structure for:

- the process of engaging experts and how to work on the case with them;
- formulating the questions to ask;
- making the right enquiries of the expert that the judge will expect to see before leave is given and doing so at the right time so that the relevant material is available on time;
- making the application (a suggested model order is available in the Appendix that fills in the gaps around the standard FPR 25 scheme);
- building better relationships with experts generally.

Some of the models that are set out in this section will be needed in word format and they are all downloadable from Sofia's site, see the www.sofiathomas.co.uk/FPR25/ tab on her site.

FIVE FLAVOURS OF EXPERT

16.05 Experts come in different flavours and how we interact with them will alter accordingly.

(1) The default[1] will be the *joint single expert or 'JSE'*; here:
   - the expert is appointed by both parties but serves the court;[2]

1 Practice Direction (PD)25D 2.1. And see Mostyn J in *J v J* [2014] EWHC 3654 (Fam).
2 Family Procedure Rules 2010 (FPR), r 25.3; and PD25B 3.1 & 4.1.

- their work will be defined by the instruction letter, prepared by the parties[3] (and in cases of conflict settled by the court[4]);
- their independence is fundamental;[5]
- there will be no separate communications by the parties with the expert or by the expert with either party:[6] communications are transparent and copied to all.

(2) There may be simpler situations where *the aligned expert* meets the needs for clarity about the situation. Here one party's own professional may provide an opinion on the complex/technical situation. This would place the expert in the position of being aligned, rather than a joint or neutral expert. They may provide an overview on which JSE input follows on … or the opinion may be adopted and not contested.

There is nothing to stop a party from attaching a short summary about the position to their form E.[7] Indeed:

- there is nothing to stop either party from instructing an expert;
- nor indeed anything to compel them to disclose a) that they have done so nor b) the report that is obtained.

What they may not do is ask for that information to be accepted as evidence without leave of the court under Family Procedure Rules 2010 (FPR), rule 25.4(3).

However, do note that where the report is disclosed then there may come into play:

- rule 25.14(3) … the court may direct that the instructions to the expert are disclosed and those instructions are not privileged against disclosure; and
- rule 25.15, which permits one party to adopt the expert's report provided by the other.

(3) In cases of complexity and/or higher conflict, either or both sides may elect to appoint their own expert, usually referred to as *a shadow expert*. This professional (who could in fact be the same person as the aligned expert, referred to above) will give guidance to the party instructing them as to:

- the form of the instructions to the JSE;
- the information to pursue to assist the JSE;
- the questions to raise on the JSE's report;
- and whether the report should be challenged in a more fundamental way (for example by seeking leave for a further report to be put in evidence).

3 The court may give permission to each side to provide their own instruction letter. This is perhaps a route that is insufficiently regularly considered (see FPR 25.12(3)).

4 FPR, r 14.12(2) and PD25D 6.1.

5 FPR, r 25.3(2) PF25B 4.1(d).

6 See Baron J in *K v K* [2005] EWHC 1070 at para 39.

7 See discussion from Mostyn J in *J v J* [2014] EWHC 3654 at para 45 quoted on page 346. We accept that this approach may arguably fall foul of the prohibition in r 25.4 against any expert evidence being put before the court in any form without permission (see r 25.4(2). However, the authority of Mostyn J seems to smooth this objection provided that the boundaries he lays out in the case are not crossed

The expert may also give help to the party directly, for example when they are concerned about how to deal with enquiries raised by the JSE.

The fact of the instruction of a shadow expert may not be apparent to the other side unless they are able to work it out, for example:

- from the quality of the input/questions being raised;
- from entries on the party's bank statement if the expert has been paid directly or from the Form H/H1.

(4) Fourth, there is *the partisan expert*:

- where there is a conflict of evidence, then:
  - the party seeking to bring in further expert evidence will need to seek permission under Part 25 for leave to give it in evidence in the proceedings;
  - if leave is given then it will be alongside procedures for identifying and narrowing of differences (see pages 290 and 377).
- the partisan expert will exist usually in two situations:
  - where each side has their own partisan expert from the outset; and
  - in the '*Daniels v Walker*' situation,[8] that is where there is a joint single expert already and an application is made (usually by one party only) for a further expert to be appointed.
- it is easy to think of this expert essentially as the shadow expert who has come out into the light, but this may not be appropriate:
  - the partisan expert will be appointed under Part 25 and so their primary duty will be to the court;
  - there are elements in the rules that are likely to call into question this former shadow expert's capacity to help the court:
    - i. (see PD25D 2.5) the letter of instructions and reports will be disclosed;
    - ii. the report must confirm the substance of the instructions and material underpinning the conclusions (PD25B 9.1);
    - iii. questions may be raised on the report by the other party (r 25.10(1)(a);
    - iv. Note too, r 25.14(3), the instructions are not privileged against disclosure.
  - these factors may make it difficult for a former shadow expert to step into the role of a partisan expert appointed under Part 25 (and even harder for an aligned expert to do so). If they are not so appointed, then their evidence cannot be put before the court anyway). In many cases, a further expert will need to be appointed.

The fifth-flavoured expert will be discussed later in the non-court dispute resolution section of this chapter.

8 This is where one party is dissatisfied with the report of the JSE and seeks leave to bring their own expert evidence in conflict with that of the JSE's evidence. This situation will need careful management as the court will generally be reluctant to permit the further expert. It is considered on page 349.

PROCESS ALTERNATIVES: FIRST: THE COURT'S APPROACH TO THE INVOLVEMENT OF EXPERTS

16.06 Not all cases work their way through the court system – and with our courts increasingly pressed, clients are increasingly engaging in non-court alternatives.

However,

- the court system provides the most exacting and detailed system for involving experts; and
- the court system is the default: only if parties agree to step away from the court and into a non-court alternative does the non-court alternative have life breathed into it.

So, in considering the position of the tax expert, it makes sense to start with the court system which provides a bedrock and which informs the other systems and how they are likely to operate.

TIMETABLING WITHIN THE COURT'S PROCESS

16.07 As we will see, meticulous compliance with the court's rules and timetabling is:

- not only required by the FPR; but
- also highly influential as to whether permission to adduce expert evidence will be granted at all.

Beyond this, well run cases are appealing to judges and they are much more likely to run with what you are seeking when you can show that the procedural rules are known and have been adopted.

16.08 The key consequences for the practitioner in operating this part of the system are as follows:

(1) *Know that it is challenging:* There is scarcely enough time to comply meticulously with the court's timetabling even when things are running well. Where, as is so often the case, forms E exchange late, then the timetabling is more pressed still.

(2) *Move early:* Assess the situation early. You don't usually need to wait until there is an exchange of form E to know whether you are going to need an expert or not. You probably can't afford to wait for exchange of forms E, to then see counsel and to then make decisions. You would be likely to run out of the time. Build the skills and take the time to assess whether expert evidence is going to be needed and move early to make progress with the procedural requirements.

(3) *Systemise:* Speed of progress will be much-assisted (and you are much less likely to put off this work until it is too late or requires additional effort, making mistakes more likely) where:

- you have precedent enquiry and instruction letters in place; and
- you build and develop a list of experts who often assist with this work;
- you have a standard application in form D11 and the accompanying draft order.

Ideally, you will reach the point where much of this work can be delegated to administrative/ secretarial support. [It is often the case that those colleagues tend to be better at meticulous management of specified steps and stages anyway]. We have provided all of this material in the Appendix.

(4) *Discuss:* Speak to your opposite number and try to agree whether there is the need for an expert.

(5) *Select:* It is best to agree the identity of your expert with your opposite number (so that a joint front can be taken at court if the judge is reluctant to give permission).

- There is a tedious instinctive-resistance that each of us seem to have for any expert proposed by the other side's team, we really need to move on from this – the bulwarks against bias within this system are pretty significant.
- If you anticipate difficulties then consider:
  - either agreeing the process first rather than discuss names and get to impasse (eg 'I will propose [3][5] names of people who can do the work in the timescale and you will select one … if you don't like that then you tell me your [3][5] names and I will select');
  - or (perhaps more risky and time-consuming) agreeing to find out timescale and cost from a fuller range and the front-runner will usually select themselves as one person is simply a lot faster and/or cheaper as well as clearly being competent to deliver, in the light of your joint past experiences.

CHRONOLOGY WHERE ONE EXPERT IS TO BE USED

16.09 The detailed rules of the FPR Part 25 and accompanying practice directions (and they are very detailed!) are set out in the Appendix of this book.

Many parts of the rules were drafted with the very different circumstances of children's cases in mind and so they may not always read as if honed for work on financial cases.[9] Whilst we have sought to strip out the children-only elements to reduce the scale of reading and highlight the significant elements, they are still a complex rule book and some patience is needed with them.

16.10 A further warning which may assist getting through the document is that is there are different – albeit it overlapping lists of requirements for the information that:

- must be provided to the expert;

9 For example 'take into consideration all of the material facts including any relevant factors arising from ethnic, cultural, religious or linguistic contexts' … not so relevant in a case involving grinding CGT calculations.

- must be included within the application to the court;
- must be included in the order.

It is another reason why systems and precedents are needed to steer you safely past the reefs of the detailed rules.

16.11 We aim for our precedent letters to provide an effective set of checklists to minimise the time spent on this exercise whilst still covering off every angle required under the scheme and promoting the smooth passage at court.

Overview of stages

16.12 In summary there will be the following steps and stages.

(1) Consider early on whether there is a need for expert evidence.[10]

(2) If so, obtain instructions from the client.

(3) Notify the other side and try to agree the identity of the expert.[11]

(4) Next or alongside:
   - draft and send out the enquiry letters as to availability and cost etc (see page 299 for a precedent); and
   - generally (we discuss this below) make clear in your enquiry, the questions to which you will be seeking answers, within the enquiry letter;
   - draft the order (see page 319);
   - make a formal application to the court (on form D11) under Part 18 (attaching the draft instructions and draft order) see page 331.

(5) Share draft order with the expert and consider a conference call (with solicitors and expert) to:
   - fine-tune instructions;
   - consider timetabling and other logistics; and
   - agree retainer and payment arrangements.

(6) On marginal cases, where difficulties are anticipated at court, consider how the evidence of the expert is 'necessary' to the disposal of the case, bearing in mind the overriding objective[12] and the need to obtain leave of the judge at the first appointment (and convince the judge of the necessity of the expert's help).

(7) Attend hearing.

(8) Serve order on expert (within two days of receipt, but generally notify immediately after the hearing so that the timetabling of the work can be put in place); issue instructions (within five days of the hearing) apply to the

10 PD25D 3.9 makes clear that an application should be made as soon as possible and usually no later than the first appointment (unless, for example, replies to the questionnaire are needed to make the decision, see PD25D 3.10).

11 PD25D 2.1

12 PD25D 3.1

court probably within the same timeframe if there remain unresolved issues on the instructions.

(9) When the report is received:
   - actively consider it – you may need to try to schedule a conference with counsel to anticipate the date of receipt. This way questions can be raised within the required ten-day timeframe (unless a longer period has been fixed by the directions order). If this is not possible and you do not feel on top of the technicalities, you may feel that you need to engage a shadow expert for guidance or (sub-optimal) raise the report as a brief stand-alone issue with counsel by phone.
   - assess answers to questions upon receipt – leave is likely to be needed to pursue matters further.

(10) Obtain and settle invoice from expert. Check that the other party has settled their part given that generally there is joint and several liability for these charges and you will not want your client being pursued for them all (perhaps long after the case is finished).

(11) Assess whether the expert will be needed at the final hearing (rarely likely to be the case as generally the report will be adopted in its entirety, following questions).

(12) Note PD25B 4.1(h) which imposes a duty on the expert to inform the instructing party if there is a change in their opinion, which may well happen with changing circumstances and tax-law. (This surely places on the instructing party the imperative at least of letting the expert know when the case is concluded).

16.13 Where relations seem good with the other party, it is easy to assume that any problems with compliance and timetabling will be forgiven. But this is a dangerous path to adopt. However good relations are with the other party's solicitor, they are still subject to their client's instructions and you can be thrown on the back foot where your conduct of the case falls foul of the FPR requirements and the other party instructs their solicitor to take the point. Instead, your aim should be to:

- resolutely operate well in-front of the moving frontier of the FPR deadlines (so that you are able to accommodate unforeseen problems); and
- make regular reference to the FPR rules (see pages 355 onwards).

SOME FUNDAMENTAL PRINCIPLES AND THEIR ORIGINS[13]

16.14

(1) In our family work, the FPR provides the detailed code for the involvement of experts.	See FPR Part 25 and its subsidiary practice directions A, B, D, E, F

13 The relevant quotes appear in the Appendix, page 341.

(2) Meticulous observance remains the requirement.	(Per Munby J @50-53 in *Re W (A Child)* [2013] EWCA Civ 1177
(3) Evidence generally is usually limited to evidence as to facts but opinion evidence is permitted where it is from an expert within their area of expertise.	Civil Evidence Act 1972, s 3
(4) Expert evidence can be submitted on any issue (save for evidence on English law).	
(5) Permission is not needed to instruct an expert …	PD25D 2.1
(6) … but court leave is required before it can be put in evidence.	FPR 25.4(2)
(7) Parties can't just attach a report to their form E …	*J v J* [2014] EWHC 3654 (Fam). Para 45
(8) … but they can – and perhaps should – attach an accountant's letter to explain their figures.	
(9) An expert is only appointed where necessary.	FPR 25.4(3)
(10) Lawyers are required to ensure experts' qualifications.	
(11) There must be no conflict of interest that would affect the independence of the expert's view.	*Toth v Jarman* [2006] All ER D 271
(12) The party seeking such evidence must usually apply before the first appointment.	FPR 25.6(d)
(13) Late applications will need to be strong.	*Cooper-Hohn v Hohn* [2014] EWCA Civ 896
(14) You only ever have a SJE	*J v J* [2014] EWHC 3654 (Fam). Para 45
∘ unless it is in the High court and you are appointing two experts to avoid 3 above; and	*SK v TK* [2013] EWHC 834 (Fam)
∘ you may be able to argue that you need a further expert (uphill task) – see these Civil Procedure Rules (pre FPR) cases – admittedly therefore weaker; and	Daniels v Walker [2000] 1 WLR 1382 CA Edwards-Tubb v JD Wetherspoon Plc. [2011] EWCA Civ 136
∘ refer here for guidance on considerations:	See *Cosgrove v Pattison* [2001] CPLR 171

(15) There should be no unilateral conversations with the expert (and see The Academy of Experts Code 2005).	*Peet v Mid Kent NHS Trust* [2001] EWCA Civ 1703; [2002] 3 All ER 688 *K v K* [2005] EWHC 1070 (Fam)
(16) You *can* sue the expert.	*Jones v Kaney* [2011] UKSC 13

PRACTICE POINTS ARISING FROM THE ABOVE AND GENERALLY

The expert is independent

16.15 This principle is clear from FPR, r 25.3(2) and PD25B 4.1(d). It is also emphasised in the code of practice of The Academy of Experts, which requires the expert not to do anything which might compromise or impair their independence, impartiality, objectivity or integrity. See www.academyofexperts.org/guidance/expert-witnesses/code-practice-experts/tae-code-practice-experts.

16.16 Unilateral conversations (ie between an expert and one party's solicitor) should be avoided:

- see quote in *Peet v Mid Kent Healthcare NHS Trust* [2001] EWCA Civ 1703 at page 351).
- Baron J in *K v K* [2005] EWHC 1070 deprecated unilateral contact with the expert saying 'When a joint valuer is appointed, then all communications should be on a joint basis (unless the parties otherwise agree in writing). Indeed, representatives from both sides (or neither) should be able to be present when valuations are undertaken (unless the parties otherwise agree in writing). If one party seeks to circumvent this simple methodology there will inevitably be a sense of unfairness, even if the resulting valuation is beyond reproach. [39] The general practice in the Family Division should be that only joint approaches are acceptable and if there is non co-operation from one side, then this cannot be circumvented by unilateral action but should be dealt with by an application.'

Confidentiality and privacy

16.17 The expert may need to carry out investigations into areas involving sensitive personal information. The parties should not, however, be concerned about that information being kept confidential as clearly the expert has a professional's duty of confidentiality in place. This duty is confirmed:

- in the academy of experts' code referred to above; and
- in the code of ethics of the ICAEW at www.icaew.com/membership/regulations-standards-and-guidance/ethics/code-of-ethics-b/part-b-200-230

and the chosen expert will no doubt have appropriate systems in place to protect all personal information.

16.18 For this reason non-disclosure agreements will generally be inappropriate. But our suggested draft order is intended to provide further reassurance to the anxious/reluctant discloser.

Clearly the expert will need such information about the client as it will enable the expert to carry out conflict of interest searches (eg required by PD25B 8.1) at the earliest stage.

Scale of report

16.19

(1) A strict reading of PD25B8.1(h) suggests that a summary is mandatory.

(2) Certainly a summary may assist the parties to meet the PD27A para 5.1 bundle limit of 350 pages (often only the summary in the report may be needed for the bundle).

(3) FPR, Part 27A, r 5.2A.1 limits the length of experts' reports (absent court permission otherwise) to 40 pages (with the executive summary at the beginning of no more than four pages).

Are we actually seeking leave to adduce expert evidence on the law, when we appoint a tax expert?

16.20 At point (4) in the above table, the prohibition on adducing expert evidence on the law is made clear. This might be a cause of difficulty, with the court saying in terms that:

- 'the maths is simple;
- it is just the tax principles that are complex;
- but those principles are simply a matter of law – and should therefore be addressed by submissions from the parties or their representatives.'

We have not heard of this argument being rolled out … presumably counsel and the judge are relieved to have an authoritative statement of the law – or rather the numbers that result from the legal principles to rely upon, in complex cases – rather than their own less expert assessment.

16.21 There is also the real value of neutrality: numbers that are generated by a non-aligned professional have the capacity to slice through situations that otherwise might be fertile ground for long-dispute.

For example, in a parallel field one saw the long-debate about pensions culminating in the reported case *WS v WS* [2015] EWHC 3941 (Fam) and (unless we have completely misread the decision) one is left with the sense that a great deal of that dispute would have been avoided had permission for a pension expert been given.

The hurdle of necessity

16.22 The high-hurdle of 'necessity' imposed by FPR, r 25.4(3) was to protect the court from delays and expanded hearings and to enable the parties to be protected from unnecessary costs.

Advocates facing resistance from a judge unwilling to give permission need therefore to base their arguments resolutely on FPR, r 25.5(2):

> (2) When deciding whether to give permission as mentioned in rule 25.4(1) … the court is to have regard in particular to –
> (a) the issues to which the expert evidence would relate;
> (b) the questions which the court would require the expert to answer;
> (c) the impact which giving permission would be likely to have on the timetable, duration and conduct of the proceedings;
> (d) any failure to comply with rule 25.6 or any direction of the court about expert evidence; and
> (e) the cost of the expert evidence.

16.23 The advocate is likely to want to:

(1) reassure the court that the objective in instructing the JSE is to provide an early and low-cost set of fixed numbers in the asset schedule (as, they will reassure the judge, will usually follow from the instruction of the JSE);

(2) point to their applications complying minutely with the rules (as will follow from use of the precedents introduced in this section); and

(3) reassure the court that the expert's costs are reasonable (and will probably result in a saving rather than having each party conduct the analysis over the febrile area).

16.24 Careful preparation is needed – it is so easy to assume that the judge will be with you – but knocked back at this stage, there may be no second chances and the processes for appealing the decision are slow and perhaps disproportionately expensive.

Conducting business with the JSE

16.25 Solicitors will be mindful that the overriding duty of the JSE is to help the court and they will be mindful of their responsibility to assist the court in line with their duties under the overriding objective.

In consequence they will be respectful of the hermetic seal around the joint single expert to maintain their independence. But this can cause practical difficulty:

- How do we complete the form E, where there are complex issues of tax arising?

- How do we even know that we need the JSE, which JSE (what specialism) or what question to ask?
- Are there occasions when we need a partisan assessment of the JSE's report, where its conclusions seem unfavourable to our client?

16.26 These considerations may necessitate the appointment, at an early stage, of a shadow expert to provide assistance on how best to outline the case and then manage the input of the JSE, as discussed above at page 261.

So far as the JSE is concerned, it will be good practice to:

(1) always copy documents and correspondence sent to the expert to the other party;

(2) avoid unilateral conversations with the expert … if they take place then a note should be taken and disclosed;

(3) support and help the expert and respect and promote their position as a non-aligned expert assisting the court.

Remember the expert can ask the court for directions in cases of difficulty (FPR, r 25.17).

Costs rules reform

16.27 It is all too easy to press on, treating our work as business as usual. However, the work of the Financial Procedure Rules Committee's Costs Working Group will (as this is written) shortly bear fruit, and is likely to result in more frequent use of inter-partes costs orders.

16.28 As one considers involving experts, a pause should be built in, permitting careful thinking ahead.

- First, in the new culture, the court may well be more willing to make costs orders where there have been time-tabling breaches.
- Second there are likely to be consequences where costs have been permitted to build disproportionately. There is a real imperative to secure the information needed to solve the case early on and avoid, as can so often happen, expert evidence becoming some sort of running sore in the case, incurring ongoing fees.
- Third, we are likely to need robust numbers from our experts as regards their fees to integrate into the costs estimates that we will be required to provide (and as we become adept at predicting how the involvement of an expert will increase our own time and fees being charged).
- Fourth, we will have in mind the imperative of being able to justify (against the 20:20 vision of hindsight) the decision to appoint a partisan expert or employ a shadow expert to assist our client in the process.

- Fifth, if we do have separate experts, then there is likely to be an additional responsibility upon us to assist their negotiating their way to either an agreed position or at least a summary of positions that will enable their attendance at court to be dispensed with because the Judge has the material upon which to make a decision, so as to avoid a judge being impatient as regards the cost incurred through an arid or unnecessary debate between experts at the final hearing.

NON-COURT DISPUTE RESOLUTION

16.29 Resolution processes generally split into two types:

(1) Those where the parties are helped to reach agreement.

(2) Those where ultimately the solution is imposed (court, as considered above and arbitration).

The map of alternatives might show as a series of rooms along a corridor as follows.

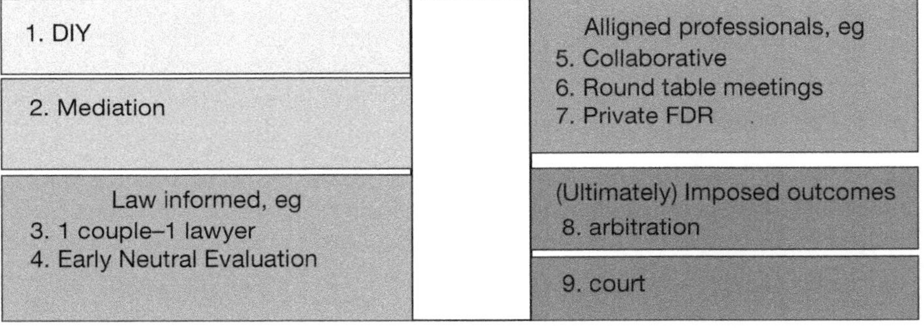

16.30 The court then is at the end of the corridor, in a process that is likely to involve:

- the most delay;
- the most expense;
- the highest level of procedural formality.

And against that backdrop 'What part is the tax expert likely to play in other processes and how should they be best involved?'[14]

16.31 In dialogue-based process, the parties will engage the expert in whatever form is helpful to them. In imposed-solution processes (for these purposes,

14 One could envisage other experts – for example the financial planner – having a larger role in some of these processes, for example providing a form of mediated service to settle the whole case but the tax expert is more likely to be having an ancillary role in the complex case to assist in refining and defining the numbers to permit others to achieve the overall agreement.

having considered court already, read simply 'arbitration') rules may be needed to ensure a fair process.

ARBITRATION

16.32 Where family law issues are addressed in arbitration, they are almost bound to be conducted under the Institute of Family Law Arbitrators ('IFLA') scheme. This has been recognised by the Family Division (for example in *S v S* [2014] EWHC 7 and so provides the faster-track to court approval of the out-turn of arbitration).

16.33 Article 3 of the IFLA scheme (currently the sixth '2018' edition of rules[15]) obliges the arbitrator to decide the substance of the dispute only in accordance with the law of England and Wales. This does not oblige them to apply the FPR (and so there is no requirement to adopt the FPR Part 25 in its entirety). However:

- the FPR is familiar and is a comprehensive short hand (that avoids rebuilding process rules from the ground upwards at great expense); and
- anecdotally, arbitrators tend to adopt the argument that as the court would have been the default, it will make sense in cases of difficulty to adopt the FPR as a guide.
- though ultimately all such decisions will be viewed through the guidance of the Arbitration Act 1996 (AA 1996, s 1) that '(a) the object of arbitration is to obtain the fair resolution of disputes by an impartial tribunal without unnecessary delay or expense;' and '(b)the parties should be free to agree how their disputes are resolved, subject only to such safeguards as are necessary in the public interest'.

16.34

Specifically, the Act and the IFLA rules provide that:

- [AA 1996, s 37] Unless otherwise agreed by the parties,
  - the tribunal may appoint experts or legal advisers to report to it and the parties or appoint assessors to assist it on technical matters and may allow any such expert, legal advisor or assessor to attend the proceedings; and
  - the parties shall be given a reasonable opportunity to comment on any information, opinion or advice offered by any such person.
- [IFLA rules, Art 8]
  - The arbitrator may appoint experts

15 Conveniently accessed at www.familyarbitrator.com.

- The arbitrator may direct a party to produce information, documents or other materials
- (In cases of default, the arbitrator can continue the proceedings in the absence of the defaulting party).

16.35 A feature of arbitration is the parties' power to agree not only what questions are determined by the arbitrator but also the form of procedure ('if necessary with the concurrence of the arbitrator' – see Art 9.1 of the rules). It is only if there is no agreement that the arbitrator has 'the widest possible discretion' to adopt the procedures the arbitrator considers suitable (Art 9.2), holding in mind the general duty under AA 1996, s 33 that they must:

– 'act fairly and impartially as between the parties, giving each party a reasonable opportunity of putting his case and dealing with that of his opponent; and

– adopt procedures suitable to the circumstances of the particular case, avoiding unnecessary delay or expense so as to provide a fair means for the resolution of the matters falling to be determined'.

16.36 This backdrop (combined with the general practice of parties selecting the arbitrator) is likely to mean the following as regards the appointment of the expert in arbitration:

(1) There is unlikely to be the same application of the 'necessary' and 'no later than first appointment' thresholds for the appointment of the expert, which may cause the solicitor such difficulty in the court process, because:
   - if both parties want the appointment, then it is almost bound to proceed (Art 9.1);
   - whilst late identification of the need for an expert might be fatal in the court process, it may not be fatal in arbitration, particularly if there is a joint request;
   - only where one party is proposing an expert and the other resisting it, will matters become more complex. Here the arbitrator is more likely to be driven by the principles provided by AA 1996, s 33 seen above.

(2) Identification of the expert, formulation of the letter of instructions and the raising of questions on the report are more likely to be dealt with flexibly:
   - Because 'directions' appointments can be conducted by phone within a matter of days of a request, there is less of an imperative to bring all the strands together at the first appointment. This may mean that the parties are left to make such progress as they can and then revert. They might also elect to have the instruction letter written by the arbitrator ... and indeed that progress with reports is chased up by the arbitrator directly by email.
   - It also makes it more likely that any points of dispute can be worked out in advance of any hearing ... or where matters are proceeding on a 'papers-only' basis, that further evidence can be obtained from the expert to fill gaps that are only identified late in the day.

OTHER 'AGREEMENT-DEPENDENT' PROCESSES

16.37 Working backwards from arbitration:

(1) There is:
- the private FDR (which may be conducted within court proceedings or prior to the issue of proceedings, or indeed within arbitration);
- the round table meeting (with/ without counsel);
- collaborative process;
- early neutral evaluation;
- 'one-couple, one-lawyer' processes offered by the bar through schemes such as www.thedivorcesurgery.co.uk;
- mediation.
- various forms of direct negotiation between the parties.

(2) The need for robust figures:
- Whether figures must be refined or not will depend upon the process. An early stage discussion may accommodate a relatively broad-brush analysis of the numbers. It can also accommodate a level of disagreement between the parties as to where ultimately the numbers will fall: they can simply agree to differ over some of the figures and perhaps still reach a solution that makes sense to both of them, albeit for different reasons, recognising the uncertainty over how key areas will, ultimately be resolved.
- However, where the process depends on perhaps quite honed advice and guidance as to the likely outcome of the case, greater clarity may well be required:
- We have all had FDRs that have collapsed or private FDRs that have cancelled late in the day because one party or their lawyers indicate that with uncertainty over one aspect or another, they are simply not able or willing to negotiate or shift from their assumptions over the numbers which renders agreement impossible.

(3) The option of dialogue and discussion:
- One of the advantages of collaborative process and other more flexible/'whole family' approaches is that the formal provision of a report may be by-passed (saving substantial costs).
- Instead the parties may prefer to meet the expert with their advice teams and have a conversation as regards the issue and options that the situation engages. In consequence the parties, in particular, are likely to achieve a deeper understanding of the issues involved and the options for progress. That in turn may promote the possibility of settlement.

(4) The existing expert:
- The procedural freedom that exists in for example mediation and collaborative process (at least when set against the steely tracks of FPR 25) open up a range of alternatives, for example the fifth of the expert 'flavours' (see page 262 above).
- Here the parties would make use of, for example, their existing professional advisor [accountant/financial planner] to advise and assist directly in the negotiations.

- It will only be appropriate where each has complete trust in the input offered by this person. Trust may depend on whether there is expected to be a continuing relationship with each party. Where the expert will be working in the future, only for one, it may be harder for the other to assume that the expert's sympathies are held evenly between the parties.
- But where it works, it can permit incredibly fast and economic progress:
  - generally the stage of disclosure and audit is completed very quickly and there is not the sort of to-and-fro debate over the numbers that so often builds costs in our court-based cases;
  - options can be raised, examined and discarded with ease, because of the advisor's knowledge of the parties and their circumstances.
- There will often be enthusiastic buy-in from the advisor who may see this as an opportunity to 'be there' for the client in their real moment of need, expand the range of services they offer and also – probably and where matters are handled well – retain both clients into the future.

(5) Further process if no agreement:

- The agreement-dependent processes will usually have a 'weather eye' on what will happen if ultimately there is no agreement.
- Where the existing expert route (point 4 above) route is not taken, then often the expert will be instructed in a formal manner and the requirements of the FPR followed to permit the safe export of their report into the arbitral or court process, for determination as the negotiations conclude without negotiation.[16]
- This may point towards a greater formality being adopted by the expert or perhaps a two-stage process:
  - their filing a report that will stand as the agreed evidence before;
  - secondly, they are involved in a more informal/solution-seeking way.
- Note PD25A3.1, which provides: 'When experts' reports are commissioned before the commencement of proceedings, it should be made clear to the expert that he or she may in due course be reporting to the court and should therefore consider himself or herself bound by the duties of an expert.'
- Appropriate adjustments will need to be made to the draft letters, to which we turn in the appendix that follows.

16 Particular attention was given to this aspect during the early stages of the development of collaborative practice. The landscape is now left open as to whether such reports are exported or not and the solicitors instructed should be careful that they are clear as to the basis on which an expert is to be involved on a case prior to the delivery of the report.

Appendices

APPENDIX 1

The detailed chronology of rules relating to the instruction of the part 25 expert

<table>
<tr><td></td><td><u>Initial timetabling</u>
The issue of the financial application will fix timetabling for:
– exchange of forms E; and
– the 1st appointment.</td><td></td></tr>
<tr><td></td><td><u>Identify the need</u>
Consideration can be given to the appointment of an expert immediately. In cases of complexity or uncertainty an early discussion with your selected counsel for the 1st appointment (if you are using one) may be needed, so as to identify:
– whether an expert will be helpful;
– what questions should be addressed;
– any particular information that the expert should be given/should be sought for the expert.</td><td></td></tr>
<tr><td></td><td><u>Discuss with the other side</u>
You must tell the other party of your intention to seek a direction and either agree the expert or identify the expert being proposed.
– The o/s has 10 days to object (this alone can wreck your timetabling if you are starting late). If they object, then they must provide an alternative.
– Each party must disclose if they have consulted this expert about this matter before.</td><td>PD25D 2.1
2.2
2.3</td></tr>
<tr><td></td><td>The scheme is made clear by PD25D 3.5.
– Ideally the parties agree who will be the expert.
– If they cannot agree then they obtain information from all experts whom they wish to put forward (for the court then presumably to make the selection if the court determines that expert evidence is necessary).</td><td>PD25D 3.5</td></tr>
</table>

	The rules say that in cases of impasse of agreeing the identity of an expert, you should not just proceed to instructing separate experts because of the risk of costs escalating (though there is nothing that actually to stop this from happening, save later court disapproval). *We consider below where multiple experts are involved.* *Assuming that one JSE can be identified then:*	2.4
	A conference call with the expert Good practice would often lead to a conference call between the parties and the proposed expert to discuss: – what is really needed by each side to present their case at the FDR/ final hearing; – how the questions should be fine-tuned in the instructions with a view to limiting costs and maximising assistance. Many experts complain that the instructions they receive are blunderbuss enquiries with too many options that are not realistically in the frame or where the focus of the instructions is incorrect. A conference call could: – eliminate these unnecessary costs; – improve trust and communications between the expert and the parties; – clarify what information the expert needs from the parties to complete the agreed task; – ensure realistic timetabling for the report; and – equip the parties with arguments to assist their dealing with objections raised by the judge at the first appointment eg as to necessity/costs capping but in particular timetabling. [1]	
	Instructions from the client Alongside this, the solicitor will want to ensure that: – they have the client's approval to the course being adopted; – the client is aware of the likely range of costs; and – that they are aware that there is joint and several liability for the fees of the JSE.	FPR 25.12(6)

1 It is unlikely to be relevant in most tax enquiries (as often reports can be short) but remember the requirements as regards the length of experts' reports in PD27A 5.2A and where shorter this will no doubt assist with the overall bundle length of 350 pages.

	Prepare for court permission by preparing application	
	Of course if the expert's evidence is agreed then there may be little more that is needed. Permission to adduce the evidence may be required as a formality but judicial resistance is unlikely as there will be no implications for cost or delay. But it is unlikely that things can move so quickly…	
	… So for safety an application will usually be issued and this will be done early on given the logistical difficulties that should be anticipated to the issue of the form prior to the 1st appointment. Leave should be sought 'no later than the first appointment.'	FPR 25.6(d)
	The information that the court will need to see before granting permission can catch up later. (If explanation is needed as to the adoption of this course before the judge, PD25D 3.6 may help '*an application … should be made as soon as it becomes apparent that it is necessary to make it.*')	PD25D3.6
	Issue the application in form D11. (part 18 FPR applies)	FPR 25.7(1)
	A draft order must be attached.	FPR 18.7(2)
	The application must state the following: (i) the field in which the expert evidence is required; (ii) where practicable, the name of the proposed expert; (iii) the issues to which the expert evidence is to relate; (iv) whether the expert evidence could be obtained from a single joint expert;	FPR 25.7(2)
	(v) the other matters set out in Practice Direction … 25D.	PD25D 3.11
	In addition to the matters specified in FPR 25.7(2)(a), an application for the court's permission to put expert evidence before the court must state – (a) the discipline, qualifications and expertise of the expert (by way of C.V. where possible); (b) the expert's availability to undertake the work; (c) the timetable for the report; (d) the responsibility for instruction; (e) whether the expert evidence can properly be obtained by only one party;	PD25D 3.11

	(f) why the expert evidence proposed cannot properly be given by an expert already instructed in the proceedings; (g) the likely cost of the report on an hourly or other charging basis; (h) the proposed apportionment (at least in the first instance) of any jointly instructed expert's fee; when it is to be paid; and, if applicable, whether public funding has been approved.	
	Prepare draft order Attach a draft order.[2] The order must set out: (a) the issues in the proceedings to which the expert evidence is to relate; (b) the party who is to be responsible for drafting the letter of instruction and providing the documents to the expert; (c) the timetable within which the report is to be prepared, filed and served; (d) the disclosure of the report to the parties and to any other expert; (e) where there are multiple experts then the organisation of, preparation for and conduct of any experts' discussion); and (f) the preparation of a statement of agreement and disagreement by the experts following an experts' discussion; (g) making available to the court at an early opportunity the expert reports in electronic form; (h) the attendance of the expert at court to give oral evidence (or how the evidence will be given unless agreement about the opinions given by the expert is reached by a specified date.)	PD25D 3.12

2 We suggest that best practice will usually involve a separate order for each expert. It is certainly quicker to manage than a composite order and likely to be more convenient for the expert to have one document that deals specifically with their involvement.

	Give information about the case to the expert Meanwhile, in the role of applicant, obtain the information required of the expert. First basic information must be provided. This is all laid out in the rules [but for convenience is reflected in the precedent letter[3]] and includes the requirement to clarify: (a) the nature of the proceedings; (b) the issues to which the evidence will relate; (c) the questions on which the expert is asked to give an opinion; (d) whether permission is being asked for experts to give evidence of the same or related questions; (e) the volume of reading; (f) the likely timetable; (g) by when the report is likely to be needed; (h) whether a hearing date has been fixed when the expert may be needed to give evidence; (i) whether the instructing party has public funding.	PD25D 3.3
	Obtain the information from the expert that the court will need And the information that must be obtained of the expert to assist the court perform its role is also laid out in the FPR (and reflected in the precedent at page 299), namely: (a) the discipline, qualifications and expertise of the expert (by way of C.V. where possible); (b) the expert's availability to undertake the work; (c) the timetable for the report; (d) the responsibility for instruction; (e) whether the expert evidence can properly be obtained by only one party;	PD25D 3.11

3 Generally an expert will need to know:
The parties' identities for conflict checks;
The scale, type and complexity of the assets involved and the work needed. (Where businesses are involved, conveniently Corporation Tax Act definitions can be used of:
- Micro
- Small <50 headcount, turnover < €10m balance sheet total
- Medium
- Large

Whether there are any international dimensions to the case and if so what countries are involved.
The purpose behind the need to know – we discuss this in the notes to the precedent letters.

	(f) why the expert evidence proposed cannot properly be given by an expert already instructed in the proceedings; (g) the likely cost of the report on an hourly or other charging basis; (h) the proposed apportionment (at least in the first instance) of any jointly instructed expert's fee; when it is to be paid; and, if applicable, whether public funding has been approved.	
	The responses will generally be shared directly with each solicitor by the expert – but if this is not done, the applicant will share the replies and seek agreement to the expert from the respondent if this has not been given already; at this stage the conference call with the expert might take place.	
	Statement of issues	
	Attention must be given to the appointment of the expert in the statement of issues under FPR 9.14(5), filed no less than 14 days before the hearing.	FPR 9.14(5)
	The rules (FPR 25.5(2)(a) are specific: the court must have regard to the issues in the case and so clearly the necessity for the appointment of the expert should be trailed in the statement of issues.	FPR 25.5(2) (a)
	Attend hearing [4]	
	Before the court, the following may be on the agenda:	
	1. whether expert evidence is necessary;	FPR 25.4(3)
	2. whether it will be given by a JSE;	FPR 25.11
	3. the form of the joint instructions; or	FPR 25.12(2)
	That each party may give separate instructions.	FPR 25.12(3)
	4. Timetabling:	
	The time for issuing the instructions (generally 5 days);	
	The time for the filling of the report;	FPR 25.8 (1)(b)
	Any extension on the time for raising questions of the expert;	FPR 25.10(2)

4 Of course attendance may be avoided through one of the protocols such as the accelerated first appointment procedure.

	The timetable for the expert's response; 5. Length of report (no longer that 40 pages including an executive summary of no more than 4 pages). 6. Access to information. 7. inspections. 6. Expenses: Perhaps the limitation of fees.	FPR 25.10(3) PD27A 5.2A(1) FPR 25.13 FPR 25.12(4) FPR 25.12(5)
	In considering whether to give leave, the court must consider the issues involved, the questions to be raised and the impacts on timetabling duration and cost and also the time when permission is being sought. Also engaged is the overriding objective.	FPR 25.5(2) FPR 25.6(d) PD25D 3.1
	Follow up and service of order The order must be served on the expert within 2 days of receipt (as must any other order that affects the expert). Best practice will be to report to the expert (copying in the other party) immediately after the hearing.	FPR 25.18
	Issue instructions If permission is given then there will usually be a jointly agreed letter of instructions for release (but see below) This must be prepared and served within 5 business days.	FPR 25.12(1) PD25D 4.1
	Exceptionally, the court may for example permit separate instructions to be given to the joint expert by each party.	FPR 25.12(3)
	Where instruction letter hasn't been approved already and is disputed Generally it will be more efficient to prepare the instructions to the JSE and attach them to the application or at least have them contained in the bundle so that any issues as to the form or scope can be settled at the hearing. Where the form of instructions has not been approved and can't be agreed, then they are emailed to the court for determination. (Presumably this must be done within the same timeframe of 5 days.)	FPR 25.12(2) & PD25D 6.1

	Requirements of instruction letter The instructions must: – set out the context (including ethnic, cultural religious or linguistic context;[5] – lay out the questions for answer; – deal with the contractual basis for payment; and – address a number of other matters that are addressed in the model instruction letter provided on page 325.	PD25D 4.1
	Considering the report and raising questions The report should be given attention as soon as it is received as all questions to the expert on the report need to be raised within 10 days: – this will mean a period of less than two weeks, given the operation of FPR 2.9 (ie received on a Monday, the questions must be raised by close of business on the Wednesday in the second week afterwards); – note too that there is no right to simply extend timeframes by agreement. So attention may be needed to extend the timeframes at the time of the order (as our draft order does). Note too restrictions on questions which must be: – proportionate; – raised once only; – be to clarify the report; They must be simultaneously copied to the other party.	FPR 25.10 FPR 2.9 FPR 4.5(3) FPR 25.10(2) FPR 25.10(2) FPR 25.10 (2)(e)
	Discharge costs Obtain invoice so that a proper report can be made in form H/H1 at the next hearing the liability is not overlooked as the litigation progresses. (Have in mind the likely expansion of such duties under anticipated 2020 costs reforms of FPR 28.)	

5 Remember that these rules were prepared with the appointment of Children Act experts also in mind.

	Preparations for Final hearing etc If the case progresses to final hearing then assess with counsel the need for the experts' attendance; and if so: – identify the period of likely cross examination; – and clarify a logical point for the evidence in the hearing.	PD25B 10.1(c) PD25B 10.2(b)
	Notify expert and obtain details of their availability before hearing dates are set. Establish substantially in advance when the expert should give evidence.	PD25B 10.1(a) PD25B 10.1
	Report to the expert on the conclusion of the final hearing within 10 days We suggest that given the expert's duty to provide updating information under PD25B 4.1(h) that it must be good practice (or even necessary practice) to notify the expert when a compromise is achieved in the case too.	FPR 25.19

APPENDIX 2

Where multiple experts are involved

Multiple experts are involved where:

- each party appointed an expert from the outset; or
- where there is an attack on the JSE report, that is one or both parties are seeking to adduce evidence from their own expert because of concerns about the joint single expert's report. Here the requirements of *Daniels v Walker* must be met for an appointment to be made, see pages 349 and 350).

However, these scenarios will come into being in very different ways:

- where each party has their own expert, this will probably have been laid out in the orders made at the first appointment;
- in the *Daniels v Walker* situation, of course:
  - first there will have been the JSE's report;
  - then there probably will have been questions on that report;
  - but then either or both parties will have taken the step of deciding to appoint a further expert ... this might be for example after a failed FDR where a contested hearing looms and would only be where there was deep dissatisfaction with the JSE report and where the really very high hurdle of judicial resistance could be overcome.

The FPR code does not really differentiate between those two scenarios. It also incorporates much of the basic code discussed on the previous pages but with an overlay, particularly around mandating discussions to:

- promote agreement;
- clarify differences.

The summary below looks at the differences.

The bulk of the procedural code is contained in PD25E.

The rules themselves are at page 377 but can also be accessed via www.sofiathomas.co.uk/FPR25/, where the parts specifically relating to multiple experts' cases are marked in blue.

We think that it would be relatively rare for there to be a *Daniels v Walker* situation re tax expert evidence and where this happens, each situation will turn on its own facts and so we have restricted our precedent letters and so on, in this edition to provision of the JSE report. Accordingly, the outline that follows is more of an introduction than a comprehensive guide.

	<u>Before the first appointment</u>	
	The court has little power, in a financial case, to prevent the parties from instructing their own expert. It simply encourages them to reflect carefully before doing so.	PD25D 2.4
	If there is an appointment, then the rules encourage the parties: ● to adopt the FPR in the form in which experts are instructed; ● to agree disclosure of the reports.	
	However, this emphasises the realities that parties are in effect free to get the expert input that they want (they may just be in difficulties persuading the court to admit the evidence when it comes to seeking permission under FPR 25.3.	
	<u>Appointment of two partisan experts</u>	
	At the first appointment (usually), the Judge will assess: ● not only whether the appointment of an expert is necessary; ● but also whether the issues demand that separate experts are appointed by each party.	
	(It will no doubt also have considered the option of the parties each giving separate instructions to the one JSE expert as is anticipated by FPR 25.12(3).	FPR 25.12(3)
	Have in mind PD25D 2.4 and the mandate to each party to 'consider carefully before instructing their own expert'.	PD25D 2.4
	Any such application is going to be met with objections from the Judge echoing the views of Mostyn J in *J v J*, set out at page 348 (but see also Moor J in *SK v TK* [2013] EWHC 834 (Fam) at page 348 below.	*J v J SK v TK*
	When appointing a second expert, the court is very likely to give directions for discussion – though these can be given at any time.	FPR 25.16
	The directions will direct discussions on specific issues (FPR 25.16(2) and be aimed at achieving an agreed opinion. They will usually mandate a joint statement setting out: agreed areas; areas of disagreement with reasons.	PD25D 3.12(e) & (f) & PD25E
	(See further details below)	FPR 25.16(3)

	Instruction	
	Raising questions where there are two partisan experts Questions can be raised not only on the joint expert's report, but also by any party on a partisan expert's report. Assuming two experts are appointed then they will each be involved in the raising of questions on the other's report. However, parties may want to consider whether the facility for questions under FPR Part 25.10 is removed as likely to simply fuel the antagonism and increase costs when much of the same outcome is better achieved through the provision for meeting and discussion under FPR 25.16, considered below.	FPR 25.10(1)(a)
	Daniels v Walker application Where however the case has proceeded to this stage with a JSE, then '25.10 questions' will certainly have been raised (presumably with the assistance of the shadow expert who will no doubt have been brought on board at an early stage in these more complex cases) … It is at this point, usually (if a decision is made that the JSE's evidence has to be challenged by another expert at the final hearing) that a new Part 18 application will be made, in form D11 for the appointment of the further expert. The lead case is *Daniels v Walker* (we provide the relevant quotes starting on page 349). These imply that the gradient is not perhaps quite as steep as we all (probably including the judge hearing your application) assume … See para 28 of the case: '*If having obtained a joint expert's report, a party, for reasons which are not fanciful wishes to obtain further information before making a decision as to whether or not there is a particular part (or indeed the whole) of the expert's report which he or she may wish to challenge, then they should, subject to the discretion of the court be permitted to obtain that evidence…*'. The objection may be made that the restrictions have tightened since 2000 when judgment was given and: • a careful survey of the relevant authorities; • a carefully constructed attack on the report contained within the D11 • (as well as a knowledge of your tribunal) will be important.	

	<u>Experts' discussion/meeting</u>	
	Only joint meetings are anticipated (rather than with one side alone).	PD25E 4.1
	Meetings should be proportionate (as well as purposeful) and further rules set out how the process is generally managed.	
	The default is that within 15 business days after the exchange of reports, the nominated professional (usually the party in the position of the applicant) will make arrangements for the experts' discussion.	PD25E 3.1
	The nominated professional must: ● prepare and circulate an agenda 5 business days before the meeting; ● provide this to each professional 2 business days before the meeting.	
	The practice direction provides further guidance as to: ● the questions to be asked; ● the chairing of the meeting; ● taking minutes.	
	Generally a Statement of Agreement and Disagreement will result.	FPR 25.16(3)
	Along with reasons.	
	And this is filed within 5 days after the meeting.	PD25E 3.1(e)

And when it comes to the hearing, parties engaging multiple experts will have very much in mind Mostyn J's comments from his case *CB v KB* [2019] EWFC 78:

[16] I heard evidence as to the value of the income streams from Mr V, Mr Stephen Marks, Mr Stuart Burns, and Mr David Greene. They were all excellent witnesses. Their evidence was clear, concise and, importantly, relevant and direct. They all answered directly the questions that were put to them. They did not dissemble, prevaricate or make self-serving speeches. To my mind answering questions directly is an important, perhaps the most important, hallmark of credibility. In my judgment all the witnesses were palpably honest.

…

18. the expert accountants, gave their evidence concurrently under the procedure colloquially known as "hot-tubbing" (see Civil Procedure 2019 at para 35.4.8). Although this procedure is referenced in CPR PD 35 at para 11, it has not found its way into FPR PD25A-E. This is not to say that the procedure has not been used in family proceedings; to my knowledge, certainly in public law children proceedings, expert evidence has been given in this way. In this case the process was extremely successful. The witnesses occupied the witness box together in close proximity. They were questioned topic by topic which from the court's point of view meant that relevant evidence on each topic was given contemporaneously and not separated by a hiatus. It was fascinating to observe little debates break out between the accountants in the witness box. After it was over Mr Greene commented that it was much more friendly than the traditional adversarial process. In my opinion this process should be considered for use in financial remedy cases where competing valuers give evidence.

APPENDIX 3

Checklist for situations where expert tax evidence may be required

We may be so used to fudging the numbers in our financial remedy cases (or relying on counsel finding a way through the problem on the day of the FDR) that we fail to spot the myriad situations where we could assist our clients through:

- obtaining more robust data;
- identifying ways for them to progress more safely through the transition of separation; or
- perhaps exploring whether there are opportunities to reduce tax/manage the various transactions at lower cost.

Here is our first list – we have no doubt that there are a vast further number out there and will welcome additions for the next edition (via jp@flip.co.uk or Tax@sofiathomas.co.uk)

RESOURCES
1. *Family home following departure by one party* [1] a. Latent CGT where there is a transfer to one spouse in the year of separation (especially now that CGT starts to accrue after 9 months – now capturing cases where one party moves out prior to 5th July in the tax year of separation). b. Triggered CGT where the transfer of the FMH happens after the tax year of separation.
2. <u>2ND properties/holiday homes/rental properties</u> a. The CGT that is generated on a transfer after the end of the tax year of separation. b. The CGT that will be latent when one party is retaining that property. c. The income tax that is due but yet unpaid [ie the rent has been received but the parties have not yet settled up for the tax that this income triggers].
<u>*Investments*</u> 3. There are myriad investments generating different issues, but essentially the questions will be focused upon:

1 CGT may also have been dormant following earlier periods of absence from the home.

a. the latent tax (ie interest or dividends have been earned on this investment but where the parties have not yet settled up for the consequent tax that falls due on that income).

b. CGT that will be triggered by the transfer of the share (cum-div/ex-div) or other asset after the end of the tax year of separation;

c. the CGT that is latent where the investment is in one party's name (or has been transferred to them as a husband-wife transfer early on in the proceedings) and is being retained.

4. *Inheritances/family gifts/trusts*

a. … realistic 'net' receipts after reallocation under deed of variation, recognising periodic charges;

b. or simply what will fall due on the vesting of various trust entitlements.

5. *Chattels*

a. chattels that are exempt;

b. chattels that will trigger a charge on transfer;

c. chattels that are to be retained but which will have an underlying latent CGT liability.

Business

6. What CGT is likely to be generated on a disposal of an interest in a business, eg holding in mind the existence of directors' loans and Business Asset Disposal relief.

7. Income tax issues relating to the business, for example:

a. the debt of income tax that falls due for payment the following Jan and July in relation to, for example:

i. Benefits;

ii. Directors' loans;

iii. Dividends.

b. Any net payment for a spouse-director being made redundant

c. more broadly an analysis of the small business and consideration of how income can best be extracted from it and what 'net' from various given gross income and expenses would look like.

Pension

8. *What* net income there will be from pensions, holding in mind state pension and likely level of pension receipt/draw down options/tax free lump sum.

9. What tax sums would be due at what points where the pensions are above LTA, including options to seeking an increased LTA.

Ordinary income issues

10. Gross to net but including complications eg where wrongly claimed allowances or child benefit.

11. An analysis of the position of the complex earner and in particular a break down over time as regards:

a. income regarded as marital, earned during the period of the marriage (albeit that it may fall in later) … so considering: i. any future [Jan/July] income tax hits; ii. the discharge of tax on the vesting of deferred shares; iii. how those shares are augmented by dividends (notional or otherwise) and how that tax is discharged … again, so as to give a 'net' figure for the parties. b. post-marital income on the same basis; c. some of this will involve a variety of categories, eg: i. shares that have been retained and which are vested (essentially only a CGT and recent dividends question); ii. shares that were awarded during the marriage and which have not yet vested; iii. shares that were earned after separation and which have not yet vested.
Foreign element 12. Any of the above where the assets is liable to foreign tax or where the asset is situated abroad.
13. Remittance from off-shore trust.
Default cases 14. Any of the above where there has been historic default in payment of tax: a. what penalties/interest are likely and what is the likely 'hit' of professional fees before this aspect is concluded; b. is the liability a joint one? Should it be treated as marital one? [2]
Assessment of schemes 15. Where the parties have engaged in a tax management scheme (film partnerships/stamp duty saving/employee benefit trusts, to name a few): a. an assessment as to whether such schemes are likely to fall under HMRC attack; b. if they are attacked, then whether HMRC is likely to be successful; c. whether any sort of assessment can be given as to (1) the likely scale of professional fees; (2) the likely scale of tax, interest, fees and penalties and (3) the sort of timescale to resolution.

2 This may be a case where:
- the tax-payer's professional team are best placed to provide the information (to avoid duplication of professional fees); and where
- the other party needs more of a watching brief/shadowing role, which can be provided through a second firm being appointed to consider the report of the tax-payer's professionals.

NEEDS
16. Stamp duty on the new purchase … options and exposure where the purchaser is still on the title of the family home or the family's second property remains in the purchasing spouse's name.
17. Any CGT that will develop in the property that will be retained for now and disposed of later, for example under a mesher/schedule 1 scheme.
18. Gaps in state pension issues.
19. Child benefit issues.
GENERALLY 20. An analysis of the impact of residence and domicile points, for example: a. where a party is non-resident but there is a risk of their facing enhanced tax liabilities owing to (1) historically having become UK-resident or (2) in the future electing to become UK-resident; or b. a party is UK resident but has options to become non-resident … consider then the likely impacts on for example income or UK state pension.

APPENDIX 4

Form of enquiry letter

INITIAL COMMENTS

The enquiry is the first of 4 steps:

1. Enquiry.
2. Court permission:
   - (all being well, the instruction of the expert is confirmed at the first appointment. Then the detailed information can be provided and the work got underway).
3. Instruction
4. Discussion:
   - at any stage along the way (but we suggest the earlier the better) 3-way discussion may be helpful between the solicitors for the reasons discussed at page 280.

At the enquiry letter stage, the following should be in mind:

ENQUIRY STAGE

Purpose

The expert is approached:

- to clarify that their appointment would not involve conflict; and
- to harvest the information (especially as to availability and fees) for the court to consider whether the appointment is necessary.

Consequence

1. ***Conflict check***: Obviously full names and information about any company are needed. For larger accountancy practices, the conflict check may be a fairly exacting and time-consuming process.
2. ***Sufficient information***: … must be given for the expert to give meaningful indications about fees they will need to be given proper information about scale and complexity of the task required of them. It is unhelpful to indicate (as some of us apparently do) 'CGT calculations on property sale…' for the expert then to receive particulars of a portfolio of 20 or more properties and the solicitor expect the fee indication and timeframe to hold up.

The expert will always need to be given sufficient information to be able to assess the work that will be required.

3. ***Purpose***: Experts say that they are helped when we are clearer about the purpose of the instructions, the options in mind or the plan. Too often solicitors coming from their position of intimate knowledge about the complexities of the case may overlook that the expert truly comes at this from a blank page. Where we can be clear and upfront about the options in mind (as we seek to illustrate in the instruction letter below) then experts are far more likely to 1. Provide honed information of use to the court; and 2, give guidance where points are being overlooked. Ultimately the expert's duty is to the court (FPR 25.3) and so we should be mindful of what will assist the court to do its job under s 25 MCA.

4. ***Question definition***: It is true that the expert may not need a completely refined question at the enquiry stage … after all, the court's permission may be granted first and then the question fine-tuned at a later stage. But we think that this approach is not to be preferred: it is better to be clear about precisely what is being sought at the start:
   - It is going to have to be done at some point, so why not do it now – rather than expanding the task by doing it incompletely at a preliminary stage and properly later, when unforeseen problems may crop up.
   - A sloppy question may cause problems when the court comes to consider the necessity of the expert's instruction at the first appointment.
   - A properly crafted set of questions will usually focus minds upon what is really needed and may permit input from the expert as to the form of the question.
   - It is more likely to 'out' differences between the solicitors as to the task required and having this clarification earlier gives more opportunity for it to be resolved, which is likely to mean that it can be done more cheaply and efficiently, because these issues can be resolved at the first appointment.

5. ***Scale of information in enquiry letter***: we appreciate that a detailed letter at the enquiry stage will often feel like an exhausting proposition and deciding the scale of the information to provide at the enquiry stage is not always an easy assessment to make.

   As indicated above, generally an expert will need to know at least:
   - the parties' identities for conflict checks;
   - the scale, type and complexity of the assets involved and the work needed;
   - where businesses are involved, conveniently CTA definitions can be used:
     - Micro;
     - Small <50 headcount, turnover < €10m balance sheet total;
     - Medium;
     - Large;
   - whether there are any international dimensions to the case and if so what countries are involved; and

- (where relevant and ideally) the purpose behind the need to know: (as discussed at 3. above, where the expert knows why you are asking the question or why you need to know the answer … ie what transition or transaction is anticipated they are much more likely to be able to provide a relevant orientation).

But whether a careful background of the various complexities is provided at this stage or the instruction stage is a moot point. Clearly when it is not provided then:

- the expert cannot give a robust indication of global costs … the parties will have to manage on the basis of an indicative hourly rate;
- they may not be able to rely on an indicated timescale where the work that is eventually sought is very substantial;
- this may not matter so much if:
  - you practice in a court where costs caps are rare; or
  - there is no immediate pressing need for the report (ie delays will not harm progress);
  - the parties recognise the need for the report and 'it will cost what it will cost' …
- but where the litigation needs to be run with greater precision then commensurately greater detail will be needed.

In many cases providing the expert with the parties' form E with minimal attachments may really assist with achieving the balance between:

- controlling the time taken to prepare the enquiry to the expert; and
- giving the expert the background information they need to provide a meaningful indication of fees and timeline…

… and perhaps help to 'out' recommendations from the expert about areas that the parties' advisors had not at that point spotted. One might say 'If you have an expert, why not use them?'.

Use replace keys in "match case mode" to change: "TP" into the Respondent/ Applicant, whoever is the tax payer; and "OP" into the Applicant/ Respondent, whoever is the other party Then delete this heading.

We have marked in shaded grey the FPR code applicable to the model documents – this obviously needs to be deleted when the letter is generated.

Dear

Enquiry as regards provision of a tax report under FPR 2010 part 25

We act for TP OP [1], the Applicant/Respondent, in family financial proceedings. [NAME OF FIRM] acts for OP TP, the Respondent/Applicant. We believe that expert evidence will be necessary for the proper and prompt resolution of the issues in the case and the court will consider whether to make orders appointing an expert for a report to be given at a hearing on [**]. If you would kindly indicate your willingness to assist the court as its joint single expert as quickly as

1 The clients' permission should be obtained for disclosure of their identity so that potential experts can undertake conflict checks.

possible it will assist us. This letter and your reply will be disclosed to the court and to the solicitors for the other party.

Background

See PD25B 6.2: The expert should be given information relating to the nature of the proceedings, the questions for the expert, the time when the report is likely to be required, the timing of any hearing and how the fees will be funded – and this is further clarified in PD25D 3.3 with the requirement to give the following information:

(a) the nature of the proceedings and the issues likely to require determination by the court;

(b) the issues in the proceedings to which the expert evidence is to relate;

(c) the questions about which the expert is to be asked to give an opinion and which relate to the issues in the case;

(d) whether permission is to be asked of the court for the use of another expert in the same or any related field (that is, to give an opinion on the same or related questions);

(e) the volume of reading which the expert will need to undertake;

(f) whether or not it will be necessary for the expert to conduct interviews and, if so, with whom;

(g) the likely timetable of legal steps;

(h) when the expert's report is likely to be required;

(i) whether and, if so, what date has been fixed by the court for any hearing at which the expert may be required to give evidence (in particular the Final Hearing); and whether it may be possible for the expert to give evidence by telephone conference or video link: see paragraphs 10.1 and 10.2 (Arrangements for experts to give evidence) of Practice Direction 25B;

(j) the possibility of making, through their instructing solicitors, representations to the court about being named or otherwise identified in any public judgment given by the court;

(k) whether the instructing party has public funding and the legal aid rates of payment which are applicable.

We believe that there are an immediate and obvious list of area where advisors should perhaps be seeking help and we provide illustrative models as to what may be required on the main types of enquiry. The list cannot be treated as exhaustive and tailoring will be required according to the circumstances of each case.

We provide background to the case and describe the task that you are asked to complete as follows:

Generic background

The parties were married in * and separated in *. [Or they are outside of the tax year of separation.] TP is aged * and OP is aged *. They have a global net worth of between * and * and

- *TP earns £* gross approximately*
- *OP earns £* gross approximately*

They are UK resident / non-UK resident.

[Consider inclusion of form Es without documents. The specific documents are then provided where this is sensible given the individual enquiries.]

1. Family home following departure by one party [2]

Background

The family home was purchased in ** for ** (a sum of £** including all stamp duty and other costs).

The parties let the property between ** and ** for a sum of approximately £* per month before returning to live in it as their marital home

[The parties will provide you with an agreed list of improvements carried out on the property and you are asked to assume that they would be able to document/ prove these to HMRC.] [You will be asked as part of your instructions to discuss with the parties what evidence of improvements will be required by HMRC for them to be taken into account and to assess the information that you are given.]

[The parties have carried out development of the property – information will be provided as to the areas involved and the chronology of disposals made/ anticipated.]

In **, TP/ OP left the property in circumstances that have proved to be permanent.

Purpose

Please assume that a transfer of this property to OP / TP will be made in [*identify month by reference to likely FDR hearing date*] and alternatively [*identify month by reference to likely final hearing date*].

Calculations

Please calculate and advise:

a) As to whether CGT would be triggered by the sale, if so in what sum and when it would be paid;

2 CGT may also have been dormant following earlier periods of absence from the home.

b) As to whether there would be a CGT liability that would be transferred to X and be latent.

You are asked to assume that the liable party's CGT allowance is [fully available] [fully accounted for by other transfers likely in the year of disposal].

2. <u>CGT on second/investment property, located in the UK</u>

<u>Background</u>

The parties have a property at *, bought in * for £* which has been let at various stages through the period of ownership and which is now worth £* (agreed valuation). The property is owned [50/50 by TP and OP] or [the property is legally owned by TP OP, however OP / TP has a beneficial interest of *%]. The parties have never lived in this property as their main home.

[The parties will provide you with an agreed list of improvements carried out on the property and you are asked to assume that they would be able to document/ prove these to HMRC.] [You will be asked as part of your instructions to discuss with the parties what evidence of improvements will be required by HMRC for them to be taken into account and to assess the information that you are given.]

[Describe and give details of any further properties on which calculations will be needed]

<u>Purpose</u>

They have various options in mind including sale / transfer to TP/ transfer to OP. Ordinarily such transfer or sale would take place in around * (if the case settles at FDR) or perhaps * if a final hearing is needed.

<u>Question</u>

Accordingly, your help please is sought to provide a report on:

1) The tax that would be triggered on those two timeframes in the event of
   a. Sale
   b. Transfer to TP
   c. Transfer to OP

2) When that tax would fall due for payment and what penalties would fall due if there were delay.

3) If there is a transfer to one party [within the tax year of separation], then what tax liabilities would be latent that would be triggered on a later sale by the retaining party.

4) Whether there are options for the parties that might mitigate the scale of liabilities they face.

5) We understand that stamp duty land tax does not need to be considered as any transfers would be by way of divorce and therefore exempt, however, please advise us if you form the view that this is incorrect.

You are asked to assume that the liable party's CGT allowance is [fully available] [fully accounted for by other transfers likely in the year of disposal].

[You are asked to note that the property is located off-shore and we understand will therefore be subject to local tax at the point of disposal with the possibility of UK tax as well, subject to off-setting, where appropriate].

3. Income tax due on rental of 2nd properties / investment properties

Background

With reference to the above property, it has been let since **. A report to the relevant tax authorities was made for the y/e 5.4.20** (relevant tax return and consequent assessments will be provided) and the instalment of taxes has been paid up to **.

Purpose and calculation

The court will want to know whether there are latent tax liabilities of significance and you will be provided with a schedule of income and relevant expenditure (which you will be asked to assume is accurate) so as to calculate what tax will fall due (and when) on the income received up to date.

[You are asked to note that the property is located off-shore and we understand will therefore be subject to local tax at the point of disposal with the possibility of UK tax as well, subject to off-setting, where appropriate].

4. Investments

Background

You are referred to the attached pages of form E and the parties' various investments. You will be provided with the acquisition costs and the name in which they are held and the latest documents relating to each of them, issued by the relevant institutions.

Purpose

Some of the investments may be sold; some transferred between the parties and some may be retained. The court will want to know:

- What CGT liabilities or other tax are likely to accrue in those different scenarios
- And when payment of the CGT will fall due
- [What penalties or interest will accrue if discharge of the CGT is delayed or reporting is only made late;]

– And what CGT would be latent during the retention of such investments (ie to fall due for payment on disposal at a later stage.

Calculation

You will be asked to carry out those calculations upon one date that we will provide to you, in anticipation of the FDR. We may need to ask for updated calculations at a later date. But that will be the subject of further instructions.

[You are asked to note that ** are held off-shore and we understand may therefore be subject to local tax at the point of disposal.]

5. Income tax on investments

In relation to the investments in the above section, you will be provided with the parties' relevant tax returns and calculation schedules for the last completed tax year [in this and in the foreign jurisdiction].

You will be provided with a schedule showing what further income has been earned on the investments to the point of instruction and will be asked to calculate

a) What income tax falls due for discharge on this income

b) When it must be reported and

c) By when the tax must be paid

d) [and what interest or penalties would accrue in the event of any late reports or delay in discharge of the tax].

6. Inheritances/

Background

The [relative] of TP / OP sadly died in * and they are a beneficiary of the estate.

Purpose and calculation

The court will want to know the likely level of receipts from the estate and whether steps might be taken that would permit there being enlarged. You will be provided with the draft probate accounts to provide these calculations

7. distributions from trusts

[*too myriad in their types to permit a meaningful outline but again, probably helpful to work through*

- *the question that the court is likely to want answered*
- *and from there the background information that the expert will need; and thus*
- *also a description of the documents to be provided*

8. Chattels

Background

You are referred to the attached form E pages concerning the parties' chattels.

A list of chattels in excel format will be provided confirming

- Date of purchase and purchase price
- Current ownership
- Anticipated end ownership where this has been identified
- Current value

Purpose

The court will want to identify the CGT that may fall on the transfer of these assets a) as shown; and b) as the parties may subsequently agree/ the court may determine.

Please will you identify whether and if so what CGT would a) accrue b) lie dormant, in the event of a future disposal by the person retaining it:

a) So far as has been identified on the list; and otherwise

b) In the event of a transfer either one way or the other between the parties.

9. Business[3]

Background

There is an [investment] [trading] business that [*describe sector]*

It has a balance sheet of approximately £*, turnover of £* and profit of approximately £*.

The shareholding is held:

- As to *% by TP

3 Generally the tax implications of dealing with the business will be wrapped within a valuation report relating to the business but there may be circumstances where no valuation is needed – for example a service company rich with cash – and the court is simply trying to understand the likely tax hits involved in the release of funds from it.

- As to *% by OP, who is also [a director/ company secretary / has some involvement in the day to day running of the business] [4] [5]

Purpose

The directors and company accountant have identified the possibility of a release of funds from the business to OP and the court will need to identify:

- What is the most tax efficient way of releasing these funds[, including by [1. The OP being made redundant and 2.] a disposal by OP of their share and the application of business asset disposal relief].
- How should the residual interest in the business fairly be valued, to include the incidence of tax, on the basis that TP intends to remain working in the business for at least the next * years

Calculation

You will be provided with the latest management accounts and asked to carry out appropriate investigations with [*the financial director/ TP / the company's accountant*] to address the above points [and will be asked to work with ** a part 25 expert appointed to value the business.]

10. Income tax issues relating to the business

Background

The company's year runs to **.

Purpose

The court will want to know:

1. The "net, in-pocket" position as regards drawings of whatever nature made from the business.
2. It will want to know whether there are directors' loans that might permit tax-free distribution of funds or which command repayment of funds to avoid tax charges that will otherwise be levied and generally what tax must be paid in respect of all distributions made to the date of enquiry and on what dates discharge of that tax must be made.
3. Looking into the future, the court will want to know what is likely to be the sustainable income that can realistically expect to be enjoyed from the company.

4 Or more simply 'the last 3 sets of accounts are attached for the business.'
5 Or equivalent information provided in relation to the Partnership / LLP etc.

Calculations

You will be asked to work with [*the financial director/ TP / the company's accountant*] to identify the likely sustainable pre tax income of the company going forward and then

The debt of income tax that falls due for payment the following Jan and July in relation to, for example, Benefits, Directors' loan, Dividends and any salary.

11. Income from business

Background

The TP draws their income from a service company, [name], which, for example had a turnover of £** in the year to ** and profits of £**; 3 years of accounts are provided.

Purpose

The court will want to know

1. What is the most efficient way of extracting funds from the company (whether the current arrangements can be improved upon)
2. Whether the current regime is likely to be challenged by HMRC such that there might be a claim for historic tax (and if so its likely scale and what penalties and interest might be charged and what professional fees involved to resolve the situation)

Calculation

You will be provided with a range of turnover and cost assumptions and asked to provide a range of net income calculations.

12. Pension

Background

[TP] [OP] [Both parties are approaching retirement. They will seek to draw down in an efficient way on the pension assets [SIPP/ defined contribution scheme / defined benefit scheme] in an efficient but prudent way.

Purpose

The court will want to know the likely scale of net income that can be enjoyed by the recipient from the pension asset.

Calculation

You will be provided with details of all other likely income and an up to date statement of the pension assets / benefits and will be asked to conclude the net income that can be enjoyed from this source.

13. Pension exceeding LTA

The parties hold pension assets in excess of the LTA.

The court will want to know what tax charges are likely to be raised and in what timeframes and whether steps can be taken to mitigate those liabilities.

You will be provided with an up to date pension statement and details of any enhanced protection and are asked to calculate the various charges that are likely to be imposed.

14. *Ordinary gross to net calculations but including complications eg where wrongly claimed allowances or child benefit … the structure of such questions will be varied but perhaps adopt the same structure of 1. Background; 2. Purpose 3. Question.*

15. Complex earners

Background

Purpose

We seek your assistance in clarifying

- TP's future income
- The sums that will in the future, 'fall-in' in respect of historic earnings (eg by way of deferred shares)
- We also seek for the court clarity as regards those that should be regarded as "generated by the marital endeavour" and those that accrue afterwards.
- The one-off tax sums that will fall due beyond those deducted by PAYE: and thus
- The extent of any cash flow pressures upon the parties.

Question

We seek please a clear schedule setting out

1. (so far as can be done) what "in pocket" sums are likely to be received by TP from the date rolling forward for the period of from the point of instruction as regards
   a. Regular monthly income

   b. Cash bonuses
   c. The vesting and realisation of deferred shares.

2. We anticipate that the court will be helped to know
   a. What deferred shares and bonus relate to the period of the marriage
   b. And we ask therefore that you clarify
      i. The resources that relate to endeavours in the period up to separation, which we ask you to take as date [x] and date [y]
      ii. The resources that relate to endeavours in the period up to the end of the company's year following separation; and
      iii. Which relate to post separation endeavours.

3. Where your projections make assumptions, please make those clear and confirm the level of certainty that you feel the court should attach to your numbers and the reasons.

16. Default cases

Background

[describe the default]

Purpose

The court will want to know what is

- The scale of exposure to claims from HMRC, including
  - Unpaid tax
  - Penalties and interest
  - Likely professional fees
  - (And whether there are any available insurances that might help defray such outlay)
- The likelihood of each postulated scenario, so as to assess from where the resources to discharge tax might come.
- It will therefore also want to know
  - The impacts of any delayed settlement
  - Whether there are steps that might be taken now to mitigate the impacts of these liabilities

Question

In addition to dealing with the above matters, please will you express an opinion on whether the liability a joint one? Should it be treated as marital one?[6]

6 This may be a case where:
- the tax-payer's professional team are best placed to provide the information (to avoid duplication of professional fees); and where
- the other party needs more of a watching brief / shadowing role, which can be provided through a second firm being appointed to consider the report of the tax-payer's professionals.

17. Assessment of schemes

Background

[Describe the scheme that the parties have engaged in (for example, film partnerships/ stamp duty saving/ employee benefit trusts).

Purpose and calculation

The court will want to be informed as to

1. Whether such schemes are under attack by HMRC/ likely to face attack from HMRC in the future;
2. If they are attacked then whether HMRC is likely to be successful;
3. Whether any sort of assessment can be given as to 1. The likely scale of professional fees; 2. The likely scale of tax, interest, fees and penalties and 3. The sort of timescale to resolution.

NEEDS

18. Stamp duty on the new purchase …

Background

As is clear from the parties' form E, enclosed herewith, the parties own in their joint names a property at []. The property will need to remain in those joint names, they are advised because of the scale of the mortgage and the limits to OP's income, being insufficient to meet the lender's requirements of such a loan.

Meanwhile TP wishes to purchase a property, of which the purchase price might be in the bracket £* to £*.

Purpose and calculation

Please advise on whether penalty stamp duty will be charged on such a purchase and describe generally the sums that would need to be paid by way of stamp duty at purchase and the circumstances in which recovery of the additional stamp duty might be possible.

19. Developing CGT on a retained property and the immediate incidence of SDLT

Background

An option being explored by the parties is the [retention of] [purchase of] a property in the name of the TP / OP / names of both parties, such a property to be retained against trigger events that will include:

- The youngest child reaching the age of **
- **

– The court ordering a disposal prior.

The proceeds will then belong to TP [will be divided between TP & OP in proportions that have yet to be determined].

To be included may be the facility to sell the property and purchase a replacement

Please assume that the purchase will be in the bracket £** to £** – the parties are each reserving their positions about this.

TP already owns a property at **, which is TP's main residence

Assistance sought

The court will want to know the financial impacts upon TP of the acquisition of such a property and this will include the likely incidence tax

– Stamp duty on acquisition

– CGT on an ultimate disposal

If there are approaches that might be adopted that might mitigate such tax, that information will be very helpful, please.

GENERALLY

20. An analysis of the impact of residence and domicile points, for example

1. where a party is non-resident but there is a risk of their facing enhanced tax liabilities owing to 1. historically having become UK-resident or 2. In the future electing to become UK-resident; or
2. a party is UK resident but has options to become non-resident ... consider then impacts on for example income or UK state pension.

In relation to the above questions, please advise if there are steps that could be taken to mitigate against the tax liabilities that you have identified.

Please indicate if there are documents that we have not identified that you will need to see to assist you. The court has power to direct production of documents and also the preparation of documents that might assist your endeavours. [7]

We will indicate if we need updating calculations if there are delays in the case accordingly please do not treat yourself as obliged to update your calculations as provided in PD25B 4.1(h). We will however, be obliged for your notifying us if you become aware of a change of practice or law that will materially affect the guidance that you have provided. For our part we will notify you when the case is settled so that you will be aware of the end of our request for help in this regard.

7 Please note analysis from counsel, Sassa-Ann Amaouche as regards the scale of the powers under FPR 20.2(l) focusing upon the facility to direct the preparation of accounts relating to a dispute.

Next steps

Please advise if you consider that any of the issues set out above require clarification/ contain omissions or whether you would consider it appropriate to discuss the parameters of instruction at this early stage e.g. by conference call with the parties' representatives.

It is anticipated that if you were to be instructed, a letter of instruction would be issued by [DATE] and that it would take a further [NUMBER OF WEEKS] weeks to provide you with the financial information that we expect you to require.

Information required

PD25B para 8.1:

(a) that acceptance of the proposed instructions will not involve the expert in any conflict of interest;

(b) that the work required is within the expert's expertise;

(c) that the expert is available to do the relevant work within the suggested time scale;

(d) when the expert is available to give evidence, of the dates and times to avoid and, where a hearing date has not been fixed, of the amount of notice the expert will require to make arrangements to come to court (or to give evidence by telephone conference or video link) without undue disruption to his or her normal professional routines;

(e) of the cost, including hourly or other charging rates, and likely hours to be spent attending experts' meetings, attending court and writing the report (to include any examinations and interviews);

(f) of any representations which the expert wishes to make to the court about being named or otherwise identified in any public judgment given by the court.

PD25D para 3.11:

(a) the discipline, qualifications and expertise of the expert (by way of C.V. where possible);

(b) the expert's availability to undertake the work;

(c) the timetable for the report;

(d) the responsibility for instruction;

(e) whether the expert evidence can properly be obtained by only one party;

(f) why the expert evidence proposed cannot properly be given by an expert already instructed in the proceedings;

(g) the likely cost of the report on an hourly or other charging basis:

(h) the proposed apportionment (at least in the first instance) of any jointly instructed expert's fee; when it is to be paid; and, if applicable, whether public funding has been approved.

For us to seek permission from the court for your report to be admitted as evidence in the case, please:

1. Indicate whether you consider this matter to be within your area of expertise and whether you are qualified to provide an opinion on the issues listed above.

2. Provide a copy of your CV.

3. Confirm that there is no conflict of interest that would preclude you from accepting instructions as a single joint expert in this matter.

4. Provide:
  a. your hourly charge out rate;
  b. your estimate for the total costs of providing the report;
  c. whether you are able to quote a fixed fee;
  d. the basis on which you would charge for further work such as responding to questions of clarification or attending court;
  e. when settlement of these fees would be due.

5. Indicate how long you would need:
  a. after confirmation of appointment to indicate your financial information requirements; and
  b. after provision of that information to prepare your report;

6. Confirm whether you are able to comply with the restrictions of PD27A, namely a report of no more than 40 pages with an executive summary of no more than 5 pages (and otherwise indicate the scale of report that is likely and the reasons why it must exceed the prescribed length).

7. Identify any other experts on whom you would anticipate wishing to rely.[8]

8. Confirm that you would have no objection to attending court to give oral evidence if required and provide an indication as to the likely period of advance notice that you would need of trial dates.[9]

9. Give an indication as to broadly what information and documentation you would anticipate requiring (or confirm that you will provide this information only after being instructed).[10]

8 This might, for example, include colleagues from within the expert's own firm from other specialist accountancy disciplines; property or pension valuation experts; or, in international cases, accountants from overseas jurisdictions.

9 If proceedings have been issued, the expert should be asked for details of any dates within the trial window on which the expert would not be available to attend court.

10 Practice will vary: some accountants will prefer to provide this information only when they are instructed.

10. State whether there are any representations that you would wish to make to the court about being named or otherwise identified in any public judgment.

We enclose, marked 'A' further information as regards the provision of experts' reports under FPR 2010. We assume that there would be no charge for your work involved in providing a response to this enquiry and prior to being instructed. If the situation is otherwise then please notify us in advance of our incurring such cost.

We look forward to hearing from you.

YF

'A' FURTHER STEPS/OTHER MATTERS

a. **Copy order:** If an order is made, we will notify you within 2 days by sending you a copy of the order and you will receive any relevant copy documents that might affect your report within the same timescale.

b. **Right to apply for directions:** You have the right to apply for further directions to enable you to carry out your function (but it will obviously be more cost-effective if we can identify those matters now and address them at the first appointment).

c. **Reporting after the final hearing:** We have an obligation to report to you within 10 days of any final hearing as to the use made by the court of your evidence. (Though, obviously, we hope that on the back of your evidence an agreement will be reached without the need for a hearing).

d. **Clarification questions:** Under FPR 25.10, questions may be put to you about your report to clarify it (only proportionate questions and only once, within 10 days of the date of service of your report unless the court directs otherwise) and it will be helpful prior to answering the questions that you indicate to us:
   1. how the answering of those questions will be charged for and the estimated fee for this work;
   2. the timetable within which you think that you will be able to provide such replies.

e. **Further data:** If, following instruction, you require further data from the parties to enable you to provide your report, please liaise with them directly. Please ensure that both parties' solicitors are copied in to such correspondence.

f. **The questions we are putting to you:** It may be that the questions that we are putting to you can be refined / improved and if so we would be pleased to have your input on that aspect.

g. **Range of expertise:** If you believe that a second expert may be required to enable you to provide the information needed, then would you:
   1. please identify this;

2. confirm the name and expertise of any such expert;
3. and answer the questions for the composite costs and indicating the timescale that will be required to complete the task.

h. **Media:** We do not anticipate any media attention in this case but we are required to make you aware that you are able to make representations to avoid being identified in any public judgment *[PD25D 3.3(j)]*.

i. **Administrative**
   1. There are no others involved in the case who are relevant to this aspect.
   2. No other experts have been instructed in the matter.
   3. You would be instructed as a joint single expert.
   4. The solicitors and the parties will have joint and several liability for your fees. Please may we be provided with an estimate of your likely fees before costs are incurred.
   5. Thereafter, when the work is completed, please will you forward to each firm for settlement an invoice showing your total fees but charging 50% to each firm – may this be done as soon as possible and in any event within one calendar month of the work being carried out. We cannot be liable for fees in excess of the estimate provided (unless subsequently revised by you and accepted by us) or where an invoice is not provided within a reasonable timeframe.
   6. Where fees are due for questions raised on the report please may these be invoiced to the party that raised the questions (with a copy being sent to the other party for information)?

j. **Part 25 FPR 2010:** You are familiar with your responsibilities under part 25. The codes are available for example at:

   www.justice.gov.uk/courts/procedure-rules/family/parts/part_25

   www.justice.gov.uk/courts/procedure-rules/family/practice_directions/practice-direction-25d-financial-remedy-proceedings-and-other-family-proceedings-except-children-proceedings-the-use-of-single-joint-experts-and-the-process-leading-to-expert-evidence-being-put-before-the-court

k. **Approach:** Generally, relevant expertise, transparency, trust and neutrality are crucial and:
   1. the report should give details of your qualifications and the information relied upon;
   2. all communications should be copied (or, if not copied, forwarded) to both sets of solicitors who will in turn copy each other with any correspondence forwarded to you;
   3. there should be no informal, unrecorded discussions or correspondence with the parties or their solicitors, other than the necessary arrangements in connection with meetings/viewings;
   4. please confirm that there is no conflict of interest of which you are aware that could affect your opinions.

APPENDIX 5

Form of draft order

ORDER 1.1: FINANCIAL DIRECTIONS ORDER

Use replace keys in 'match case mode' to change: 'TP' into the Respondent/ Applicant, whoever is the tax payer; and 'OP' into the Applicant/ Respondent, whoever is the other party Then delete this heading.

In the Family Court **No: [Case number]**

Sitting at [Court name]

The Matrimonial Causes Act 1973 The Marriage / [Civil Partnership] / [Relationship] / Family] of TP and OP

After hearing [*name the advocate(s) who appeared*] After consideration of the documents lodged by the parties

ORDER MADE BY [*NAME OF JUDGE*] ON [*DATE*] SITTING IN PRIVATE AT A FIRST DIRECTIONS APPOINTMENT

WARNING: IF YOU DO NOT COMPLY WITH THIS ORDER, YOU MAY BE HELD TO BE IN CONTEMPT OF COURT AND YOU MAY BE SENT TO PRISON, BE FINED, OR HAVE YOUR ASSETS SEIZED.

The parties

1. The Applicant is TP OP

The Respondent is OP TP

The Tax Payer shall refer to the Applicant / Respondent The Spouse shall refer to the Respondent/ Applicant [1]

Definitions

2. The "Expert" shall refer to [name] of [organisation]

1 We appreciate that some courts will require use of the term 'Applicant'/'Respondent' throughout – other courts may prefer the clarity and the usability that these terms confer (and the likelihood of mistakes being avoided.

Recitals

3.

Agreements

4.

Undertakings to the court

5.

Orders

IT IS ORDERED (BY CONSENT) THAT:

Appointment

6. The parties shall jointly instruct the Expert as a single joint expert to provide a report, addressing for the court:

EITHER (where the instructions have been agreed) the questions set out in the instructions attached to this order [2]

OR (where the instructions have yet to be clarified) the following tax issues:

a.

b.

OR (perhaps better:) the matters set out in the enquiry letter of the Applicant / Respondent addressed to the Expert and dated **

Instructions

7. The letter of instruction [and [*insert any other documents*]] shall be sent to the expert by [*time and date*].[3] It need not be filed at court[4]

8. Application shall be made to the court by the Applicant / Respondent by [** *default is 5 days after the permission hearing*] in the event that the form of instructions cannot be agreed by then. The provisions of PD25D 6.1 to apply. The email address to be used is [**].

2 Where the instructions are amended during the hearing, the judge may be invited to leave the amended copy on the file initialled in the event of subsequent disagreement over the terms of amendment.

3 Due within 5 business days after the permission hearing PD25D 4.1

4 Otherwise PD25D 4.1 would require this to be done.

Information

9. Absent further permission, the parties and the expert are restricted by operation of the Contempt of Court Act 1981, and FPR 9.46 and PD9B from disclosing to any third party (other than the parties to these proceedings or their advisors, the court and experts appointed by the court or as is provided by those provisions) information provided by the parties pursuant to their obligation to disclose or directions of the court. A non-disclosure agreement shall *not* be required by either party.

10. Henceforth, all communications to or from the Expert shall be made simultaneously with both parties, save:

a. The expert may meet and correspond with the Tax Payer in the absence of the Spouse (or the Spouse's representative), where, nonetheless copies of the correspondence or a note of the substance of the discussions is kept and is (subject to para ** below) made available to the Spouse's legal representative.

b. The expert may meet and correspond with the accountant of the Tax Payer and the Spouse [*consider with whom else meetings might be needed, eg Financial Director of the various companies comprising the Business Interests or their Accountants*] in the absence of the Spouse or the Spouse's representative, where, nonetheless copies of the correspondence or a note of the substance of the discussions is kept and is (subject to para [15] below) made available to the Spouse's legal representative.[5]

11. In any event the substance of all material information provided to the Expert shall be recorded in the Expert's report.

Further documents

12. The Tax Payer shall provide to the Expert [and the Spouse's legal representative] the documents set out in the schedule by no later than 4pm on [date].[6]

Further assistance

13. The parties shall each provide the Expert with any assistance reasonably requested by the Expert within a reasonable timeframe of a request in writing being delivered to their solicitors, (such request being simultaneously copied to the other solicitor) and in default application shall be made by the [Expert or either party] [party refusing provision of such assistance] [7] for further directions.

5 Consider whether a distinction is to be drawn between communications with the Tax Payer and the finance director/accountants … For example, the spouse's solicitor may want to receive contemporaneous copies of correspondence with the spouse but not with the FD or accountant. Where no distinction is drawn, these paragraphs may conflated.

6 See powers set out at 25.13. This provision is used where the expert has already identified requirements. Otherwise the expert will set out what they require once instructions are issued and the paragraph is likely to be removed in favour of the following paragraph, 13.

7 We suggest the latter provision is preferable so that party who objects must apply. Remember that the expert may be subject to a capped fee and so should not be burdened.

14. In the event that the Tax Payer shall object to the provision of information as being commercially sensitive then (in the absence of further application being made immediately) they shall nonetheless provide that information without redaction. The Expert will not produce that information to the Spouse without the Tax Payer's having had reasonable opportunity to make application to this court for further directions [*further directions may be wanted as to form of application and whether reserved to a specific Judge if available*].

Timetable for provision of the report

15. The report shall be sent to the parties simultaneously by [*time and date*]. It need not be filed with the court save as is required by FPR part 27A.

Scale of report

16. Permission is given for a report of up to ** pages[8].

Further questions

17. The parties may raise questions on that report no later than 4pm 14 days after delivery of the report [FPR 2.10, acknowledged] and will be acknowledged by the Expert within 2 days and answered by the Expert within a reasonable time of the delivery of such questions, proportionate to the scale of the enquiry made.[9]

Costs[10]

18. (Without prejudice to the parties' joint and several liability to the Expert for the costs of the Expert), those costs shall be met by the [Applicant / Respondent / parties in equal shares] in the first instance.

19. (Without prejudice to the parties' joint and several liability to the Expert for the costs of the Expert), the party raising questions on the report shall be responsible for the costs of the Expert in answering them. A separate invoice or invoices shall be raised by the Expert for the time spent in providing replies to questions raised on the report.

8 PD27A para 5.2A.1 limits reports to 40 pages and the executive summary at the front of the report to 4 pages unless directions are given to permit a longer report. Presumably the court will need reasons.

9 This provision changes the timetable of 10 days otherwise provided by 25.10, which may simply be too quick. The rules also provide detail as regards the form in which questions are raised and their scope and scale. A longer period may be needed and the point should be assessed carefully.

10 FPR 25.12(6) clarifies that there is joint and several liability for fees so any variance to this arrangement should be addressed in the order. A common variation is to provide that the report is paid for equally, but each party should pay for the costs of answering any questions they raise, in the first instance.

Attendance

20. Save as may be ordered by the court the Expert's written report and answers to the rule 24.10 questions shall be admissible as evidence without the attendance of the Expert. However, the Expert shall attend the final hearing to give oral evidence unless the parties agree that this is not needed no less than [28][56] days prior to the final hearing.

No other expert evidence without the court's permission

21. Save as is expressly ordered by the court, no further expert evidence shall be admissible before the court.

Unavoidable delay

22. In the event of unavoidable delay in the provision of the report and answering of questions by the Expert, extension of time to the timetabling may be agreed:

a. In writing between the parties and the Expert; and otherwise

b. On application for further directions, on reasonable notice to the Expert

Dated [*date*] **Approved by [*name*]**

Schedule of documents to be provided by the Tax Payer under para 10

APPENDIX 6

Form of instructions

Requirements of PD25D4.1:

The party responsible for instructing the expert shall, within 5 business days after the permission hearing, prepare (in agreement with the other parties where appropriate), file and serve a letter of instruction to the expert which shall –

(a) set out the context in which the expert's opinion is sought (including any ethnic, cultural, religious or linguistic contexts);

(b) set out the questions which the expert is required to answer and ensuring that they –
   (i) are within the ambit of the expert's area of expertise;
   (ii) do not contain unnecessary or irrelevant detail;
   (iii) are kept to a manageable number and are clear, focused and direct; and
   (iv) reflect what the expert has been requested to do by the court;

(c) list the documentation provided, or provide for the expert an indexed and paginated bundle which shall include –
   (i) an agreed list of essential reading; and
   (ii) a copy of this Practice Direction and Practice Directions 25B, 25E and where appropriate Practice Direction 15B;

(d) identify any materials provided to the expert which have not been produced either as original medical (or other professional) records or in response to an instruction from a party, and state the source of that material (such materials may contain an assumption as to the standard of proof, the admissibility or otherwise of hearsay evidence, and other important procedural and substantive questions relating to the different purposes of other enquiries);

(e) identify all requests to third parties for disclosure and their responses in order to avoid partial disclosure, which tends only to prove a case rather than give full and frank information;

(f) identify the relevant people concerned with the proceedings and inform the expert of his or her right to talk to them provided that an accurate record is made of the discussions;

(g) identify any other expert instructed in the proceedings and advise the expert of their right to talk to the other experts provided that an accurate record is made of the discussions;

(h) subject to any public funding requirement for prior authority, define the contractual basis upon which the expert is retained and in particular the funding mechanism including how much the expert will be paid (an hourly rate and overall estimate should already have been obtained), when the expert will be paid, and what limitation there might be on the amount the expert can charge for the work which they will have to do. In cases where the parties are publicly funded, there may also be a brief explanation of the costs and expenses excluded from public funding by Funding Code criterion 1.3 and the detailed assessment process.

Dear [ ],

We write to confirm your appointment to act as the part 25 expert in this matter on a SJE basis to report to the court on [the questions set out in the letter of enquiry sent to you by us and dated **] [the following matters: ***].

Please be advised as follows:

Target date for provision of your report

Information as regards fees

We attach:

1. The following documents to supplement those provided with our enquiry: **a.**

No doubt you will advise us as to what further information is required.

2. Order made by DJ ** in the form in which it was granted (and we will forward the sealed copy when it is to hand)

You will note that by [date]. [name] should have provided you with the following: **a. b.**

Please indicate to us if these documents are not delivered by then.

3. Basic contact information etc for the parties as "B"

4. Attachment "C" as a checklist for your report.

Please advise if anything else is needed.

We are copying this note to our counter-parts **. Please may all future communications about these instructions be had with both of us simultaneously.

Yours Faithfully

**

'B'

	Applicant	**Respondent**
Title		
Full name		
Any other names known by		

	Applicant	**Respondent**
Date of birth		
Occupation		
Nationality		
Residency for tax purposes		
Approximate annual income		
Approximate income	Basic/higher/additional rate taxpayer	Basic/higher/additional rate taxpayer
Addresses		
Telephone		
Email		
Solicitors		
• Names		
• Firm		
• Address/		
• Telephone/		
• Email		
Date of marriage	Court:	
	Court ref no:	
	Date of next hearing:	
Date of separation (if not agreed each party to make separate entries in the table)		

'C' CHECKLIST FOR PROVISION OF REPORT

PD25B		√
9.1(a)	My report provides details of my qualifications and experience.	
9.1(b)	I have identified the documents containing the material instructions I have received and the substance of any oral instructions.	
-„-	I have summarised the fact and instructions that are material	
9.1(c)	No test, examination or interview has been carried out save for interviews that I have conducted myself	

PD25B		√
9.1(f)	Where I have expressed an opinion, it takes into account all the material facts I have described my risk assessment process where relevant I have indicated where my conclusions are an hypothesis or where my opinions are qualified or provisional (indicating the qualification and the reasons for it.	
9.1(g)	Where I have given **a range** of opinion ● I have summarised the range, ● I have identified any unknown cause (i.e. something arising from the facts of the case or from the limits to my experience or the lack of research, peer review or support in the relevant field of expertise). ● I have given reasons for any opinion expressed and where possible have adopted a balance sheet approach to the factors.	
9.1(h)	I have provided a summary of my conclusions and opinions	
9.1(i)	I confirm that there is no conflict of interest engaged in my giving this report and that I will notify of any such conflict that emerges prior to the final hearing	
PD25(B) 4.1(a)	I understand my duties and confirm that I have complied with them. My duties include helping the court in relation to matters within my expertise (I acknowledge that this duty overrides any obligation to the person from whom I have received instructions or by whom I am paid.)	
-,,-	I am aware of my duty to the court and have complied with this duty I am aware of the requirements under FPR part 25 and the associated practice directions, including those under PD25B at 4.1, namely (a) to assist the court in accordance with the overriding duty; (b) to provide advice to the court that conforms to the best practice of my profession; (c) to answer the questions about which I am required to give an opinion …; (d) to provide an opinion that is independent of the party or parties instructing me;	

PD25B	√

(e) to confine my opinion to matters material to the issues in the case and in relation only to the questions that are within my expertise (skill and experience);

(f) where a question has been put which falls outside my expertise, to state this at the earliest opportunity and to volunteer an opinion as to whether another expert is required to bring expertise not possessed by those already involved or, in the rare case, as to whether a second opinion is required on a key issue and, if possible, what questions should be asked of the second expert;

(g) in expressing an opinion, to take into consideration all of the material facts including any relevant factors arising from ethnic, cultural, religious or linguistic contexts at the time the opinion is expressed;

I have complied with those duties.

9.1(j) I confirm that I have made clear which facts and matters referred to in this report are within my own knowledge and which are not. Those that are within my own knowledge I confirm to be true. The opinions I have expressed represent my true and complete professional opinions on the matters to which they refer

4.1(h) I will inform those instructing me without delay if, prior to any final hearing that I am notified about my opinions change, providing also details of the reasons for such change.

Signed:

Dated:

APPENDIX 7

Model form D11

APPLICATION NOTICE

To be completed by the relevant party	
The Family Court sitting at Bury St Edmunds	Case No.
Name of Petitioner/Applicant Velma Dinkley	
Name of Respondent Shaggy Rogers	
Name of Co-respondent (if applicable) N/a	
Solicitor's fee account no. 76447767	
Help with Fees – Ref no. (if applicable)	

If completing this form by hand, please use **black ink and BLOCK CAPITAL LETTERS** and tick the boxes that apply.

1. Please state your name or, if you are a solicitor, the name of your firm.

   Harvey Birdman LLP

2. Are you the ☐ Petitioner ☐ Applicant ☐ Respondent ☐ Co-Respondent ☐ Solicitor

   in the main proceedings, or

   ☐ Other?

   (if Other, please specify)

   If you are a solicitor, whom do you represent? The applicant

3. What order are you asking the court to make and why?

   Permission for the appointment of an expert under FPR25 to give evidence on the following tax questions:

   1. the net income likely to be derived from the operation of the Respondent's business ** Ltd
   2. The likely scale of tax applicable upon a disposal of the Respondent's interest in that business.

   Or as appropriate

   Please attach a draft copy of the order you are applying for.

4. This application may be considered by a judge on the information you have set out in your application notice. The judge may make an order on that information, without a hearing. However, any party who objects to an order made in this way may apply to the court within 7 days of it being made, for a hearing, at which all parties can attend, when the application will be reconsidered.

   Are there any reasons why this application should not be dealt with on paper by a judge? ☐ Yes ☐ No

   If Yes, please provide details.

   It can more conveniently be dealt with at the first appointment listed on **

5. Are there any reasons why this application should not be dealt with at a telephone hearing? ☐ Yes ☐ No

   If Yes, please provide details.

   As above

6. How long do you think the hearing will last?

   within 1st appointment listing

   Is this time estimate agreed by all parties? ☐ Yes ☐ No

7. Give details of any fixed hearing date or period?

   See first appointment listing referred to above

8. Does this application need to be heard by a specific judge/ level of judge? ☐ Yes ☐ No

   If Yes, please enter name/level of judge

9. Who should be served with this application? (If necessary, please continue on a separate sheet)

   Give names and addresses, including postcodes:

   The Respondent

10. What information will you be relying on?

    ☐ the attached statement.

    ☐ the divorce/dissolution/nullity/(judicial) separation petition

    ☐ the affidavit in support of the divorce/dissolution/nullity/(judicial) separation.

    ☐ the evidence set out in the box below.

A. BACKGROUND

By way of background as to the issues in the case and the questions that the expert would address:

–

–

B. INFORMATION

Permission is therefore sought for the appointment of an expert and the following information is provided in compliance with FPR 25.7(2) and PD25D 3.11

FPR 25.7(2)

(i) the field I which the expert evidence is required

TAX

(ii) where practicable, the name of the proposed expert;

TO FOLLOW

(iii) the issues to which the expert evidence is to relate;

I would be interested in our listing out all likely options here

(iv) whether the expert evidence could be obtained from a single joint expert;

IN OUR VIEW YES

PD25D 3.11

(a) the discipline, qualifications and expertise of the expert (by way of C.V. where possible);

Qualified accountant under *

Member of the Academy of Experts

Member of ICAEW

(b) the expert's availability to undertake the work;

The expert proposed will be available.

(c) the timetable for the report;

Within a matter of weeks of permission

(d) the responsibility for instruction;

Should be given to the Applicant

(e) whether the expert evidence can properly be obtained by only one party;

We suggest that the Joint Single Expert is the more appropriate vehicle for such evidence as is confirmed by PD25D 2.1. And see Mostyn J in J v J [2014] EWHC 3654 (Fam).

(f) why the expert evidence proposed cannot properly be given by an expert already instructed in the proceedings;

There is none yet instructed

(g) the likely cost of the report on an hourly or other charging basis:

This information is being obtained; and application is made in anticipation given the imminence of the first appointment.

(h) the proposed apportionment (at least in the first instance) of any jointly instructed expert's fee; when it is to be paid; and, if applicable, whether public funding has been approved.

The costs should be met equally in the first instance

C. ARGUMENT

The appointment is necessary (FPR 25.3 applied) in our submission given the tests provided under FPR 25.5 and the overriding objective, specifically:

1) The complexity of the issues involved
2) The relatively high value of what is at stake as against the relatively low costs of obtaining the report
3) The risk of the parties falling into dispute in the absence of the expert assistance, (thereby
   a. incurring greater cost to themselves
   b. creating risk to the progress of the case
   c. reducing the chances of settlement; and
   d. risking greater time being needed to ultimately dispose of the case
4) Giving leave
   a. will not delay timetabling of the case
   b. should reduce the duration of attendance upon the court
5) This application is made in compliance with FPR 25.6 (making application no later than the first appointment).

Statement of Truth

This section must be completed by the person making this application (referred to in this section as the 'Applicant'), or by a solicitor acting for the Applicant.

The Applicant believes that the facts stated in this section (and any continuation sheets) are true

I am duly authorised by the Applicant to sign this statement

Signed: Harvey Birdman — Dated: [ ][ ] / [ ][ ] / [ ][ ][ ][ ]

Applicant's solicitor

Print full name	Harvey Birdman
Name of Applicant's solicitor's firm	Harvey Birdman, Attorney at Law LLP
Position or office held	Principal

(if signing on behalf of firm or company)

Proceedings for contempt of court may be brought against a person who makes or causes to be made, a false statement in a document verified by a statement of truth.

11. Signature and address details

Signed: — Dated: [ ][ ] / [ ][ ] / [ ][ ][ ][ ]

Applicant's solicitor

Position or office held:

(if signing on behalf of firm or company)

Applicant's address to which documents about this application should be sent:	If applicable	
	Telephone no.	
	Fax no.	
	DX no.	
	Your ref.	

E-mail	HB@HBProdns.co.uk

NOTICE OF APPLICATION – NOTES FOR GUIDANCE

Court Staff cannot give out legal advice. If you need information or advice on a legal problem you can contact Community Legal Advice on 0845 345 4 345 or www.communitylegaladvice.org.uk, or a Citizens Advice Bureau. Details of your local offices and contact numbers are available on their website www.citizensadvice.org.uk.

Paying the court fee

A court fee is payable depending on the type of application you are making. For example:

- To apply for leave to issue a divorce petition without a marriage certificate.
- To apply for an order within existing proceedings.
- To apply for directions to be given by the judge in existing proceedings.
- To ask for a hearing to be adjourned.

For more information on court fees, please refer to booklet **EX50 – Civil and Family Court fees**.

This booklet is available from your local court or on the internet at hmctsformfinder.justice.gov.uk.

What if I cannot afford to pay a court fee?

If you cannot afford to pay a court fee, you may be eligible for help with your court fee in full or in part. The booklet **EX160 Guide – How to apply for help with court fees** gives all the information you need. You can get a copy from any court office or online at hmctsformfinder.justice.gov.uk.

Completing the form

Question 3

Set out what order you are applying for and why; eg to adjourn the hearing because…, to apply for leave to issue my divorce petition without my marriage certificate because… etc. If you are applying to vary an existing order or to re-activate proceedings you should enter the details here. A draft copy of any order you are applying for must be attached to your application. The draft should state the amount of any costs to be paid by the other party and a brief calculation of how it was arrived at.

Question 4 and 5

Most applications will require a hearing and you will be expected to attend. The court will allocate a hearing date and time for the application. Please indicate in a covering letter any dates that you are unavailable to attend within the next six weeks.

The court will only deal with the application 'without a hearing' in the following circumstances:

- where all the parties agree to the terms of the order being asked for;
- where all the parties agree that the court should deal with the application without a hearing; or

- where the court does not consider that a hearing would be appropriate.

Telephone hearings are only available in applications where at least one of the parties involved in the case is legally represented.

Not all applications will be suitable for a telephone hearing and the court may refuse your request.

Question 6

If you do not know how long the hearing will take do not guess, instead leave these boxes blank.

Question 7

If your case has already been allocated a hearing date or trial period please insert details of those dates in the box.

Question 8

Enter the details if there is a requirement for your case to be heard by a specific judge or level of judge.

Question 9

Please indicate in the box provided who you want the court to send a copy of the application to.

Question 10

In this section please set out the information you want the court to take into account in support of the application you are making. If you wish to rely on:

- a **witness statement**, tick the first box and attach the statement to the application notice. A witness statement form is available on request from the court office.
- a **statement of case**, tick the second box if you intend to rely on your particulars of claim or defence in support of your application.
- **written evidence** on this form, tick the fourth box and enter details in the space provided. You must also complete the statement of truth. Proceedings for contempt of court may be brought against a person who signs a statement of truth without an honest belief in its truth.

Question 11

The application must be signed and dated and your current address and contact details completed. If you agree that the court and the other parties may communicate with you by Document Exchange, telephone, facsimile or email, please complete the details.

Before returning your form to the court

Have you:

- signed the form on page 3?
- enclosed the correct fee or an application for fee remission?
- if you have applied for your Help with Fees online please insert your Help with Fees reference number in the box provided at the top right hand side of this form.
- made sufficient copies of your application and supporting documentation? You will need to submit one copy for each party to be served and one copy for the court.

APPENDIX 8

Possible agenda points for telephoned discussion with expert

1. Any additional informational needs on part of expert to give guidance at this stage.
2. Consideration of the question posed:
   a. What is missing.
   b. What other tax-planning options need to be explored.
3. Likely objections on the part of the judge to the instruction of the expert and how those should be addressed.
4. What information will the expert need upon instruction:
   a. Whether this could more conveniently be secured from the parties directly and if so;
   b. How will the solicitors be kept informed of the progress of that process.
5. Timescale and cost of report ... when are the fees due for settlement on the report.
6. FPR 25.10 questions:
   a. Whether they can be raised within 10 days of the report – if not what longer period will be needed.
   b. Likely period for provision of responses by expert – any pressing hearings/ deadlines or dependency for those answers.
   c. That the question raiser will discharge the costs arising in the first instance ... timeframe for delivery of bill and when due for settlement.

Other situation-specific considerations

7. On income issues:
   a. What has been the position historically? Eg was one joint accountant filing for both?
   b. What tax returns have been filed and what is outstanding.
8. On non-disclosure issues – possibly an area where a shadow expert would be helpful.
   a. Set out at the forefront the SJE's duty/or non duty to disclose to HMRC.
   b. Be considerate in what you tell the SJE.
   c. How many years does the non-disclosure affect?
   d. Is the purposes to get a figure for exposure or is the purpose to disclose to HMRC?
9. On complex issues:
   a. Set out the background briefly, eg:
      i. first or second marriages;
      ii. do any parties receive income from trusts;
      iii. Any residence or domicile issues.

APPENDIX 9

Case quotes for fundamentals and principles table from page 266

Key elements of text are underlined.

Costs management

22. By this stage, around £1 million in costs had been expended but much uncertainty and lack of information about important matters existed. However, one thing was very clear from the limited information that had been gathered, and this was that the preparation of the case had failed to identify material concerning the hotel and the business carried on at it that would almost inevitably have a significant impact on the cases being advanced by both parties. So, it was correctly recognised by counsel for both parties that the trial could not continue on the basis of the information then available, and that there was a need for the parties to gather further information and evidence and, in the light of that, to consider their positions at law.

23. This result is lamentable.

Charles J in *X v X* [2012] EWHC 538 (Fam)

THE LITIGATION COSTS

[18] The total bill is some *£930,000* in the round. This, in the context of assets currently worth just over £6m. Accordingly, the costs represent about 15% of this family's worldly wealth. This is a tragedy particularly as I am not convinced that the sums in issue, in reality, ever amounted to anything approaching £1m.

Baron J in *K v K* [2005] EWHC 1070 (Fam)

9. In this case since the failure of the FDR a mere eight months ago the parties have between them spent on costs the staggering sum of just under £700,000. I must confess to have been almost lost for words when the scale of this madness was revealed to me. They have spent a total of £920,000 in costs. Of this they have spent, as I have said, £154,000 on forensic accountants

Mostyn J in *J v J* [2014] EWHC 3654 (Fam)

And later in the same case:

16. In my opinion only if these two steps [fixed pricing and a court-imposed costs cap] are taken will the grotesque leaching of costs, such as has occurred in this case, be arrested. It might also have the beneficial consequence that the present volume of self-representation deriving from the wholesale withdrawal of legal aid from private family law cases is reduced. If a litigant on the cusp of self-representation knew at the start of the case how much it was going to cost for each phase then he may well opt for representation. The benefits of representation are too obvious to spell out extensively. Far more cases with the benefit of representation settle, with the resultant avoidance of the legacy of heartache that contested litigation engenders. Those cases that do fight will be on rational and properly pleaded justiciable issues. The lengthy delays in the court system caused by the explosion in self-representation may be reduced.

5. As can be seen, the parties are £687,000 apart. Not very surprisingly, the combined costs of the parties amount to £652,000. It seems to be an iron law of ancillary relief proceedings that the final difference between the parties is approximately equal to the costs that they have spent.

Mostyn J in *N v F* [2011] EWHC 586 (Fam)

MEETING DEADLINES

50. It is, unhappily, symptomatic of a deeply rooted culture in the family courts which, however long established, will no longer be tolerated …

51. I refer to the slapdash, lackadaisical and on occasions almost contumelious attitude which still far too frequently characterises the response to orders made by family courts. There is simply no excuse for this. Orders, including interlocutory orders, must be obeyed and complied with to the letter and on time. Too often they are not. They are not preferences, requests or mere indications; they are orders…

52. The law is clear. As Romer LJ said in *Hadkinson v Hadkinson* [1952] P 285, 288, in a passage endorsed by the Privy Council in *Isaacs v Robertson* [1985] AC 97, 101:

> 'It is the plain and unqualified obligation of every person against, or in respect of whom, an order is made by a court of competent jurisdiction, to obey it unless and until that order is discharged. The uncompromising nature of this obligation is shown by the fact that it extends even to cases where the person affected by an order believes it to be irregular or even void.' …

53. Let me spell it out. An order that something is to be done by 4 pm on Friday, is an order to do that thing by 4 pm on Friday, not by 4.21 pm on Friday let alone by 3.01 pm the following Monday or sometime later the following week. A person who finds himself unable to comply timeously with his obligations under an order should apply for an extension of time *before the time for compliance has expired.*

Sir James Munby, former President of the Family Division, originally from In re W [2013 EWCA Civ 1177 but quoted with approval just about everywhere ever since and ensuring the principle has jumped to financial remedy proceedings.

BUNDLES

***Re L (Procedure: Bundles: Translation)* [2015] EWFC 15**

Munby P

[20] I make two final observations about PD27A, both of which bear on the crucial issue of the size of the bundle – something which is at the core of the difficulties in the present case. The first is that PD27A para 4.1 spells out the fundamental principle that:

> 'The bundle shall contain copies of only those documents which are relevant to the hearing and which it is necessary for the court to read or which will actually be referred to during the hearing (emphasis added).'

In other words, there is a double requirement to be satisfied before any document is included in the bundle: it must be relevant and it must be a document which will used, in the sense that it will either be read or referred to. This principle is reinforced by the list of documents which PD27A para 4.1 states 'must not be included in the bundle unless specifically directed by the court'.

[21] The other observation is the desirability of documents being, to adopt the language of PD27A para 4.4, 'as short and succinct as possible'…

…

[23] This endemic failure of the professions to comply with PD27A must end, and it must end now. Fifteen years of default are enough. From now on:

i) Defaulters can have no complaint if they are exposed, and they should expect to be exposed, to public condemnation in judgments in which they are named.

ii) Defaulters may find themselves exposed to financial penalties of the kind referred to by Mostyn J in *J v J*.

iii) Defaulters may find themselves exposed to the sanction meted out by Holman J in *Seagrove v Sullivan*.

THE ALTERNATIVE OF ARBITRATION

53. I would remark that if parties wish to have a trial with numerous bundles then it is open to them to enter into an arbitration agreement which specifically allows for that.

Mostyn J in *J v J* [2014] EWHC 3654 (Fam)

if parties wish, at their own expense, to litigate to their hearts' content, with thousands and thousands of pages of documents, there is a mechanism available to them known as private arbitration. But litigation within the courts has to be the subject of much more rigorous discipline and structure, precisely because the courts have a duty to ensure that an appropriate, but only an appropriate, share of the court's resources are allocated to any one case. The same judges have to deal also with an enormous number of very difficult cases involving the future of vulnerable children, and the care and treatment of sick people, including mentally incapacitated people. It is simply not tolerable that we go on and on affording to people like Sandra and Larry an estimated eight days of court time on a dispute that ultimately is measured in something not exceeding about £500,000.

Holman J in *Seagrove v Sullivan* [2014] EWHC 4110 (Fam)

A FUNDAMENTAL CHALLENGE?

30. I would add that, in my view, the application of the sharing rationale, particularly in non-paradigm cases, and so where it does not apply with full force, has introduced into this field of litigation property and commercial issues which the present system was not designed to deal with, and which historically practitioners in this field have not had to deal with.

31. These property and commercial issues have introduced a need (a) to identify property interests by applying property, company, trust and tax law, (b) to consider commercially and pragmatically viable options, particularly for private companies that are difficult to value, whose shares may not have a market, which it may be unfair to sell and which cannot provide funding to meet a clean break solution, (c) to consider, on an asset and case specific basis, apportionment and division of assets and their value at various times and (d) to identify relevant matrimonial choices. This is a far cry from an approach based on the payee's reasonable requirements and, it follows that, a system that has been developed against that overall approach (found to be wrong in White), is highly likely to need significant adjustment, that involves significant changes in the mind set of those applying it, to focus on the legal, commercial and evidential issues that arise and form the essential building blocks upon which the s. 25 exercise now has to be carried out.

32. Problems of the types I have identified, and which were acknowledged to exist by counsel, relate primarily to big money cases, and disproportionate costs burdens are more likely to arise in cases where the money is not that big.

33. In my view, the key to their solution is that in those cases there should be a change of practice to ensure that at an early stage the relevant issues, and thus the relevant facts and factors, that the court will be invited to find and take into account are identified. It this is done properly, and at an appropriate stage, it should provide the platform for:

i) the identification of the documents that need to be produced, inspected and considered; (here the transfer of the hotel, the leases, company documents and documents relating to the transfer and the leases – which it seems were not properly disclosed, sought or considered),

ii) the identification of the expert evidence that needs to be gathered, and so the drafting of appropriately focused instructions to the experts; (here the valuation of the freehold of the hotel – which was not done before trial), and

iii) the identification of the other evidence that needs to be gathered, which will generally need to be served much earlier than is often now the case; (here the husband's explanation of the gift and the wife's case that the freehold of the hotel should be treated as a matrimonial asset – both of which were deficient).

34. If this change is it to bring about a significant improvement it will have to be accompanied by a change in approach by practitioners and courts to the preparation of cases for hearing that adds a focus on:

i) the property and other issues referred to in paragraph 31,

ii) the application of the relevant substantive law to those issues,

iii) the law of evidence, and

iv) the range of practical and commercial options available to achieve a fair result.

Charles J in *X v X* [2012] EWHC 538 (Fam)

CASELAW ON EXPERTS

'The problem does not lie with the experts themselves. It lies in the use we make of them.' (Sir James Munby)

'Three things are needed

1) A reduction in the use of experts

2) A more focussed approach in the cases where experts are still needed

3) A reduction in the length of reports.'

Opinion evidence permissible where from an expert

The prohibition on a witness giving evidence of an opinion rather than a fact is relaxed where the witness is an expert giving evidence in their area of expertise:

S3 Civil Evidence Act 1972: where a person is called as a witness in any civil proceedings, his opinion on any relevant matter on which he is qualified to give expert evidence shall be admissible in evidence.

Practitioners must be meticulous to ensure that information is given about an expert's qualifications, expertise and experience

Don't just append report to the form E and sit back and wait for questions

> *'but it is quite wrong to append a very full expert report and yet more wrong then to turn up at the first appointment and argue that that report should stand as the only evidence about the value of those shares and that the wife should be confined merely to asking questions of the husband's expert. For that is what happened here. In those circumstances the Deputy District Judge was persuaded, wrongly in my view, to allow the wife to have her own expert. He should have ordered that a SJE be instructed'.*

Mostyn J in *J v J* [2014] EWHC 3654 (Fam). Para 45

But it is permissible to append an accountant's letter seeking to justify a Form E figure:

It is of course permissible to append a short accountant's letter justifying a Form E figure; this is what the Form requires.

An expert is only appointed where necessary FPR:

Control of expert evidence in proceedings other than children proceedings 25.4

(1) This rule applies to proceedings other than children proceedings.

(2) A person may not without the permission of the court put expert evidence (in any form) before the court.

(3) The court may give permission as mentioned in paragraph (2) only if the court is of the opinion that the expert evidence is necessary to assist the court to resolve the proceedings.

In re: P (Children) (placement orders: parental consent)[3] in which Lord Justice Wall (as he was then) stated,

> "'Necessary' takes it colour from the context that in the Strasbourg Jurisprudence has a meaning lying somewhere between 'indispensable' on the one hand and 'useful', 'reasonable' or 'desirable' on the other hand. It implies the existing of what the Strasbourg Jurisprudence calls a 'pressing social need'."

in *Re H-L (A Child)* [2013] EWCA Civ 655, [2013] All ER (D) 112 (Jun), Munby P said:

> 'The short answer is that "necessary" means necessary [...] This court said it "has a meaning lying somewhere between 'indispensable' on the one hand and 'useful', 'reasonable' or 'desirable' on the other hand', having 'the connotation of the imperative, what is demanded rather than what is merely optional or reasonable or desirable."' (para [3])

The application for an expert must have appended a draft order

PD25C, paragraph 3.11, requires a draft order to be attached to the application setting out various matters, including the following:

> '(a) the issues in the proceedings to which the expert evidence is to relate and which the court is to identify;
>
> (b) the questions relating to the issues in the case which the expert is to answer and which the court is to approve ensuring that they –
>
> (i) are within the ambit of the expert's area of expertise;
>
> (ii) do not contain unnecessary or irrelevant detail;
>
> (iii) are kept to a manageable number and are clear, focused and direct;
>
> (c) the party who is responsible for drafting the letter of instruction and providing the documents to the expert;
>
> (d) the timetable within which the report is to be prepared, filed and served'.

Late applications will need to be strong

[27] FPR 2010 Rule 25.4 provides that a person may not without permission put expert evidence before the court. That does not prevent a party obtaining expert evidence. In a case such as this, it would usually be expected that a party wishing to adduce expert evidence would obtain that evidence and then seek permission to adduce it. That is what the wife did, probably earlier this year, but certainly before 11 March 2014.

[28] By FPR 2010 Rule 25.4(3), formerly Rule 25.1 when this application was considered by Coleridge J, the court may give permission to adduce the evidence: 'Only if the court is of the opinion that the expert evidence is necessary to assist the court to resolve the proceedings.'

[29] The language of the rule is discretionary and an opinion upon the evidence is necessary. It is also permissive. Evidence may be admitted if the court is of the opinion that it is necessary, but cannot be admitted if the court is not of that opinion. In order to decide whether the expert evidence is necessary, the court must consider a number of factors set out in FPR 2010 Rule 25.5(1), specifically including: 'Any failure to comply with rule 25.6 or any direction of the court about expert evidence.'

[30] FPR 2010 Rule 25.6 provides the mandatory timetable for seeking expert evidence: '...parties must apply for permission... as soon as possible; (d) in proceedings for a financial remedy, no later than the first appointment...'

[31] Again, the emphasis is on steps being taken early and promptly.

[32] It follows that one of the matters which the court is obliged to consider when deciding whether expert evidence is necessary is whether it has been sought as soon as possible and if not by the date of the first appointment, which in this case was the directions order made by Eleanor King J on 14 June 2013, the reason why it was not sought at that time. The fact that in June 2013 all other valuations were directed is relevant.

[33] 'Necessary' in the context of FPR 2010 Part 25 has a meaning: 'Lying somewhere between 'indispensable' on the one hand and 'useful', 'reasonable' or 'desirable' on the other hand', having 'the connotation of the imperative, what is demanded rather than what is merely optional or reasonable or desirable.' per Sir James Munby P in *Re: HL (A Child)* [2013] EWCA Civ 655.

Cooper-Hohn v Hohn [2014] EWCA Civ 896

Only ever a SJE says Mostyn J in J v J

One reason why so much forensic acrimony was generated, with the consequential burgeoning of costs, was that the Deputy District Judge at the first appointment on 9 November 2012 permitted each party to have their own expert to value the husband's business interests, notwithstanding the terms of Part 25 FPR which clearly stated then (and even more strongly states now – see PD 25D para 2.1) that a SJE should be used 'wherever possible'. Not 'ideally' or 'generally' but 'wherever possible'. In this case the forensic accountants have filed a total of no fewer than six expert reports and have prepared a joint statement setting out their extensive disagreements. They have charged a total of £154,000 in fees. The husband has been permitted during the course of the case to ditch his expert and to instruct a new one.

On 17 June 2014 Judge Bancroft actually mooted the instruction of a SJE in respect of the husband's business interests but I was told that both counsel 'poo-poo-ed' the idea, and in such circumstances the judge acquiesced. Again, in my view that was the wrong decision. On neither occasion was it demonstrated that the appointment of a SJE was impossible, which is what PD25D para 2.1 literally requires. (para 46)

… Unless per Moor J it is High court business and you are appointing 2 experts to avoid 3:

68. The Husband was not happy with her report. He asked detailed questions to her more than once. He then sought permission to rely on his own expert forensic accountant, Sally Longworth of Grant Thornton. Almost inevitably, the Wife then sought permission for her own expert, Peter Smith of Quantis.

69. Ironically, this meant that an attempt to reduce the accountancy evidence to one expert rather than two has led to there being three experts. This is not the first time this has happened before me. As far as I can see, it has become

almost the norm in contested litigation in the Family Division where there is an issue as to the value of a privately owned business. It has led me to wonder whether it is ever appropriate to have a Single Joint Expert accountant in a High Court case. I do accept that it would be wrong to dictate the position without regard to those High Court cases that settle on the basis of just one Single Joint Expert. I will therefore say no more about it at the moment. It may be that there should be some research into this issue. Moreover, I am making absolutely no criticism of orders for Single Joint Expert accountants in non-High Court cases where such an order is not only sensible but absolutely essential to save costs. Equally, Single Joint Expert property valuations are always required, regardless of the value of the property concerned.

SK v TK [2013] EWHC 834 (Fam)

Persuading the court to have a second expert

(pre FPR civil cases)

***Daniels v Walker* [2000] 1 WLR 1382 CA**, a case involving a party unhappy with the jointly appointed single expert now seeking a further such:

'28. … The correct approach is to regard the instruction of an expert jointly by the parties as the first step in obtaining expert evidence in a particular issue. It is to be hoped that in the majority of cases it will not only be the first step but the last step. If having obtained a joint expert's report, a party, for reasons which are not fanciful wishes to obtain further information before making a decision as to whether or not there is a particular part (or indeed the whole) of the expert's report which he or she may wish to challenge, then they should, subject to the discretion of the court be permitted to obtain that evidence.

29. In the majority of cases, the sensible approach will not be to ask the court straight away to allow the dissatisfied party to call a second expert. In many cases it would be wrong to make a decision until one is in a position to consider the position in the round. You cannot make generalisations, but in a case where there is a modest sum involved a court may take a more rigorous approach. It may be said in a case where there is a modest amount involved that it would be disproportionate to obtain a second report in any circumstances. At most what should be allowed is merely to put a question to the expert who has already prepared a report.

30. …31. In a case where there is a substantial sum involved, one starts, as I have indicated, from the position that, wherever possible, a joint report is obtained. If there is disagreement on that report, then there would be an issue as to whether to ask questions or whether to get your own expert's report. If questions do not resolve the matter and a party, or both parties, obtain their own expert's reports, then that will result in a decision having to be reached as to what evidence should be called. That decision should not be taken until there has been a meeting between the experts involved. It may be that agreement could then be reached; it may be that agreement is reached as a result of asking the appropriate questions. It is only as a last resort that you accept that it is necessary for oral evidence to be given by the experts before the court. The expense of cross examination of expert witnesses at the hearing, even in a substantial case, can be very expensive.

32. The great advantage of adopting the course of instructing a joint expert at the outset is that in the majority of cases it will have the effect of narrowing the issues. The fact that additional experts may have to be involved is regrettable, but in the majority of cases the expert issues will already have been reduced. Even if you have the unfortunate result that there are three different views as to the right outcome on a particular issue, the expense which will be incurred as result of that is justified by the prospects of it being avoided in the majority of cases.

Lord Woolf MR

- ***Stallwood v David*** [2006] All ER (D) 286 (Oct)

Held – The appeal would be allowed. The scheme of CPR 35 concerning experts' discussions did not rule out the granting of permission to call a further expert following an experts' discussion. It would, however, be a rare case where that would be appropriate. Where a court was asked for permission to adduce expert evidence from a new expert in circumstances where the applicant was dissatisfied with the opinion of his own expert following the experts' discussion it should do so only where there was good reason to suppose that the applicant's first expert had agreed with the expert instructed by the other side or had modified his opinion for reasons which could not properly or fairly support his revised opinion. Such reasons would include that the expert had clearly stepped outside his expertise or brief, or otherwise had shown himself to be incompetent. It was likely that it would be a rare case in which such a good reason could be shown. Where good reason was shown, the court would have to consider whether, having regard to all the circumstances of the case and the overriding objective, it could properly be said that further expert evidence was reasonably required to resolve the proceedings.

In the circumstances of the instant case, the judge below had not had regard to all the relevant matters when he had considered the claimant's application. That application should be considered afresh. The way in which the judge had dealt with the application, and the claimant's sense of grievance, was an additional and exceptional reason why the application should be considered afresh. If the claimant was not permitted to rely upon the evidence of the new expert and the court subsequently accepted the evidence of the original expert, she would understandably have a sense of grievance judged objectively. Having regard to the very special circumstances of the case, dealing with the case justly required that permission be granted to the claimant to rely upon the expert evidence of the new expert.

***Cosgrove & Anor. v Pattison & Anor.* 2000 WL 1841601 (2000)**

After quoting Lord Woolf's para 31 from *Daniels v Walker*, above Lord Neuberger continued:

> 'In my judgment although it would be wrong to pretend that this is an exhaustive list, the factors to be taken into account when considering an application to permit a further expert to be called are these. First, the nature of the issue or issues; secondly, the number of issues between the parties; thirdly, the reason the new expert is wanted; fourthly, the amount at stake and, if it is not purely money, the nature of the issues at stake and their importance; fifthly, the effect of permitting one party to call further expert evidence on the conduct of the trial; sixthly, the delay, if any, in making the application, seventhly, any delay that the instructing and calling of the new expert will cause; eighthly, any other special features of the case; and, finally, and in a sense all embracing, the overall justice to the parties in the context of the litigation.'

The case then turns to a careful examination of those elements and so provides an illustration as to the exercise and how the question of costs should be dealt with.

'No unilateral conversations'

Peet v Mid Kent Healthcare NHS Trust – court of appeal' .

Lord Woolf CJ, Simon Brown and Buxton LJJ, November 2001

The claimant and his legal representatives wished to have a conference with the joint experts, in order to discuss the evidence and their view of it, and wanted that conference to take place without any of the defendant's representatives being present. The defendant applied to the judge for ruling on that issue. The judge took the view that it was not appropriate for a conference of that nature to take place and ordered, inter alia, that no conference be conducted by the claimant with the joint experts without the written consent of the defendant. The claimant appealed.

The appeal would be dismissed.

The framework was designed to ensure an open process so that both parties knew what information had been placed before the single expert. Whilst there was nothing against discussion taking place with a joint expert where both sides were present, to do so in the absence of the other party was impermissible. The protocol of the Academy of Experts (published 1 June 2001) specifically stated that a single joint expert should not attend a meeting with one side unless the other side had agreed in writing. The critical message in relation to litigation in the nature of that in the instant case was that there was a need for co-operation and openness on both sides, which would go a long way to meeting the concerns of people in the position of the claimant and his family. If an open approach were not adopted, it would lead to an unnecessary adversarial approach which would only increase the concerns of a claimant and his family.

[38] In addition to this perceived difficulty. There was an order for property to be valued on a joint basis. This was done but the wife's solicitors sought updated values from the joint valuer and wrote directly without reference to the husband's team. This is not acceptable. When a joint valuer is appointed, then all communications should be on a joint basis (unless the parties otherwise agree in writing). Indeed, representatives from both sides (or neither) should be able to be present when valuations are undertaken (unless the parties otherwise agree in writing). If one party seeks to circumvent this simple methodology there will inevitably be a sense of unfairness, even if the resulting valuation is beyond reproach.

[39] The general practice in the Family Division should be that only joint approaches are acceptable and if there is non co-operation from one side, then this cannot be circumvented by unilateral action but should be dealt with by an application. I am aware of the terms of CPR r 38.8 but it seems to me that in matrimonial cases, where emotions often run high, it is prudent to act co-operatively and therefore jointly. Moreover the Best Practice Guide for Instructing a Single Joint Expert sub-r 9 appears to confirm that in family cases supplementary instructions should not be given 'unless the other party has agree or the court has sanctioned them'.

Baron J in K v K (ancillary relief: management of difficult cases) [2005] EWHC 1070 (Fam)

TAE CODE OF PRACTICE FOR EXPERTS

This code of Practice should be followed by all Academy of Experts members. It may also be considered Best Practice for other Experts both in England and Wales and around the world.

The Code was endorsed on 22nd June 2005 by Rt Hon Lord Phillips of Worth Matravers Master of the Rolls and Chairman of the Civil Justice Council and again on 26th June 2006 the Code was endorsed by the Master of the Rolls, Rt Hon Sir Anthony Clarke and the President of the Queen's Bench Division, Rt Hon Sir Igor Judge for use in Criminal proceedings.

Preamble

This Code of Practice shows minimum standards of practice that should be maintained by all Experts.

It is recognised that there are different systems of law and many jurisdictions in Europe, any of which may impose additional duties and responsibilities which must be complied with by the Expert.

There are in addition to the Code of Practice, General Professional Principles with which an Expert should comply.

These include the Expert:

- Being a 'fit and proper' person
- Having and maintaining a high standard of technical knowledge and practical experience in their professional field
- Keeping their knowledge up to date both in their expertise and as Experts and undertaking appropriate continuing professional developments and training.

The Code

1. Experts shall not do anything in the course of practising as an Expert, in any manner which compromises or impairs or is likely to compromise or impair any of the following:
   a. the Expert's independence, impartiality, objectivity and integrity,
   b. the Expert's duty to the Court or Tribunal,
   c. the good repute of the Expert or of Experts generally,
   d. the Expert's proper standard of work,
   e. the Expert's duty to maintain confidentiality.
2. An Expert who is retained or employed in any contentious proceeding shall not enter into any arrangement which could compromise his impartiality nor make his fee dependent on the outcome of the case nor should he accept any benefits other than his fee and expenses.
3. An Expert should not accept instructions in any matter where there is an actual or potential conflict of interests. Notwithstanding this rule, if full disclosure is made to the judge or to those appointing him, the Expert may in appropriate cases accept instructions when those concerned specifically acknowledge the disclosure. Should an actual or potential conflict occur after instructions have been accepted, the Expert shall immediately notify all concerned and in appropriate cases resign his appointment.
4. An Expert shall for the protection of his client maintain with a reputable insurer proper insurance for an adequate indemnity
5. Experts shall not publicise their practices in any manner which may reasonably be regarded as being in bad taste. Publicity must not be inaccurate or misleading in any way.
6. An Expert shall comply with all appropriate Codes of Practice and Guidelines.

Note:

1: The Academy has a prescribed minimum requirement for £1m for professional indemnity cover.

APPENDIX 10

Part 25

EXPERTS AND ASSESSORS

A stripped-down version of the FPR relating to experts in financial proceedings with underlining of key elements. (The elements relating only to partisan experts are in italics).

EXPERTS' OVERRIDING DUTY TO THE COURT

25.3

(1) It is the duty of experts to help the court on matters within their expertise.

(2) This duty overrides any obligation to the person from whom experts have received instructions or by whom they are paid.

(Particular duties of an expert are set out in Practice Direction 25B (The Duties of an Expert, the Expert's Report and Arrangements for an Expert to Attend Court.).

CONTROL OF EXPERT EVIDENCE IN PROCEEDINGS OTHER THAN CHILDREN PROCEEDINGS

25.4

(1) This rule applies to proceedings other than children proceedings.

(2) A person may not without the permission of the court put expert evidence (in any form) before the court.

(3) The court may give permission as mentioned in paragraph (2) only if the court is of the opinion that the expert evidence is necessary to assist the court to resolve the proceedings..

FURTHER PROVISIONS ABOUT THE COURT'S POWER TO RESTRICT EXPERT EVIDENCE

25.5

(1) …

(2) When deciding whether to give permission as mentioned in rule 25.4(1) in proceedings other than children proceedings, the court is to have regard in particular to –
   (a) the issues to which the expert evidence would relate;
   (b) the questions which the court would require the expert to answer;
   (c) the impact which giving permission would be likely to have on the timetable, duration and conduct of the proceedings;
   (d) any failure to comply with rule 25.6 or any direction of the court about expert evidence; and
   (e) the cost of the expert evidence..

WHEN TO APPLY FOR THE COURT'S PERMISSION

25.6 Unless the court directs otherwise, parties must apply for the court's permission as mentioned in … rule 25.4(2) as soon as possible and –

…

(d) in proceedings for a financial remedy, no later than the first appointment; ….

WHAT AN APPLICATION NOTICE REQUESTING THE COURT'S PERMISSION MUST INCLUDE

25.7

(1) Part 18 applies to an application for the court's permission as mentioned in … rule 25.4(2).

(2) In any proceedings –
   (a) the application notice requesting the court's permission as mentioned in … rule 25.4(2) must state –
      (i) the field in which the expert evidence is required;
      (ii) where practicable, the name of the proposed expert;
      (iii) the issues to which the expert evidence is to relate;
      (iv) whether the expert evidence could be obtained from a single joint expert;
      (v) the other matters set out in Practice Direction … 25D, as the case may be; and
   (b) a draft of the order sought is to be attached to the application notice requesting the court's permission and that draft order must set out the matters specified in Practice Direction25D ….

WHERE PERMISSION IS GRANTED

25.8

(1) In any proceedings, where the court grants permission as mentioned in … rule 25.4(2) –

(a) it will grant permission only in relation to the expert named or the field identified in the application notice requesting the court's permission; and
(b) the court will give directions specifying the date by which the expert is to provide a written report..

GENERAL REQUIREMENT FOR EXPERT EVIDENCE TO BE GIVEN IN A WRITTEN REPORT

25.9

(1) Expert evidence is to be given in a written report unless the court directs otherwise.

(2) The court will not direct an expert to attend a hearing unless it is necessary to do so in the interests of justice.

WRITTEN QUESTIONS TO EXPERTS

25.10

(1) A party may put written questions about an expert's report to –
  (a) *an expert instructed by another party*; or
  (b) a single joint expert appointed under rule 25.11.

(2) Unless the court directs otherwise or a practice direction provides otherwise, written questions under paragraph (1)–
  (a) must be proportionate;
  (b) may be put once only;
  (c) must be put within 10 days beginning with the date on which the expert's report was served;
  (d) must be for the purpose only of clarification of the report; and
  (e) must be copied and sent to the other parties at the same time as they are sent to the expert.

(3) An expert's answers to questions put in accordance with paragraph (1) –
  (a) must be given within the timetable specified by the court; and
  (b) are treated as part of the expert's report.

(4) Where –
  (a) a party has put a written question to an expert instructed by another party; and
  (b) the expert does not answer that question,

  the court may make one or both of the following orders in relation to the party who instructed the expert –
  (i) that the party may not rely on the evidence of that expert; or
  (ii) that the party may not recover the fees and expenses of that expert from any other party..

COURT'S POWER TO DIRECT THAT EVIDENCE IS TO BE GIVEN BY A SINGLE JOINT EXPERT

25.11

(1) Where two or more parties wish to put expert evidence before the court on a particular issue, the court may direct that the evidence on that issue is to be given by a single joint expert.

(2) Where the parties who wish to put expert evidence before the court ('the relevant parties') cannot agree who should be the single joint expert, the court may –
   (a) select the expert from a list prepared or identified by the relevant parties; or
   (b) direct that the expert be selected in such other manner as the court may direct..

INSTRUCTIONS TO A SINGLE JOINT EXPERT

25.12

(1) Where the court gives a direction under rule 25.11(1) for a single joint expert to be used, the instructions are to be contained in a jointly agreed letter unless the court directs otherwise.

(2) Where the instructions are to be contained in a jointly agreed letter, in default of agreement the instructions may be determined by the court on the written request of any relevant party copied to the other relevant parties.

(3) Where the court permits the relevant parties to give separate instructions to a single joint expert, each instructing party must, when giving instructions to the expert, at the same time send a copy of the instructions to the other relevant parties.

(4) The court may give directions about –
   (a) the payment of the expert's fees and expenses; and
   (b) any inspection, examination or assessments which the expert wishes to carry out.

(5) The court may, before an expert is instructed, limit the amount that can be paid by way of fees and expenses to the expert.

(6) Unless the court directs otherwise, the relevant parties are jointly and severally liable for the payment of the expert's fees and expenses..

POWER OF COURT TO DIRECT A PARTY TO PROVIDE INFORMATION

25.13

(1) Subject to paragraph (2), where a party has access to information which is not reasonably available to another party, the court may direct the party who has access to the information to –

(a) prepare and file a document recording the information; and
(b) serve a copy of that document on the other party.

....

CONTENTS OF REPORT

25.14

(1) An expert's report must comply with the requirements set out in Practice Direction 25B.

(2) At the end of an expert's report there must be a statement that the expert understands and has complied with the expert's duty to the court.

(3) The instructions to the expert are not privileged against disclosure.

(Rule 21.1 explains what is meant by disclosure.).

USE BY ONE PARTY OF EXPERT'S REPORT DISCLOSED BY ANOTHER

25.15 Where a party has disclosed an expert's report, any party may use that expert's report as evidence at any hearing where an issue to which the report relates is being considered..

DISCUSSIONS BETWEEN EXPERTS

25.16

(1) The court *may, at any stage, direct a discussion between experts* for the purpose of requiring the experts to –
 (a) *identify and discuss the expert issues* in the proceedings; and
 (b) where possible, *reach an agreed opinion* on those issues.

(2) The court may specify the issues which the experts must discuss.

(3) The court *may direct that* following a discussion between the experts *they must prepare a statement* for the court *setting out those issues* on which –
 (a) *they agree*; and
 (b) *they disagree, with a summary of their reasons* for disagreeing.

EXPERT'S RIGHT TO ASK COURT FOR DIRECTIONS

25.17

(1) Experts may file written requests for directions for the purpose of assisting them in carrying out their functions.

(2) Experts must, unless the court directs otherwise, provide copies of the proposed requests for directions under paragraph (1) –
   (a) to the party instructing them, at least 7 days before they file the requests; and
   (b) to all other parties, at least 4 days before they file them.

(3) The court, when it gives directions, may also direct that a party be served with a copy of the directions.

COPIES OF ORDERS AND OTHER DOCUMENTS

25.18 Unless the court directs otherwise, a copy of any order or other document affecting an expert filed with the court after the expert has been instructed, must be served on the expert by the party who instructed the expert or, in the case of a single joint expert, the party who was responsible for instructing the expert, within 2 days of that party receiving the order or other document.

ACTION AFTER FINAL HEARING

25.19

(1) Within 10 business days after the final hearing, the party who instructed the expert or, in the case of a single joint expert, the party who was responsible for instructing the expert, must inform the expert in writing about the court's determination and the use made by the court of the expert's evidence.

(2) Unless the court directs otherwise, the party who instructed the expert or, in the case of the single joint expert, the party who was responsible for instructing the expert, must send to the expert a copy of the court's final order, any transcript or written record of the court's decision, and its reasons for reaching its decision, within 10 business days from the date when the party received the order and any such transcript or record.

ASSESSORS

25.20

(1) This rule applies where the court appoints one or more persons under section 70 of the Senior Courts Act 1981 as an assessor.

(2) An assessor will assist the court in dealing with a matter in which the assessor has skill and experience.

(3) The assessor will take such part in the proceedings as the court may direct and in particular the court may direct an assessor to –
   (a) prepare a report for the court on any matter at issue in the proceedings; and

(b) attend the whole or any part of the hearing to advise the court on any such matter.

(4) If the assessor prepares a report for the court before the hearing has begun –
(a) the court will send a copy to each of the parties; and
(b) the parties may use it at the hearing.

(5) Unless the court directs otherwise, an assessor will be paid at the daily rate payable for the time being to a fee-paid deputy district judge of the principal registry and an assessor's fees will form part of the costs of the proceedings.

(6) The court may order any party to deposit in the court office a specified sum in respect of an assessor's fees and, where it does so, the assessor will not be asked to act until the sum has been deposited.

(7) Paragraphs (5) and (6) do not apply where the remuneration of the assessor is to be paid out of money provided by Parliament.

PRACTICE DIRECTION 25A – EXPERTS AND ASSESSORS IN FAMILY PROCEEDINGS

This Practice Direction supplements FPR Part 25

INTRODUCTION

1.1 This Practice Direction and Practice Directions 25B to E relate to expert evidence and supplement FPR Part 25. This Practice Direction applies to children proceedings and all other family proceedings.

EMERGENCY AND URGENT CASES

2.1 In emergency or urgent cases – for example, where, before formal issue of proceedings, a without-notice application is made to the court during or out of business hours; or where, after proceedings have been issued, a previously unforeseen need for (further) expert evidence arises at short notice – a party may wish to put expert evidence before the court without having complied with all or any part of Practice Directions 25B to E. In such circumstances, the party wishing to put the expert evidence before the court must apply forthwith to the court – where possible or appropriate, on notice to the other parties – for directions as to the future steps to be taken in respect of the expert evidence in question.

www.justice.gov.uk/courts/procedure-rules/family/practice_directions/pd_part_25a – pagetop

PRE-APPLICATION INSTRUCTION OF EXPERTS

3.1 When experts' reports are commissioned before the commencement of proceedings, it should be made clear to the expert that he or she may in due course be reporting to the court and should therefore consider himself or herself bound by the duties of an expert set out in Practice Direction 25B (The Duties of An Expert, the Expert›s Report and Arrangements for An Expert To Attend Court). In so far as possible the enquiries of the expert and subsequent letter of instruction should follow … 25D (Financial Remedy Proceedings and other Family Proceedings (except Children Proceedings) – the Use of Single Joint Experts and the Process Leading to Expert Evidence Being Put Before The Court).

…

3.3 It should be noted that the court's permission is required to put expert evidence (in any form) before the court in all family proceedings (see (see section 13(5) of the 2014 Act and FPR 25.4(2)) … The court's permission will be needed to put any expert evidence before the court which was obtained before proceedings have started.

…

PRACTICE DIRECTION 25B – THE DUTIES OF AN EXPERT, THE EXPERT'S REPORT AND ARRANGEMENTS FOR AN EXPERT TO ATTEND COURT

This Practice Direction supplements FPR Part 25

SCOPE OF THIS PRACTICE DIRECTION

1.1 This Practice Direction focuses on the duties of an expert including the contents of the expert's report and, where an expert is to attend court, the arrangements for such attendance. …

www.justice.gov.uk/courts/procedure-rules/family/practice_directions/practice-direction-25b-the-duties-of-an-expert,-the-experts-report-and-arrangements-for-an-expert-to-attend-court – pagetop

THE MEANING OF 'EXPERT'

2.1 In accordance with FPR 25.2(1), 'expert' means a person who provides expert evidence for use in family proceedings. …

2.2 An expert includes a reference to an expert team which can include ancillary workers in addition to experts. … The purpose of the term 'expert team' is to enable a multi-disciplinary team to undertake the assessment without the order having to name everyone who may be involved. The final expert's report must, however, give information about those persons who have taken part in the assessment and their respective roles and who is responsible for the report.

www.justice.gov.uk/courts/procedure-rules/family/practice_directions/practice-direction-25b-the-duties-of-an-expert,-the-experts-report-and-arrangements-for-an-expert-to-attend-court – pagetop

THE EXPERT'S OVERRIDING DUTY

3.1 An expert in family proceedings has an overriding duty to the court that takes precedence over any obligation to the person from whom the expert has received instructions or by whom the expert is paid.

www.justice.gov.uk/courts/procedure-rules/family/practice_directions/practice-direction-25b-the-duties-of-an-expert,-the-experts-report-and-arrangements-for-an-expert-to-attend-court – pagetop

PARTICULAR DUTIES OF THE EXPERT

4.1 An expert shall have regard to the following, among other, duties –

(a) to assist the court in accordance with the overriding duty;

…

(b) to provide advice to the court that conforms to the best practice of the expert's profession;

(c) to answer the questions about which the expert is required to give an opinion …;

(d) to provide an opinion that is independent of the party or parties instructing the expert;

(e) to confine the opinion to matters material to the issues in the case and in relation only to the questions that are within the expert's expertise (skill and experience);

(f) where a question has been put which falls outside the expert's expertise, to state this at the earliest opportunity and to volunteer an opinion as to whether another expert is required to bring expertise not possessed by those already involved or, in the rare case, as to whether a second opinion is required on a key issue and, if possible, what questions should be asked of the second expert;

(g) in expressing an opinion, to take into consideration all of the material facts including any relevant factors arising from ethnic, cultural, religious or linguistic contexts at the time the opinion is expressed;

(h) to inform those instructing the expert without delay of any change in the opinion and of the reason for the change.

www.justice.gov.uk/courts/procedure-rules/family/practice_directions/practice-direction-25b-the-duties-of-an-expert,-the-experts-report-and-arrangements-for-an-expert-to-attend-court – pagetop

THE REQUIREMENT FOR THE COURT'S PERMISSION

5.1 The general rule in family proceedings is that the court's permission is required to put expert evidence (in any form) before the court … The court is under a duty to restrict expert evidence to that which in the opinion of the court is necessary to assist the court to resolve the proceedings. The overriding objective in FPR1.1 applies when the court is exercising this duty …

www.justice.gov.uk/courts/procedure-rules/family/practice_directions/practice-direction-25b-the-duties-of-an-expert,-the-experts-report-and-arrangements-for-an-expert-to-attend-court – pagetop

PRELIMINARY ENQUIRIES WHICH THE EXPERT SHOULD EXPECT TO RECEIVE

6.1 In good time for the information requested to be available for –

(a) the court hearing when the court will decide whether to give permission for the expert evidence to be put before the court .. or

(b) the advocates' meeting or discussion where one takes place before such a hearing,

the party or parties intending to instruct the expert shall approach the expert with some information about the case.

6.2 The details of the information to be given to the expert are set out in … Practice Direction 25D paragraph 3.3 and include the nature of the proceedings, the questions for the expert, the time when the expert's report is likely to be required, the timing of any hearing at which the expert may have to give evidence and how the expert's fees will be funded.

…

BALANCING THE NEEDS OF THE COURT AND THOSE OF THE EXPERT

7.1 It is essential that there should be proper co-ordination between the court and the expert when drawing up the case management timetable: the needs of the court should be balanced with the needs of the expert whose forensic work is undertaken as an adjunct to his or her main professional duties.

www.justice.gov.uk/courts/procedure-rules/family/practice_directions/practice-direction-25b-the-duties-of-an-expert,-the-experts-report-and-arrangements-for-an-expert-to-attend-court – pagetop

THE EXPERT'S RESPONSE TO PRELIMINARY ENQUIRIES

8.1 In good time for the court hearing when the court will decide whether or not to give permission for the expert evidence to be put before the court … or for the advocates' meeting or discussion where one takes place before that hearing, the party or parties intending to instruct the expert will need confirmation from the expert –

(a) that acceptance of the proposed instructions will not involve the expert in any conflict of interest;

(b) that the work required is within the expert's expertise;

(c) that the expert is available to do the relevant work within the suggested time scale;

(d) when the expert is available to give evidence, of the dates and times to avoid and, where a hearing date has not been fixed, of the amount of notice the expert will require to make arrangements to come to court (or to give evidence by telephone conference or video link) without undue disruption to his or her normal professional routines;

(e) of the cost, including hourly or other charging rates, and likely hours to be spent attending experts' meetings, attending court and writing the report (to include any examinations and interviews);

(f) of any representations which the expert wishes to make to the court about being named or otherwise identified in any public judgment given by the court.

www.justice.gov.uk/courts/procedure-rules/family/practice_directions/practice-direction-25b-the-duties-of-an-expert,-the-experts-report-and-arrangements-for-an-expert-to-attend-court – pagetop

CONTENT OF THE EXPERT'S REPORT

9.1 The expert's report shall be addressed to the court and prepared and filed in accordance with the court's timetable and must –

(a) give details of the expert's qualifications and experience;

(b) include a statement identifying the document(s) containing the material instructions and the substance of any oral instructions and, as far as necessary to explain any opinions or conclusions expressed in the report, summarising the facts and instructions which are material to the conclusions and opinions expressed;

(c) state who carried out any test, examination or interview which the expert has used for the report and whether or not the test, examination or interview has been carried out under the expert's supervision;

(d) give details of the qualifications of any person who carried out the test, examination or interview;

(e) answer the questions about which the expert is to give an opinion and which relate to the issues in the case;

(f) in expressing an opinion to the court –
   (i) take into consideration all of the material facts including any relevant factors arising from ethnic, cultural, religious or linguistic contexts at the time the opinion is expressed, identifying the facts, literature and any other material, including research material, that the expert has relied upon in forming an opinion;
   (ii) describe the expert's own professional risk assessment process and process of differential diagnosis, highlighting factual assumptions, deductions from the factual assumptions, and any unusual, contradictory or inconsistent features of the case;

(iii) indicate whether any proposition in the report is an hypothesis (in particular a controversial hypothesis), or an opinion deduced in accordance with peer-reviewed and tested technique, research and experience accepted as a consensus in the scientific community;

(iv) indicate whether the opinion is provisional (or qualified, as the case may be), stating the qualification and the reason for it, and identifying what further information is required to give an opinion without qualification;

(g) where there is a range of opinion on any question to be answered by the expert –

(i) summarise the range of opinion;

(ii) identify and explain, within the range of opinions, any 'unknown cause', whether arising from the facts of the case (for example, because there is too little information to form a scientific opinion) or from limited experience or lack of research, peer review or support in the relevant field of expertise;

(iii) give reasons for any opinion expressed: the use of a balance sheet approach to the factors that support or undermine an opinion can be of great assistance to the court;

(h) contain a summary of the expert's conclusions and opinions;

(i) contain a statement that the expert–

(i) has no conflict of interest of any kind, other than any conflict disclosed in his or her report;

(ii) does not consider that any interest disclosed affects his or her suitability as an expert witness on any issue on which he or she has given evidence;

(iii) will advise the instructing party if, between the date of the expert's report and the final hearing, there is any change in circumstances which affects the expert's answers to (i) or (ii) above;

(iv) understands their duty to the court and has complied with that duty; and

(v) is aware of the requirements of FPR Part 25 and this practice direction;

...

(j) be verified by a statement of truth in the following form –

"I confirm that I have made clear which facts and matters referred to in this report are within my own knowledge and which are not. Those that are within my own knowledge I confirm to be true. The opinions I have expressed represent my true and complete professional opinions on the matters to which they refer."

(FPR Part 17deals with statements of truth. Rule 17.6 sets out the consequences of verifying a document containing a false statement without an honest belief in its truth.)

Appendix 10

ARRANGEMENTS FOR EXPERTS TO GIVE EVIDENCE

Preparation

10.1 Where the court has directed the attendance of an expert witness, the party who instructed the expert or party responsible for the instruction of the expert shall, by a date specified by the court prior to the hearing at which the expert is to give oral evidence ('the specified date') ... ensure that –

(a) a date and time (if possible, convenient to the expert) are fixed for the court to hear the expert's evidence, substantially in advance of the hearing at which the expert is to give oral evidence and no later than a specified date prior to that hearing ...;

(b) if the expert's oral evidence is not required, the expert is notified as soon as possible;

(c) the witness template accurately indicates how long the expert is likely to be giving evidence, in order to avoid the inconvenience of the expert being delayed at court;

(d) consideration is given in each case to whether some or all of the experts participate by telephone conference or video link, or submit their evidence in writing, to ensure that minimum disruption is caused to professional schedules and that costs are minimised.

Experts attending court

10.2 Where expert witnesses are to be called, all parties shall, by the specified date ... ensure that –

(a) the parties' advocates have identified (whether at an advocates' meeting or by other means) the issues which the experts are to address;

(b) wherever possible, a logical sequence to the evidence is arranged, with experts of the same discipline giving evidence on the same day;

(c) the court is informed of any circumstance where all experts agree but a party nevertheless does not accept the agreed opinion, so that directions can be given for the proper consideration of the experts' evidence and opinion;

(d) in the exceptional case the court is informed of the need for a witness summons.

PRACTICE DIRECTION 25D – FINANCIAL REMEDY PROCEEDINGS AND OTHER FAMILY PROCEEDINGS (EXCEPT CHILDREN PROCEEDINGS) – THE USE OF SINGLE JOINT EXPERTS AND THE PROCESS LEADING TO EXPERT EVIDENCE BEING PUT BEFORE THE COURT

This Practice Direction supplements FPR Part 25

SCOPE OF THIS PRACTICE DIRECTION

1.1 This Practice Direction applies to financial remedy proceedings and other family proceedings except children proceedings and contains guidance on –

(a) the use of single joint experts;

(b) how to prepare for the hearing at which the court will consider whether to give permission for putting expert evidence (in any form) before the court including –
  (i) preliminary enquiries of experts;
  (ii) information to be given to the court before the hearing;

(c) the letter of instruction to the expert.

SINGLE JOINT EXPERTS

2.1 FPR 25.4 applies to a single joint expert ('SJE') in addition to an expert instructed by one party. This means that the court's permission is required to put expert evidence from an SJE (in any form) before the court. However, in family proceedings (except children proceedings) there is no requirement for the court's permission to be obtained before instructing an expert. Wherever possible, expert evidence should be obtained from a single joint expert instructed by both or all the parties ('SJE'). To that end, a party wishing to instruct an expert should first give the other party or parties a list of the names of one or more experts in the relevant specialty whom they consider suitable to be instructed.

2.2 Within 10 business days after receipt of the list of proposed experts, the other party or parties should indicate any objection to one or more of the named experts and, if so, supply the name(s) of one or more experts whom they consider suitable.

2.3 Each party should disclose whether they have already consulted any of the proposed experts about the issue(s) in question.

2.4 Where the parties *cannot agree on the identity of the expert, each party should think carefully before instructing their own expert and seeking the* *permission of the court to put that expert evidence before it because of the costs implications*. Disagreements about the use and identity of an expert may be better managed by the court in the context of an application for the court's permission to put the expert evidence before the court and for directions for the use of an SJE (see paragraph 2.6 below).

Agreement to instruct separate experts

2.5 If the parties *agree to instruct separate experts and to seek the permission of the court to put the separate expert evidence before it* –

(a) *they should agree in advance that the reports will be disclosed*; and

(b) *the instructions to each expert should comply, so far as appropriate, with paragraphs 4.1 and 6.1* below (Letter of instruction).

Agreement to instruct an SJE

2.6 If there is agreement to instruct an SJE, before applying to the court for permission to put the expert evidence before it and directions for the use of an SJE, the parties should –

(a) so far as appropriate, comply with the guidance in paragraphs 3.3 (Preliminary enquiries of the expert) and paragraphs 3.11 and 3.12 below;

(b) receive the expert's confirmation in response to preliminary enquiries referred to in paragraph 8.1 of Practice Direction 25B;

(c) have agreed in what proportion the SJE's fee is to be shared between them (at least in the first instance) and when it is to be paid; and

(d) if applicable, have obtained agreement for public funding.

2.7 The instructions to the SJE should comply, so far as appropriate, with paragraphs 4.1 and 6.1 below (Letter of instruction).

THE TEST FOR PERMISSION AND PREPARATION FOR THE PERMISSION HEARING

3.1 The test in FPR 25.4(3) which the court is to apply to determine whether permission should be given for expert evidence to be put before the court has been altered from one which refers to expert evidence being restricted by the court to that which is reasonably required to resolve the proceedings to one which refers to the expert evidence being in the opinion of the court necessary to assist the court to resolve the proceedings. The overriding objective of the FPR, which is to enable the court to deal with cases justly, having regard to any welfare issues involved, continues to apply when the court is making the decision whether to give permission. In addition, the rules (FPR 25.5(2)) now tell the court what factors it is to have particular regard to when deciding whether to give permission.

3.2 Paragraphs 3.3 to 3.12 below give guidance on how to prepare for the hearing at which the court will apply the test in FPR 25.4(3) and the factors in FPR 25.5(2) and decide whether to give permission for expert evidence to be put before the court. The purpose of the preparation is to ensure that the court has the information required to enable it to exercise its powers under FPR 25.4(2) and 25.5(2) in line with FPR 25.4(3).

Preliminary enquiries of the expert

3.3 In good time for the information requested to be available for the hearing at which the court will consider whether to give permission for expert evidence to be put before the court, the party or parties intending to instruct the expert shall approach the expert with the following information –

(a) the nature of the proceedings and the issues likely to require determination by the court;

(b) the issues in the proceedings to which the expert evidence is to relate;

(c) the questions about which the expert is to be asked to give an opinion and which relate to the issues in the case;

(d) whether permission is to be asked of the court for the use of another expert in the same or any related field (that is, to give an opinion on the same or related questions);

(e) the volume of reading which the expert will need to undertake;

(f) whether or not it will be necessary for the expert to conduct interviews and, if so, with whom;

(g) the likely timetable of legal steps;

(h) when the expert's report is likely to be required;

(i) whether and, if so, what date has been fixed by the court for any hearing at which the expert may be required to give evidence (in particular the Final Hearing); and whether it may be possible for the expert to give evidence by telephone conference or video link: see paragraphs 10.1 and 10.2 (Arrangements for experts to give evidence) of Practice Direction 25B;

(j) the possibility of making, through their instructing solicitors, representations to the court about being named or otherwise identified in any public judgment given by the court;

(k) whether the instructing party has public funding and the legal aid rates of payment which are applicable.

Expert's response to preliminary enquiries

3.4 In good time for the hearing at which the court will consider whether to give permission for expert evidence to be put before the court, the solicitors or party intending to instruct the expert must obtain the confirmations from the expert referred to in paragraph 8.1 of Practice Direction 25B. These confirmations include that the work is within the expert's expertise, the expert is available to do the work within the relevant timescale and the expert's costs.

3.5 Where parties cannot agree who should be the single joint expert before the hearing at which the court will consider whether to give permission for expert evidence to be put before the court, they should obtain the above confirmations in respect of all experts whom they intend to put to the court for the purposes of rule 25.11(2)(a) as candidates for the appointment.

The application for the court's permission to put expert evidence before the court

Timing and oral applications for the court's permission

3.6 An application for the court's permission to put expert evidence before the court should be made as soon as it becomes apparent that it is necessary to make it. FPR 25.6 makes provision about the time by which applications for the court's permission should be made.

3.7 Applications should, wherever possible, be made so that they are considered at any directions hearing or other hearing for which a date has been fixed or for which a date is about to be fixed. It should be noted that one application notice can be used by a party to make more than one application for an order or direction at a hearing held during the course of proceedings. An application for the court's permission to put expert evidence before the court may therefore be included in an application notice requesting other orders to be made at such a hearing.

3.8 Where a date for a hearing has been fixed, a party who wishes to make an application at that hearing but does not have sufficient time to file an application notice should as soon as possible inform the court (if possible in writing) and, if possible, the other parties of the nature of the application and the reason for it. The party should provide the court and the other party with as much as possible of the information referred to in FPR 25.7 and paragraph 3.11 below. That party should then make the application orally at the hearing. An oral application of this kind should be the exception and reserved for genuine cases where circumstances are such that it has only become apparent shortly before the hearing that an expert opinion is necessary.

3.9 In financial remedy proceedings, unless the court directs otherwise, parties must apply for permission to put expert evidence before the court as soon as possible and no later than the first appointment. The expectation is that the court will give directions extending the time by which permission should be obtained where there is good reason for parties to delay the decision whether to use expert evidence and make an application for the court's permission.

3.10 Examples of situations where the time for requesting permission to put expert evidence before the court is likely to be extended are where –

(a) a decision about the need for expert evidence cannot be made until replies to questionnaires in relation to Forms E have been fully considered; or

(b) valuations of property are agreed for the purposes of the Financial Dispute Resolution appointment but no agreement is reached to resolve the proceedings at that appointment and the court cannot make a consent order as mentioned in FPR 9.17(8). In these circumstances, it may become clear to a party that he or she will want to use expert valuations of property and an application for the court's permission for such valuation to be put before it may be made orally at the end of the appointment to avoid the need for a separate hearing about this issue. As with other oral applications, the party should provide the court and the other party with as much as possible of the information referred to in FPR 25.7 and paragraph 3.11 below. FPR 9.17(9) requires the court to give directions for the future course of the proceedings where it has not made a consent order including, where appropriate, the filing of evidence.

The application

3.11 In addition to the matters specified in FPR 25.7(2)(a), an application for the court's permission to put expert evidence before the court must state –

(a) the discipline, qualifications and expertise of the expert (by way of C.V. where possible);

(b) the expert's availability to undertake the work;

(c) the timetable for the report;

(d) the responsibility for instruction;

(e) whether the expert evidence can properly be obtained by only one party;

(f) why the expert evidence proposed cannot properly be given by an expert already instructed in the proceedings;

(g) the likely cost of the report on an hourly or other charging basis:

(h) the proposed apportionment (at least in the first instance) of any jointly instructed expert's fee; when it is to be paid; and, if applicable, whether public funding has been approved.

The draft order to be attached to the application for the court's permission

3.12 FPR 25.7(2)(b) provides that a draft of the order giving the court's permission to put expert evidence before the court is to be attached to the application for the court's permission. That draft order must set out the following matters –

(a) the issues in the proceedings to which the expert evidence is to relate;

(b) the party who is to be responsible for drafting the letter of instruction and providing the documents to the expert;

(c) the timetable within which the report is to be prepared, filed and served;

(d) the disclosure of the report to the parties and to any other expert;

(e) the organisation of, preparation for and *conduct of any experts' discussion* (see Practice Direction 25E – Discussions between Experts in Family Proceedings);

(f) the *preparation of a statement of agreement and disagreement by the experts* following an experts' discussion;

(g) making available to the court at an early opportunity the expert reports in electronic form;

(h) the attendance of the expert at court to give oral evidence (alternatively, the expert giving his or her evidence in writing or remotely by video link), whether at or for the Final Hearing or another hearing; unless agreement about the opinions given by the expert is reached by a date specified by the court prior to the hearing at which the expert is to give oral evidence.

LETTER OF INSTRUCTION

4.1 The party responsible for instructing the expert shall, within 5 business days after the permission hearing, prepare (in agreement with the other parties where appropriate), file and serve a letter of instruction to the expert which shall –

(a) set out the context in which the expert's opinion is sought (including any ethnic, cultural, religious or linguistic contexts);

(b) set out the questions which the expert is required to answer and ensuring that they –
  (i) are within the ambit of the expert's area of expertise;
  (ii) do not contain unnecessary or irrelevant detail;
  (iii) are kept to a manageable number and are clear, focused and direct; and
  (iv) reflect what the expert has been requested to do by the court;

(c) list the documentation provided, or provide for the expert an indexed and paginated bundle which shall include –

(i) an agreed list of essential reading; and
(ii) a copy of this Practice Direction and Practice Directions 25B, 25E and where appropriate Practice Direction 15B;

(d) identify any materials provided to the expert which have not been produced either as original medical (or other professional) records or in response to an instruction from a party, and state the source of that material (such materials may contain an assumption as to the standard of proof, the admissibility or otherwise of hearsay evidence, and other important procedural and substantive questions relating to the different purposes of other enquiries);

(e) identify all requests to third parties for disclosure and their responses in order to avoid partial disclosure, which tends only to prove a case rather than give full and frank information;

(f) identify the relevant people concerned with the proceedings and inform the expert of his or her right to talk to them provided that an accurate record is made of the discussions;

(g) identify any other expert instructed in the proceedings and advise the expert of their right to talk to the other experts provided that an accurate record is made of the discussions;

(h) subject to any public funding requirement for prior authority, define the contractual basis upon which the expert is retained and in particular the funding mechanism including how much the expert will be paid (an hourly rate and overall estimate should already have been obtained), when the expert will be paid, and what limitation there might be on the amount the expert can charge for the work which they will have to do. In cases where the parties are publicly funded, there may also be a brief explanation of the costs and expenses excluded from public funding by Funding Code criterion 1.3 and the detailed assessment process.

ADULT WHO IS A PROTECTED PARTY

5.1 Where the adult is a protected party, that party's representative shall be involved in any instruction of an expert, including the instruction of an expert to assess whether the adult, although a protected party, is competent to give evidence (see Practice Direction15B – Adults Who May Be Protected Parties and Children Who May Become Protected Parties in Family Proceedings).

ASKING THE COURT TO SETTLE THE LETTER OF INSTRUCTION TO A SINGLE JOINT EXPERT

6.1 Where possible, the written request for the court to consider the letter of instruction referred to in rule 25.12(2) should be set out in an e-mail to the court and copied by e-mail to the other instructing parties. The request should be sent to the relevant court or (by prior arrangement only) directly to the judge dealing with the proceedings. Where a legal adviser has been appointed as the case manager, the request should also be sent to the appointed legal adviser. The court will settle the letter of instruction, usually without a hearing to avoid delay; and will send (where practicable, by e-mail) the settled letter to the party responsible for instructing the expert for transmission forthwith to the expert, and copy it to the other instructing parties for information.

PRACTICE DIRECTION 25E – DISCUSSIONS BETWEEN EXPERTS IN FAMILY PROCEEDINGS

This Practice Direction supplements FPR Part 25

SCOPE

1.1 This Practice Direction supports FPR25.16 by providing details about how and when experts discussions are to be arranged, their purpose and content. This Practice Direction applies to children proceedings and all other family proceedings.

EXPERTS' DISCUSSION OR MEETING: PURPOSE

2.1 In accordance with FPR 25.16, the court *may, at any stage, direct a discussion between experts for the purpose* outlined in paragraph (1) of that rule. FPR 25.16(2) provides that *the court may specify the issues* which the experts must discuss. The expectation is that those issues will include –

(a) *the reasons for disagreement on any expert question* and *what, if any, action needs to be taken to resolve* any outstanding disagreement or question;

(b) an *explanation of existing evidence or additional evidence in order to assist the court to determine the issues.*

One of the aims of specifying the issues for discussion is *to limit, wherever possible, the need for the experts to attend court to give oral evidence.*

EXPERTS' DISCUSSION OR MEETING: ARRANGEMENTS

3.1 Subject to the directions given by the court under FPR25.16, the solicitor or other professional who is given the responsibility by the court ('the nominated professional') ***shall within 15 business days after the experts' reports have been filed and copied to the other parties****, make arrangements for the experts to have discussions.* Subject to any specification by the court of the issues which experts must discuss under FPR 25.16(2), the following matters should be considered as appropriate –

(a) where permission has been given for the instruction of experts *from different disciplines, a global discussion may be held relating to those questions that concern all or most of them*;

(b) *separate discussions may have to be held among experts from the same or related disciplines*, but care should be taken to ensure that the discussions complement each other so that related questions are discussed by all relevant experts;

(c) *5 business days* **prior to a discussion or meeting**, *the nominated professional should formulate an agenda* including a list of questions for consideration. The agenda should, subject always to the provisions of FPR 25.16(1), *focus on those questions which are intended to clarify areas of agreement or disagreement.*

Questions which *repeat questions asked in the court order giving permission for an expert to be instructed or expert evidence to be put before the court or the letter of instruction or which seek to rehearse cross-examination in advance of the hearing should be rejected* as likely to defeat the purpose of the meeting. The agenda may usefully take the form of a list of questions to be circulated among the other parties in advance and should comprise all questions that each party wishes the experts to consider.

The agenda and list of questions should be *sent to each of the experts* ***not later than 2 business days before the discussion***;

(d) the nominated professional may exercise his or her discretion to accept further questions after the agenda with the list of questions has been circulated to the parties. ***Only in exceptional circumstances should questions be added to the agenda within the 2-day period before the meeting. Under no circumstances should any question received on the day of or during the meeting be accepted.*** This does not preclude questions arising during the meeting for the purposes of clarification. Strictness in this regard is vital, for adequate notice of the questions enables the parties to identify and isolate the expert issues in the case before the meeting so that the experts' discussion at the meeting can concentrate on those issues;

(e) the discussion should be *chaired by the nominated professional. A minute must be taken* of the questions answered by the experts. Where the court has given a direction under FPR 25.16(3) and subject to that direction, a *Statement of Agreement and Disagreement* must be prepared which should be agreed and signed by each of the experts who participated in the discussion. In accordance with FPR25.16(3) the statement *must contain a summary of the experts' reasons for disagreeing*. The statement should be served and filed **not later than 5 business days after the discussion has taken place**;

(f) in each case, whether some or all of the experts participate by telephone conference or video link to ensure that minimum disruption is caused to professional schedules and that costs are minimised.

MEETINGS OR CONFERENCES ATTENDED BY A JOINTLY INSTRUCTED EXPERT

4.1 Jointly instructed experts *should not attend any meeting or conference which is not a joint one*, unless all the parties have agreed in writing or the court has directed that such a meeting may be held, and it is agreed or directed who is to pay the expert's fees for the meeting or conference. Any meeting or conference attended by a jointly instructed expert should *be proportionate* to the case.

(… Practice Direction 25D paragraphs 2.1 to 2.7 deals with single joint experts in relation to other family proceedings).

…

Index

[all references are to paragraph number]